Conservative
Nationalism in
Nineteenth-Century
Russia

Conservative Nationalism in Nineteenth-Century Russia

BY EDWARD C. THADEN

UNIVERSITY OF WASHINGTON PRESS   SEATTLE   1964

TO THE MEMORY OF MY FATHER

Preface

CONSERVATIVE nationalism in nineteenth-century Russia grew out of the endeavor of Russian conservative intellectuals to create national ideals that would serve to bring together the Russian state, the mass of the people, and the educated elite in harmonious and organic unity. Although the political application of conservative nationalism, especially in the western borderlands of the tsarist empire, will not be closely examined in this study, the practical implications of this ideology cannot be completely ignored. Theory and practice in intellectual history are inextricably interrelated. In Russia the cultural and political struggle between the government and publicists on the one hand and various national minority groups on the other exercised a profound influence on the thinking of Russian conservative nationalists. Many of them undertook studies and developed persuasive arguments that provided historical and theoretical justification for the centralizing and Russifying tendencies of the St. Petersburg bureaucracy. However, since the emphasis of this study is on intellectual, not on administrative and political history, I will not discuss in detail the actual policies of the Russian state.

Few historians since 1917 have given serious attention to the thinkers who are considered in this study. Fedor Dostoevskii is, of course, well known. He is included here because of his great influence on and his close relation to such relatively little-known figures as Apollon Grigor'ev and Nicholas Strakhov. Russia's conservative writers have often been dismissed as mere reactionaries; seldom have historians seen them in terms of their own ideals and intellectual development. Conservative and nationalistic intellectuals admittedly lost their battle against Westernism and Russian radicalism. Their ultimate defeat and failure, however, do not justify an almost exclusive emphasis on the importance of Russia's radical intelligentsia, for the picture of nineteenth-century Russian life is distorted if one fails to understand the radicals' opponents—Russia's conservative nationalists.

This study was conducted over a period of ten years at libraries and universities in the United States, Europe, and the Soviet Union. I therefore have many obligations to acknowledge to those who gave me encouragement and assisted me in my research. My interest in the general subject of Russian conservatism and nationalism was first aroused by the lectures of Professor Victor-L. Tapié at the Sorbonne in 1950. I began research on this subject while I was at the University of Washington during 1951–52. Criticisms and suggestions made at that time by Professors Donald W. Treadgold, Victor Erlich, and Herbert J. Ellison were most helpful to me in investigating the intellectual and historical background of Russian conservatism. This investigation led to an article, "The Beginnings of Romantic Nationalism in Russia," published in the *American Slavic and East European Review* in 1954. After 1952 I continued my research at the libraries of California, Columbia, Harvard, Helsinki, Moscow, and Pennsylvania State universities as well as the New York Public Library, the Library of Congress, the Hoover Institute and Library on War, Revolution, and Peace, the Saltykov-Shchedrin Public Library, and the Library of the Institute of Russian Literature (Pushkinskii Dom) of the Academy of Sciences in Leningrad, the Lenin Public Library in Moscow, and the Bibliothèque Nationale in Paris. Thanks are due to the staffs of all these libraries for the kind assistance they extended to me, especially to librarians in the manuscript rooms of the Lenin Library, the Saltykov-Shchedrin Library, and the Pushkinskii Dom; to the Inter-Library Loan staff at Pennsylvania State University; and to Sergei Sergeevich Bulich, Nina Nikolaevna Hippius, Magister Elisabeth Tokoi, Dr. Maria Widnäs, Dr. Sulo Haltsonen, and Dr. Jorma Vallinkoski of the University of Helsinki Library. I am grateful to the Harvard and Moscow University libraries and Professors Robert E. MacMaster, S. L. Evenchik, and Sidney Monas for saving me many hours of note taking by permitting me to have microfilmed dissertations on Nicholas Iakovlevich Danilevskii, Constantine Petrovich Pobedonostsev, and the Third Section during the reign of Nicholas I.

I am grateful to Professor Edgar H. Lehrman of Emory University, who read the entire manuscript for literary style and gave many helpful suggestions. Numerous discussions with Professor Oswald P. Backus of the University of Kansas while we both were Fulbright scholars in Helsinki during 1957–58 were a constant source of encouragement. Professor Harry D. Harootunian of the University of Rochester read most of the manuscript and made many penetrating observations that persuaded me to reformulate some of my ideas on the nature of nineteenth-century Russian conservative nationalism. I am indebted to Professor Walter Ralls of Hobart College and Professor Ari Hoogenboom of Pennsylvania State University for having critically examined early chapters of the manuscript and final revisions. Thanks are also due to the Conference Board of Associated Research Councils, the Inter-University Committee on Travel Grants, and the Social Science Research Council for grants that permitted me to spend fourteen months of research in Helsinki, Moscow, and Leningrad between 1956 and 1958. Finally, I wish to express my appreciation to the College of the Liberal Arts and the Administrative Committee on Research of Pennsylvania State University for having granted me released time from teaching and for numerous grants during the preparation of this book.

EDWARD C. THADEN

University Park, Pennsylvania

Contents

PART I

*The Traditional and
Romantic Background*

Introduction

JEAN Jacques Rousseau was among the first of a small number of intellectuals in eighteenth-century Europe to suggest how governments could make use of national sentiment. Especially in his *Considérations sur le gouvernement de Pologne*, he urged the use of the army, national institutions and customs, a national theater, and education as means of developing cohesion in society and serving the interests of the nation state. The Poles, however, obviously were not in a position at the time to follow Rousseau's advice. Instead, his Jacobin admirers in France were the first to have the opportunity to adopt and apply his suggestions in their attempt to weld together French revolutionary society and attach French citizens to *la Patrie* and the ideals of the Revolution. They were at least partly able to attain this goal, especially in the army and at Paris, by exploiting such patriotic symbols as the "Marseillaise," the tricolor, revolutionary monuments and fêtes, and the idea of the "nation in arms."

The French Revolution opened the eyes of many intellectuals and political leaders in Europe to the importance of nationalism as a potential source of national strength and unity. It was clear from the beginning that the Jacobins' use of nationalism represented but one of many possible applications. There was no good reason why conservative governments, too, could not make use of nationalism to inculcate in the minds of their subjects attitudes of loyalty to the state and of emotional attachment to the traditional values and institutions of their country. The society of early nineteenth-century Europe, however, was not quite ready for such use of nationalism. Several additional generations of dedicated work and agitation on the part of intellectuals and scholars, of improvement in communications, and of industrial, political, and social progress were

3

needed before nationalism could become an effective instrument of national policy in the hands of European governments.

In England and France the development of nationalism during the nineteenth century was greatly facilitated by the earlier efforts of English and French kings to achieve a degree of political unity and uniformity in both countries. Equally important, relatively homogeneous English and French national languages and cultures had gradually evolved since the Middle Ages. Other nationalities were not as fortunate. The Germans, to a large extent, had been united culturally and linguistically by 1800, but still were almost hopelessly divided politically and economically. The peoples of central and eastern Europe generally lacked not only political but also social, cultural, and economic unity. Russia, of course, enjoyed the advantages of political unification and of a strong unitary state, but the extensive Westernization of the upper strata of the Russian population had deprived tsarist society of cultural cohesion and internal moral and spiritual unity.

Nineteenth-century Russian conservative nationalists were heavily indebted to German philosophy, romantic literature, and scholarship in their efforts to formulate a new philosophy of life based on Russian nationalism and the customs and institutions of traditional Russian society. Germany, as Karl Mannheim has pointed out, "achieved for the ideology of conservatism what France did for the Enlightenment—she exploited it to the fullest extent of its logical conclusions."[1] Most of the basic ideas of this ideology can be detected in the essays and reflections of Edmund Burke. However, when such German writers as Novalis, Friedrich von Schlegel, Adam Müller, and Friedrich von Savigny developed and reworked Burke's empirical and practical conservatism, it acquired a new, more theoretical and philosophical formulation. The resulting philosophical outlook and conservative ideology that emerged in Germany at the beginning of the nineteenth century have subsequently been referred to as historicism. This view was characterized by its emphasis on the fundamental irrationality of reality, on national individuality, and on organic historical development.[2] Historicism in Germany was not always associated with nationalism, but the widespread reaction after 1800 in German intellectual circles against Napoleonic rule caused most early German historicists to identify themselves closely with either German or Prussian nationalism.

The general historicist view of life later proved to be of great use to nationalists throughout central and eastern Europe. In Russia the organic concepts of the German idealists and romantics were especially appreciated by the Lovers of Wisdom (the *liubomudry*), a group of young men who, in the 1820's, fervently believed in the necessity of developing

Russian national feeling and uniquely Russian forms of literature, philosophy, and art.[3] The Society of the Lovers of Wisdom existed for only a few years prior to the Decembrist uprising of 1825; but the efforts of its members, among whom were such future Slavophiles as I. V. Kireevskii and A. I. Koshelev, to adapt German idealist philosophy and romantic esthetics to the intellectual needs of Russian society represented a highly significant point of departure for the further development of Russian nationalistic thought.

The first Russian conservative who fully understood some of the possible uses the Russian state could make of modern nationalism was the novelist and historian Nicholas M. Karamzin, whose basic philosophy of life remained largely unaffected by German romanticism and idealism. Even though he rejected the ideas of the French Revolution and cosmopolitanism, Karamzin was always strongly influenced by the rationalism of the Enlightenment. Thus the nationalism he advocated in his series of articles in the *Messenger of Europe* (*Vestnik Evropy*) between 1801 and 1803[4] was entirely in keeping with the emphasis put on education and environment by Montesquieu, Rousseau, and other eighteenth-century French writers. In these articles Karamzin urged that Russians should be educated in their own country so that they could acquire feelings of national pride and become accustomed to its climate, customs, laws, and way of life.[5] In the nineteenth century, he predicted, only those states which promoted the arts and sciences through a national and patriotic form of education would be strong and enjoy the esteem of civilized mankind.[6] Specifically in regard to Russia he wrote:

> It is necessary to inculcate in Russians a consciousness of their own value; it is necessary to show them that their past is capable of furnishing subjects of inspiration for the artist, of encouraging works of art, of making hearts palpitate. Not only the historian but also the poet, the sculptor, and the painter can be organs of patriotism.[7]

The Russians Karamzin referred to, however, were not ready for the widespread inculcation of patriotism. The educated upper strata of Russian society had been so profoundly influenced by the intellectual world of Western Europe that to them concepts of patriotism and nationalism usually had little meaning except in the narrow sense of loyalty to the tsar and faith in the strength and greatness of the Russian state. In other words, patriotism and nationalism were instinctive and associated with the duty every Russian subject owed to his ruler and country; but they were not related to any distinctly Russian conception of life or cultural heritage. It was difficult for the Russian poet, writer, or artist to become an organ of patriotism because the artistic forms and intellectual materials he used were generally of Western European origin. Even in the 1840's and 1850's, by which time Russian literature and national thought had developed impressively, the continued existence of serfdom prevented the majority of the people from being educated in the spirit of Russian nationalism. Until the serfs were freed in 1861, elementary education for the peasant masses was practically nonexistent. Therefore only after 1861 could Russian intellectual and political leaders seriously envisage the use of nationalism in education as an effective means of promoting the social, political, and cultural goals of the Russian state.

For this reason, the main emphasis of the present study will be on the period following the emancipation proclamation of 1861. The ideology of conservative nationalism that emerged during this period, however, can only be understood properly against the background of traditional Russian society and of the romantic nationalism developed by the Slavophiles and others during the first part of the nineteenth century. Therefore, the first three chapters of Part I will concern themselves with this basic traditional and romantic background. The fourth chapter will discuss the curious fashion in which traditional Russian conservatism and nationalism mingled with romantic nationalism in the journalism of Michael Nikiforo-vich Katkov during the decades following the death of Nicholas I.

Part II will examine the formulation of conservative nationalism as an ideology and philosophy of life by a group of writers that gathered about two journals edited by the Dostoevskii brothers during the early 1860's. Through Nicholas Strakhov they were also associated with Nicholas Danilevskii, whose famous work, *Russia and Europe,* Strakhov described as being a "catechism or codex of Slavophilism."[8]

From the beginning there were many internal inconsistencies and weaknesses in the thinking of Russian conservative nationalists. These became particularly apparent during the 1870's, 1880's, and 1890's when such writers as General Rostislav Fadeev, Constantine Leont'ev, and Constantine Pobedonostsev sought to adapt conservative nationalism to the needs of a society that was experiencing the anguish of internal dissension and rapid social and economic change. Their modification of its theory and practice and their ultimate failure will be discussed in Part III, "The Dissolution of Conservative Nationalism."

CHAPTER ONE

Traditional Russian Society

TRADITIONALLY Muscovite and Petrine Russia was above all a service state that required everyone to perform his prescribed duties and to remain in his designated place in society. The gentry, for example, were largely the creation of the Muscovite grand princes and tsars and consisted mainly of the descendants of people who had entered the service of the Muscovite state during the fifteenth, sixteenth, and seventeenth centuries. The Moscow rulers commonly referred to the gentry as "serving people" (*sluzhilye liudi*). Being "servants" of the tsar, the Russian gentry of the sixteenth and seventeenth centuries lacked the traditional privileges and independent position in society of both the old Russian princes and boyars and the Western European nobility. They differed from other groups of the Muscovite population mainly because of the nature of the military and administrative obligations they owed to the state. In exchange for their services to the state, they received control of a large part of the land and the serf population of the Russian countryside. Originally, however, they did not own the land assigned to them but only held it contingent upon the services they performed for the tsar.[1]

The other strata of the population also had their respective duties and obligations. The peasants were bound to the land by either tax obligations or their servile status and were liable to compulsory labor and military service. Similar obligations tied the townspeople to their communes, but they at least enjoyed certain trading privileges within the limits of their towns. The clergy had the task of administering to the religious needs of the population and giving moral support and sanction to the authority of the tsar's government. They were freed from many of the service and tax obligations of the other groups of the population, but were given little protection against abuses on the part of the state and gentry. After

7

the sixteenth century the clergy became more and more a closed caste, above all because of the common interest of state and gentry in discouraging social mobility in Russia. During the seventeenth and eighteenth centuries ecclesiastical schools were restricted almost exclusively to preparing children of priests for positions as parish priests or monks; this tended to separate the clergy from the rest of the population and make its membership almost hereditary.[2]

The tsar stood at the head of traditional Russian society. From the end of the fifteenth century, polemicists, genealogists, clerks, and monks in the service of the Muscovite state had asserted that the grand prince, and later tsar, at Moscow was the legitimate "Sovereign of all Russia" by divine will and through inheritance from his ancestors, who, in previous times, had ruled in Moscow, Kiev, and, allegedly, in Prussia and Rome. According to the official ideology, the tsar was the protector of the Orthodox Church, the defender of the interests of the Russian state, the spiritual father of the Russian people, and a firm and just ruler who sought to promote the good and welfare of his subjects. This conception was, of course, a political and social myth created for the purpose of justifying the position of the Muscovite rulers, but it conformed sufficiently to the needs of Russian society to become the dominant view of political and social reality for a number of centuries in Muscovite and Petrine Russia.[3]

Both church and state did their utmost to keep this conception of politics and society alive in the minds of Russians. In the church it was an integral part of the religious instruction of the masses, whereas the state gave it legal sanction by making it part of the fundamental law of the Russian empire. Thus Article I of every edition of the *Collected Laws of the Russian Empire* published between 1832 and 1905 read: "The Russian Emperor is an autocratic and unlimited monarch. His supreme power is not only to be obeyed from fear but also as a matter of conscience and as commanded by God."[4] Jurists in tsarist Russia, however, usually carefully distinguished between Russian autocracy and despotism. Indeed, Article XLVII of the *Collected Laws of the Russian Empire* referred to Russia as being governed on a firm basis of law.[5] In theory, of course, law in tsarist Russia originated in the authority of the Russian autocrat. But the tsar was always implicitly expected to rule justly and in accordance with custom, the will of God, moral law, and the traditions of the Orthodox Church. The tsar was accordingly viewed as the benevolent and Christian father of the Russian people who had the responsibility of watching over his children and looking out for their interests and welfare.

The notion that all that was good and beneficial in Russia originated in the authority and leadership of the tsar was again and again reiterated by Russian publicists and in the manifestoes of tsars, especially at the time of their ascension to power. A particularly good example is the manifesto made by Nicholas I on July 13, 1826, a little more than six months after the Decembrist uprising:

> Let all classes unite in confidence in the Government. In a state in which love of the Monarch and loyalty to the throne are based upon the innate qualities of the people; where there are national laws and firmness in their administration, all the efforts of ill-intentioned men will ever be vain and frantic. . . . In this condition of the body politic, every man may be confident of the unshaken solidity of the order which will protect his person and his property, and, tranquil in the present, may look forward with hope to the future. It is not by means of insolent and impracticable projects, which are destructive, but it is from above, that national institutions are gradually improved, defects remedied, and abuses reformed. In this regular progress of gradual amelioration, every moderate desire for reform, every project for the dissemination of true enlightenment and industry, brought to Our knowledge through a legal channel, which is open to every man, will ever be received by Us with goodwill and attention; for We neither have nor can possibly have, any other desire than that of seeing our country at the highest pitch of happiness and glory which Providence may have destined it to attain.[6]

The Russian gentry, which represented the principle source of political and social support for the tsar's authority, generally accepted the official version that autocracy was the best and only practical system of government for Russia. They, of course, enjoyed important social and economic advantages and, perhaps for this reason, displayed surprisingly little interest in acquiring for themselves a corporate status in Russian society and political control of the government. Challenges to the autocratic powers of the tsar were usually considered by them to be challenges to their own special position in society. Thus they almost invariably rallied to the defense of autocracy in the face of popular uprisings and the various intrigues and conspiracies of the upper nobility to limit the powers of the tsar and establish some form of aristocratic rule in Russia. Even Catherine II's granting of special privileges and a corporate status in society to the gentry in 1785 did little to alter their traditional political attitudes, for they showed a singular lack of desire to use the elective posts reserved for them in the provinces to strengthen their influence in the Russian countryside and gain political control over local government.[7]

The idea of service owed to the state also did not die out among a good part of the Russian gentry during the second half of the eighteenth century. It is true that obligatory state service was widely resented by the Russian gentry earlier in the century. Nevertheless, a substantial number remained in service in the army and bureaucracy after being freed from obligatory state service in 1762. They probably did so mainly for economic reasons, for the majority of the Russian gentry lived in straitened circumstances. But habit, custom, and a sense of duty also played their respective roles. Many families sent their sons into state service, especially the army, generation after generation. Certainly loyal and devoted servants of the Russian autocrat such as Maksim Maksimych in Lermontov's *Hero of Our Time* and Nicholas Rostov in Tolstoi's *War and Peace* were fairly common figures among Russian gentry during the first part of the nineteenth century. Such gentry included even the proud but usually impoverished descendants of boyars and Kievan princes. An outstanding representative of this group was Prince Vladimir Odoevskii, who was a well-known writer and government official during the reign of Nicholas I. In 1835 he wrote concerning the importance of government service in Russia:

> Service here in Russia is the *only way to be useful to the Fatherland.* . . . [In Russia] there is no inborn . . . aspiration for enlightenment. Tell me, who among us builds schools? The government. Who builds factories and machines? The government. Who makes discoveries possible? The government. Who supports companies? The government and only the government. All these things do not—and will not in the future—occur to private individuals. [But] the government needs people for its undertakings. Dissociating oneself from it means dissociating oneself from that which moves all of Russia forward and gives her life and air to breathe.[8]

The French Revolution did much to enhance the prestige of autocratic government in the eyes of the Russian gentry as the principal source of progress and social stability in Russia. Both Catherine II and the gentry soon realized that the Revolution threatened the very existence of established order everywhere in Europe.[9] Hence there was a natural tendency for the gentry and the throne to join forces in keeping the influence of revolutionary ideas and institutions out of Russia.

But certain obstacles stood in the way of truly intimate cooperation between the gentry and the government. The government, for its part, was never completely satisfied with the low cultural and educational level of the bulk of the gentry nor with the lack of interest in civic affairs and public life so many of them displayed. The gentry, in their turn, had always resented the government's willingness to permit a number of people from the lower strata of the population, especially from the clergy, to occupy responsible posts in the bureaucracy. At the beginning of the nineteenth century the gentry were particularly alarmed by the rapid growth of the bureaucracy and by the influence exercised by Michael Speranskii, the son of a priest, over Alexander I during the years immediately preceding the War of 1812. They were irritated not only by specific measures of Speranskii, such as the requirement made in 1809 that promotion to the higher posts in the bureaucracy should be made only on the basis of examination and university credentials, but also by his general plans for the reform of the Russian government. Above all, they feared that the implementation of Speranskii's proposed reforms would undermine the position of the gentry as a privileged social group and the main ally of the autocrat in maintaining order in Russian society. The most sophisticated expression of their fears at this time was Karamzin's famous *Memoir on Ancient and Modern Russia*.[10] Less sophisticated accusations were hurled indiscriminately against Speranskii in gentry circles before 1812. He was accused of Jacobinism, of wanting to abolish serfdom, of subservience to the interests of France, and of encroachments on the rights of the gentry and on the autocratic powers of the tsar. Although these accusations were half-truths at best, the gentry were certainly quite right in their conviction that the very principle of reform could, in many ways, adversely affect them in the future. Speranskii's ideal was that of a Russia run by an official bureaucracy recruited from various strata of the population, whose selection would be based on efficient service for the state. Trained bureaucrats and functionaries were obviously best suited for such a system, not the gentry and aristocrats of the old regime.[11]

Speranskii, however, was sacrificed for the sake of peace and harmony between the tsar and the gentry. After this, Russian rulers seldom risked antagonizing the gentry by allowing commoners to occupy positions high enough in the Russian bureaucracy to influence decision making and the conduct of official policy. Thus, at the end of Alexander I's reign and under Nicholas I, Admiral A. S. Shishkov, Count S. S. Uvarov, Count A. Kh. Benckendorff, and other defenders of the vested interests of the gentry in Russia were placed in charge of such important activities as education, censorship, and the police. Under Nicholas I, especially, they worked determinedly to defend established social order in Russia against the influence of European liberal and revolutionary ideas, to discourage social mobility in Russian society by keeping the lower classes out of secondary and higher schools, and to stifle criticism at all levels of the social and political *status quo* through the strict regulation and control of society by police and censorship authorities.[12] The reforms introduced by Alexander II after the Crimean War did little to alter the predominance of the gentry in government circles. They were, it is true, obliged to agree to the emancipation of the serfs; but they were permitted to control the commissions and committees that worked out the details of emancipation. Of course, they made certain that their own special interests were given more than fair consideration in the final emancipation settlement in 1861.

At the same time, the gentry continued to have their duties and responsibilities. There is evidence that, as a whole, they took, or were obliged to take, these duties and responsibilities more seriously than before. Nicholas I expected every young person of noble birth to serve either in the bureaucracy or in the army. "We are all," he once commented characteristically, "in service."[13] Nicholas made every effort to raise the standards of performance of the gentry in the civil service and army. One example was the founding of the School of Jurisprudence at St. Petersburg in 1835, which had the special task of preparing children from the gentry for service as legal experts in the bureaucracy. Both Constantine Pobedonostsev, the future Over Procurator of the Holy Synod, and the Slavophile Ivan Aksakov attended this school. Indeed, all of the thinkers who formulated the ideology of conservative nationalism during the 1860's, 1870's, and 1880's attended either service schools or a university and spent some time in the bureaucracy or army, although they did not always find such service to their liking. Four of the conservative nationalists who will be discussed in subsequent chapters—Nicholas Strakhov, Rostislav Fadeev, Constantine Leont'ev, and Constantine Pobedonostsev—spent most of their adult lives in state service. This is not coincidental, for the defenders of conservative order and nationalism in nineteenth-century Russia came primarily from among the service gentry.

Two of these theoreticians of conservative nationalism in Russia, however, came from families that did not originally belong to the service gentry. Nicholas Strakhov's father was educated at the Kiev Ecclesiastical Academy, from which he received a Master's degree; and Strakhov, himself, after having been orphaned, was educated by his uncle (also a member of the academically trained upper white clergy) in church seminaries before entering the University of St. Petersburg in 1845. Constantine Pobedonostsev's grandfather was a simple priest. His father, however, was educated at the Moscow Ecclesiastical Academy and later became a professor of Russian literature at the University of Moscow. Constantine Pobedonostsev was permitted to attend the School of Jurisprudence, which was intended for children of the gentry, because of his father's standing as a university professor. His general philosophy of life, however, was characteristic of the upper clergy's and not of the gentry's.

The appearance of two descendants of the academically trained clergy among the defenders of established order in Russia suggests the importance of the church in Russian society during the nineteenth century. In previous times, of course, the Orthodox Church had played a highly significant role in Russian history and had been very useful to the state in establishing in the popular mind the notion that the tsar's power had divine sanction and that all authority in society was part of the natural order and originated in God.[14] During the eighteenth century the Westernization and secularization of Russian politics and upper-class culture greatly diminished the influence of the church on the thinking and policies of governmental leaders.[15] After the French Revolution and the French invasion of Russia in 1812, however, Alexander I and others in governmental circles again came to have a greater appreciation of the importance and usefulness of religion as a source of moral unity in Russian society. But they did not, interestingly enough, turn immediately to Orthodox Church traditions in their efforts to further the cause of religion in Russia. Instead, they initially gave at least semiofficial sanction to the activities of Freemasons and others to disseminate Western European mystical and Protestant religious ideas throughout Russia.[16] Only toward the end of Alexander I's reign, especially as a result of the intrigues of such figures as Metropolitan Seraphim of St. Petersburg and Admiral A. S. Shishkov,[17] did the Russian emperor and government come under the influence of official Orthodoxy. From then on Orthodoxy was a primary consideration in the mind of every Russian emperor and statesman who sought to maintain established order in Russia in the face of the challenge of liberal and revolutionary ideas coming from Western Europe.

The Orthodox Church remained, however, the humble servant of the Russian state. Under Nicholas I, who in his own way was most dedicated to the cause of Orthodoxy, the Russian church was more rigidly and hopelessly subordinated to the bureaucratic control and minute regulation of the government than ever before.[18] The upper clergy sometimes resented this bureaucratic control of church affairs, but they never questioned the fundamental correctness of the premise that one of the most important responsibilities of the church was to aid the state in maintaining order in society. Thus such an influential and respected church figure as Metropolitan Filaret of Moscow constantly emphasized in his sermons and writings the tsar's role as the living instrument of God's will and the need for unquestioning obedience to established authority in society.[19] On the tenth anniversary of the coronation of Nicholas I, Filaret celebrated Russia's good fortune in having a people whose obedience to established authority was a result of their natural love for ruler and country:

> This is a vital warmth in the body of a state, a self-generating movement in the direction of social unity; it is a winged chariot of authority, free submission and submissive freedom. We Russians, fed by our mother's milk with love for ruler and country, know from past and present experience how strengthening this nourishment has been for the most formidable exploits in times of great difficulty.[20]

Filaret felt that the parish clergy had a special role in Russia as examples of obedience and loyalty to the government, as interpreters for the common people of the tsar's will and governmental decrees, and as spiritual leaders in the struggle against disorder and disrespect for authority in the Russian countryside.[21] During the 1850's and 1860's he was particularly disturbed by opinions expressed in radical and liberal journals, which he considered a threat to Orthodox Christianity, public morality, and social order. He therefore condemned freedom of the press as a harmful innovation in Russia.[22] He also was afraid that the emancipation of the serfs could lead to undesirable repercussions. Although he came to accept the inevitability of emancipation, Filaret's sympathies were not on the side of the peasants. He defended corporal punishment and argued that any promise to the peasants of permanent possession of land formerly held by the gentry would adversely affect the gentry's economic interests and, therefore, weaken their confidence in the wisdom of the government's policies.[23] Filaret, it should be recalled, was entrusted by Alexander II, the so-called tsar-liberator, with the drafting of the text of the emancipation proclamation of February 19, 1861.[24] This is really not surprising, for Alexander never broke completely with traditional Russian society. In the final analysis, the main source of social order and unity in this society had always been the close alliance between the autocrat, the upper clergy, and the gentry.

CHAPTER TWO

Traditional Russian Nationalism

In the Troitse-Sergiev Monastery at Zagorsk stands a monument erected in 1792 which records how this monastery allegedly helped save Russia from the Tatars in 1380 and from the Poles and two serious internal crises during the seventeenth century. This monument is interesting not only because it is a surprisingly early example of patriotic architecture but also because it suggests how closely associated traditional Russian nationalism always was with both the Orthodox Church and the Russian state.

During the centuries of Tatar domination the Orthodox Church remained the only institution that continued to represent the idea of political and national unity implanted in the minds of the Orthodox Eastern Slavs by the religious and political leaders of Kievan Rus'. The religious unity of the former lands of Kievan Rus' was, however, not politically meaningful as long as the greater part of the Eastern Slav Orthodox population lived under the authority of the Catholic Polish-Lithuanian state or of petty Russian princes subjected to the control of Mohammedan Tatars. Therefore the church clearly had an interest in supporting the strongest among the Orthodox princes in the hope that he would someday reunite the so-called Russian land.

Although the Kievan metropolitanate had been located in Moscow as early as the first part of the fourteenth century, only after the Battle of Kulikovo Field in 1380 did the Orthodox Church begin to praise the Muscovite princes as the defenders of the religious and national traditions of the "Russian land."[1] It is, of course, a matter of conjecture to what extent the Muscovite princes in the late fourteenth and early fifteenth centuries accepted this version of their role as the continuers of the Kievan political and Orthodox Christian traditions. By the end of the fifteenth century, however, Ivan III had officially announced himself to be the

15

"Sovereign of all Russia" by the grace of God and through inheritance from his ancestors. This was a clear indication of his determination to bring under his rule all of the lands formerly included within Kievan Rus' or inhabited by Orthodox Eastern Slavs.

The official ideology of the Muscovite state that emerged around 1500 is related to the theocratic theories of Orthodox churchmen and to popular nationalism in a complicated fashion. The state was naturally quite eager to strengthen its position by making use of Byzantine political ideas and by identifying itself with the popular image of a Russian national and Orthodox monarchy. This was especially true under Ivan IV. Ivan's famous correspondence with Prince Andrew Kurbskii reflects the profound influence of Byzantine thought and Orthodox Russian nationalism on the official ideology of the Muscovite state by the mid-sixteenth century. Certain examples of icon art of that era give the same impression. "The Church Militant," now in the Tretiakov Gallery at Moscow, is one such icon. Here Ivan, after his victory over the Tatars at Kazan in 1552, is allegorically represented in the company of Dmitrii Donskoi, Saint Vladimir, Alexander Nevskii, the Archangel Michael, and the Virgin with the Christ child as one of the great national and religious heroes of Russian history.[2] But the Muscovite rulers, apparently fearing that the church might encroach on some of the tsar's sovereign powers, did not allow themselves to become completely identified with the Orthodox Church's conception of a Russian national and Christian monarchy. To the contrary, they were usually cautious in their acceptance of ideas from the clergy and Byzantine Greeks. Thus the designation of Moscow as the Third Rome remained largely confined to clerical circles and never became part of the official terminology of the Muscovite grand princes and tsars. Likewise, the Muscovite rulers were cool to the suggestion that they should legitimize their position by basing it on the Byzantine inheritance through Ivan III's marriage with Zoe Palaeologus. They preferred a simple appeal to their rights as the descendants of the Kievan rulers of "all Russia."[3]

In any event, Orthodox churchmen must be given credit for helping the Muscovite state popularize the image of the tsar as the defender of the national and religious interests of Russia. The support the state derived from this notion was particularly apparent in times of crisis, especially in connection with the anti-Polish and anti-Catholic sentiment resulting from foreign intervention in Russia at the beginning of the seventeenth century. The popular view of the Catholic Lithuanians and Poles as the national and religious enemies of Russia and of the tsar as her protector was, of course, useful to the political and religious leaders of Muscovy in their efforts to re-establish political and moral order at the time.[4]

During the eighteenth century, however, the Russian government tended to discourage rather than encourage xenophobia and religious nationalism, for it was then mainly preoccupied with the adaption of Western technology and civilization to the needs of Russian society. There were, nevertheless, numerous individual Russians who continued to have strong patriotic and religious feelings. The warnings of monks concerning the heresies and intrigues of foreigners,[5] the criticisms of gallomania made by such writers as Nicholas I. Novikov and Denis I. Fonvizin, the hostility displayed by so many Russians during the eighteenth century toward Germans in the government, army, and Academy of Sciences, and even the support Catherine II gave to Russian Orthodoxy in what was formerly eastern Poland[6]—all indicate that traditional nationalism remained at least a powerful undercurrent in Russian life during the period when Russians supposedly "became citizens of the world but ceased in certain respects to be citizens of Russia."[7] The government, however, gave little more than token support to the cause of Russian nationalism. It was obviously more interested in improving the administrative efficiency of the civil service, in maintaining existing political and social order, and in raising the cultural level of the Russian gentry than it was in developing social cohesion through an appeal to Russian national and religious traditions.

The challenge to traditional society represented by the French Revolution, however, sooner or later made it clear to conservative governments that henceforth no European state could afford to neglect developing feelings of patriotism among its subjects. The historian Nicholas Karamzin realized this at the very beginning of the nineteenth century. Thus he criticized Peter I in his *Memoir on Ancient and Modern Russia* for having failed to realize that "national spirit constitutes the moral strength of states"[8] and for having "weakened the spirit of brotherly national unity binding the estates of the realm"[9] by separating the upper classes from the lower through the introduction into Russia of the manners and customs of Western European nations. He commented concerning the differences between the old and the new Russia:

> In the reigns of Michael and of his son, our ancestors, while assimilating many advantages which were to be found in foreign customs, never lost the conviction that an Orthodox Russian was the most perfect citizen and Holy Rus' the foremost state in the world. Let this be called a delusion. Yet how much it did to strengthen patriotism and the moral fibre of the country! Would we have today that audacity, after having spent over a century in the school of foreigners, to boast of our civic pride?[10]

Karamzin's appeal in the name of Russian nationalism was but one— and a moderate one at that—among many in Russia during the period of the Napoleonic wars. One of the more bizarre exponents of exaggerated patriotism at the time was Karamzin's literary opponent and critic, Admiral Shishkov. Shishkov equated morality and the purity of Russian religion with the use of Old Church Slavonic. He therefore not only vehemently denounced all traces of revolutionary ideas in Russia but also went so far as to condemn the influence of French on the Russian literary language.[11] Such a condemnation was clearly not in keeping with the thinking of most educated Russians at the beginning of the nineteenth century. In 1812, however, Shishkov was made state secretary, replacing the disgraced Speranskii.[12] During 1812 and 1813 Alexander made frequent use of Shishkov for the drafting of patriotic manifestoes to the army, but he did not allow the subject of educating Russians in the spirit of Orthodoxy and Russian nationality to be given serious consideration in government circles until the end of his reign.

Alexander's change of policy was much influenced by a campaign against foreign religious influences in Russia, which was begun in the early 1820's by Metropolitan Seraphim of St. Petersburg, Minister of War A. A. Arakcheev, Admiral Shishkov, and other conservative figures in church government. The logical starting point for this campaign was the removal of the Minister of Ecclesiastical Affairs and Public Instruction, Prince A. N. Golitsyn, who was the principal supporter in the government of foreign religious influences. The major instrument of intrigue against Golitsyn was the monk Fotii Spaskii, the Archimandrite of the Iurev Monastery near Novgorod. Fotii's friends arranged for him to be given two interviews with the emperor on the assumption that the eloquence and complete devotion of this ardent and emaciated monk would move the emperor, who was then undergoing a severe spiritual crisis, to favor the Orthodox Church more than he had previously. Their plan succeeded after Fotii had his second interview with Alexander in 1824. In this interview Fotii warned the emperor against the forces plotting to weaken the religious foundation of the Russian state. He fulminated especially against certain German writers whose religious activities and works had allegedly prepared many Russians for revolution. To avert general calamity for Russia, Fotii implored the emperor to deal firmly with foreign religious ideas and groups in Russia and to abolish the Ministry of Ecclesiastical Affairs and Public Instruction (which had combined educational and church affairs under Golitsyn's direction since 1817).[13] These cries of alarm and importunities apparently made a deep impression on Alexander, for he removed Golitsyn from his post as Minister of Ecclesiastical Affairs and Public Instruction several weeks later. The ministry itself was abolished. The Holy Synod assumed its old position in the Russian bureaucracy, the Over Procurator no longer being subordinated to a special ministry but once again having direct access to the emperor.[14] The new Minister of Public Instruction was Admiral Shishkov.

As minister, Shishkov was determined to do his utmost to curtail the influence of revolutionary and non-Orthodox religious ideas in Russia and to organize public instruction in accordance with "purity of faith," loyalty to ruler and country, and the tranquillity of society. In December, 1824, he proposed an ambitious program, whose aim was to teach all students in the schools under the jurisdiction of the Ministry of Public Instruction patriotism, Russian history, literature, and language, Church Slavonic, the doctrines of the Orthodox faith, and Christian morality. Shishkov's plans for the education of upper-class Russians in the spirit of patriotism and Russian Orthodoxy never got much beyond the initial planning stage in government committees by the time he retired in 1828.[15] However, several years later, in 1833, when S. S. Uvarov, a well-educated and competent administrator, became Minister of Public Instruction, the Russian state finally attempted in earnest to exploit the latent possibilities of nationality as a source of social cohesion and moral strength for Russia.

Uvarov's main service was to formulate a much more convincing theory of official nationality[16] than Shishkov had ever been able to do. Indeed, his articulation of the formula "Autocracy, Orthodoxy, and Nationality" was an accomplishment in itself. He first suggested this phrase shortly before he became Minister of Public Instruction when, in December, 1832, he reported to Nicholas I concerning conditions at the University of Moscow.[17] In this as well as in subsequent reports, Uvarov emphasized the necessity of protecting Russian youth from the contagion of European ideas. He urged that they should be transformed into loyal and patriotic servants of the Russian state by developing in them respect for patriotic subjects and the conviction "that only an adaption of general, universal enlightenment to our national way of life, our national soul, can bring true fruits to each of us."[18] As minister he was eager that the Ministry of Public Instruction should assume a role of leadership in accomplishing this task. Thus in 1843 he assured Emperor Nicholas:

> In the reign of Your Majesty the chief task of the Ministry of Public Instruction consisted in gathering together and uniting all the intellectual forces which until now have been dispersed, all the means of general and private education which have remained without respect and partly without supervision, all the elements which have had an unreliable and even false orientation; in adapting the development of minds to the needs of the government; and in making sure of the future now as much at this is humanly possible.[19]

Nationality (*narodnost'*) was clearly the most ambiguous term in Uvarov's trinity.[20] Of course, all Russian nationalists agreed that *narodnost'* suggested the basic notion that the preservation and development of Russian national individuality represented an intrinsically noble and worthwhile aspiration. They were, however, often in disagreement concerning the nature of this individuality. The Slavophiles and other romantic nationalists, for example, sought it in terms of the manifestations of Russian national originality in music, poetry, literature, folklore, and the life of the common people. Uvarov, on the other hand, being an aristocrat and reactionary bureaucrat, displayed little interest in the culture and customs of the common people. Characteristic of his attitude toward them was his defense of the utility and necessity of serfdom in Russia and his efforts to exclude the lower classes from the secondary schools and universities of the Russian empire.[21] Uvarov, in contrast to the Slavophiles and other romantic nationalists, assigned a passive and secondary role to the people in Russian national life. In the introduction to the first issue of the *Journal of the Ministry of Public Instruction,* which Uvarov founded in 1834, he stated: "Here [in Russia] the Tsar loves the Fatherland in the person of the people whom he rules as a Father . . . ; and the people are unable to separate Fatherland from Tsar and see in Him their happiness, strength, and glory."[22]

In practice, Uvarov's official nationality meant, above all, three things: (1) the teaching of the tsar's subjects to be loyal to the government and true to the Orthodox Church, (2) the encouragement of Russian patriotism through emphasis on national subjects in the education of the upper classes, and (3) support for the cause of Russian national culture and the increased use of the Russian language in Poland and in the western and Baltic provinces. The first-mentioned objective of Uvarov's ministry was hardly a novel one, for the tsarist government had traditionally sought to promote political loyalty and religious conformity in Russia. Moreover, the critical attitude of so many educated Russians toward autocracy and Orthodoxy during the 1830's and 1840's suggests that Uvarov was not particularly successful in instilling the proper political and religious principles and attitudes in the minds of young Russians. His emphasis on nationality, however, though he was certainly vague concerning the meaning of this term, was in keeping with the spirit of the time and, perhaps for this reason, enjoyed relative success. The support that his ministry gave to the cause of Russian national culture in Poland and in the western and Baltic provinces was also of great importance to the subsequent history of Russia, for during the 1830's and 1840's the Russian government first seriously experimented with techniques to oblige the children of the gentry and the middle class in these areas to learn the Russian language and more about Russian culture and history.

The Russian government was especially unrelenting in its efforts to uproot Polish and Catholic culture and influence in the western provinces after the Polish uprising of 1830–31. Russian authorities were particularly anxious to curtail the church schools of Roman Catholic monasteries and replace them with Russian schools under the jurisdiction of the Ministry of Public Instruction. In 1832 the Polish university at Vilna was closed; it was replaced by the Russian Saint-Vladimir University at Kiev in the following year. In 1836 the teaching of Polish was discontinued in state schools.[23] Another heavy blow to Polish Catholic influence in the western provinces was the success of the Russian government and church authorities during the 1820's and 1830's in persuading key figures among the Uniate clergy to leave the Uniate Church and declare their adherence to the official Russian church. In 1839 the reunion of the Uniates in the western Ukraine with the Orthodox Church was formally proclaimed.[24]

The Baltic Germans, whose personal loyalty to the throne was above reproach, were treated more considerately. But here, too, there was no question about the special rights of the Orthodox Church and the necessity of greater use of the Russian language in the schools of the Baltic provinces.[25] Indeed, Nicholas I's concern about the special rights of the Orthodox Church even persuaded him to permit Orthodox priests to convert almost 100,000 Latvian and Estonian Lutheran peasants to Orthodoxy.[26] In the context of the economic and social grievances these peasants had against their German landowners, mass conversion among them had dangerous implications for established order in the Baltic provinces. Influential Baltic barons naturally pointed this out to Nicholas I, who soon took measures to restrain the zeal of the more militant advocates of the interests of Russian Orthodox culture in the Baltic region.[27] This episode is instructive for the light it throws on the nature of Nicholas I's policy. The main difference between it and the Russification of a later date is that Nicholas I unmistakably attached greater importance to the maintenance of established order than he did to the propagation of Russian nationality and the Orthodox faith. Nonetheless, champions of Russification toward the end of the nineteenth century nearly always regarded Nicholas I as one of the few Russian rulers prior to Alexander III who had an adequate understanding of the true interests of Russian nationality and religion in the Baltic region.

Nicholas V. Riasanovsky has emphasized that there was considerable support of official nationality among two groups of Russian intellectuals during the reign of Nicholas I: the nationalists on the one hand, and those who viewed Russia in terms of the traditionally dynastic state on the other.[28] The nationalists were profoundly influenced by German romanticism and not only championed the cause of freedom for their "brother Slavs" but also favored the emancipation and education of the Russian serfs. Moreover, they challenged the caste privileges of the Baltic Germans in Kurland, Livonia, and Estonia in the name of Russian nationality. The dynastic supporters of official nationality identified Russian nationality narrowly with the traditional devotion of the Russian people to tsar and church and with the existing social *status quo* in Russia. They usually viewed the nationalists' sympathies for Russian peasants and Balkan Slavs with suspicion and esteemed the Baltic Germans as loyal servants of the Russian emperor.[29]

There was also a third group of supporters of official nationality: those who continued the tradition of moralistic and nationalistic Orthodoxy advocated by Admiral Shishkov and Archimandrite Fotii.[30] General S. A. Burachek, a retired naval engineer, sought to defend this point of view during the early 1840's as the principal editor of *The Lighthouse: A Journal of Contemporary Enlightenment, Art, and Education in the Spirit of Russian Nationality* (*Maiak, zhurnal sovremennago prosveshcheniia, iskusstva i obrazovaniia v dukhe narodnosti russkoi*). Burachek was especially concerned with the success of secular literature in Russia at the time. He equated secular literature with paganism and argued that the proper task of literature after the French Revolution was not the battle of romanticism versus classicism but the battle of Christianity with paganism, of the spiritual with the secular.[31] He was particularly offended by Lermontov's *Hero of Our Time* because it was not inspired by Orthodoxy and Russian nationality but, instead, by destructive egotism and pessimism.[32] Rather than follow the example of Lermontov, he wanted the writers of his time to turn to Russian nationality (*narodnost'*). "Tsar, faith, and language, autocracy, Orthodoxy, and speech (*slovo*) . . . ," he explained, "here truly is the cornerstone of Russian nationality."[33]

One advantage of Burachek's conception of Russian nationality over the dynastic view was that it at least sought to relate nationality to the actual life of the common people in Russia. Thus the *Lighthouse* not only accepted contributions of semiliterate Russian peasants but also displayed interest in folklore by publishing ethnographic studies and examples of Eastern Slav, especially Ukrainian, popular poetry and prose.[34] But the uncritical naïveté of Burachek and other contributors to the *Lighthouse* made it difficult for the general reading public to take this journal seriously. Buracheck, himself, hardly contributed to the *Lighthouse*'s popularity by publishing in it his own articles, which were full of mathematical formulae, pious religious sentiments, and figures of speech taken from elementary physics (such as the "parallelogram of forces" between the will of God and the will of man[35]). The *Lighthouse* had its maximum number of 800 subscribers during its first year of publication in 1840, and this number progressively diminished until Burachek stopped publishing it in 1845.[36]

The dynastic interpretation of official nationality was equally unpopular among intellectuals interested in the development of Russian national culture. The dynastic view attracted few intellectuals because it had little to do with nationality in the usual sense of the word and because it was so clearly associated with the efforts of the government of Nicholas I to control the thought of Russian intellectuals through rigid censorship. Moreover, the opposition of so many proponents of this view to the education and emancipation of the serfs could only alienate an increasing number of Russian intellectuals ranging from the socialist left to the Slavophile right.

Hence, among the supporters of official nationality, only the nationalists had much chance for any lasting influence on Russian intellectuals. Among such nationalists, two Moscow University professors, M. P. Pogodin and S. P. Shevyrev, were particularly important. Their lectures and writings had considerable impact on the thinking of such promising young Muscovites of the 1830's and 1840's as the Slavophiles, Apollon Grigor'ev, A. N. Ostrovskii, and T. I. Filippov.[37] Since Shevyrev and Pogodin lacked the originality and personal magnetism required to make them the nucleus of an intellectual movement, their journal, *The Muscovite* (*Moskvitianin*), attracted relatively few readers. This journal did, it is true, briefly attain a degree of popular success in the early 1850's, when Pogodin was assisted by a group of "junior editors" including Grigor'ev, Filippov, Ostrovskii, and E. N. Edel'son. But Pogodin's interference and tightfisted financial policies soon offended the "junior editors." Without their cooperation, Pogodin was obliged to discontinue publication of the *Muscovite,* which could not compete with the new journals founded at the beginning of Alexander II's reign.

Both Pogodin and Shevyrev, however, are probably best understood not in terms of their defense of official nationality but, instead, in terms of their general contribution to Russian romantic nationalism during the first part of the nineteenth century. It is probably true that they often were little better than apologists for and glorifiers of Nicholas I's official policies. At the same time, their extravagant praise of the Russian people, their romantic view of Russian nationality, and their championing of the cause of the Balkan Slavs were hardly compatible with the traditional conception of Russian nationality and the inflexibly dynastic views of Nicholas I and his principal advisers. The nationalism advocated by Pogodin, Shevyrev, and other romantic nationalists found its final justification in the way of life and customs of Slavic peasants scattered throughout eastern Europe and the Balkans. As such, this nationalism could easily become associated with the idea of the liberation of the Balkan Slavs from the Turks and Austrians, of Russians (i.e., Ukrainians and Belorussians) from Polish landowners, and even Estonians and Latvians (who supposedly yearned to become Russian Orthodox Christians) from the Baltic Germans. Nicholas I feared that nationality conceived in these terms might be used to challenge established authority in society, thereby undermining the foundations of traditional order throughout central and eastern Europe.

Romantic nationalism later came to be associated much more with conservatism in Russia than with social criticism and revolt against authority. Thus the radical thinkers of the 1860's were prone to criticize the idealism and romanticism of early Russian utopian socialists, while contemporary conservative nationalists consciously identified themselves with the romantic and idealistic philosophy of life that had been so popular in Moscow intellectual circles during the 1830's and 1840's. This philosophy was, of course, politically neutral and also provided considerable stimulus to the development of the revolutionary nationalism of Alexander Herzen and the populists. Most of its advocates during the 1830's and 1840's, however, never broke with the traditional Muscovite patriotism and devotion to tsar and Orthodox Church which they had learned at home as the offspring of well-established, conservative gentry families. At times they were critical of Nicholas I's official policies, but they never lost faith in the essential soundness of traditional Russian values and institutions. The conservative nationalists of the 1860's usually belonged to the same social group as the earlier romantic nationalists and generally shared their attitudes and philosophical outlook. In more than one way, the conservative nationalists inherited an earlier intellectual tradition and sought to modernize it and adapt it to the needs and exigencies of a new era.

CHAPTER THREE

Russian Romantic Nationalism[1]

THE MAJOR goal that nineteenth-century Russian romantic nationalists set for themselves was to define the nature of Russian national character and historical individuality. The definition they sought had to be in conformance with both traditional Russian attitudes and current Western European philosophical and social views, for the romantic nationalists themselves and the audience for whom they intended their theories had been educated not only in the school of traditional Russia but also in that of contemporary Western Europe. This often placed them in a somewhat difficult and even ambiguous position. They approved of autocracy and Orthodoxy as being properly part of the Russian way of life; but the European form of their education made it impossible for them to accept the naïve xenophobia, the moralistic and exclusively nationalistic Orthodoxy, and the narrowly dynastic autocracy of such figures as Admiral Shishkov, Archimandrite Fotii Spaskii, and General Burachek. At the same time, they were always on guard against European influences. They accepted what they considered valid in the European inheritance but sought to be independent in their interpretation of it. In this endeavor they were but partly successful.

The problem was not a new one, for Russians had long been concerned about preserving their country's national identity. However, only toward the end of the eighteenth century did such Russian intellectuals as the dramatist D. I. Fonvizin, the publisher and journalist N. I. Novikov, the actor and journalist P. A. Plavil'shchikov, and the general and amateur historian I. N. Boltin first give serious attention to the task of describing the nature of Russian national character and historical individuality. Fonvizin, Novikov, and Plavil'shchikov emphasized certain positive sides of Russian character and customs and pointed to the originality and freshness

25

of the Russian mind as evidence of the brilliant future that was in store for the Russian people.[2] Boltin, in his turn, sought to find certain principles and laws governing Russia's historical development as a nation. His immediate objective was to refute the thesis of N. G. Le Clerc's *Histoire physique, morale et politique de la Russie ancienne et moderne* (Paris: Froullé, 1783–94) that the main connecting link in Russian history had been the tyranny of Russia's rulers and the backwardness and servitude of her people. He experienced little difficulty in finding historical evidence to demonstrate that Russia's development had been a complex one and that its earlier stages had been similar to those through which the Western European nations had passed. As a follower of Montesquieu and other eighteenth-century writers, he insisted that Russian history had to be viewed strictly in accordance with the special conditions created by Russian geography and climate. He had a profound respect for these conditions—especially in the form of traditions, customs, and the political institutions of Russian society—and therefore argued that European standards could not always be applied in judging Russia.[3] He also believed that changes in customs and ancestral usages should be gradual. For this reason he criticized Peter I's reforms for their abruptness and forced character. Or, as H. Rogger has summarized in his study of Boltin:

> To Boltin's quite modern perception, a culture was all of one piece. Destroy the old Russian bath-house, accustom stomachs to the refinements of French cuisine and you destroy at the same time vital elements of the culture which have enabled Russians to adapt to the rigors of their climate and to use to best advantage the products of their soil.[4]

But Boltin did not precisely define the nature of the elements that constituted Russia's cultural heritage any more than did Novikov, Fonvizin, and Plavil'shchikov. He remained too cosmopolitan, rational, and pragmatic in outlook to attach primary importance to the specific manifestations of Russian nationality in the folklore, popular songs, and daily life of the Russian people. Investigation of these manifestations was reserved for a subsequent generation of Russian intellectuals.

Karamzin, who belonged to the generation following Boltin's, also did not undertake this task. Admittedly, his *History of the Russian State* did contribute significantly to the awakening of patriotic pride among educated Russians by describing the past achievements of Russian autocracy in a polished and readable Russian prose style. He sentimentally yearned for those former times when Russians dressed themselves as Russians, spoke their own language, and faithfully maintained their own customs.[5] But his conception of Russian individuality and uniqueness was largely a political one. That is, he was above all interested in the defense of traditional autocratic government and of the power interests and political unity of the Russian state. His concern with the unity and power interests of the Russian state was particularly evident in his statements about Poland, which he wanted to keep under the firm and unrelenting control of Russia.[6] Moreover, his interest in the life of the common people was at best a superficial one, for his history did not describe the development of the Russian people's national culture and character but, instead, that of the Russian state.

A new attitude toward Russian nationality, history, and culture emerged only after the Napoleonic wars and largely as the result of the influence of German romantic nationalism. This new philosophy of life and nationality praised the intuitive imagination and simplicity of peoples not corrupted by civilization and sought expressions of the spontaneous art of primitive peoples (such as the Slavs and German peasants) in the form of folklore, popular songs, and language. Before the end of the Napoleonic era such thinkers as Herder, Friedrich Schlegel, Schleiermacher, Friedrich Ludwig Jahn, and Friedrich von Schelling had formulated a romantic theory of esthetics, nature, and life and had coined or adopted such words as *Volkstümlichkeit, nationale Eigenart,* and *Volksgeist* to express the idea of national individuality.

Friedrich Meinecke and other recent writers have described the romantic nationalists' conception of history and life as historicism. Meinecke associated historicism primarily with what he called the *Individualitäts-gedanke* and the *Entwicklungsgedanke.* By *Individualitätsgedanke* he meant the consideration of historical forces in terms of individual cultural and social structures. This new view was chiefly developed in the eighteenth and early nineteenth centuries, when it began more and more to challenge prevailing rationalistic ideas derived from classical antiquity, medieval Christianity, and the Enlightenment. The old view had conceived of history and human society in terms of generalizations such as natural law and model institutions, which could be applied at any time and any place. In contrast to this, the historicists stressed the importance of individuality—that there is so much variety in human experience that it is utterly impossible to comprehend society and history in abstract and general terms alone. Instead, they felt, it was necessary to consider historical development in a more organic manner. Applied to nationality, this meant that each people had its own national character and individuality, which were expressed in its history, literature, religion, art, customs, and, especially, its language. The essence of such individuality, Meinecke wrote, "is revealed only in development."[7] He insisted on the importance of the idea of development (*Entwicklungsgedanke*) because almost invariably the writers concerned with the individuality of collective entities such as peoples and nations had attempted to understand their uniqueness in terms of development. The principal expression of this idea is, of course, history; and the study of history has played a dominant role in the thought of European nationalists and intellectuals since the end of the eighteenth century.[8]

German romantic nationalism was introduced into Russia during the 1820's and 1830's by a small but influential group of young Russian professors and intellectuals. They were attracted by German theories of nationalism because the efforts of German intellectuals to gain cultural and national independence from the influence of French civilization and the ideas of the French Revolution so closely paralleled their own efforts to develop a uniquely national culture and philosophy of life in Russia. Moreover, the relatively low level of philosophical culture in Russia at the beginning of the nineteenth century handicapped them in elaborating philosophical concepts and terminology sufficiently sophisticated and convincing to justify abandoning the prevailing cosmopolitan *Weltanschauung* they had learned from the French Enlightenment. In time, Russian nationalists probably would have independently developed their own terminology and concepts for a new nationalistic philosophy of life. But since the Germans had already done so, their ideas understandably had a powerful attraction for many patriotic young Russians.

Moscow was the center in which German romantic nationalism took root in Russia during the 1820's and 1830's. Here such professors as I. I. Davydov, M. G. Pavlov, and N. I. Nadezhdin popularized German idealistic philosophy and ideas on organic development and romantic esthetics.[9] Their students were especially interested in using these ideas to lay the foundations for a new national school of Russian literature. In 1823 a group of students organized themselves into the Society of the Lovers of Wisdom, which included in its ranks not only several future Slavophiles but also Pogodin and Shevyrev. The leader of the society was Prince V. F. Odoevskii and its most gifted member D. V. Venevitinov, who died in 1827 at the age of twenty-two.[10]

In his brief career as a literary critic Venevitinov, influenced by Schelling, Friedrich Schlegel, Fichte, and other German idealists and romanticists, gave expression to the main outlines of the ideas of romantic nationalism which were to preoccupy so many Russian thinkers during the nineteenth century. He regretted Russia's failure up to this time to make important contributions to world literature. He attributed this failure to the circumstance that Russia, so to speak, had had journals before textbooks. That is, Russian literature had borrowed foreign literary forms and ideals and was not based on distinctly Russian ideas and principles of national life. Russia, he wrote, needed to conserve her own national originality (*samobytnost'*) and to follow her own course of development so that Russian literature could take a form that would correspond to the essence of Russia's own national being. To attain this end he considered it necessary to isolate Russia intellectually and to develop a national literature based not on imitation but on a philosophical and critical analysis that would enable her to become aware of her own mission.[11]

A second group of students who worked for a more national orientation of Russian literature was the circle that gathered around N. V. Stankevich during the 1830's. Stankevich was another tragic young man who died before he reached the age of thirty. At the end of the 1830's, it is true, his circle came to be dominated by the philosophy of Hegel (who definitely was not a romanticist),[12] and during the 1840's some of its members, such as Belinskii and Bakunin, largely abandoned the romantic idealism of their youth. During the early and mid-1830's, however, Schelling, Fichte, and similar German idealists and romanticists were zealously studied, though hardly digested and comprehended, by the members of Stankevich's circle. Whatever political or philosophical camp the individual members of this circle belonged to later, they never ceased to be dedicated to the cause of furthering the development of Russia's national identity—or *narodnost'* as it was called since the early 1820's.[13]

The importance of romantic nationalism in the Stankevich circle is also suggested by the careers of several of its more conservative members. For example, after the death of Stankevich, the Slavophile Constantine Aksakov came to be generally ridiculed by Moscow intellectuals for his excessive romanticization of the history, institutions, and customs of Muscovite Russia.[14] The future journalist M. N. Katkov gave lectures at the University of Moscow between 1845 and 1850 which were strongly influenced by German romanticism and idealism, especially by the philosophy of Schelling, whose lectures Katkov personally attended in 1841 and 1842 while he was a student in Berlin. Katkov's student, Bestuzhev-Riumin, who later became a well-known historian, wrote concerning his teacher's lectures:

> The lectures of M. N. Katkov . . . had a special fascination: he exposed for us Schelling's system of mythology in a well-organized and elegant manner; all marvelled at the unusual ability to convey the most abstract notions clearly and in concise and sharply drawn detail. In this regard, the lecture is especially remembered in which [was presented] the teaching of Schelling on the early stage of religious consciousness. . . . Out of these lectures we derived an awareness of the historical significance of the world process, its influence on destiny and the development of mankind, its first-rate historical importance.[15]

It should be noted, however, that Katkov did not become a disciple of Schelling while a member of the Stankevich circle, for he joined it late in the 1830's when Hegel was its principal object of philosophical venera-tion.[16] But Katkov's Hegel was adulterated by idealistic and romantic no-tions concerning creativity, organic development, and Russian nationality, which he had probably picked up from his professors and fellow students at the University of Moscow.

Illustrative of Katkov's state of mind while he belonged to the Stanke-vich circle is the review he published in 1839 in the *Annals of the Father-land (Otechestvennyia Zapiski)* of I. Sakharov's collection of Russian popu-lar songs. In addition to assessing the significance of Sakharov's collection, Katkov also expressed great admiration in this article for the marvel of the Russian nation as a result of a long and necessary historical evolution. This evolution was conceived of in terms of a curious mixture of notions derived from traditional religious teachings, Hegel, and German romanticism, ac-cording to which all peoples developed not only organically and biologi-cally in much the manner of plants but also culturally and intellectually as part of the general unfolding of the spirit in world history. All significant peoples, he emphasized, became carriers of the revealed word of God once they reached a certain stage of maturity.[17] He believed that the Rus-sian people had reached such a stage more than a century before his own time when the "voice of God" enlightened it through the lips of Peter the Great.[18]

Katkov, however, was far from being the first to apply romantic and organic theories of development specifically to Russian history, for in the late 1820's and early 1830's such writers as Pogodin and the journalist Nicholas Polevoi had affirmed that history is governed by laws and that each people, sooner or later, must pass through the respective stages of the universal historical process.[19] In regard to Polevoi, it is significant that he undertook to write a history of the Russian *people*—not of the Russian state as did Karamzin. In a passage in the second volume of his work, which he dedicated to the German historian Barthold Niebuhr, his roman-tic and nationalistic philosophy of history is expressed especially well:

> Peoples, like individual human beings, are born, grow, attain maturity, get old, and die; that is, they exist in the manner of man with a childhood, maturity, and old age. Each society represents a victory of the human spirit over nature. The Secret Wisdom of Providence . . . consists in this: each society appears at its own time and in its own place in order to fulfill its particular duty in the general life of mankind.[20]

Pogodin expressed similar views as early as 1827 in his *Historical Apho-risms.*[21] As a trained historian his contribution to the study of Russian his-tory was much more important than that of the amateur Polevoi. Pogodin's serious works, however, were noteworthy for their systematic examination of source materials rather than for their synthetic grasp of the spirit of

Russian history. Thus his popularization of a nationalistic and romantic view of Russian history was done mainly through his lectures and activities as a journalist. It is true that his nationalism was on occasion so uncritically emotional and even bombastic that it was decidedly not in good taste, which made it easy for a clever young man like Alexander Herzen to ridicule him.[22] Pogodin's lectures and articles were, nevertheless, significant for their discussion of the nature of Russian historical individuality. His best discussion of this subject was in an article of 1845 in the *Muscovite* (*Moskvitianin*).[23] Here he emphasized the uniqueness of the Russian state as contrasted with the states of Western Europe. Using chiefly the evidence of Augustin Thierry's *Histoire de la conquête de l'Angleterre par les Normands* (Paris: Firmin Didot, 1825), Pogodin argued that the state in Western Europe had been founded on the basis of force and conquest.[24] In Russia, on the other hand, there had allegedly been no slavery, no hatred, and no conflict. The Russian people had invited Rurik to come to Novgorod, and they had accepted Oleg at Kiev without resistance. Thus from the very beginning Russian history had been characterized by peace, unity, and love; and Western history, by war, discord, and conflict.[25] In the course of time, according to Pogodin, these differences were further accentuated by the beneficial influence of Slavic character, Russian geography and climate, and the Eastern Orthodox Church.[26] Needless to say, such an evaluation of the differences separating Russia from the West was flattering to the national pride of Russians. At a later date, the Slavophiles, Dostoevskii, Danilevskii, and other writers made Pogodin's hypothesis concerning the respective origins of the state in Russia and in Western Europe one of the classical arguments of Russian conservative nationalism.

Another variant on the theme of Russian uniqueness was the notion that Russian Orthodoxy remained the one pure form of Christianity in nineteenth-century Europe. Pogodin's friend and colleague Shevyrev was one of the early defenders of this point of view. Shevyrev experienced religion with an intensity that occasionally reached the point of ecstasy in connection with the traditional festivals of the Orthodox Church.[27] He closely associated nationality (*narodnost'*) with religion, defining it as "the combination of all spiritual and physical forces given to a people by Providence so that it [this people] could fulfill its destination on earth."[28] Each nationality was therefore for Shevyrev the "vessel of the Divine"[29] in history. The principal task for Russia in the nineteenth century, according to Shevyrev, was to preserve her own nationality and religion and to free herself from harmful and negative Western European influences.[30] He was troubled by what he considered the decline of morality, culture, and, especially, religion in Western Europe; he clearly felt that Europe had passed its zenith and would soon need the moral assistance of the Russian spirit, which he described as a Christian one of tolerance and universal communion.[31] Or, as he wrote to the German romantic religious philosopher Franz von Baader in 1840: "It is especially in Russia that one can hope for a development of universal Christianity apart from European prejudices, from the petrifying egoism of the Roman Church, and from the principle of dissolution unfortunately introduced by Protestantism."[32]

Much the same idea was expressed by Prince Vladimir Odoevskii, the leader of the Society of the Lovers of Wisdom, in his book *The Russian Nights* (*Russkiia nochi*), which was first published in 1844. Odoevskii, too, believed that the West was declining and that it needed to be revitalized with the spiritual forces of the Slavic East. In speaking of the Slavic East, he was, of course, thinking mainly of Russia as the hope of the West, because he believed that Russia, after Peter I, combined the strongest elements of Western civilization (science and art) with those of Slavic civilization (love and faith) and had developed them together into a new synthesis. Russia was therefore capable of saving Europe by providing her with the elements necessary for a more harmonious existence. When this would take place, Russia would have performed her "great calling" and would "take first place among nations." "The nineteenth century belongs to Russia!"[33]

During the 1840's and 1850's this vision of a declining West being eclipsed by the awakening Russian East was widely popularized by the Slavophiles of Moscow.[34] Their attempts to define and describe the nature of Russian *narodnost'* were of immense importance for the further development of nationalistic thought in nineteenth-century Russia. They were vociferous and consistent advocates of the need for returning to the original and native sources of Russian life. To effect this goal, many of them took action: Peter Kireevskii collected folk songs,[35] Ivan Kireevskii helped the monks at the Optina Pustin' monastery to edit the works of fathers and monastic reformers of the Eastern Church,[36] Constantine Aksakov and Alexis Khomiakov wrote books or articles concerning Russian history and Orthodox Church theology,[37] Constantine Aksakov studied Russian peasant customs and traditions,[38] and Iurii Samarin participated in the preparatory committees whose work paved the way for the emancipation of the Russian serfs.[39]

Similar to the German romanticists, the Slavophiles believed that every society had its own uniquely national origins and peculiar laws of individual organic growth. Peter the Great, they thought, had interrupted Russia's natural organic development and imposed on her the alien rationalistic, bureaucratic, and utilitarian ideas and practices of Western Europe. Hence the Slavophiles believed that the true nature of Russian national character and culture was to be sought in the history of pre-

Petrine Russia. They idealized the earlier Muscovite and Kievan period of Russian history as a harmonious epoch without the bureaucracy, class divisions, and conflict that allegedly characterized the history of Western Europe.

In defining the nature of the historical individuality of pre-Petrine Russia, the Slavophiles, like other Russian conservatives and nationalists, accepted autocracy, Orthodoxy, and *narodnost'* as the distinguishing features of Russian civilization. But they did so in their own individual and independent manner. The word autocracy, for example, meant something different to the Slavophiles than it did to the supporters of official nationality, who usually equated autocracy with unquestioning belief in the sanctity of established order in Russian society. For the Slavophiles the tsar was above all the living symbol of the political and spiritual unity of the Russian people. He was responsible for defending the interests of the Russian nation and traditionally consulted his people through such institutions as the Council of the Land (*zemskii sobor*) and the Boyar Council (*boiarskaia duma*) in regard to matters of vital national importance.[40] For the sake of the welfare of the Russian people, his political power was unlimited. Yet he did not, according to the Slavophiles, properly have the right to interfere with his people's freedom of thought and expression. Thus Constantine Aksakov, in his "supplement" to the letter he addressed to Alexander II in 1855, implied that the reign of Nicholas I had been a period of "spiritually harmful despotism."[41] Accordingly, he urged Alexander II to return to the traditions and principles that had once been the basis of political and social life in Russia: unlimited political power in the hands of the government, and freedom of opinion and expression for the people.[42] Unlimited power in the hands of the tsar was necessary, Aksakov held, because the Russians were an unpolitical people who did not want to rule. "Not wanting to rule," he emphasized, "the people reserved for the government unlimited state power."[43] In return for this, the Russian people "reserved for itself moral freedom, freedom of life and spirit."[44] In the past the government had violated these basic principles of Russian political and social life. This, Aksakov concluded, was the "source of all the evils of Russia."[45]

Orthodoxy, like autocracy, had a different meaning for the Slavophiles than it did for followers of official nationality. For the latter it meant little more than complete acceptance of the established Orthodox Church as it was at the time. The Slavophiles, on the other hand, had an idealized conception of Orthodoxy. They denied that the state had the right to interfere with religion and therefore disapproved of the almost complete dependence of the Russian church on the bureaucratic and secular state since the time of Peter the Great.[46] It was largely in protest against this dependence

as well as against what the Slavophiles termed the formalism and rationalism of Western Catholicism and Protestantism that they developed their
idealization of Russian Orthodoxy. Of all the Slavophiles, Khomiakov, in
particular, formulated the Slavophile philosophy of religion. The essence
of this philosophy is contained in the Russian word *sobornost'*,[47] a term
that has no exact equivalent in English. It was derived from *sobor*, meaning assembly or council, and therefore connoted that important issues of
dogma were decided by church councils, not by the authority of a pontiff
as in the Roman Catholic Church. *Sobornost'* was interpreted by the Slavophiles to mean the organic unity of all Christians in the Church headed by
Christ and founded on the principles of love and inner freedom, which
enabled the Eastern Church to avoid both the Protestants' rejection of the
unity of all Christianity and the Catholics' acceptance of the principle of
external religious authority.[48]

In addition to idealized autocracy and *sobornost'*, the Slavophile conception of Russian nationality was also characterized by a third unique
feature: the peasant commune, or *obshchina*. The Slavophiles were not
alone in their interest in the *obshchina*, for a Decembrist, P. I. Pestel, and
a bureaucrat, Count P. D. Kiselev, had already considered the Russian
peasant commune as a possible means of avoiding the economic ills of
Western Europe before the Slavophiles first discussed it seriously in 1839;[49]
and somewhat after this date such Russian socialists as Herzen, Chernyshevskii, and members of the Petrashevskii circle defended the *obshchina*
as a means of transforming Russia into a socialist state. For the Slavophiles,
the *obshchina* was, however, much more than merely a form of economic
and social organization. It was also a moral and spiritual way of life, a
manifestation of the principles of brotherly love, unity, and personal freedom implicit in Slavic tradition and Orthodox Christianity.[50] Thus the
Slavophiles played a pioneer role in identifying the *obshchina* as one of
the principal characteristics that distinguished the Russian people from all
others. It was, in their opinion, the one uniquely national civil institution
that had survived from the past and continued to preserve the Russian
people's original customs and usages, folklore, songs, dress, and philosophy
of life.[51]

The Slavophile conception of Russian *narodnost'* was clearly much more
a romantic idealization of what Russia should be than a true description of
Russian reality. Indeed, the Slavophile viewpoint was essentially opposed
to the official policies of the Russian government at the time. Instead of
accepting the spiritual guidance of Nicholas I's government, the Slavophiles sought an ideal world in the theology of isolated monks and in the
folksongs, customs, and way of life of simple peasants. Nicholas I's bureaucracy, therefore, perhaps rightfully considered the Slavophiles to be dan-

gerous, for their dream of a new Russian cultural synthesis and civilization could only make those whom it influenced dissatisfied with existing conditions in Russia. For this reason the Slavophiles were constantly under suspicion, harassed by censorship officials, and even briefly imprisoned (Ivan Aksakov and Iurii Samarin). Nevertheless, there is little doubt that they performed an important service for the government by popularizing and giving deeper meaning to a distinctly Russian conception of civilization and cultural development.

A few governmental officials in mid-nineteenth century Russia, at least, realized the potential usefulness of the Slavophiles as defenders and exponents of Russian nationalism. One such official was Vladimir Ivanovich Nazimov, who had been an army general, provincial administrator, and official in the service of the Ministry of Public Instruction during the reign of Nicholas I. In 1855 he defended the utility of the Slavophile journal then proposed by Alexander Koshelev and Tertii Filippov. He did so by emphasizing the desirability of injecting new life into Russian journalism, which had ceased to play an important role in Russian life as a result of the severe censorship practiced after 1848. Nazimov admitted that this censorship had apparently been necessary in order to meet the danger of the revolutionary ideas then current in Europe. He insisted, however, that time had shown that these ideas, "being completely foreign to us and contrary to the fundamental principles of Russian life, can have no effect on the majority of our society."[52] He felt that the Russian government had little reason to fear that the majority of Russians would be influenced by false revolutionary principles because the government was firmly established in its historical role as the tutor and educator of the Russian people. But this did not mean that the government could afford to ignore public opinion. Nazimov believed that it was definitely to the interest of Russia to enable writers to turn from the harmful state of inactivity in which they found themselves to "useful and exalted" undertakings.[53] He therefore considered the permission granted to Katkov to start a new literary and political journal in Moscow, the *Russian Messenger* (*Russkii Vestnik*), to be a necessary step forward. "Let our literature work," he urged, "allow it to express its thoughts so that it will be easier for the government to follow and, if need be, to direct the course of public opinion."[54]

In order to support more specifically the idea of the usefulness of a new Slavophile journal, Nazimov briefly traced an increasing interest in national history and traditions in all the Slavic countries during the first part of the nineteenth century.[55] In Russia there had been a sharp decline of the former infatuation with European ideas and customs and a revived interest in the study of the Russian national past. The imperial government had encouraged such study by establishing the Archaeographical Commission

and by publishing historical and juridical documents. Thus the Slavophiles, Nazimov suggested, were only one group among many concerned
with Russia's national past.[56] Their views regarding the harmful influence
of Peter the Great were, he admitted, rather extreme. On the other hand,
none of their ideas had political implications, for they were pious fathers
and landowners who never would have thought of violating the lawful
order of things: "One may reject the extreme implications of their thinking,
but one may not condemn completely the movement itself because it is
based on pure love for everything Russian, the regulations of our church,
our national customs, and our native language. . . ."[57] Nazimov associated
the Slavophiles with a number of great names in Russian literature—
Karamzin, Pushkin, Griboedov, and Gogol—for these writers had also admired ancient Russia and sought inspiration from her history. Such
talented Slavophiles as Khomiakov, the Kireevskiis, and the Aksakovs were
therefore continuing a tradition in literature representative of the opinions
of the most reliable and loyal elements in Russian society. Accordingly,
Nazimov reasoned, the journal requested by Filippov and Koshelev was
bound to serve the purposes of the government inasmuch as it would enable the Slavophiles to render useful and devoted services to their country.[58]

Nazimov undoubtedly exaggerated the usefulness of the Slavophiles at
the beginning of Alexander II's reign. At the time they were generally regarded to be too doctrinaire and extreme in their views to be taken very
seriously by most educated Russians. Ivan Aksakov himself admitted, in
writing to his parents concerning provincial Russia in 1856, that the Slavophiles were then given scant attention, while there was hardly a provincial teacher who did not know Belinskii's letter to Gogol by heart.[59]
The *Russian Conversation* (*Russkaia Beseda*), the journal the Slavophiles
began publishing in 1856, had only a limited circulation and was abandoned in 1859 after only three years of publication.[60] This journal and subsequent Slavophile publications did not, however, remain completely un-
noticed. Their articles on freedom of conscience, the peasant commune,
and the emancipation of the Russian serfs were sometimes even regarded
with favor by writers inclined to socialism and liberalism. Ivan Aksakov's
newspaper, *Day* (*Den'*), was also able to attract a respectable number of
readers between 1861 and 1866, especially during the Polish crisis of 1863.
However, the specifically Slavophile interpretations of history, science,
and nationality were not shared by many Russians at the time. Certainly
there were few members of the reading public who disagreed with Katkov
in 1856 when he criticized the Slavophiles for describing science as a
function of nationality and for viewing history as a product of the development of tribes and peoples instead of humanity as a whole.[61] A negative

view of the Slavophiles was so prevalent by the early 1860's that any journal identified too closely with them was hurt by the association. Accordingly, Michael Dostoevskii, who then edited the journal *Time* (*Vremia*), urged the literary critic Apollon Grigor'ev to be more sparing in his praise of the Slavophiles because such praise would probably make an unfavorable impression on readers.[62] In 1864 Fedor Dostoevskii explained his brother's attitude by pointing out that Michael had been reluctant to associate *Time* with the name of the Slavophiles because the mass of Russian readers then regarded writers like Ivan Kireevskii and Khomiakov as "retrogrades, though this mass had never read them."[63] Fedor, himself, in November, 1861, wrote disapprovingly about the Slavophiles' stubborn defense of their own vague and indefinite ideal and their romanticization of the Muscovite past.[64] He asked sarcastically whether only Slavophiles had the privileges of being honorable and of loving their country.[65]

Another limitation on the use of the Slavophiles as patriotic and loyal instruments of government policy was that they were too independent in their judgment of official policies during the 1860's and 1870's. This was particularly the case for Ivan Aksakov, whose personal courage and integrity won general respect and qualified admiration even among the majority of the Russian intelligentsia who were in basic disagreement with most of the favorite doctrines of the Slavophiles. The Slavophiles, however, seldom bothered to take the elementary precaution of assuring themselves the protection of officials within the government whose power and influence were equal to that of the minister or ministers whom they were attacking in their publications.

At a later date the Slavophiles enjoyed much favor and esteem in official and conservative circles. By the time of Alexander III, officials and writers with conservative views of one shading or another often identified themselves, usually erroneously, with the Slavophile label. Various passages in Dostoevskii's *Diary of a Writer* are probably the best-known example of this particular trend in Russian intellectual life around 1880. Alexander III, himself, was an enthusiastic admirer of Ivan Aksakov, but this admiration did not alter the fact that Ivan Aksakov had been forced to suspend his activities as an editor between 1867 and 1880.[66] His activities in the Moscow Slavic Benevolent Committee during these years hardly compensated his loss of the right to use the printed word to help shape public opinion in Russia.

CHAPTER FOUR

Katkov and His Time

MICHAEL Nikiforovich Katkov, in contrast to Ivan Aksakov, was able to use the printed word to influence public opinion in Russia for more than three decades following the Crimean War. Unlike Aksakov, he only risked major battle with high officials when he was sure of powerful support at the court or in one of the various ministries at St. Petersburg. As a practical and hardheaded businessman, Katkov was not particularly interested in abstract truth or even accuracy in his debates with opponents; nor did he hesitate to alter the texts of contributors if he thought this was necessary for the purposes of his own publications.[1] Such editorial practices naturally did not endear Katkov to Russian writers and intellectuals.

Symbolic of the attitude of Russian writers toward Katkov during the 1870's and 1880's was Ivan Turgenev's snubbing of him at the Pushkin commemoration at Moscow in 1880, where Katkov delivered one of the speeches. This speech was not only intelligent, but also, apparently as a result of the general atmosphere of friendship and good-fellowship that prevailed at this celebration in honor of Pushkin, conciliatory toward many members of the intelligentsia whom he had previously treated as enemies. Most of those present were temporarily moved to forgive Katkov for his previous attacks against themselves and therefore lifted their champagne glasses in his direction at the end of the speech in a sort of token reconciliation. Turgenev, who was sitting across the table from Katkov, did not follow the example of the majority of those present. Katkov noticed this and extended his glass in the direction of Turgenev. Turgenev answered with a weak, unenthusiastic nod. After the general clinking of glasses was over, Katkov seated himself and lifted his glass toward Turgenev for the second time. Turgenev merely looked at him coldly and placed the palm of his hand over his glass.[2]

Unfavorable opinions of Katkov were not confined to Russian writers, but were shared by practically all liberal and revolutionary members of the intelligentsia. This was particularly true in the decades following the late 1870's, by which time he had abandoned his earlier liberalism and espousal of reform and had become closely associated with some of the most reactionary elements of Russian society. One of the common charges leveled against Katkov was, in the words of A. F. Koni, that he followed "the exclusive cult of naked power, as a self-sufficient goal, as power *an und für sich*."[3] The censor Nikitenko described him as a power-hungry, ambitious individual who wanted to arrogate to himself the right to determine who and what were patriotic and loyal in Russia.[4] Another popular view was that Katkov was a renegade liberal who had turned reactionary.[5] Lenin was one of those who wrote in this vein somewhat later: "At the time of the rise of the democratic movement in Russia . . . , the liberal . . . landowner Katkov turned to nationalism, chauvinism, and raging black hundredism."[6] Others accused him of being inconsistent because at one time or another he had defended and attacked the jury system, ardently advocated free trade and then subsequently supported protectionism, stood for hard currency and later extolled paper money, defended the university statute of 1863 and later saw in it the cause of the decline of science in Russia.[7]

Although there are elements of truth in all of these charges, Katkov's significance as a journalist and public figure cannot be denied. His very adroitness, hardheadedness, and ability to identify himself as a loyal defender of Russian national interests prevented him from having his journalistic career cut short, as was the case for such publicists as Pisarev, Chernyshevskii, and Ivan Aksakov. Because his career was not cut short, Katkov was able to publish, practically uninterruptedly, his *Russian Messenger* (*Russkii Vestnik*) and *Moscow News* (*Moskovskiia Vedomosti*) over periods of thirty-one and twenty-four years respectively. These two publications can therefore be considered as a sort of mirror of Russian society between 1856 and 1887 as viewed from a generally conservative and nationalistic point of view.

It should be emphasized that Katkov's influence during this period was not solely negative. His *Russian Messenger* published much of the best literature and many of the most stimulating essays written in Russian during the decades following the mid-1850's. Turgenev's *Fathers and Children* and *Smoke*, Dostoevskii's *Crime and Punishment, Idiot, Demons,* and *Brothers Karamazov*, Tolstoi's *Anna Karenina*, and brilliant essays by such writers as S. M. Solov'ev, Constantine Leont'ev, General Rostislav Fadeev, Nicholas Strakhov, and V. V. Rozanov—all were among the contributions published in the *Russian Messenger* after 1860. Katkov clearly tried to publish literature that would attract public interest and was therefore ready to pay well for contributions from popular writers.[8] His business acumen in such matters undoubtedly greatly contributed to the success of all of his publications.

Katkov's ability to adapt the editorial policies of his publications to the changing directions of Russian state policy over a period of years was of equal importance for this success. He was always able to appear patriotic and in favor of solutions that ostensibly served state interests and were acceptable to a strong component of the Russian officialdom in St. Petersburg. In so doing he must have been at least partly motivated by considerations of expediency. At the same time, it should be added that certain basic attitudes in Katkov's orientation toward life and society can be detected in his writings and thinking. In the course of a lifetime he often changed his ideas. However, his fundamental attitudes toward life and society were only modified, never radically altered. There is therefore an inner consistency that can be traced in Katkov's development, despite the numerous *volte-faces* he made on such matters as education, economics, law, and public policy.

The two attitudes that underlay practically all of Katkov's opinions and changing social and economic views were his nationalistic conception of life and his basic conservatism in viewing the problems of Russian society; but his thoughts on nationalism and conservatism were rarely profound. Notwithstanding his early philosophical training, Katkov's journalistic writings show little evidence of any attempt to think through the philosophical premises of the views he expressed in his publications. In the absence of such philosophical self-examination, it was easy for him to be inconsistent and to adjust his opinions to the various contingencies of public life in the manner of successful modern journalists everywhere. Indeed, it was mainly Katkov's journalistic success and political influence and prestige that made him so important for the history of conservative nationalism in Russia. Almost all of the conservative nationalists who will be discussed in subsequent chapters published contributions in Katkov's journals, were at one time or another his allies, or, though they often differed with him, at least admired him for his alleged patriotic services to Russia.

Katkov emphasized the importance of nationalism for a Russia that had been humbled on the field of battle as early as 1855—the very beginning of Alexander II's reign. At that time he attempted to obtain permission to found and edit an independent journal. In justifying the need for such a journal, Katkov, in a special memorandum to the Minister of Public Instruction, pointed to the progress made in developing a new form of art and literature based on Russian nationality during the preceding thirty years.[9] He argued that it was highly desirable that this trend in Russian intellectual life should be reinforced in order that:

> . . . a characteristically Russian view might be more and more used to explain everything; in order that the Russian mind might throw off the yoke of foreign thought just as it had already thrown off the yoke of foreign letters; in order that our literature, maturing and enriching itself, might provide satisfaction for all of the intellectual needs of Russian man.[10]

Katkov regretted that there were two few reliable journals in Russia to further this task. The existing journals, he claimed, tended to be monopolized by a small group of men whose editorial policies satisfied only a small part of the Russian public.

The Minister of Public Instruction was assured that Katkov's own proposed journal would satisfy a larger segment of the Russian reading public and that it would help strengthen the national element in Russian intellectual life. Concerning his own personal convictions, he wrote: ". . . I feel the entire importance of my calling. I shall never betray my duty, and in my service I shall zealously act as is befitting a sincere Christian, a loyal Russian subject who is profoundly convinced of the destiny of his country."[11] These assurances were obviously received with favor by the Minister of Public Instruction, for Katkov was granted permission to publish his new journal, the *Russian Messenger*, toward the end of 1855. In the first issue of this journal (January, 1856), Katkov reaffirmed the creed he had formulated in his memorandum of 1855:

> We shall firmly believe that Divine Providence reigns in the life of humanity and in the destinies of peoples, that it permits without purpose neither creation nor destruction, and that in a people which was born and matured so long and with such pains there is concealed great strength and a great future. With pure and sincere love we turn our eyes to the Throne. We give our strength and enthusiasm to our Imperial Leader. With joy and with full devotion we shall go forward onto a good path under his banner; we shall proceed with complete faith that the banner of our Leader is the true honor, light, and welfare of our country.[12]

It is interesting to note that Katkov chose to use the conventional language of the Russian church and of Nicholas I's official nationality in his efforts to obtain approval and support for his plans to play an important role in Russian public life as the editor of a patriotic journal. His choice of language was probably dictated in part by the realization that it was unlikely that Russian officialdom had radically changed its attitudes just because Nicholas I had died shortly before. It was therefore precisely the conventional language used in Nicholas' time that was likely to reassure them in regard to the loyalty and reliability of any individual writer or thinker. At the same time, it would be unjust to assume that Katkov was completely opportunistic and insincere in his statements of patriotism during 1855 and 1856, for he used much the same language in expressing his attachment to crown and country and determination to serve the government on various occasions during the remainder of his career as a journalist and editor.

Despite his solemn affirmation of belief in Divine Providence's benevolent direction of Russia's fate, he did not attract much attention to himself as a defender of Russian national interests during his first years as editor of the *Russian Messenger*. Most thinking Russians realized that the Crimean War had demonstrated the glaring contrast between the official picture of an all-powerful, stable, and orderly empire and the actual picture of internal dissension, backwardness, and weakness. This realization persuaded many of them that Russia needed reform much more than endless discussions concerning the goals and nature of Russian nationality. Accordingly, Katkov's journal initially concerned itself with such issues as serfdom, freedom of the press, and legal reforms rather than the defense of Russian national interests. Katkov, himself, took up the study of English political and legal institutions and acquired a reputation as an Anglophile during these years. It is symptomatic of his attitude at the time that his first polemics were directed against those who most loudly championed the cause of Russian cultural independence, the Slavophiles of Moscow.[13] Katkov began these polemics in 1856 with a criticism of the views of Iurii Samarin on nationality and science,[14] and continued them during the next several years by publishing a series of articles written by various authors and directed against the Slavophiles. In 1856 and 1857 rather convincing articles by B. N. Chicherin and S. M. Solov'ev questioned the historical validity of the theories of the Slavophiles in regard to the economic, social, and cultural life of pre-Petrine Russia;[15] and in 1858 a number of authors stressed the economic inefficiency of the peasant commune, contrasting the duplication of labor and peasant apathy which they attributed to it with the manifold advantages of private property and a free peasant economy. Katkov's editorial comments in the "Contemporary Chronicle" section of his *Russian Messenger* clearly indicate that he was in complete agreement with such views.[16] Not until several years later did he become personally, but not necessarily theoretically, reconciled with the Slavophiles.

The *Russian Messenger*'s Anglophilia during the early part of Alexander II's reign is well illustrated by the enthusiasm for England that Katkov displayed in an editorial of 1858: "Here there are no written words, ready formulas, abstract ideas; the English system is not a constitution on paper, it is not a book, it is not even a science; it is life and nature in their development, in their real creation. . . ."[17] The particular words Katkov chose to express this enthusiasm are, of course, more suggestive of the intellectual atmosphere of romantic Russia in the 1830's and idealistic Germany in the early nineteenth century than of mid-century England. The historical parallel of ancient Rome that he selected to illustrate the significance of England for his own time was inspired in part by his earlier interests—especially his study of classical civilization. He emphasized this parallel by paraphrasing the words of the Swiss-German political thinker Bluntschli: ". . . what Rome was in ancient times in regard to the development of law and governmental order is now represented by England."[18]

The desire for law and order reflected in these words was doubtless strengthened in Katkov's mind by the turmoil and internal dissension in Russia that followed the emancipation of the serfs in February, 1861. Toward the end of that year Katkov complained about the large number of empty heads everywhere in Russia, especially in St. Petersburg, that could only repeat meaningless phrases about progress, the social contract, revolution, liberalism, and public opinion. He felt that such people were like Khlestakov, the superficial, light-minded, and irresponsible adventurer depicted by Gogol in the *Inspector General*.[19] The student disturbances of the early sixties, the revolutionary movement, and the Polish uprising in 1863—all were events that disconcerted the conservative-minded Katkov concerning the soundness and reliability of the views of the Russian intelligentsia. He accordingly ridiculed the utopianism of the radical *Contemporary (Sovremennik)* as early as 1861 and criticized Herzen during the following year for his irresponsibility in stirring up dissident thoughts and feelings among Russian youth.[20] Katkov's concern about the problem of young Russia undoubtedly made him most pleased to receive Turgenev's manuscript of *Fathers and Children*, which was published in the *Russian Messenger* during 1862. He wrote a special article apropos of Turgenev's work that July. Here he spoke disapprovingly of the spirit of negation that had taken hold of so many Russian minds. He pointed to the forces of civilization—education, science, industrial development, political maturity, freedom of conscience, and the living force of tradition—as a counteracting influence to this spirit. In Russia, however, he admitted regretfully, such forces were rather weak:

> . . . in our civilization, which does not have in itself any independent forces, in our small intellectual world where nothing stands firmly, where there is not one cause which would not be ashamed and confused with itself and would just believe a little in its own existence—[here] the spirit of nihilism can develop and acquire significance.[21]

Despite his pessimism about the state of mind of Russian society, Katkov continued to defend the various political, social, and economic reforms of

Alexander II until the late 1870's.[22] There is no doubt that his pessimism about Russian society's independent forces increased as the years passed; therefore, it is strange that he did not turn to reaction sooner than he did. One reason that he did not was that he continued to believe for many years that it was possible for the government to strengthen the forces of civilization in Russia through enlightened public policy.

Perhaps the best example of this is Katkov's advocacy of a system of education based on the classics, which would provide young Russians with a foundation upon which to build their future careers as citizens, scholars, and scientists. He felt that more emphasis on Greek, Latin, and classical literature would definitely raise educational standards in Russia, thus, he reasoned, avoiding the crowding of Russian universities with badly educated and poorly prepared students, as had been the case in the late 1850's and early 1860's. He even went so far as to attribute the rise of nihilism to the inadequate educational system in Russia after 1848, which had deemphasized classical studies, and he suggested that a system of classical education similar to the one established in Germany during the nineteenth century would contribute greatly toward remedying the principal evils and weaknesses of Russian society.[23]

Katkov's doubts about the internal strength and stability of Russian society are clearly seen in the thread of caution and conservatism that runs throughout his journalistic writings—even at the height of his liberalism and Anglophilia in the early 1860's. This conservatism, it should be mentioned, was not only a reaction to the Polish uprising and the revolutionary views of the radical intelligentsia, for many of the articles and memoranda written by Katkov prior to the 1860's, especially where he expressed his desire to do his duty by serving the throne and advancing the interests of his country, are suggestive of a basically conservative attitude toward life. Certainly the ability of nineteenth-century England to make reforms without revolution recommended it to cautious and moderate Russian liberals such as Katkov. On the other hand, Katkov's earlier proclivity toward conservatism was strengthened as a result of his journalistic wars against nihilists, *emigré* intellectuals, and Polish rebels.

At the beginning of the 1860's Katkov's discussions of the organization of the zemstvos first unmistakably demonstrated his conservatism. Early in these discussions he affirmed that the leadership in the zemstvos should be in the hands of Russia's ablest and most experienced class in political matters—the gentry.[24] But he did not favor equal treatment for all members of the gentry. Instead, he argued that only the larger landowners and wealthier townspeople should be represented directly in the zemstvos because of their greater maturity and reliability; and if he was not convinced that the smaller landowners and ordinary merchants in the towns were prepared for direct participation in zemstvo affairs, he naturally was even less in favor of participation by the peasants. He considered the peasants unsuited for any leading role in Russian society because of the narrowness of their background and views. He did not, however, want to exclude them entirely from the zemstvos, insisting that zemstvo institutions in Russia should have an all-Russian and all-class character.[25]

Katkov was decidedly opposed to any suggestion that the gentry should exercise exclusive control over zemstvo affairs as a separate caste. He insisted that the idea of caste had been imported into Russia from Germany and therefore was foreign to Russian society, where everyone in previous times had been regarded solely in terms of service and social categories.[26] At that time he even favored the abolition of the gentry's special privileges, pointing out that the government did not exist for the gentry but the gentry for the government.[27] After the mid-1860's, however, Katkov became more and more favorably disposed toward the Russian gentry because of the support they gave him in his campaigns for more militantly nationalistic governmental policies. It is also clear that the larger landowners appreciated Katkov's advocacy of a leading role for themselves in the zemstvos. In 1865, according to popular rumor, Katkov was the instigator of the address the Moscow gentry made to Alexander II. In this address they urged the emperor to call together a special assembly of those among his subjects who had always been the most loyal and dependable connecting link between the tsar and his people, namely themselves, in order to consider the current and future needs of the Russian state. Whatever his role actually was in the instigating and drafting of the Moscow gentry's address, Katkov's intimate relationship with the gentry at that time is clear.[28]

In an editorial in the *Moscow News* of November, 1865, for example, he heaped praise on the gentry as the one group in Russia that had taken a firm stand in defense of Russia's national interests. In December of the same year, the Moscow gentry presented to Katkov a special inkstand as a token of their appreciation of his journalistic services. At the base of this inkstand were represented such objects as books, a shovel, a sickle, a rake, and unrolled plans—all of which were obviously intended to suggest Katkov's constructive activities in behalf of Russia. Standing on this base in the armor of a medieval Russian knight was Katkov with a shield held close to his left side in one hand and a banner, upon which were inscribed the words "unity of Russia," held aloft in the other. The importance of this rather melodramatic and flattering representation of Katkov as the heroic champion of Russian state interests certainly should not be exaggerated, but it is at least symbolic of his changing and increasingly cordial relations with the Russian gentry. By 1874 he had openly accepted the gentry's own version of themselves as the dedicated servants of the tsar who, more than any other single group in Russian society, united him organically with the Russian people.[29] In 1885 he even published in the *Russian Messenger* the influential article by A. D. Pazukhin that pleaded for the restoration of the corporate rights of the gentry as a means of reinforcing the authority of autocracy in Russia.[30] It is, however, not certain to what extent Katkov was prepared to identify himself with the plans of the gentry that assured them not only a leading role but also a separate corporate status in Russian society, for the organic unity of this society unmarred by any rigid caste distinctions and special prerogatives given to any one group remained one of Katkov's most cherished ideals throughout his career as a journalist.

The desire for harmonious unity in Russia became a characteristic feature of the conservative view of society that gradually developed in Katkov's mind after the early 1860's. As early as 1864 he asked:

> Where is there . . . a people more strongly and firmly interested in conserving the Supreme Power? Where does it have such great, indisputable, unshakable significance? Where do we find such profound conviction in its inviolability and sanctity? What guardianship can replace this great interest? National forces to which it will be entrusted or the mercenary who comes from God knows where and who has God knows what in his mind? Can there be any doubt whatsoever about the existence of this interest inculcated by our history? Can there be any doubt about the existence of another great interest inextricably interwoven with our national life—the interest of the integrality and unity of the state, of its greatness, honor, and strength. . . . Really, do the dynastic and radical parties that exist in Western Europe serve as better indications of maturity than this integrality of the national mind?[31]

At the time Katkov expressed these thoughts, he was still generally known as an Anglophile and liberal; but his words reflect a conception of the Russian nation that was based much more on old Muscovite ideas concerning the unlimited faith of Russians in their Orthodox tsar as the defender of national unity and protector of his people than on any political or social notions that he might have borrowed from Western Europe.

A year earlier Katkov had greatly improved his position as an influential journalist and public figure when, together with his friend P. M. Leont'ev, he became coeditor of the *Moscow News*. Although he shared the direction of the *Moscow News* with Leont'ev until 1875, Katkov's influence was the prevailing one until his death in 1887. As coeditor, and later editor, of a daily newspaper, Katkov was in a position to reach a much wider audience than he had with the monthly journal *Russian Messenger,* which he continued to publish. It was indeed fortunate for Katkov that he was able to reach such an audience even shortly before the beginning of the Polish uprising, for this event outraged a large segment of the relatively small Russian reading public in the early 1860's, making it receptive to the emotional appeals of a self-appointed champion of Russian national interests such as Katkov.

In the very first issue for 1863 of the *Contemporary Chronicle,* which then became the Sunday supplement to the *Moscow News,* Katkov began his patriotic campaign against the Poles. This campaign was apparently first suggested to Katkov by a series of five articles that had appeared during 1862 in the *Messenger of Southwestern and Western Russia (Vestnik Iugo-zapadnoi Rossii),* which was then published by K. Govorskii in Kiev. The major question discussed in the five articles concerned the dangerous influence of Polish propaganda in the western Ukraine. Taking his cue from this discussion, Katkov indignantly commented that the Poles only constituted one-seventh of the total population in this region and emphasized that the agitation of the Polish party should therefore be regarded mainly as an attempt to create a Poland in an area where Poland had never really existed.[32] He continued this polemic in the first issue of the *Russian Messenger* for 1863, prior to the beginning of actual fighting in Poland. Here he referred to the historic battle for existence between the Russians and the Poles in this region. He insisted that Polish-Russian relations should not be considered a simple rivalry but a life-and-death struggle between two enemies over the question of which of them was to continue to exist as a nation. Thus the whole issue was, in Katkov's eyes, more than a simple matter of giving Poland a new constitution; it was a struggle against Polish aspirations to replace Russia as the dominant power in eastern Europe. He therefore considered any concession made to Polish patriotism to be not only inadmissible but also a "death certificate for the Russian people."[33]

After the beginning of the revolt, Katkov pushed for vigorous measures to defend Russia's vital interests in the southwestern provinces. He advocated, at one time or another during the next several years, the termination of the dependence of the Russian (i.e., Ukrainian) peasants in southwestern Russia on Polish landowners, the expropriation of Polish landowners involved in the revolt, increasing the number of Russian clergymen in the southwestern region, the expansion of Russian schools, tax relief for Russian peasants, the introduction of the Russian language into Roman Catholic church services in the region, diminishing the influence of the Catholic clergy, the construction of railroads to speed up Russification, and the like.[34] In so doing he gave full support to the brutal policies of General M. N. Murav'ev in the Vilna region and campaigned against the liberal or humanitarian policies favored by many bureaucrats, intellectuals, and journalists.[35] Among those against whom he polemicized at the time were the Slavophiles, who, although they were also generally in favor of Murav'ev's "firm" measures, defended the right of the Poles to have their own

culture and nationality. Katkov reproached the Slavophiles most merci-
lessly and sarcastically for having lost sight of Russia's real interests in their
constant chatter about nationality and national principles.[36] These attacks
against the Slavophiles, however, were rather short-lived. His repeated and
often virulent diatribes against the liberal bureaucrats of St. Petersburg,
on the other hand, continued throughout the 1860's.

The key to Katkov's violent polemics against leniency in Poland was his
belief that the Polish revolt was part of a general European conspiracy
against Russia. Like so many other Russian nationalists, he was convinced
that there was no popular basis for revolution in Russia but felt nevertheless that Russia's enemies could weaken her and cause her embarrassment
by using the allegedly insignificant Russian revolutionary movement as a
means of undermining Russia's position in Europe.[37] These enemies were
aided, Katkov suggested in the *Moscow News* as early as 1863, by bureaucrats in St. Petersburg who had liberal and pro-Polish sentiments.[38] In his
private utterances at the time he even went so far as to name individual
ministers. Toward the end of 1864, for example, he inveighed bitterly, in
the presence of E. M. Feoktistov, against A. V. Golovnin, who was then
Minister of Public Instruction. Katkov blamed Golovnin for having influenced the Grand Duke Constantine Nikolaevich, who had been Viceroy
of Poland for a little more than a year between 1862 and 1863, to favor a
conciliatory policy in Poland and claimed that Golovnin was working
with "Palmerston, Mazzini, with all our enemies and breeders of European
revolutions."[39] When Feoktistov protested that this was perhaps an exaggeration, Katkov answered: "I am not at all joking and am firmly convinced
that Golovnin is in close contact with the foreign revolutionists."[40] But even
Katkov never dared to publish such extreme attacks against government
officials. The theme of the Polish revolutionary conspiracy was, however,
one that he could harp on with impunity. He therefore returned to it again
and again whenever a proper occasion presented itself. The 1866 attempt
of Karakozov on the life of Alexander II presented such an occasion. Upon
hearing of this deed Katkov rhetorically proclaimed that its perpetrator
could not have been a Russian. When it turned out that he actually had
been a Russian, Katkov only modified his line somewhat, affirming that
Karakozov had been the instrument of Polish intriguers and European
revolutionists. At the same time, he suggested that elements in the St.
Petersburg bureaucracy probably had also been involved in this affair.[41]

The Poles were not the only minority group within the Russian empire
to arouse Katkov's anger during the 1860's. For, while he harangued
against the Poles, he was also highly incensed over the attempts of the
Finns, Germans, Georgians, and Armenians to achieve or maintain special
autonomous rights and privileges within the framework of the empire.[42]

He was particularly concerned about the Baltic Germans, who were tenaciously fighting to maintain and even strengthen their position as the dominant group in the Baltic provinces. Katkov bitterly opposed even the smallest concession to the political demands of the Baltic German nobles. Accordingly, he was very much against the proposals made by the Baltic German press in 1864 to unite Estonia, Livonia, and Kurland administratively into one province. He argued that the single and strengthened "German state" resulting from such a union would be only nominally united with Russia and would therefore be a likely area for the eastward expansion of Prussia, which he described as the "outpost of German nationality."[43] Another sore point for Katkov was the dominant position of the German language in the Baltic provinces. He found it an intolerable state of affairs that Russia allowed the Germans to use public educational institutions and religion as instruments of Germanization in the Baltic provinces.[44] Hence he recommended that the Russian language should be introduced as at least one of the principal instructional subjects in the schools, and he wanted Russian to be assured an official place in the public life of the Baltic provinces as well as elsewhere in the tsarist empire.[45]

Katkov's defense of the Russian language and of the authority of the empire was not confined to the territorial limits of Russia. After the mid-1860's he became an ardent advocate of closer relations between Russia and the Slavs of central and eastern Europe; but his interest in the Slavs outside of Russia considerably antedated his journalistic activities of the 1860's. Indeed, one can observe traces of such an interest even before Katkov studied in Germany in the early 1840's.[46] In 1858 Katkov had difficulties with Russian censorship authorities because of having published an article in support of the Bulgarian church against the patriarch of Constantinople;[47] and that same year he became a member of the newly founded Moscow Slavic Benevolent Committee.[48] After 1863 he usually was in agreement with Ivan Aksakov concerning Poland and the Baltic provinces. He published an increasing number of articles not only on Poland and other areas of the empire containing national minorities but also on the Slavic peoples of eastern and central Europe.[49] This was particularly the case in 1867, both during and after the Slavic Ethnographic Exhibition, which was held in Moscow in the fall of that year. Katkov then reflected the common excitement about the Slavic world in nationalistic circles at Moscow and St. Petersburg. He spoke of the necessity of putting an end to the weakness of the Slavs arising out of their disunity through the acceptance of a common Slavic language (such a language could, of course, only be Russian), which would give them the consciousness of solidarity they needed in order to be unified and strong.[50] The ethnographic exhibition was hailed as a great success by Katkov.[51] He did not forget the Slavs after the exhibition, for the internal crisis of Austria-Hungary between 1867 and 1870, which was brought about by the refusal of the Austrian government to grant the Czechs the same rights it had given to the Hungarians in 1867, provided him ample opportunity to continue to affirm the brotherly feelings of Russian society toward the Austrian Slavs.[52] After 1870, however, the strict and inflexible application of censorship regulations temporarily obliged Katkov to tone down the stridently nationalistic emphasis of his journalism.[53] However, the Russo-Turkish War of 1877–78 once again permitted him to speak out loudly in the name of Russian and Slavic nationalism. Thus Russia's declaration of war against Turkey on April 12, 1877, was jubilantly greeted by Katkov as a "great event," one which "had been long in the making," and long awaited by the "entire Russian land."[54]

Katkov's ardent, if sometimes condescending, advocacy of friendship with the Slavs is often difficult to reconcile with his brutally realistic appraisal of the internal problems of Russian nationalism. This conflict between Katkov's Pan-Slavism and his political realism suggests certain internal inconsistencies in his nationalistic philosophy of life. On the one hand, realism and expediency characterize his discussions of Russia's minority problems. He advocated a policy of force in Poland, apparently in the belief that the Poles had to be taught that the historical battle for existence between Russia and Poland had been definitely decided in favor of Russia. His opposition to the aspirations for autonomy of various groups within Russia seems to have been based on a conviction that federation could only weaken Russia and lead to the dissolution of the unified and powerful state that had been inherited from Muscovite times.[55] In regard to the Slavs, on the other hand, his views can hardly be considered to have the same realistic tenor. He did, it is true, speak of the unity and strength the Slavs would achieve through common action, which in its turn would tend to improve the position of Russia in Europe by giving her dependable and sympathetic neighbors.[56] However, together with such ostensibly realistic ideas there were many extremely vague ones; and it is certainly not at all clear that the pro-Slav policy of Katkov and the Pan-Slavists would have actually furthered the real power interests of Russia any more effectively than the policy pursued by the Russian foreign office, which was usually so bitterly criticized by them for not being sufficiently nationalistic. Katkov rarely made such criticisms of the policies of the Russian foreign office, however, and he was usually in agreement with official Russian foreign policy until he began to advocate a Franco-Russian alliance in the late 1880's.[57] This agreement implied acceptance of the official Balkan policy of the Russian foreign office, which hesitated to give open support to the Slavic peoples in the Balkans during the 1860's and 1870's because of its

fear of diplomatic complications in Europe.[58] Moreover, there was no assurance to what extent the Balkan peoples could be counted on as dependable allies, which was another practical justification for the note of caution
in the Balkan policy of the Russian foreign office. Hence Katkov's emotional attitudes toward these peoples cannot easily be reconciled with the
considerations of *Realpolitik* that apparently persuaded him, on an intellectual level, to approve the general lines of Russian diplomacy prior to
the 1880's.

Katkov may have realized some of the weaknesses and inconsistencies of
his own reasoning concerning Russian nationality, politics, and foreign
policy. After the Polish uprising of 1863, he tried repeatedly to formulate
a personal creed of nationalism, perhaps to serve as both an acceptable
conceptual framework and as a moral basis for his activities as a publicist.
Such attempts were, however, usually sporadic and in response to some
direct challenge to Katkov in his self-appointed role as the defender of
Russian national interests. One such challenge was made by the French
publicist, Charles de Mazade, who attacked Katkov in the *Revue des deux
Mondes* in March, 1866, for his demagogic use of Russian nationalism following the Polish uprising of 1863. Katkov was, of course, indignant and
enraged by Mazade's attack and answered him before the end of March
in the *Moscow News*. He explained his own conception of the role of a
publicist in Russia in the following words:

> The political character of our activity we have understood in the sense of a
> most binding obligation and we have not forgotten for a moment what
> activity of a political nature requires of every honorable man. . . . We
> have been able to judge all the questions subjected to public consideration
> exclusively from the point of view of Russian state interest. Our opinions
> might have been mistaken, but we have resolved not to say anything before
> we have convinced ourselves that it corresponds to the interests of Russia.
> The more profoundly we have been convinced of this, the more decisively
> and perseveringly we have considered it our duty to give our opinion.[59]

A little later that same year, in celebrating the resumption of publication
of the *Moscow News* after a successful struggle against the measures taken
by the Minister of the Interior to curtail his activities, Katkov formulated
his own conception of the nature of a journalist's duty in Russian society.
This conception was a simple one: the patriotic journalist was a sort of
civil servant who was bound by oath to perform his duty as a loyal subject.
This, Katkov affirmed, was the only basis for the activity of a public figure
in Russia.[60]

Twenty years later, shortly before his death, Katkov reaffirmed this conception of patriotic duty in an article published in the December, 1886,
issue of the *Moscow News*. At the time, Katkov was once again under the

attack of the St. Petersburg officialdom. His position was an especially weak one at that moment because Alexander III, who still favored continuing Russia's traditional ties of friendship with Austria-Hungary and Germany, strongly disapproved of Katkov's advocacy of a rapprochement with France during 1886 and 1887. He was, therefore, obliged to defend the image he had been so successful in creating of himself as a patriotic Russian publicist. He attempted to do this by emphasizing the peculiar role played by the press in Russian life. "Every Russian subject," he wrote, "is obliged to stand watch over the rights of the Supreme Power and to be solicitous about the interests of the government." This obligation was regarded as a sort of unwritten Russian constitution—one that was concisely expressed in the loyalty oath every Russian owed to his government. Thus the proper task of the Russian political press was to look out for the interests of "Crown and country" by conscientiously uncovering what was bad and speaking the truth fearlessly. "Here is what a serious political organ should be in Russia," he concluded. "This is not the path of power or to power; it is the path of service according to conscience."[61]

Katkov's final statement of his philosophy of patriotism and loyal service to the government hardly went beyond the conventional concepts of duty and loyalty to be found in the civil and, especially, military services of practically all modern nations. It was, therefore, too undifferentiated and unfinished to be convincing to his contemporaries or perhaps even to Katkov himself. Moreover, its meaning was so indefinite and vague that it could be associated with just about any social or political program and point of view. This is well illustrated by Katkov's own career: originally, he was an Anglophile and champion of liberal reform; at the end of his life, he came to be identified with reaction and obscuration.

More than any other single event, the trial, acquittal, and escape of Vera Zasulich, who had attempted to assassinate the military governor of St. Petersburg, General F. F. Trepov, in 1878 marked a turning point in Katkov's gradual transformation from a conservative-minded liberal into a reactionary. At this time he seemed to lose completely his already weakened faith in the presence of a sufficient degree of loyalty and maturity in educated Russian society to justify the hope that it would cooperate spontaneously with the government in the common task of strengthening Russia through reform. In 1878 he bitterly compared the patriotism of educated Russians at the time of Karakozov's attempt to assassinate Alexander II in 1866 with their open sympathy with a revolutionist and terrorist such as Vera Zasulich twelve years later.[62] Continued unrest among university students, the assassination of the governor-general of Kiev, and renewed attempts on the life of Alexander II, culminating in his assassination on March 1, 1881, provided Katkov with additional reasons for bitterness and anger in his thoughts concerning the loyalty and political maturity of the intelligentsia. He began to demand that severe measures be taken similar to those of Murav'ev in the western provinces in 1863 and at St. Petersburg in 1866 after the Karakozov affair.[63] His attitude toward the court reforms of the 1860's almost necessarily changed as he became progressively more and more disenchanted with Russian educated society. He accused judges and lawyers of having used the special position they had acquired as a result of Alexander II's legal reforms as a means of opposing the will and policies of the government.[64]

Katkov also discerned a feeling of hostility toward the government among zemstvo leaders. He attributed to them the desire to gain political control in Russia.[65] Such an aspiration was, of course, rejected by Katkov. He also condemned the notion that the Russian people should be given political rights. For Katkov, this was empty talk, and he denied that such rights had any place in Russian society. As opposed to political *rights*, he repeatedly emphasized the importance of the political *obligations* of every Russian subject and Orthodox Christian: "We are obligated to respect authority. The Church teaches that authority is from God. We are bound to respect authority not only out of fear but also out of conscience. Not only our conscience as citizens but also as Orthodox Christians commits us to this."[66] This traditional[67] and narrow definition of civic conscience led Katkov to condemn *in toto* the institutions introduced by the reforms of Alexander II once they had become strong enough to exercise some sort of independent influence in Russian society. Accordingly, during the 1880's he urged the abolition of the jury system, the termination of university corporate autonomy, and the strict subordination of all judges and court officials to the Ministry of Justice[68]—all of which he had supported during the 1860's and even into the 1870's. In regard to zemstvo institutions, Katkov's publishing of Pazukhin's article[69] on the desirability of strengthening the position of the gentry in the zemstvos indicates the trend of his thought on this subject, but this question was not argued energetically in the *Russian Messenger* or in the *Moscow News* during Katkov's lifetime.

Other differences between Katkov and the Russian liberals during the 1880's concerned his attitude toward education and tariffs. The Russian intelligentsia generally detested the system of classical education that Katkov continued to defend.[70] In respect to the tariff question, Katkov had previously taken the economic position of English liberalism, having argued that low tariffs were in the interest of Russian industry and commerce.[71] After the Russo-Turkish War of 1877–78, however, he discontinued his support of economic liberalism and declared that the time had come to make a clean break with the free-trade doctrines of the liberals. Now he advocated a narrowly nationalistic economic policy and claimed that Russia could only speed up her own industrialization and protect the Russian home market from the competition of foreign industry by the systematic application of high tariffs.[72]

This complete break with liberalism greatly simplified Katkov's system of conservatism and nationalism by eliminating some of the inner inconsistencies and irreconcilable elements within it. But consistency was gained at the price of making his own basic position incompatible with the ideals held by a majority of the educated public in Russia. Katkov's only answer to such nineteenth-century ideas as freedom and progress was his creed of patriotic duty, according to which every Russian was expected to do his utmost to further the interests of the Russian state. This patriotic duty was usually interpreted by Katkov to mean that the ideal Russian subject and citizen should make every effort to support the government in encouraging it to act resolutely, boldly, and if necessary, even brutally in defense of Russian national interests in the face of the various intrigues and threats he attributed to Poles, foreigners, and revolutionaries. Officials deemed by Katkov incapable of such action were accused, early in his career by insinuation and later by open personal attack, of having an antinational and antigovernmental attitude.[73] As long as Katkov's criticisms were tempered by his advocacy of reforms aimed at the improvement of Russian society, they could always be interpreted as exaggerations made by a publicist for the sake of progress and enlightenment. But once he had decided that reform was bad for Russia, that it was dangerous to allow any suggestion of independent and autonomous political activities whatsoever, then his ideal of a good society became so narrow that it was intolerable for the overwhelming majority of his contemporaries.

It is also difficult to visualize how Katkov's society was to function. He wanted everyone to serve the tsar and Russia, but he regarded the existing institutions in Russia that provided the best opportunities for such service —the zemstvos and the bureaucracy—with the greatest suspicion. Moreover, the system of education he favored in the 1880's was hardly designed to serve the true interests of the Russian state at the end of the nineteenth century. In this system future scientists and public servants were to receive a classical education. The education of the common people, on the other hand, was to be limited to the "three R's" and taught by church deacons who would, Katkov felt, provide them with all the knowledge they needed to learn and also give them some idea about Divine Law, thus bringing them closer to the church.[74] Such educational ideas were quite compatible with a static, agrarian society; Katkov, however, was far from being an agrarian idealist or populist. He viewed Russia's future in terms of a rapid industrialization to be stimulated through high protective tariffs. But his educational system was designed to produce an obedient people and a duty-conscious elite, who would be unfit to provide Russian industry with the large number of skilled laborers, technicians, engineers, and resourceful managerial leaders it needed for internal development and expansion.

The ideal world of Michael Nikiforovich Katkov was, therefore, a strange combination of static and dynamic elements. The static element in his thought was conservatism—the clinging to traditional concepts and ways of action. The dynamic element was nationalism. Russia's national interests, he felt, had to be spelled out and interpreted, and public opinion had to be aroused in support of Russia's foreign and domestic policies. Such interpretations and publicizing were, of course, the responsibilities of loyal and reliable leaders of public opinion—especially of Katkov himself; and decision-making was only to be entrusted to the hands of nationalistically inclined and highly placed figures in the St. Petersburg bureaucracy whose views Katkov happened to approve of.

The question of just how Russian national interests were to be interpreted was one that Katkov never answered satisfactorily. Indeed, his lack of success in dealing with this question is not surprising because, as even Katkov's admirer Nevedenskii admitted,[75] he did not begin to study politics, law, and economics until relatively late in his life. He was approximately forty years old when he began this study and so deeply involved in the movement of contemporary events that he certainly lacked the time to acquire a thorough understanding of these subjects. Accordingly, his thinking shows little evidence of clearly formulated ideas based on carefully reasoned theoretical and practical knowledge. Lacking such knowledge, he often changed his opinion on basic issues. In the last stage of his development, he did the very thing against which he had warned earlier: he became a conservative with the *status quo* as his slogan.[76] Everyone, according to Katkov's scheme of things during the 1880's, was to be obedient, perform his duty, stay in his proper place in society, and remain loyal to the sovereign power as was fitting for good Christians and subjects. Science and learning were not for the common man[77] but only for a select few who attended the classical gymnasiums. The courts were to be subordinated to the central administration. Local government was to be controlled by the most loyal element of the population—the gentry. The interests of the industrialists were to be protected by high tariffs; but those of the ordinary Russian had no protection, and the average Ivan Petrovich was expected to be absorbed into an amorphous unity of people, state, and tsar that permitted him no rights, hopes, or advantages but only prescribed Christian duties owed to the Supreme Power.

From the standpoint of conservative nationalism, it was particularly important that Katkov failed to perform well the tasks he had outlined for himself when he founded the *Russian Messenger* in the mid-1850's. He then had announced that he was resolved to serve the ends of the government by awakening the moral and intellectual forces of the country and strengthening the national element in the life of Russian society. On only one occasion was Katkov truly instrumental in rallying public opinion in defense of Russian national interests: this was in 1863 at the time of the Polish uprising. On that occasion he successfully identified himself with the cause of the Russian nation and became a figure of national significance. His *Moscow News*, with 12,000 subscribers,[78] became one of the most widely read newspapers in Russia at the time. His reputation as a defender of Russian national interests won him powerful support in governmental and court circles, which he was able to use in 1866 to humble Valuev, the Minister of the Interior.[79] After this, however, Katkov's influence gradually declined. He was not able to find another issue comparable to the Polish crisis that he could use to fire the imagination of the reading public. In the long run, he offered relatively few constructive ideas and could not hold the sustained interest of a large number of readers over a protracted period of time. The number of subscribers to the *Moscow News* therefore soon fell below 6,000 and never again rose above this figure.[80]

Katkov once again played an influential role as a public figure after 1881 as a result of Alexander III's official policies, but this did little to improve the popular appeal of his publications. Indeed, Katkov's open espousal of reaction at that time made him even less popular than he had been before. Thenceforth few first-rate authors were willing to submit their novels or articles to Katkov for publication, and the general level of the works published in the *Russian Messenger* was unquestionably lower than ever before.

In 1862 Katkov had, in his review article of Turgenev's *Fathers and Children*, pointed to such civilizing forces as education, science, industrialization, and the living force of tradition as necessary antidotes to the powerful spirit of negation in Russian society. In the 1880's, educated Russians ceased to associate Katkov with these forces of civilization. He, therefore, tended to lose any potential usefulness that he might have otherwise had in aiding the government to assume a role of leadership in Russian society; for the decline in his popularity made it difficult for him to continue to use nationalism effectively as a means of awakening the moral and intellectual energies of the country on the behalf of the government. In the final analysis, he failed to bring into existence a flourishing tradition of patriotic journalism along the lines advocated by Nazimov and other writers a generation earlier. Instead, Katkov served primarily as sort of a barometer for the changing opinions of conservatively and nationalistically inclined Russians during a period of reform, revolutionary agitation, and reaction.

PART II

The New Ideology

Introduction

To GAIN wide acceptance among educated Russians in the second part of the nineteenth century, conservative nationalism needed champions who could intellectually meet the challenge that socialism and nihilism represented for Russian society. Katkov had been too much an opportunist in his journalistic tactics and too much a vacillating eclectic in his philosophical, social, and economic views to undertake this task. Such Slavophiles as Ivan Aksakov and Iurii Samarin also were unsuited to it, for their doctrinaire and rather inflexible adherence to the ideas formulated by their predecessors in the 1840's usually offended their contemporaries, who felt that Slavophilism was no longer applicable to the conditions and problems of Russian society in the 1860's. There were, however, other conservative nationalists at the time whose ideas were philosophically more consistent than those of Katkov and more closely attuned to the popular tastes and attitudes of the period than those of the Slavophiles. Among such conservative nationalists, the *pochvenniki* (enthusiasts of the soil), who organized themselves around the Dostoevskii brothers' two journals, *Time (Vremia)* and *Epoch (Epokha)*, were particularly important. Closely allied to the *pochvenniki* was Nicholas Danilevskii. Danilevskii's original inspiration and point of departure were radically different from those of the *pochvenniki*, but he later came to be intimately associated with many of their ideas, and his book *Russia and Europe* became a sort of Bible for conservative nationalists in Russia during the 1880's and 1890's.

The *pochvenniki's* first journal, *Time*, was founded in 1861 and edited by Michael Dostoevskii. Michael's brother Fedor (who then could not serve as editor because of his recent penal servitude in Siberia), Apollon Grigor'ev, and Nicholas Strakhov, however, unquestionably provided the principal intellectual inspiration for the ideas expressed in *Time* and *Epoch*. The name of the group, *pochvenniki,* suggested the nature of these ideas. It was derived from *pochva,* or soil, and was symbolic of the desire of Grigor'ev, Strakhov, and the Dostoevskii brothers to get as close as possible to the Russian people and the national sources of Russian cultural life. From the outset they were convinced of the original organic unity of Russian society, of its lack of class antagonisms and distinctions;[1] they were also conscious of the historic cleavage in Russian society between the people and the educated minority. At the same time, they believed that civilized society was beginning to come once again into closer contact with the common people. Fedor Dostoevskii felt that such contact was necessary for Russia's future development and progress.[2] He dreamed of a new intellectual leadership in Russia that would arise and identify itself intimately with the Russian people and give it knowledge and enlightenment after a "long journey from the Russian soil into German lands."[3] This gift, Dostoevskii thought, would justify the intelligentsia's long separation from the Russian people.

However similar these aspirations might seem to those of the Slavophiles, it should be emphasized that the *pochvenniki* consciously strove to disassociate their journals from all party labels. They therefore tried to strike a compromise between Westernism and Slavophilism. As they wrote in their 1863 subscription announcement for *Time:*

> We did not go to ancient Moscow for ideals; we did not say that everything first had to be forced into a German mold so that our nationality could be considered as suitable material for a future permanent edifice. Our point of departure was what is, and in addition to this we only want the greatest possible degree of freedom of development. With freedom of development we believe in Russia's future; we believe in her independent potentiality.[4]

Russia's "independent potentiality" was certainly a vague formulation and could be interpreted in a variety of ways. It could, for example, be regarded from either a Slavophile or a Westerner point of view. The editors of *Time* seem to have been divided on this matter. Strakhov tended to identify himself with Slavophilism almost at the very beginning of his association with *Time.* Apollon Grigor'ev, on the other hand, often spoke highly of the Slavophiles but always had many reservations concerning their literary and historical arguments. The Dostoevskii brothers had even stronger reservations about the Slavophiles. It has already been pointed out that Michael Dostoevskii advised Grigor'ev to be more sparing in his praise of the Slavophiles so that *Time* would not be too closely associated with the Slavophile label in the minds of readers. In 1861 Fedor Dostoevskii contrasted the inflexibility and fanaticism of the Slavophiles with the more realistic attitude of the Westerners.[5] Dostoevskii seems to have held this opinion only temporarily, since after 1861 he became relatively more sympathetic toward the Slavophiles.

Dostoevskii's change of position was, however, a gradual one, and his general attitude as well as the editorial policies of *Time* and *Epoch* were characterized by a moderate liberalism. Strakhov referred to this position as "pure liberalism," by which he meant the support of such abstract principles as "freedom of thought, freedom of speech, freedom of trade, etc.," whenever there were no "clear grounds for another manner of action."[6] Accordingly, liberalism, for Strakhov, was a teaching without definite content—one that could be adapted to any social or political system.[7] Certainly Dostoevskii must have envisaged liberalism in similar terms, although there seems to be little precise information concerning his political, social, and economic views at the time. In any case, many of the articles in *Time* and *Epoch* testify to the moderately liberal, though also nationalistic, ideas of their editors. The emancipation of the Russian serf was thus described in glowing terms as the "beginning of a new life" and as a distinctly Russian reform, which liberated the peasant *with land,* thereby avoiding the duplication in Russia of Europe's proletarian problem.[8] The dissemination of education and literacy among the people was hailed as the "principal task of our time," and even the Sunday schools of the early sixties, which the government soon closed for security reasons, were viewed by Dostoevskii as a sign of a new positive view toward education.[9] Such an example of economic progress as the construction of railways was also greeted by the editors of *Epoch* as a means of strengthening the Russian nation.[10] This liberalism of *Time* and *Epoch,* however, had no solid basis in political and economic theory but was essentially an emotional attitude reflecting the general enthusiasm for reform then current in Russian public life.

The *pochvenniki* certainly failed to understand the social and economic implications of the reforms of the 1860's. The emancipation of the peasants, the establishment of the zemstvos, the expansion of education, the construction of railways, and the reform of the Russian legal system were all calculated to strengthen the Russian state vis-à-vis the states of Western Europe by utilizing the country's natural resources more rationally and by tapping new sources of human energy, intelligence, and initiative. The *pochvenniki* accepted these reforms in principle, but they did not perceive the difficulty an underdeveloped country has in catching up with more advanced nations. Capital must be accumulated; technicians, specialists, and leaders must be trained. Furthermore, the people of backward countries must be sacrificed if their leaders are bent on rapid progress. The land is not cultivated intensively and labor productivity is low in these countries. The peasant is therefore in no position to bear the heavy tax burden made necessary by the state's sponsorship of industrialization. The growing labor force, on the other hand, is poorly paid and housed because the workers' initial lack of the skills and training required by modern industry puts them at a disadvantage in dealing with their employers.

Yet Russian intellectuals in the second part of the nineteenth century commonly argued that Russia could avoid the evils of Western European industrialization and bourgeois society. Russian populists, as late as the 1890's, even denied the possibility of a capitalistic development in Russia.[11] The *pochvenniki* and Danilevskii never went to these lengths in combating the industrialization of Russian society. Unlike the populists, they desired a strong Russian state that could defend its power interests; they realized how indispensable railways and factories were for the smooth and effective functioning of modern armies. But they were poor economists and did not foresee how the costs of industrialization would be borne mainly by the peasant, therefore producing a desperate agricultural crisis that poisoned the atmosphere in the countryside and further alienated the peasant from society. The growing proletariat in the mines and towns would be equally alienated. In addition, the hundreds of thousands of economists, agronomists, engineers, lawyers, doctors, statisticians, and teachers who had been trained since the early 1860's for service in the zemstvos, courts, schools, businesses, and the bureaucracy represented a new force in Russian society. Although the conditions of Russian life did not permit them to lead society as did the bourgeoisie of Western Europe, their training and practical experience taught them self-confidence. Many became liberals and demanded a greater role in national politics. Others favored the radical and revolutionary transformation of society as the best assurance for Russia's future. Meanwhile, the continued growth of the Russian revolutionary movement during the latter part of the nineteenth century demonstrated the illusory nature of the *pochvenniki's* dream of a harmonious Russian society that possessed unique organic unity and was devoid of the class antagonisms of Western Europe.

The *pochvenniki* were idealists and romanticists in their basic philosophical orientation. This orientation was both their weakness and their strength. It was their weakness in that their idealization of the Russian past and present obscured for them the economic and social forces transforming Russian society. Hence they were poor prophets of Russia's future. On the other hand, their idealization of traditional institutions and values made them aware of the continuity of Russian history. Believing that the past could not be ignored in planning for the future, they understood how well traditional attitudes, values, and ideals form the base of a people's conscious national identity. They knew far better than the majority of their contemporaries how important national cohesion is for modern society.

The ideal of Russian nationality championed by the *pochvenniki* influenced many educated Russians between 1860 and 1890, particularly through Fedor Dostoevskii's novels and articles. Many of the ideas expressed in these novels and articles were inspired by Apollon Grigor'ev, who, although highly erratic, was the most brilliant contributor to *Time* and *Epoch*. Dostoevskii's colleague Nicholas Strakhov was the first to appreciate fully the importance of Apollon Grigor'ev's "organic" conception of Russian literature. Later, Strakhov also became the leading defender of Danilevskii's theory of cultural-historical types. Danilevskii claimed to have proved "scientifically" that Russia should reject liberalism and other Western ideas and follow her own path of historical development.

CHAPTER FIVE

Organic Criticism

APOLLON Grigor'ev first advanced the basic philosophical ideas underlying the *pochvennik* ideal of Russian culture and society. In literary understanding and erudition, linguistic competence, and philosophical instruction, Grigor'ev was certainly among the best prepared and most able literary critics and thinkers on the Russian scene during the 1850's and 1860's. Early in his youth, during the 1830's, he had become intimately acquainted with Russian and foreign romantic and sentimental literature. He was also able to share some of the excitement of university students for Polevoi's journalism and the poetry of Pushkin and Byron long before he became a student at the University of Moscow, for his tutor, referred to in his memoirs as Sergei Ivanych, often allowed him to sit in on the meetings of a small circle of university students. While at the University of Moscow between 1838 and 1842, Grigor'ev was initiated into some of the ideas of European idealistic and romantic philosophy, especially as expressed in the works of Schelling and Hegel. Unlike so many of his fellow students, Grigor'ev mastered German well enough to read Hegel in the original. It is not known exactly which of Hegel's works Grigor'ev read, but his subsequent writings suggest that Hegel's general emphasis on ideas in the development of mankind made a profound impression on him.[1]

During his university years, Grigor'ev was greatly influenced by Shevyrev and, especially, Pogodin, who were among the few professors at the University of Moscow in the early 1840's whom he respected.[2] After his graduation, Grigor'ev remained in close contact with Pogodin. He contributed poems to Pogodin's journal *Muscovite* (*Moskvitianin*) and became one of its junior editors. Grigor'ev later looked back with pleasure to the struggle he waged on behalf of Russian nationality "in life, art, and science" during his years of association with the *Muscovite*.[3] Grigor'ev was hardly ever guilty of the tasteless and sometimes vulgar chauvinism of his two mentors, Shevyrev and Pogodin; nevertheless, the Muscovite patriotism of his favorite teachers must have been a significant factor in molding his world of ideas.

Grigor'ev's early sources of intellectual inspiration were not limited to Moscow university professors and German philosophers. While still a student, he must have also read Belinskii's articles on Russian literature with avid interest. At a later date Belinskii was often mentioned and quoted in Grigor'ev's literary criticisms in a most favorable manner. Grigor'ev's approval, however, was of the romantic and idealistic Belinskii of the thirties, the author of the *Literary Reveries,* and not of the realist of the forties and author of the *Letter to Gogol.* Grigor'ev appreciated Belinskii's fine feeling for good literature and his ability to paint a vivid and living picture of Russian literature in terms of the general development of Russian culture and of humanity.[4] Grigor'ev refused to believe that Belinskii's realism of the forties represented more than a passing stage in his development. Thus he wrote in 1861 that if Belinskii had lived on he would have become a Slavophile. But this too, he quickly added, would have been no more than a brief moment in his development as a critic.[5]

Grigor'ev only became acquainted with the views of the Slavophiles several years after he graduated from the University of Moscow in 1842. During the first several years following his graduation he associated primarily with such Westerners as Professor Granovskii, the Korsh brothers, and M. V. Butashevich-Petrashevskii.[6] Not until 1845, while in St. Petersburg, did Grigor'ev probably first acquire a more or less accurate and complete impression of the views of the Slavophiles through the articles of Khomiakov and the Kireevskii brothers in Pogodin's *Muscovite,* which was then briefly under the editorial leadership of Ivan Kireevskii.[7] The editor of the last attempt to publish a complete edition of Grigor'ev's works, V. Spiridonov, argued in 1918 that these articles most likely exercised an important influence over Grigor'ev's thinking during 1845 and 1846. To support this theory Spiridonov pointed especially to Grigor'ev's articles of 1846 in the *Finnish Messenger (Finskii Vestnik),* in which Grigor'ev emphasized the importance of nationality in Russian history and culture as well as the deficiencies of Western civilization and Catholic Christianity as compared with the truth and vitality of the Eastern Church.[8] These were themes that were also close to the heart of Grigor'ev's teachers, Pogodin and Shevyrev, and, therefore, are not necessarily indicative of any Slavophile influence. Moreover, Grigor'ev did not mention the Slavophiles by name on the pages in the *Finnish Messenger* referred to by Spiridonov;[9] he did, however, specifically speak of the Romantic movement and of the German philosopher Schelling.[10]

Grigor'ev was usually quite independent in his use of the ideas of others and accepted only those elements of such ideas that he found compatible with his own general philosophy of art, esthetics, and society. Because of this independence of mind it is inadvisable to attempt to identify Grigor'ev as a follower of any given school of thought, whether Slavophilism, German romanticism, or the official nationality of Pogodin and Shevyrev. With specific reference to the Slavophiles, it is true that Grigor'ev subsequently nearly always spoke respectfully of them, especially of Khomiakov. At the same time, he found their general position to be entirely too theoretical and doctrinaire and therefore out of touch with Russian national life and contemporary culture. "Slavophilism," he remarked in an article of 1862 concerning the early works of Leo Tolstoi, "simply rejects both in literature and even in national life all phenomena that are not in conformance with its own ideal, calling them corruption in literature and perversion, deformity, etc. in national life."[11]

In the early 1850's Grigor'ev received an opportunity to develop his own ideas on Russian nationality and literature when he became one of the junior editors of Pogodin's *Muscovite*. By the end of the 1840's the subscriptions to this journal had fallen to a little over three hundred because few readers were attracted by Pogodin's official nationality.[12] Pogodin therefore decided to bring into his journal a number of gifted younger writers, such as A. N. Ostrovskii, T. I. Filippov, A. F. Pisemskii, and Grigor'ev.[13] The junior editors of the *Muscovite* greatly differed from one another in their attitudes, but they all, with the exception of T. I. Filippov,[14] had a less official and more subtle view of Russian nationality than Pogodin did. Moreover, figures like Pisemskii, Ostrovskii, and Grigor'ev contributed creative works and essays of great value, thus attracting a greater number of readers to the *Muscovite*. Its total number of subscribers soon tripled.[15]

Grigor'ev's first serious attempt to formulate a literary *profession de foi*, "Russian Literature in 1851," appeared in the *Muscovite* at the beginning of 1852.[16] He began this article with a discussion of historical criticism as the most representative approach to an analysis of the literature of his epoch. He admitted that the historical method often had been abused but nevertheless declared himself to be an adherent of it and insisted that in his age no other approach was possible.[17] In order to avoid any ambiguity concerning his interpretation of historical criticism, he prefaced his discussion of Russian literature in 1851 with a definition of the historical method. First of all, historical criticism considered literature "as the organic product of an age and people in connection with the development of state, social, and moral conceptions."[18] Grigor'ev, however, hastened to add that every age also was part of the eternal and invariable. Therefore, he reasoned, the literature of every epoch did not fall outside the sphere of generally valid laws of esthetic criticism. In other words, he believed that there was such a thing as good taste in literature and did not want to associate himself with those critics among his contemporaries who tried to replace literary taste with historical generalities.[19] The second characteristic feature of historical criticism, in Grigor'ev's opinion, was its view of literary works "in their successive and consequential connection, deducing them, so to speak, one from the other, comparing them, verifying them with one another, but not destroying one in favor of another, not elevating the last-written at the expense of the preceding."[20] He again emphasized that the good historical critic must not only analyze a literary work as an organic product of life but also in accordance with the absolute laws of esthetics. This was, of course, a difficult task, but Grigor'ev believed that the analyses made by the German critic and historian Gervinus of the works of Goethe, Schiller, and Shakespeare were examples of the successful application of this type of historical criticism.[21] The third aspect of Grigor'ev's system of historical criticism might be considered as a form of humanism. He affirmed that the historical method of literary criticism must necessarily view a literary work in terms of the "new strings it has touched in the human soul, or the old strings upon which it has played skillfully."[22] In a word, he asked that a first-rate literary work should somehow contribute to the understanding of man and his emotions,[23] in which way he again attempted to set himself apart from the cruder practitioners of historical criticism.

In his 1852 article, and subsequently, Grigor'ev applied these criteria to the analysis of Russian literature. Generally speaking, this analysis perhaps had more in common with the philosophy of literary history than it did with literary criticism in the usually accepted sense of the term. For Grigor'ev was always primarily concerned with finding writers who represented their periods, with describing their philosophy of life and art as a means of understanding an entire epoch, and, especially, with showing the manner in which Russian nationality was embodied and expressed in their creative works. In regard to nineteenth-century Russian literature, Grigor'ev's representative authors were Pushkin, Gogol, Lermontov, and Ostrovskii.[24] He was particularly enthusiastic about Pushkin, whom he described as being the only full expression "of our national personality" and of "our national essence."[25] Of all the characters created by Pushkin, Grigor'ev considered Ivan Petrovich Belkin to be especially important as a Russian national type. Belkin represented for Grigor'ev the "gentle and peaceful" Russian[26] who was later to become so popular in Russian literature. After Pushkin's Belkin, the next example of such a figure cited by Grigor'ev was Lermontov's Maksim Maksimych in *The Hero of Our Time*.

Lermontov, however, did not satisfy Grigor'ev completely as a characteristically Russian writer because he thought him to be too much under the influence of foreign models; Grigor'ev, however, praised him enthusiastically as the outstanding representative of the phase of Byronic romanticism in Russian literature.[27] Gogol came closer to Grigor'ev's ideal of a Russian national writer, especially because Gogol's humor cast much light on the moral nature of Russian man. But Gogol, too, was found to have weaknesses, for Grigor'ev considered his ideas to be often too narrow and his views too negative to be representative of all sides of Russian national character.[28] Ostrovskii, on the other hand, was warmly commended for his success in depicting Russian national life, especially for his having turned to the undeveloped strata of Russian society for the characters in his dramas. Ostrovskii was not the first writer in Russia to attempt this, Grigor'ev pointed out, but his dramatic representation of Russian national types was finer, clearer, and simpler than what had been done previously. In his plays, Grigor'ev wrote in 1859, Ostrovskii altered many stereotypes concerning native Russian customs and traditions and acquainted his audience with Russian types and aspects of the "Russian soul" which they had never before suspected.[29]

Apollon Grigor'ev continued to have a high opinion of the *Muscovite* after he left its editorial board in 1855. He and the other junior editors had, however, found themselves constantly at odds with Pogodin on money matters and editorial policy. Pogodin not only was unreasonably stingy in his relations with the junior editors, but he often disagreed with them publicly—even adding his own footnotes to their articles.[30] Nevertheless, after 1855 Grigor'ev made every effort to resume his collaboration with Pogodin under improved working conditions. The *Muscovite*, however, died a natural death at the end of 1857 before any suitable agreement could be arranged. In 1860 Grigor'ev attempted to persuade Pogodin to revive the *Muscovite*, offering to serve as its editor provided that he had full editorial control.[31] He assured Pogodin that he had able, potential coworkers at his disposal for the threefold task of the new *Muscovite*: (1) the struggle for the "idea of nationality in life and literature," (2) the struggle against materialism "in the name of idealism and Orthodoxy," and (3) the struggle for freedom "against despotism on the one hand and against Tushino Fourierism on the other."[32] Grigor'ev's outline of the task of a new *Muscovite* is suggestive of how close he then stood to Pogodin in his interpretation of nationality, politics, and Orthodoxy. He also, as is evident from his letter to Pogodin of March 7, 1857, accepted Pogodin's division of Europe into a West and an Orthodox East, regarding the East to be the repository of spiritual life as contrasted with the abstract theory of the West.[33] In regard to politics, Grigor'ev wrote to Strakhov in 1861 that he knew of no more reliable guide than Pogodin's letters to Nicholas I.[34] These letters, of course, represented Pogodin at his best, for in them he not only expressed traditionally Russian thoughts on the relation of the Russian people to their tsar but also courageous criticisms of some of the negative aspects of the policies of the Russian government during the reign of Tsar Nicholas I. In any case, Grigor'ev was not able to collaborate with Pogodin in 1860 in developing publicly the ideas they held in common. Permission was not granted to revive the *Muscovite* because of the disinclination of official circles to see Grigor'ev as the editor of a literary journal.[35]

It was, however, possible for Grigor'ev gradually to redefine and perfect his rather nebulous conception of literature and life during his last eight years (1856–64). He did this especially under the general heading of organic criticism and in four articles appearing in such divergent periodicals as the *Russian Conversation* (*Russkaia Beseda*), the *Library for Reading* (*Biblioteka dlia Chteniia*), the *Russian Word* (*Russkoe Slovo*), and *Epoch*.[36] These years were, it should be emphasized, ones of personal crisis for Grigor'ev. He not only underwent great inner spiritual conflict but also had such serious differences with his wife that he ceased living with his family at the end of 1858. In the face of these mounting difficulties, he seemed to find solace and consolation only in excessive drinking. This, of course, did not aid his straitened financial circumstances. In the early sixties he fell so deeply into debt that he was obliged to spend much time in a debtor's jail cell. His friends often tried to help him, but his temperamental instability tended to undo their best efforts.[37] Indeed, this instability reached such dimensions that Fedor Dostoevskii's brother Michael once suggested in jest that he should give Grigor'ev a short-term note and then have him placed in jail so that Grigor'ev could write brilliant articles for him.[38] However, in spite of Grigor'ev's turbulent existence during these last years of his life, many of his best and most original articles belong to this period.

One of Grigor'ev's first applications of his organic theory was to what he called "national organisms." In this context he wrote on one occasion in the late 1850's in a spirit reminiscent of Danilevskii's formulations which appeared approximately a decade later: "Each such organism is self-contained in itself, is in itself necessary, has in itself full power to live according to laws peculiar to it, and is not obliged to serve as an ephemeral form for another [organism]. . . ."[39] Grigor'ev attributed to these national entities certain organic principles which were, in one way or another, formed in the course of their historical development and contributed to "world life." He did not, however, go as far as Danilevskii in denying the existence of universal humanitarian values and ideals.[40]

Despite envisaging history in terms of "national organisms" and despite continued references to literature as the "organic fruit of an age and a people,"[41] Grigor'ev carefully distinguished his theory of organic criticism from the "one-sided historical view." His own view of literature, he wrote in 1864, had as its point of departure ". . . the creative, immediate, natural, vital forces; in other words, it is not the mind alone with its logical demands and theories to which these demands necessarily give birth but the mind and its logical demands *plus* life and its organic manifestations."[42] This emphasis on the irrational sides of culture and historical development was certainly not absent from Grigor'ev's earlier writings, but it occupied a much more central position in his thinking after 1856 than it ever had during his years of association with the *Muscovite*. Leonid Grossman has suggested that Schelling's influence, in particular, led Grigor'ev, after 1856, to underline the importance of intuition, organic development, and creative life for literature.[43] Grigor'ev, in his student days at the University of Moscow, had, of course, read Schelling, but he rediscovered the implications of Schelling's ideas for his own theories on Russian literature and society when, in 1856, he read the posthumously published *Philosophy of Mythology*. This work returned Grigor'ev to the excited philosophical discussions of his university years, and, in his own words, "the transcendental tendency, *sub alia forma*, again captivated and took possession of me."[44]

Grigor'ev's conception of literature as an organic manifestation of life had little influence on Russian society in the early sixties. There were relatively few in the Russian reading public who had the philosophical, historical, and literary background to understand his ideas; and the minds of most young people were then dominated by the realism and materialism of Chernyshevskii, Dobroliubov, and Pisarev. Certainly, the views of these authors were much less complicated, more concrete, and easier to understand than those of Grigor'ev, whose theories were developed in an abstract philosophical language understandable only to readers with a great deal of patience and interest as well as a solid educational background in the humanities.

The theory of organic criticism was nevertheless of considerable importance as a serious attempt to oppose nihilism. It was a rival conception of life, not only romantic and idealistic but also solidly based on philosophical arguments gradually developed over an eight-year period. Grigor'ev's friends were not alone in acknowledging his importance; even the radical critic Pisarev paid him a form of homage in 1864, after Grigor'ev's death in September. In so doing, Pisarev deftly attempted to disassociate Grigor'ev from his friends on the editorial board of the Dostoevskii brothers' journal *Epoch* by emphasizing some of the differences that had arisen between them and Grigor'ev in the early sixties. Indeed, Pisarev used materials published in *Epoch* as a means of suggesting that the talented defender of idealism and romanticism had been prevented from fully developing his ideas before a broad public by the lack of understanding he encountered among his own associates and friends.[45] This insinuation was, of course, not just, for the Dostoevskii brothers, Strakhov, and others associated with *Time* and *Epoch* had both respect for and patience with Grigor'ev, whose temperament was, as Fedor Dostoevskii once remarked, such that he could hardly accustom himself to work "tranquilly with a single editorial board in the world."[46] The high regard the editors of *Epoch* had for Grigor'ev is amply demonstrated by the articles they published about him toward the end of 1864 and the beginning of 1865. Thus Strakhov related how he had read aloud almost all of the letters he had received from Grigor'ev during 1860 and 1861, commenting that the opinions expressed in these letters "always had great weight in [the editorial board of] the journal."[47] Strakhov quoted a number of these letters in the two articles he wrote concerning Grigor'ev shortly before the latter's death. Here he quoted Grigor'ev's words, "the Slavophiles have won," which apparently had reference to the nationalistic feeling aroused in Russia in response to the Polish uprising of 1863. Grigor'ev also, according to Strakhov, recommended that this nationalistic enthusiasm be made use of to encourage even more zealous efforts on the behalf of furthering Russian national and cultural originality.[48] These efforts were clearly to be directed against the materialism of the nihilists, although Strakhov did not spell out exactly what he meant by this or engage in direct polemics with the nihilists in his two commemorative articles on Grigor'ev.

It is interesting that the editors of *Epoch* realized how much their struggle against materialism was based on the ideas of German romanticism and idealism. In August, 1864, they published an article by one of their less well-known contributors, Dmitrii Averkiev, on the close relationship between Grigor'ev and Schelling. Averkiev greatly appreciated the negative attitude that Grigor'ev had taken toward the "useful" and "naturalist" school of Russian criticism and attributed his success in countering this school to his having based his ideas on Schelling's philosophy. This philosophy, Averkiev believed, had been the point of departure for the independent study of Russian life because it had obliged Russian thinkers to view their country in terms of its own "peculiar laws" and "original development" and, accordingly, to consider Russian art as the organic creation of the Russian "national soil." Schelling's philosophy had, Averkiev somewhat optimistically claimed, enabled Grigor'ev to lay the foundations of "scientific" literary criticism in Russia.[49]

Averkiev was no doubt correct in opposing the organic theories of

Schelling and Grigor'ev to those of the Russian materialists of the early 1860's. He was, however, much too sanguine in his evaluation of the future of such organic theories in Russian society. Only a minority of educated Russians accepted these theories during the following decades. The *pochvenniki* were among the intellectual leaders of this minority; their self-imposed task of leadership was made much easier by Grigor'ev's efforts to create a new terminology and a new conceptual framework for describing Russian national life and literature.

CHAPTER SIX

Russia's Orthodox, Humanitarian Mission

A NUMBER of Russian critics have theorized that Apollon Grigor'ev must have exercised an important influence over the development of Fedor Dostoevskii's ideas during the early sixties. Dostoevskii's first biographer, Nicholas Strakhov, suggested that Grigor'ev was instrumental in bringing Dostoevskii closer to the Slavophiles, with whom he was "almost entirely unaquainted" at the time of his return from exile.[1] Father George Florovskii saw Grigor'ev's influence on Dostoevskii in the form of the romantic view of life seen as an integral and organic phenomenon. This was, in Florovskii's opinion, the basic philosophy underlying Dostoevskii's insistence that the Russian educated class should return to the people in an attempt to restore organic unity to Russian society.[2] V. V. Zenkovskii's variant on this theme was that Grigor'ev was largely responsible for Dostoevskii's acquaintance with earlier Russian thought, in the tradition of Herder and Schelling, which saw the national individuality of a nation as the key to its mission in world history.[3]

All these inferences contain elements of truth; but certainly others, such as Belinskii, Strakhov, and Vladimir Solov'ev, were equally, if not more, important than Grigor'ev in making Dostoevskii familiar with the tradition of German idealism and romanticism in Russia.[4] Belinskii, who even as a socialist during his last years still displayed many traces of German idealism and Russian romantic nationalism in his thinking, must have especially influenced Dostoevskii during their two years of rather close personal relations between 1845 and 1847.[5] Strakhov, who had an excellent theoretical grasp of German idealistic philosophy, was intimately associated with Dostoevskii during the 1860's, and they had frequent, long conversations on philosophical subjects. Dostoevskii apparently learned much from these conversations—so much that he admitted to Strakhov on one occasion, if one can believe Strakhov's own testimony, that "half of my ideas are your ideas."[6] As for Vladimir Solov'ev, his contact with Dostoevskii was too late to have been an influence in forming his basic ideas, though Solov'ev did perhaps aid Dostoevskii considerably in their final formulation.

It would be a mistake to exaggerate the importance of philosophy for Dostoevskii, for he was educated in a military engineering school instead of in the lecture halls of the University of Moscow and later lacked the time to make a systematic study of philosophy. What philosophical knowledge he did have was gained largely through his contacts with literary and political circles during the 1840's in St. Petersburg and later with Strakhov and Grigor'ev after his return from Siberia. The very fragmentary nature of this knowledge makes it difficult to analyze satisfactorily and in accurate detail the various philosophical ideas that might have influenced the development of his ideas on Russian society and nationality. It is therefore advisable not to ascribe too much importance to philosophy in discussing Dostoevskii but, instead, to describe the development of his ideas in terms of his family background and subsequent experiences as a convict, editor, and writer.

Certainly the roots of Dostoevskii's conservatism are to be sought in the pious, patriotic, and disciplinarian family milieu of his early years. "In our family," he wrote in 1873, "we knew the Gospels from early childhood. By the time I was ten years old I already knew almost all of the principal episodes in Russian history from Karamzin, which father read to us aloud evenings."[7] The belief in God which was implanted in his mind by a devout family was apparently weakened by his contact with Belinskii. According to the testimony of his friend Dr. Ianovskii, however, he returned to the church after his break with Belinskii in 1847.[8] Such a reconciliation, assuming that Ianovskii's testimony is accurate, could hardly have been a complete one, for Dostoevskii continued to be attracted to socialist and radical ideas until his arrest as a member of the Petrashevskii circle in the spring of 1849.

The explanations Dostoevskii made to a special investigating committee in 1849 concerning his participation in the Petrashevskii circle indicate how uncertainly he then wavered between traditionally Russian concepts of political and social order on the one hand and the new and alien concepts of Fourier socialism on the other. He understandably attempted to demonstrate to his questioners that the views of the *Petrashevtsy* were completely harmless and that it was quite possible for someone like himself to be a loyal Russian subject and a *Petrashevets* at the same time. He naturally did not want to divulge details concerning the *Petrashevtsy's* discussions that might have compromised them in the eyes of the government.[9] Dostoevskii's testimony was entirely in keeping with the views on political and social order in Russia that consistently reappeared in his writings during the remainder of his life. Thus he firmly denied that he was a free thinker and an enemy of autocracy. He even gave his questioners a lesson in history in order to demonstrate the importance of autocracy for Russia. Russia, he pointed out, had been saved twice through the strengthening of autocracy: "the first time from the Tatars, the second time in the reform of Peter the Great, when only a warm childlike faith in her great helmsman gave Russia the possibility to endure such a sharp turn into a new life."[10] Reforms in Russia, he argued, had to come from above, for all that was good in Russia since the time of Peter had come from the throne.[11] He declared that his whole outlook and upbringing were alien to the idea of republicanism in Russia. Republicanism and revolution belonged to the sphere of the Western world, where they were rooted in the old and "most stubborn struggle of society with an authority which was founded on a foreign civilization by conquest, force, and oppression."[12] Fourierism, like republicanism and revolution, Dostoevskii claimed, was a phenomenon that had been produced by Western conditions and therefore could not constitute a serious threat to Russian society:

> . . . Fourierism, together with every other Western system, is so unsuited for our soil, so much not in accordance with our conditions, so much not in the character of our nation, and, on the other hand, so much of Western derivation, so much a product of the state of affairs existing in the West, in the midst of which the proletarian question is being decided in one way or another, that Fourierism, with its persistent necessity at the present time, would be comically ridiculous for us, among whom there are no proletarians.[13]

However much Dostoevskii might have or have not believed in these opinions expressed before the special investigating committee for the Petrashevskii affair in 1848, their content indicates clearly that he was at least superficially acquainted with many of the ideas of the conservative historicist school of thought in Russia during the reign of Nicholas I. This does not necessarily mean that Dostoevskii had studied the writings of Pogodin, Shevyrev, the Slavophiles, and their followers, but that historicist interpretations of Russia's unique path in world history and culture were commonplace in the Russia of the 1840's. Dostoevskii could have picked them up, in one way or another, from a variety of sources.

If Dostoevskii in 1849 was not yet completely won over to the conservative opinions he expressed before the investigating committee, facing the prospect of death while standing before the firing squad and living four years as a Siberian convict seem to have persuaded him that the *Petrashevtsy* had been wrong in seeking to improve Russia through the introduction of a foreign ideology. His contact with his fellow convicts revealed to him not only many positive attributes of the common people in Russia

but also how difficult it was for an educated Russian to overcome the instinctive distrust the average uneducated Russian felt for all noblemen.
His spiritual isolation caused him to turn to religion and to study over and
over again the New Testament, which the wives of the Decembrists had
given him in 1849 at Tobolsk.[14] Whether or not he actually was able to
recover the naïve faith of his childhood, he earnestly sought God and
Christ during the four years he spent in the prison compound at Omsk. In
1854 he wrote to one of the Decembrist wives who had given him his New
Testament concerning the spiritual peace he had achieved in finding for
himself a symbol of faith:

> This symbol is very simple. Here it is: to believe that nothing is more
> beautiful, more profound, more sympathetic, more reasonable, more manly,
> and more perfect than Christ—and not only is there nothing but nothing
> can be; this I say to myself with jealous love. Moreover, if someone would
> prove to me that Christ is outside of the truth, and that *really* the truth is
> outside of Christ, then I should prefer remaining with Christ rather than
> with the truth.[15]

After his transfer from Omsk to Semipalatinsk, Dostoevskii's intense yearn-
ing for God reached a climax in an ecstatic religious vision. Dostoevskii
was arguing with an atheist friend about the existence of God. As Dostoevskii shouted the words "there is a God, there is," he was seized by an
epileptic fit. Before he lost consciousness nearby church bells began to
ring. "And I felt," he related in a conversation a number of years later,
"that the sky descended to the earth and swallowed me up. I really reached
God and was permeated by him. Yes, there is a God!—I shouted—and there
is nothing more that I remember."[16]

This "regeneration," as Dostoevskii later referred to it,[17] also applied to
the development of his ideas on politics. Thus Dostoevskii's patriotic
poems of 1854 and 1856 reveal great respect and veneration for Nicholas
I and Alexander II.[18] Most interesting is his attitude toward Nicholas I. It
seems that he did not bear any grudge against Nicholas for having exposed
him to the horror of a mock execution or for having sentenced him to four
years of Siberian imprisonment. In 1856 he wrote to Todleben, the hero
of Sevastopol, whose aid he wanted in an attempt to improve his position
in the army at Semipalatinsk: "I was guilty, I acknowledge this fully. I was
found guilty of [having had] the intention (but no more) of acting against
the government; I was condemned legitimately and justly. . . ."[19] A few
years later, this time petitioning directly to Alexander II for permission to
reside in St. Petersburg, Dostoevskii praised the emperor in the most hy-
perbolic language, likening him to the sun because of the light he brought
as the benefactor of his people to both "the just and the unjust."[20] Statements made in letters of petition are of course not always to be taken at

face value. In Dostoevskii's case, these expressions of esteem for autocracy and of guilt concerning his own past actions conform so well with his general philosophy of life that they must certainly be taken seriously. Dostoevskii later expressed similar sentiments in private conversations, where there was no personal gain involved for himself. One such conversation in which Dostoevskii praised Nicholas I was overheard by the Scottish student of Russia, Donald MacKenzie Wallace. When Wallace expressed surprise that Dostoevskii had spoken so highly of the man who had sent him to Siberia, he received the following answer from Dostoevskii's friends: "This is difficult for you to understand as a foreigner . . . , but for us it is understandable as a completely national trait."[21]

The Dostoevskii who returned to St. Petersburg in 1861 was therefore much more conservative and much more prone to accept traditional Russian values and institutions than the *Petrashevets* who had been sent to Siberia in 1849. This reaffirmation of Russian tradition necessarily influenced Dostoevskii's attitude toward the radical intelligentsia at St. Petersburg. He became highly critical of their materialistic philosophy of life. As a creative artist and believer in the freedom of art, Dostoevskii could not accept their injunction that literature should be primarily useful and serve the cause of material progress.

Dostoevskii began his polemics against the esthetics of the *Contemporary*, the leading journal of the radical intelligentsia, in February, 1861, with his article "Mr. ——bov and the Art Question." Here, in the name of the freedom of art, he attacked the utilitarian views on art expressed in the *Contemporary*, especially those of Dobroliubov. He insisted that art should not be hindered in the freedom of its development; that the freer and more naturally art could develop, the more useful it would become. For Dostoevskii, artistic creativity and beauty lived in the individual human being.[22] "Beauty is useful," he declared, "because it is beauty, because humanity has an eternal need for beauty and its higher ideal."[23] Such words certainly represent the standpoint of European idealism and romanticism and can be attributed, as Florovskii and Zenkovskii have done, to the influence of figures such as Grigor'ev and Strakhov. However, they can just as well be interpreted as the instinctive reaction of the creative artist to the abstract theories of the professional critic. The latter interpretation is borne out by the nature of the fictional works Dostoevskii wrote after 1864, when he published his *Notes from the Underground* in *Epoch*. Dostoevskii, in this work, clearly accentuated the differences between his individualistic, irrational, and religious conceptions of man and the utopian and utilitarian ones of such writers as Chernyshevskii, Dobroliubov, and Pisarev. The *Notes from the Underground* marked, as many critics have pointed out,[24] a turning point in Dostoevskii's artistic activity. Thereafter the theme of fallen and sinful man, for whom salvation was impossible through his own efforts but possible through faith in God and Christ, constantly recurred in Dostoevskii's works.

Various changes and events taking place in Russian society and in Dostoevskii's own life during the course of the 1860's soon broadened the range of his conservative traditionalism beyond the spiritual sphere of esthetics and religion to include that of practical politics. These changes and events in Russian society were the same ones that excited Katkov at the time: the increasingly extreme attitudes of the radical intelligentsia, the student disturbances, nihilism, and the Polish uprising. In Dostoevskii's case, the impact of these events was further complicated by his extremely negative reaction to Western Europe upon seeing it firsthand—a reaction greatly intensified by his own despair in not being able to cope successfully with mounting financial and personal difficulties during the 1860's and early 1870's.

The unrest among university students did not, it seems, immediately alarm Dostoevskii after his return to St. Petersburg in 1859.[25] He did not even learn of the revolutionary objectives of an organized group among the Russian youth until the latter part of 1862. It was at this time that he found the proclamation "To the Young Generation" attached to his door.[26] The contents of this proclamation disgusted and depressed him:

> Although I had already lived in Petersburg three years and had examined carefully other events, this proclamation that morning stunned me, as it were, appeared to me as a completely new and unexpected discovery: never until this day had I supposed such nullity. And the very degree of this nullity was terrifying.[27]

The Polish question proved fatal for Dostoevskii's journal *Time* because an article written by Strakhov on this subject, "The Fatal Question," and published in April, 1863, was misunderstood by censorship officials and led to the suppression of the journal. This article, seemingly because of its lack of clarity, was interpreted by Katkov, Ivan Aksakov, and the censors as containing unpatriotic thoughts at a time of national crisis. Actually, Strakhov's intentions had been most patriotic; he had only wanted to emphasize that, in addition to being a material affair, the Polish question had an intellectual and cultural aspect that had to be considered if Russia were to emerge completely victorious in her duel with Poland. Unfortunately, his moderation in discussing the Polish view of Russo-Polish relations was more apparent than his patriotism. For this, *Time* was handled even more severely than the *Contemporary* had been in the previous year, even though the Dostoevskii brothers and Strakhov were able to persuade Katkov and the censor A. V. Nikitenko that Strakhov had had the best of intentions. Eight months later, however, the editors of *Time* were allowed to begin a new journal, *Epoch,* in which they repeatedly discussed the Polish question in accordance with the nationalistically Russian views they had always held.[28] The heavy hand of censorship had, however, already dealt a decisive blow, for the financial difficulties caused by the suppression of *Time* in 1863, together with other adverse circumstances, made it impossible for Dostoevskii to publish *Epoch* after February, 1865.[29]

Probably even more important than the revolutionary movement and the Polish question in the development of Dostoevskii's conservatism in politics were his first encounters with Western Europe in 1862, 1863, 1865, and between 1867 and 1871. A. P. Miliukov, who was then a fairly close acquaintance of Dostoevskii, noticed a change in Dostoevskii's attitude toward Europe after he returned from his first trip abroad in 1862. Miliukov found that Dostoevskii's encounter with Europe had greatly weakened his sympathy for European civilization and strengthened his belief in the necessity for a more independent development of Russian life and society, commenting that Dostoevskii "returned almost a Slavophile."[30] Credence is given to Miliukov's observations by Dostoevskii's own words in his *Winter Notes on Summer Impressions,* which was published in 1863. As a result of Dostoevskii's subsequent visits to Europe these opinions became even more extreme. Much of the time he was sick and beset with almost insoluble personal and financial problems, all of which most definitely did not make him any more receptive to the positive sides of European civilization. His success with *Crime and Punishment* and the *Gambler* did little to improve his finances, and after April, 1867, he was obliged to spend four years abroad in order to avoid being thrown into a debtor's prison cell. During these four years of exile, his ideas on Russian society and its relations to Western Europe crystallized.

Almost at the beginning of this stay Dostoevskii had a violent argument with Turgenev about Russia, religion, and civilization. Turgenev's favorable comments concerning Germany and his critical ones concerning Russia infuriated Dostoevskii, who referred to Turgenev as a "Russian traitor"[31] in a letter of August 16/28, 1867, to the poet Apollon Maikov. Turgenev had also, Dostoevskii wrote, declared that he was an atheist. This alleged admission prompted Dostoevskii to make the following comments concerning Turgenev and other Russian liberals and sympathizers with Western ideas:

And what do these Turgenevs, Herzens, Utins, Chernyshevskiis represent for us? In the place of Supreme Divine beauty, upon which they spit, all of them are so vilely egotistical, so shamelessly exasperating, so frivolously proud that it is simply incomprehensible. In what do they trust and who follows them? He [Turgenev] insulted Russia and Russians without measure, terribly. But this is what I have noticed: all these so-called liberals and progressives, still pre-eminently of the school of Belinskii, find their first pleasure and satisfaction in reviling Russia.[32]

In other letters to Maikov during the remainder of his four-year stay in Western Europe, Dostoevskii continued to fulminate against Russian liberals and radicals, at the same time speaking of the great Orthodox mission of Russia for which these same liberals and radicals had so little understanding.[33]

Once Dostoevskii began to concern himself actively with the relation of Russia to Europe and with the thought of Russia's mission in world history, he almost inevitably turned his attention to the nature of political order in Russia as one of those peculiarities which distinguished her from the other countries of Europe. Thus in 1868 he wrote to Maikov that only while abroad had he become a "complete monarchist."[34] He described his own conception of monarchism in terms of the mutual love between monarch and people in Russia, which he referred to as "our constitution." Love, he claimed, was the foundation of the Russian state, as contrasted with the Western European state, which had been founded through conquest.[35] This view of monarchism in Russia and of the foundation of the Russian state was, of course, one that had been rather common among Russian conservatives after the early 1840's. Dostoevskii himself had expressed it as early as 1849 during his interrogation and, thereafter, probably always held it in one form or another. True, in the mid-1870's he did become more conciliatory toward Russian liberals and radicals like Belinskii, Chernyshevskii, Nekrasov, and Turgenev; but there is no evidence that he ever abandoned his traditionalist view of the tsar's political authority in Russia. Thus a little less than a year before his death, on February 14, 1880, he described the tsar as the father of the Russian people in commemorating the twenty-fifth year of the reign of Alexander II in a speech before the St. Petersburg Slavic Benevolent Society. Commenting on how the members of the society regarded their tsar and conceived of freedom in Russia, he stated: "We believe in a freedom [which is] true and complete, living, and not formal and contractual, in the freedom of children in the family of a father who has confidence in the love of [his] children. . . ."[36] Shortly before his death, almost a year later, Dostoevskii returned to this theme in the last issue of his *Diary of a Writer*. At this time, he placed the tsar alongside of God as one of the two most cherished and vital realities for the Russian people.[37] He described the relationship of the Russian people to the tsar as its most important distinguishing feature as compared with the other peoples of Europe and the world.[38] Because of this relationship between tsar and people in Russia, he declared, it was possible for Russians to have more freedom than "anywhere else in the world, whether in

Europe or even in North America."[39] This freedom, he explained, was not based on any written document but on the childlike faith of the people in the tsar as a father; for a father, out of the love felt for his children, could permit much that would be "inconceivable in the case of contractual peoples."[40]

If the relation of the Russian people to its tsar was its most important distinguishing feature, this relationship did not constitute the essence of Russia's mission in world history. Russia's historical mission was, of course, especially closely associated with the Orthodox Church and the religious ideal of the Russian people. Like his political views, Dostoevskii's ideas on Russia's historical individuality and mission were already present in his thinking during the decade following his arrest in 1849. He expressed his belief in the historical individuality of Russia, for example, at the time of his arrest. The experience of living in Siberia with convicts from the common people intensified his patriotism. While still in Siberia he took great pride in his knowledge of Russian national types and characters, for which he had boundless enthusiasm.[41] And in 1856 he expressed his complete agreement with Apollon Maikov's poetical vision of Russia's historical mission and significance for both Europe and the world of the Slavs:

> I read your verses and found them beautiful; I fully share with you the patriotic feeling of the *moral* liberation of the Slavs. This is the role of Russia, noble great Russia, our holy mother. How good the ending is of the final lines in your "Clermont Council"! Where do you find such language in order to express such a magnificent thought? Yes, I share with you the idea that Russia will be the culmination of Europe and of her mission. This has been clear to me for a long time.[42]

But such messianic thoughts did not occupy a central place in Dostoevskii's thinking during the following decade of his life at Semipalatinsk, Tver, and St. Petersburg. Perhaps this was because he was too preoccupied with winning recognition as a novelist and assisting in forming public opinion as one of the *pochvenniki* in an era of reform.

As a publicist he was particularly concerned with persuading the intelligentsia that any meaningful improvement of the condition of Russian society had to be accompanied by a cultural and spiritual reconciliation between Russia's educated minority and the mass of the common people. In Dostoevskii's case such notions were necessarily nationalistic because of his conviction that the common people stood in a more intimate relationship with the soil and sources of national life than any other group in Russian society. At the time, he did not choose to emphasize Russia's moral and historical significance for Europe and the world.[43] Such an emphasis reappeared only gradually in Dostoevskii's thinking as a result of his trips abroad and of his reaction to the optimistic, Western-inspired views of the Russian liberals and radicals during the early sixties. Thus, in his *Winter Notes on Summer Impressions* of 1863, he took violent exception to the bourgeois way of life in Western Europe and to its affirmation of material progress, individualism, and of abstract, rationalistic principles such as liberty, equality, and fraternity.[44] His polemics on esthetics with the *Contemporary* and his unorthodox work, *Notes from the Underground,* were part of this same battle. He implicitly waged this battle against the entire rationalistic and materialistic tradition of thought that had become firmly established in both Russia and Europe as a result of the eighteenth-century European Enlightenment. In the second part of the sixties, Dostoevskii temporarily lost all sense of measure in his struggle against this tradition, apparently because of his increasing bitterness in the face of such events as the Polish uprising, the excesses of nihilism, and the revolutionary movement in Russia. His branding of Turgenev as a "Russian traitor" is an example of his state of mind by 1867. In reacting to the negative attitude of the liberals and radicals toward aspects of Russian civilization which Dostoevskii valued highly, he exaggerated the positive features of that civilization. Accordingly, he predicted a role of cultural and moral leadership for Russia among nations and expressed his "passionate faith" in the future "great renewal" of the whole world through the "Russian idea."[45]

This notion of the possible role of the "Russian idea" in world history further developed in Dostoevskii's mind as a result of reading Nicholas Danilevskii's *Russia and Europe* in 1869. Dostoevskii had known Danilevskii personally as one of the *Petrashevtsy* in the late forties. He was therefore thrilled when he learned through his friend Strakhov that a former fellow Fourierist had returned to the traditions of his childhood "to become a Russian again and to come to love his own soil and essence."[46] On March 18/30, 1869, he wrote enthusiastically to Strakhov about the great significance of what Danilevskii had said in the first chapters of *Russia and Europe,* which had just been published in Strakhov's journal *Dawn (Zaria).* He described his surprise in finding Danilevskii's views so close to his own conclusions and convictions and, at the same time, so well supported by logical and scientific arguments. However, even after a reading of only the first chapters of Danilevskii's work, Dostoevskii was apprehensive about whether Danilevskii's approach to the history of culture in further chapters would permit him to describe adequately the nature of Russia's mission in history. For Dostoevskii, Russia's mission consisted in revealing to the world the Russian Christ contained in "our own Orthodoxy."[47] After he had read all of Danilevskii's work, he decided that there was little trace in it of "this thought about Russia, i.e., about her exclusively Orthodox, humanitarian mission."[48]

After 1870 Dostoevskii continued to develop his religious and national-istic views, and he gradually made them known to the general Russian reading public through such works as *The Possessed, The Brothers Kara-mazov,* and *The Diary of a Writer.* Dostoevskii wrote *The Possessed* while living abroad at a time when his rancor against the West and the socialists and his messianic faith in the Russian people were at a high point. In this novel Shatov voiced many of Dostoevskii's innermost thoughts on na-tionalism, religion, and Russia. Thus Shatov, in an argument with Stavro-gin, described how all great peoples had believed in their own gods, in their own truths, in placing themselves in the vanguard of humanity.

> If a great people does not believe that truth is in itself alone . . . , if it does not believe that it alone is able and called to raise up everyone and to save everyone with its truth, then it at once is transformed into ethnographical material, and not into a great people. A truly great people can never be satisfied with a second-rate role in humanity or even with a first-rate one, but invariably and exclusively the first role. Whoever loses this faith ceases to be a nation.[49]

Dostoevskii did not mean to imply with these words that truth as repre-sented by various nations was a relative matter. There was only one truth, he insisted through Shatov. This truth was contained in the ideal of God the Russian people carried within itself. The Russian god was therefore the only true one, though the gods of other peoples had often been great.[50]

Seven years later and shortly before the beginning of the Russo-Turkish War, Dostoevskii, in *The Diary of a Writer,* echoed Shatov's words on the necessity for every people to have faith in itself and to believe that in it alone "is contained the salvation of the world."[51] Each people, he con-tinued, should only live "to stand at the head of peoples, to join all of them to itself, to lead them in a harmonious choir toward the final goal for which they are all preordained."[52] Dostoevskii admitted that this proposition was a controversial one, but he argued, giving examples from history, that this had been the natural attitude of every great historical people. In this ar-gument, he stood unmistakably close to the historical philosophy of Hegel with its emphasis on the importance of peoples identified with great his-torical ideas in furthering the progress of mankind. He, however, differed from Hegel, as Reinhard Lauth has pointed out, in that he felt the Russian idea developed independently of other historical ideas and did not enter into any necessary dialectical relationship with them.[53]

Four months later, when Russia declared war against Turkey, Dostoev-skii was no longer so concerned about the harmonious choir of mankind, for he found the thought of war exciting and stimulating. He even praised war as uplifting and beneficial as opposed to the stagnation, greed, and egoism produced by long periods of peace.[54] War was more than just a psychological experience for Dostoevskii, because he was also mindful of possible material gains for Russia from the war. "Constantinople must be *ours*," he wrote, "conquered by *us* Russians from the Turks and remain ours forever."[55] Dostoevskii considered the diplomatic situation in Europe at the time to be most favorable for Russian initiative in regard to Constantinople because of what he regarded to be the impending showdown between Germany and France.[56] He was then, though he had earlier been quite critical of Germany in the letters he wrote during the Franco-Prussian War, exceedingly pro-German and greatly admired Bismarck.[57] He attributed to Bismarck ideas similar to his own on the relation between Catholicism and socialism. According to these views, French socialism was regarded as being a product of Roman Catholicism and as possessing Catholicism's alleged materialism and despotism, even though it was, in Dostoevskii's opinion, a reaction to the Papacy's various distortions of Christianity. Therefore he considered France as the embodiment of the ideas of both Catholicism and socialism. Hence Protestant Germany, Dostoevskii thought, was obliged to move against France and to destroy her politically in order to strike a blow against socialism, the heir of Catholicism.[58] The "Western world" would thereafter belong to Germany and the East would go to Russia; but Russia had to "seize the moment," Dostoevskii argued, and take advantage of German friendship and the existing diplomatic conditions in Europe, for there was no assurance how long these conditions would continue to be so favorable for Russia.[59]

Despite this affirmation of power politics, Dostoevskii never completely lost sight of his previously expressed ideas on Russia's mission to lead mankind toward its final and preordained goal. In addition to serving mankind, Russia also had the task of assisting her "Slavic brethren" in winning and maintaining their independence. This specific task seems to have been always subordinated in Dostoevskii's mind to the more exalted one of bringing a new message to the world that would "save European humanity."

> Russia already becomes aware . . . that she alone is the bearer of the idea of Christ, that the word of Orthodoxy transforms itself in her into a great cause, that this cause has already begun with the present war, and that ahead of her there are still centuries of self-sacrificing labor, of the propagation of the brotherhood of peoples and of ardent maternal service to them as to dear children.[60]

Indeed, Dostoevskii's militant Pan-Slavism and Pan-Russianism was relatively short-lived. During the last years of his life he returned to the much purer variety of Christian humanitarianism that characterized his writings of the period preceding the Russo-Turkish War of 1878. In the figure of the *Starets* Zosima in *The Brothers Karamazov,* for example, Dostoevskii's vision of salvation coming from the faith and humility of the Russian people[61] was expressed in a more spiritualized form than ever before. He spoke in the same spirit toward the end of his famous speech on Pushkin before the meeting of the Society of Lovers of Russian Literature on June 8, 1880. Here he sought to make Pushkin a symbol of Russian nationalism and universalism and to unite the Russian Westerners and Slavophiles, whose differences he labeled a "misunderstanding," in a common consciousness of Russia's significance for Europe and all of the "Aryan peoples." The spiritual unity of future Russians, he declared, was to be based on the following aspirations:

> . . . to seek a final reconciliation of the European contradictions, to show the solution of European anguish in our own universal and all-unifying Russian soul, to contain in it all our brethren through brotherly love, and, finally, perhaps, to utter the ultimate word of the great, general harmony, of the brotherly, definitive accord of all peoples in keeping with the law of Christ's Gospel![62]

There is, however, little reason to believe that these lofty enunciations of Russian spirituality meant that Dostoevskii necessarily had rejected the glorification of war and the justification of power politics and Russian conquest that he had preached in 1877. The nebulous nature of his religious ideal of the Russian people as the bearer of Christ and the uncritical fervor with which he advocated this ideal made him, and others who shared his views, easy prey for the currents of chauvinism, imperialism, and religious prejudice which afflicted Russian society in the late 1870's and early 1880's. Certainly, for example, his simplistic and crude ideas on the Jewish problem in Russia and on the alleged Jewish financial mastery of Europe, which he developed especially during the last few years of his life, are not to be ignored any more than his anti-Catholic prejudices.[63] His attraction to vistas of Russian imperialistic expansion was definitely more than a form of temporary madness produced by the war hysteria and Pan-Slav exaltation of 1877. Several years later another Russian military victory, namely Geok-Tepe, again excited the novelist's imagination about the future material greatness and strength of Russia. He demanded that "the name of the White Tsar should stand above those of the khans and emirs, above that of the Empress of India, even above that of the Caliph."[64] Asia, with its vast resources and possibilities for development, was to be a sort of North America for Russia, a vast storehouse of raw materials which only needed Russian enterprise and imagination in order to be developed. Russian development of Asia, he averred, would give Russians a "civilizing mission" that would restore their confidence in themselves and therefore contribute to making them independent of Europe.[65] Like many of his American, English, and German contemporaries who held similar opinions about their nations' respective missions, Dostoevskii did not bother to inquire whether the Asians really wished to be civilized by the Russians. His obsession with Russia's national destiny assumed a militant note in the concluding words of *The Diary of a Writer*, which he wrote shortly before his death: "Yes, hail the victory of Geok-Tepe! Hail Skobolev and his soldiers, and the eternal memory of the heroic knights who 'were withdrawn from the rolls.' We shall inscribe them on our rolls."[66]

This bizarre combination of imperialism, narrow religious prejudices, Russian Orthodox messianism, and conventional Muscovite political attitudes made it easy for more than one Russian reactionary to identify his views with those of Dostoevskii. Even during his lifetime Dostoevskii was closely associated with such notorious leaders of reaction in Russia as Prince Vladimir Meshcherskii, publisher of the journal *Citizen* (*Grazhdanin*), and Constantine Pobedonostsev, the tutor of the future Alexander III and, later, the Over Procurator of the Holy Synod. He served as editor of Meshcherskii's journal between January 1, 1873, and March 19, 1874;[67] and his relations with Pobedonostsev were particularly close between 1873 and 1881.[68] During these years Dostoevskii often spent Saturday evenings at Pobedonostsev's house in order to discuss various ideas which he was developing in his novels. Pobedonostsev even claimed that Dostoevskii had created the figure of the *Starets* Zosima in *The Brothers Karamazov* "according to my suggestions."[69] Certainly, this was an exaggeration, for Dostoevskii had worked on the prototype of the *Starets* Zosima as early as 1870.[70] In addition there were many important differences in outlook between Dostoevskii and Pobedonostsev. Dostoevskii's conciliatory attitude during the late seventies toward such heroes of the radical intelligentsia as Belinskii and Nekrasov in *The Diary of a Writer*, his notion that the Russian peasant could become the teacher of the intellectual in a *zemskii sobor*, and his belief in civic, artistic, and religious freedom[71]—all clearly represented ideas that were unacceptable to Pobedonostsev, who was a grim, inflexible, and persistent enemy of all freedom for nonconformist artistic and intellectual expression. On the other hand, Pobedonostsev could only approve Dostoevskii's hostility toward Jews, Catholics, Western-oriented liberals, radicals, and bureaucrats as well as his emphasis on the importance of religion and nationalism in Russian life. He was therefore able to write in all honesty to the future Alexander III, early in 1881: "The death of Dostoevskii is a great loss for Russia. In the circle of the literati he almost alone was an ardent advocate of the fundamental principles of faith, nationality, and love of fatherland."[72]

CHAPTER SEVEN

Philosophical Struggle with the West

THE THIRD important representative of the *pochvennik* group, Nicholas Nikolaevich Strakhov, was a philosopher and scholar by training and temperament. This prevented him from being carried away by the naïve and emotional mixture of religion, idealistic nationalism, and great-power chauvinism that characterized Dostoevskii's last years as a publicist and novelist. Strakhov, having been born in 1828, was seven to eight years younger than Apollon Grigor'ev and Fedor Dostoevskii. As has been already pointed out, Strakhov's family did not come from the service gentry —as did the Grigor'evs and Dostoevskiis—but from the upper strata of the white clergy. Strakhov was educated by his uncle, who was successively rector of the ecclesiastical seminaries at Kamenets-Podolsk and Kostroma.[1] In these seminaries Strakhov received a very thorough and systematic, but conventionally ecclesiastical, education. The nature of this education is suggested by the 258-page essay he composed in 1844, shortly before he entered the Mathematical Faculty of the University of St. Petersburg, on the "Governmental Institutions of the Russian Empire."[2] This essay clearly represented the study notes of an unusually diligent and conscientious teen-age student who had written into his copybook the tedious and legalistic formulations of law manuals of the period. It was filled with such phrases as "The governmental law of the Russian Empire is a part of Russian law";[3] "Russian law is the systematic exposition of the laws of the Russian Empire";[4] and "The authority of the Russian Emperor is *autocratic, unlimited,* and *hereditary.*"[5] Strakhov's intellectual horizons later were extended far beyond the narrow limits of his early education; but he never forgot the lessons this education inculcated in him concerning the nature of political order and of religious truth, for he remained a conservative in politics and religion throughout his life.

Apollon Grigor'ev first brought Strakhov into contact with the other *pochvenniki*. Grigor'ev had noticed Strakhov as early as 1858, when the latter's article, "Letters about Organic Life," appeared in the *Russian World (Russkii Mir)*.[6] Strakhov, in his turn, was greatly impressed by Grigor'ev's organic view of literature, which became the point of departure for his own subsequent activities as a literary critic. What influence Grigor'ev's ideas did have on Russian literary thought was to a large extent the result of Strakhov's efforts to popularize them. He began these efforts in the early 1860's, when he read the letters Grigor'ev wrote him from Orenburg to the editorial committee of *Time*, and continued to include them in a number of his articles during the 1860's, 1870's, and 1880's. In 1876 he published Volume I of what was intended to be a collection of all of Grigor'ev's important works, but he never completed this project because of public indifference to Grigor'ev at the time.[7]

Dostoevskii, on the other hand, seems to have been of little importance for the intellectual development of Strakhov. On the contrary, Strakhov, despite being younger and less experienced than Dostoevskii, was intellectually the stronger of the two. He was, therefore, in the opinion of the Soviet authority on Dostoevskii, A. S. Dolinin, able to exercise what was probably a decisive influence over the editorial policies of the Dostoevskii brothers' journal *Time*.[8] It should also be mentioned that apparently Strakhov had been negatively impressed by Dostoevskii as a human being as early as 1862, when they spent some time together in Western Europe. In November, 1883, shortly after his "Recollections Concerning F. M. Dostoevskii" were published, Strakhov confessed to Count Leo Tolstoi that he had found the task of writing about Dostoevskii a distasteful one.[9]

In Strakhov, the Dostoevskii brothers came into contact with one of the most broadly educated minds in Russia at the time, for Strakhov wrote well and authoritatively on such subjects as philosophy, physiology, zoology, psychology, and literature. His university education was mainly in the natural sciences. In 1857 he defended a Master's dissertation in zoology, which was written on the rather narrow and specialized subject "Concerning the Wrist Bones of Mammals" ("O kostiakh zapiast'ia mlekopitaiushchikh"). During the 1850's he had taught physics, mathematics, and the natural sciences in secondary schools at Odessa and St. Petersburg.[10] During these years of teaching he familiarized himself with German idealistic philosophy, which he regarded throughout his life as the high point in the development of philosophical thought. In his own words, he had always been the typical intellectual of the 1840's whose ideal of education was "to understand Hegel and to know Goethe by heart."[11] He therefore strongly believed in the "usual German theory of the freedom of art, that theory which originated in German philosophy, which came to us during the lifetime of Pushkin, and to which our literature is so much obligated."[12] But Strakhov's understanding of German philosophy was much more thorough and complete than that of the generation of the 1840's, as was clear as early as 1860 when Strakhov's article on the philosophy of Hegel was published in the journal *Torch* (*Svetoch*). He later became one of the most important popularizers of German idealistic philosophy in Russia for the rapidly expanding reading public of the 1860's, 1870's, and 1880's.[13]

Strakhov's activities as a literary critic must also not be overlooked. He was a particularly enthusiastic exponent of Grigor'ev's esthetic theories, which he used rather effectively to review such works as Turgenev's *Fathers and Children* and Tolstoi's *War and Peace*.[14] The intrinsic value of these and other reviews by Strakhov during the 1860's and later definitely entitles him to more serious consideration than he has received in the past from both Western and Soviet literary critics, who have pretty much ignored him in their almost exclusive emphasis on the importance of such figures as Chernyshevskii, Pisarev, and Dobroliubov. Certainly, this emphasis cannot be justified on purely esthetic grounds. The radical critics were, of course, of great historical significance; but one gets a one-sided and distorted picture of the intellectual life of the 1860's by almost completely ignoring their opponents.[15]

Neither literature nor philosophy, however, represented Strakhov's major preoccupation during his thirty-five year career as a Russian publicist. His main concern was with the "struggle with the West," which was the title of his three-volume collection of polemical articles directed against the influence of Western European ideas in Russia.[16] *Argumenta ad hominem* were relatively rare in these articles. Indeed, for a man engaged in public discussions in Russia during the second part of the nineteenth century, Strakhov usually (with the notable exception of the last years of his life when he engaged in polemics with Vladimir Solov'ev and other writers concerning Danilevskii's *Darwinism* and *Russia and Europe*) displayed an almost surprising degree of lucidity and calmness in his writings. These qualities of mind, as well as Strakhov's erudition and interest in religion undoubtedly recommended him to Count Leo Tolstoi, who was his close friend from 1871 until Strakhov's death in 1896.[17]

Two letters exchanged between Strakhov and Tolstoi during March, 1882, cast much light on both the fundamental nature and weakness of Strakhov's struggle with the West. The first of these letters was written by Tolstoi on March 14. It was brief, but in it Tolstoi reproached Strakhov for the purely negative character of the essays he had just written concerning Herzen, Michelet, and Renan.[18] Strakhov was hurt by these reproaches from Tolstoi, for whom he had boundless admiration. In his attempt to answer them honestly, he explained to Tolstoi some of the reasons for his negative attitude toward Europe and modern society. Since the time of the Reformation, he wrote, European history had been characterized by a gradual disintegration of the moral foundations of its society, which had been inherited from medieval times. The various movements of his own time—those of liberalism, revolution, socialism, and nihilism—had, in his opinion, a purely negative character, and the ideals of these movements— freedom and equality—were only "idols for the many," banners of battle and revolution, which in themselves had "not the slightest attraction or any positive content that could give them genuine value or lead to positive goals."[19] Modern society, he suggested, was only held together by old elements—remnants of faith, patriotism, and morality—and these were increasingly losing ground:

> But since these principles were inculcated by Christianity to an unheard of [degree of] strength, mankind carries them ineffaceably within itself, and they will long suffice for its sustenance. But mankind does not live by them, but against them or without them. All of the new principles are a direct avowal of a mundane, worldly life—and this is why life now has been developed so sumptuously. There is latitude for everything, for every sort of activity, for science and art as well as for service to Mars, Venus, and Mercury.[20]

Such a moral criticism of the premises of modern civilization, in order to be convincing, also demanded the exposition of positive principles to replace the ones branded as false. Strakhov recognized this and admitted to Tolstoi that he would have been much more effective if he had presented "an entire system, a clear idea."[21] But he lacked the powers of synthetic thinking needed to create such a system, so his only recourse was to do his utmost to oppose the negative movement of modern ideas, explaining that in negating modern ideas "I negate negation."[22]

The positive elements in Strakhov's thought must therefore be sought not in any original system of ideas intended primarily for the future but rather in those particular principles and values inherited from the past which he hoped to conserve and defend. He believed that more of the heritage of the past had been preserved in Russia than elsewhere.[23] Given this belief, he naturally considered the struggle with the West—that is, the struggle against its negative movements and ideals—to be the primary task of every true Russian conservative.

Strakhov seldom discussed political questions, but when he did there was little mistaking the conservative nature of his views. Like so many other conservative Russians, he had been nurtured on Karamzin's history of Russia. As a result, he identified himself closely with this historian of the Russian state in regard to politics.[24] He, therefore, was indignant when the fourth chapter of A. N. Pypin's "Studies of the Social Movement under

Alexander I" appeared in the *Messenger of Europe* (*Vestnik Evropy*) in 1870, for here Pypin concluded that Karamzin had been in many ways a harmful influence on the society of Alexander I.[25] This was particularly the case, Pypin had written, in regard to Karamzin's views on serfdom, Poland, and autocracy. Strakhov attempted to defend Karamzin by arguing that any emancipation of the serfs at the beginning of the nineteenth century would have been ill-advised because at that time the peasants could only have been emancipated without land.[26] As for Poland, Strakhov claimed that it was clear that Alexander I's liberal plans for that country had been against the interests of the Russian state and of the Russian people, whereas Karamzin had been entirely correct in his insistence that the interests of Poland had to be subordinated to those of Russia.[27] With reference to autocracy and Karamzin's relationship to this institution, Strakhov wrote:

> Authority belongs to the tsar, but honor and conscience as well as thought and moral judgment do not constitute subjects for this authority. These are blessings, the right to which Russian citizens have never consciously given up to anyone. It has of course happened that rulers have erred in [interpreting] the meaning of their authority; it has also happened that subjects have distorted the [proper] conception of their relations with authority. But the true sense of the union between tsar and people has been sometimes manifested in all its purity, and Karamzin belongs to the number of most magnificent examples of this phenomenon.[28]

The union between tsar and people was, in Strakhov's opinion, peculiar to Russia and gave her a governmental structure that protected her from such evils as revolution, the struggle between property owners and proletarians, and the passion for political power, which were then allegedly undermining Western European society.[29] The Russian state was unique in history. It was monarchical without having an Old Regime, democratic without socialism, and martial without feudalism and a feudal nobility. Political ambition, he believed, was completely foreign to the Russian people. The Russian was willing to sacrifice everything for his country but did not seek to take part in ruling it. Indeed, the ordinary Russian regarded participation in the governing of his country more as an obligation than as a right, for the "equality, liberty, and fraternity" that the Russian sought and demanded did not lie in material interests and political rights.[30] The actual sphere where the Russian did seek and demand equality, liberty, and fraternity was not made explicit by Strakhov in this context. It is, however, clear from his other writings that he must have meant the spheres of morality and religion.

In 1890 Strakhov's friend and disciple V. V. Rozanov described religion as the central issue of Strakhov's entire life and career as a writer.[31] Strakhov's correspondence with Tolstoi strongly suggests that Rozanov was correct in his emphasis of the role of religion in Strakhov's works. But Strakhov's religious outlook was more original and less dependent on traditional Russian sources than was his view of politics. In fact, after the 1860's, Strakhov rarely referred to the Orthodox Church as such, although he often discussed the importance of religion for any society. Strakhov's tendency to drift away from the narrow confines of the official church probably resulted from the inherent difficulties he found in trying to reconcile Orthodox dogmas and practices with the historical and philosophical views of religion that he encountered in the works of such philosophers as Schelling, Spinoza, Hegel, and Fichte and in his conversations with Vladimir Solov'ev and Leo Tolstoi. By the late 1880's he had associated himself with the "pure religion" of the mystics and philosophers, who were, he wrote to Tolstoi in October or November, 1887, almost always misunderstood and distrusted by the organized religious communities to which they belonged.[32]

These unorthodox and independent opinions, however, did not alter his conviction that religion and religious feeling were natural and necessary parts of human existence. He therefore was very much disturbed by the rationalistic and materialistic interpretation of religion then popular in Germany and France. Thus he described David Friedrich Strauss's attempt (in *Der alte und der neue Glaube;* Leipzig: S. Hirzel, 1872) to preserve religious feeling without belief in God as a "striking inconsistency," because religious feeling, he insisted, was inconceivable without God.[33] Strakhov believed that it was not possible for man to confront the "moral ugliness" surrounding him unassisted by religious faith. An ideal representing purity and perfection was necessary, and he rejected the assumption of an optimist like Strauss that man alone could create such an ideal for himself.[34] He felt that Strauss's assumption could only lead to the direst consequences.

He was able to find at least partial support for this view in *La réforme intellectuelle et morale* of Ernest Renan. Renan, as a believer in science and progress and as a follower of Strauss in writing a naturalistic life of Jesus, was a rather strange ally for Strakhov. But the Renan of *La réforme intellectuelle et morale,* which was published in 1871, was a sharp critic of the materialistically and democratically oriented France that had just been defeated by Prussia. Renan's criticism of democracy and materialism in France was a welcome confirmation of the view held by Strakhov and numerous other Russian conservatives[35] that France was weak and divided because French civilization was materialistic, rationalistic, and individualistic, therefore lacking in the sound moral principles necessary for the survival of any society. Religion, in the opinion of Russian conservatives, was one of the most important sources of such sound principles. Accordingly, Strakhov argued that any decline of religion could only have an adverse effect on society, for the fervor that once was expressed through religion had to find new and less desirable outlets. In Western Europe politics, especially, replaced religion; and politics assumed all of the fanaticism, proselytism, and even martyrdom which had once been associated with religion. Strakhov considered this substitution of politics for religion as most unsatisfactory and therefore praised Renan for having described so well the lowering of moral standards that resulted from it.[36] Renan obviously would not have agreed with this commentary on his brochure of 1871, for he, like Strauss, was an anticlerical and a believer in science as the key to the future of mankind.[37]

Emphasis on the decline of morals during the nineteenth century is a recurring theme in Strakhov's essays. He regarded this decline to be especially the result of nineteenth-century Europe's preoccupation with material things and progress rather than with eternal values.[38] Russia, he believed, was only affected by nineteenth-century materialism to the degree that she was influenced by Western Europe. As the revolutionary movement in Russia increased in intensity toward the end of the 1870's and at the beginning of the 1880's, he was, however, obliged to concede that in many respects the Russian nihilists had outdone their European mentors in carrying nihilism to greater extremes of terror and crime against society.[39] The root of the evil was, nevertheless, to be found in the spirit of negation characteristic of European enlightenment. Strakhov was willing to admit that many of the Russian professors and writers who preached the current European ideas were men of good intentions and personal integrity. They were protected from the extremes of nihilism, he claimed, by remnants of positive principles from the past in their thinking; but their students were not restrained by the heritage of the past, for it no longer had a central place in their education.[40] From their teachers these students learned to be proud and confident of their own intellectual ability and knowledge and to be critical of the existing order of things in society. They also learned that the highest goal in life was to be active politically and to work for the general welfare of society.[41] This political idealism became a surrogate for religion, though a poor one in Strakhov's opinion, because it aimed at an external, material result. It therefore "sooner or later had to lead to the notion that the end justifies the means, that it is necessary to sacrifice even conscience if an undertaking indubitably demands this."[42] Strakhov believed precisely this had happened in the case of the Russian nihilists. Because of their failure to master science, to come into contact with the common people, and to propagate the ideas of European socialism through literature, they had, he reasoned, been disillusioned, lost their conscience, and tried to attain their goals through murder and terror.[43]

Despite his condemnation of the Russian revolutionists, particularly harsh in the period immediately following the assassination of Alexander II,[44] it is not certain that Strakhov was in sympathy with the views of such spokesmen of reaction as Pobedonostsev and Katkov during the 1880's and 1890's. For one thing, Strakhov's friendship with Leo Tolstoi almost necessarily prevented him from being very close to Pobedonostsev. In regard to Katkov, it is true that Strakhov had been greatly heartened by Katkov's championing of Russian interests in Poland during the 1860's; but even then he disapproved of Katkov's lack of consistency and of solid philosophical principles.[45] When Katkov died in 1887, Strakhov commented in a letter to Tolstoi about the futility of Katkov's efforts to spur on the Russian government to more resolute and energetic policies:

> The Polish uprising and the *Moscow News* coincide: 1863. And from that time on our affairs proceed worse and worse. Meanwhile he, stimulated by his success in the Polish affair, worked indefatigably, and several times he announced loudly and solemnly: finally, we are on the right path, finally everything is coming along beautifully. You are right, Lev Nikolaevich, people are marionettes whom someone moves, and they only imagine that they move themselves.[46]

He did not confine such criticism to Katkov, for in the early 1880's he complained to Nicholas Danilevskii about the type of reactionary views then being expressed in Russia and more specifically about the many senseless opinions published in Prince Vladimir Meshcherskii's *Citizen* (*Grazhdanin*) and in Ivan Aksakov's *Rus'*.[47] In 1890, in the introduction to Volume II of the second edition of his *Struggle with the West*, Strakhov wrote with similar disapproval about the many conservatives, monarchists, nationalists, and defenders of Orthodoxy who had appeared at the time. For Strakhov their patriotism and conservatism were too instinctive and therefore not based on valid philosophical principles. He felt that Russian patriotism and conservatism could only acquire meaning and stability if they were made meaningful through an elucidation of "Slavophile" ideas. Russian conservatism, however, generally lacked the solid foundation that a further development of "Slavophile" ideas could have given it and therefore, Strakhov concluded, had relatively little impact on Russian public opinion.[48]

Strakhov constantly emphasized the importance of critical thinking and philosophical principles in his essays. In his opinion it was not possible for a society to lead a normal existence without having valid guiding principles. This was one of his major complaints against Western Europe during the second half of the nineteenth century: "The West now lives *with-*

out philosophy," he wrote, "that is, without any higher scientific view which could pose and decide basic questions of knowledge."[49] He believed that the skepticism and materialism of European thought had brought about this result. Germany had long been protected from the negative influence of skepticism and materialism by her school of philosophical idealism, which Strakhov considered, especially as expressed by Hegel, to be the apogee of European philosophical development.[50] But Germany, too, had lost her intellectual independence, and, rather than developing her own philosophical tradition, had turned for inspiration to English thinkers such as John Stuart Mill and Charles Darwin, who in Strakhov's eyes were just as much popularizers as they were philosophers or scientists. As such they were merely another manifestation of what Strakhov termed "our sad time," that is, the time when every fool had the right to ask questions which wise men were expected to answer.[51]

When Strakhov spoke of the place of philosophy in the intellectual life of a society, he had especially in mind the need for disciplined thinking in accordance with certain laws of philosophical reasoning. This was already evident in his article of 1860 on Hegel, where he particularly stressed the importance of Hegel's writings on logic.[52] But he expressed himself with much greater clarity, little more than a decade later, when he wrote an article on John Stuart Mill's book *The Subjection of Women* (London, 1869). The heart of Mill's argument, in Strakhov's opinion, was that no fundamental differences existed between men and women as rational and moral beings. Strakhov admitted that Mill made many clever and generally correct remarks about the difficulties inherent in discussing the question of differences between the two sexes; but he regretted that Mill did not confine himself to his role as a skeptical philosopher. In this role he was a worthy continuer of the tradition of Hume, to which Strakhov was willing to assign historical significance although he personally was not sympathetic toward it. Mill, however, Strakhov declared, had gone considerably beyond the limits of his métier as a skeptical philosopher and had sought to advocate and demonstrate a positive argument: that there are no emotional and mental differences between men and women.[53] Strakhov conceded that the legal discrimination practiced against women in England was at least a subjective justification for this argument. But he quickly added that Russian women were in a much more satisfactory legal position than their English sisters and that the question of women's rights was therefore a meaningless one in Russia.[54] Although Strakhov was correct in claiming that the legal position of Russian women was superior to that of women in the West, it might be remarked here that Strakhov, a bachelor until his death, apparently was never very familiar with the opinions and feelings of his Russian feminine contemporaries.

The denial of the differences existing between things in life and nature, Strakhov reasoned, made it impossible to know anything about their relative value, their degree, and their place in creation.[55] Mill, in denying the differences between man and woman, made much the same mistake that so many so-called enlightened people did,[56] whose new truths, Strakhov believed, were essentially characterized by the denial of all differences between phenomena. They denied the difference between God and nature, between spirit and matter, between man and woman, man and animal, soul and body, between the beautiful and the useful, between morality and the aspiration for happiness, and the like.[57] This inability to recognize the differences between things was in effect, Strakhov argued, an admission that one knew nothing, because true understanding demanded the ability to discern and to distinguish the characteristic features of phenomena.

> In each thing it is necessary to be able to distinguish the essential from the accidental, the important from the unimportant, spirit and content from form and appearance. . . . As *seeing* means to discern subjects in space by color, size, form, and distance, so *understanding* means to classify things mentally by their quality, value, essence, and importance. Knowing something means to be able to distinguish the known thing from all other things. And, consequently, the new wisdom, which affirms that for it things are not distinguishable from one another, really asserts that it knows nothing about them, that it disavows knowledge, that it has forgotten, or has lost, even that first knowledge which the first man received from holy traditions and which also consisted in the ability to distinguish, namely to distinguish good from evil.[58]

The struggle Strakhov waged on behalf of philosophical reasoning, moral and religious principles, and civic duty represents one of the most positive and attractive aspects of his career as a Russian publicist. He was one of the few thinkers in Russia during the second part of the nineteenth century who not only opposed the various intellectual fads then dominating the Russian public mind but who also did so out of convictions based on independent thinking and considerable philosophical and scientific erudition. Unfortunately, however, he based much of his criticism of the negative ideas and values of his time on the untenable proposition that they were exclusively Western European in origin and were only present in Russia to the extent that they had been borrowed from the West. To support this contention he borrowed another Western idea, namely the romantic theory of the organic development of peoples and civilizations, and used it in an attempt to demonstrate Russia's uniqueness as a historical entity. In so doing, he was guilty of following the most typical of all nineteenth-century Europe's intellectual fads: nationalism. Moreover, the particular type of nationalism advocated by Strakhov proposed no humanitarian ideas similar to those of Renan, Mazzini, or Dostoevskii (at his best). Instead, Strakhov's nationalism had unmistakable undertones of a form of national exclusiveness which had little ultimate purpose other than that of furthering the narrowly interpreted power and national interests of the Russian state.

In the early 1860's Strakhov's organic thinking had influenced him to advocate ideas that were later taken up by reactionary and ultranationalistic advocates of ruthless Russification in the 1880's and 1890's. True, Strakhov never consciously associated himself with such excesses of nationalism, but his organic view of nationality undoubtedly contained the germs of a narrower and more intolerant view of nationalism—one that considered non-Russian groups within the tsarist empire as a cause of national weakness. In 1864 he even advocated Russification of one small group of people within the empire, namely the Baltic Germans. He felt particularly strongly that the Baltic Germans should learn to love Russia and all things Russian so that they could become "living members of the organism of which we are a part."[59] Later that year he explained the need for the Baltic Germans and other minorities to come into organic unity with the Russians in greater detail. "It is not only possible," he wrote, "but necessary for each nationality . . . to desire success in its development, the fullest development of the peculiarities of its spiritual organism." Accordingly, he reasoned:

> Russian Germans, Russian Catholics, Russians of the Mosaic Law, etc.—this entire phenomenon is in no way conducive to any rich and fruitful development, but, on the contrary, they represent the possibility of an uninterrupted deviation from a sound development.
>
> A man who finds himself between two nationalities is not in a normal situation. It is understood that he will strive to get out of it and, sooner or later, he does get out of it, having completely attached himself to one of the nationalities. Thus life itself does not tolerate these intermediate states; it does not allow them to settle and to assume solid forms. In these cases we, as Russians, not only can but also must desire that our non-Russian groups should be Russified; in their Russification we should see for them the pledge of a more normal spiritual life, see their fusion with our great national organism and, in consequence, their own welfare.[60]

In regard to Poland, Strakhov did not demand that the Poles should form an integral part of the Russian national organism. Instead, he merely emphasized the benefits that had accrued to the Polish peasants after 1863 as a result of their being in the Russian empire rather than in Austria or Prussia.[61] Even the Polish uprising did not influence Strakhov to follow Katkov's example in urging the use of force and suppression as the only practical ways to solve the Polish question. As has already been pointed out, Strakhov's moderate position in regard to the Polish question in 1863 so aroused the anger of professional Russian patriots like Katkov that the

Dostoevskii brothers' journal *Time* was suspended for having published Strakhov's article, "The Fatal Question." Strakhov continued to hold moderate views concerning the nationality question in Russia's border-lands as well as to believe in the mild and beneficial nature of Russian rule in the non-Russian parts of the empire as late as 1890.[62] Until the time of his death in the mid-1890's he seems to have remained largely oblivious of the policies of the Russian government during the reign of Alexander III, which aimed at assuring Russia's organic unity through the forceful Russification of the borderlands and of the various non-Russian and non-Orthodox groups in all parts of the empire. The excesses of Russification during the 1870's, 1880's, and 1890's perhaps escaped his notice because he paid little attention to political matters after the mid-1860's; or perhaps his belief in the desirability of organic unity in Russia blinded him to the extent of the injustices committed by the Russian bureaucracy in the name of national unity.

The question of non-Russian nationalities only occupied Strakhov's mind for a period of several years during and immediately following the Polish uprising. Thereafter, he devoted himself almost exclusively to philosophi-cal, scientific, and literary studies. In his treatment of these subjects, he accentuated organic thinking and Russian nationalism even more than he had previously, in accordance with what he regarded to be the tradition of the Slavophiles and of Apollon Grigor'ev in Russian thought. This trend in Strakhov's further intellectual development may be seen especially in his reviews of Tolstoi's *War and Peace* and of N. Ia. Danilevskii's *Russia and Europe*, which appeared in Strakhov's journal *Dawn (Zaria)* between 1869 and 1871.

Approximately one-fourth of Strakhov's long review of *War and Peace* was taken up with a discussion of Apollon Grigor'ev's views on literature and nationality. Strakhov displayed great admiration for Grigor'ev in this article. Thus he described Grigor'ev as superior to all other Russian critics, as the "real founder of Russian criticism," and as the only critic who had a comprehensive view of Russian literature.[63] Strakhov summarized what he interpreted to be the essence of Grigor'ev's literary theory in the fol-lowing words: "Ap.[ollon] Grigor'ev, examining modern Russian literature from the standpoint of nationality, saw in it the *constant conflict of Euro-pean ideals, of a poesy foreign to our spirit, with the aspiration for original* [artistic] *creativity, for the creation of purely Russian ideals and types.*"[64] These words, of course, represent a summary of Strakhov's views more than those of Grigor'ev, although the latter admittedly did express similar opinions in various contexts at one time or another.

Strakhov believed that Grigor'ev's general view of Russian literature after Pushkin had made it possible to see Tolstoi in the perspective of the long search of Russian writers for purely national types and ideals in Russian literature.[65] Pushkin, whom both Strakhov and Grigor'ev regarded to be the founder of an independent Russian literature, did not succeed in giving full expression to what Strakhov interpreted to be Russia's national ideal. Gogol revealed much of the sense of Russian life, but his relationship to it was negative. Only Tolstoi, Strakhov concluded, created types that embodied the positive sides of Russian life.[66] Thus Strakhov described the simplicity, goodness, self-sacrifice, and sense of justice of such figures in *War and Peace* as Princess Mary, Pierre Bezukhov, and the peasant Platon Karataev as representative of the highest ideals of the Russian people.[67] He felt that these ideals were still very much alive among the mass of the Russian people, who remained untouched by the corrupting influences of the nineteenth century, and he believed that any healthy development of Russian society in the future had to take the living ideals of the people as its point of departure.[68]

Such virtues as simplicity, goodness, self-sacrifice, and a sense of justice were, however, hardly sufficient in themselves to establish Russia's identity as an organic entity distinct from the rest of Europe. Strakhov clearly had to establish the fact of Russia's uniqueness if he was to be successful in his efforts to demonstrate that the negative currents of thought of his time had no roots whatsoever in Russia's past and present and that they had no application to her future, representing instead a phenomenon that belonged exclusively to the cultural sphere of Western European civilization. But Strakhov lacked the synthetic ability to support his assumptions with any new and original formulation of the organic theory of historical and cultural development. In 1868, however, someone else provided him with such a formulation.

In January of that year Nicholas Danilevskii appeared in St. Petersburg with the completed manuscript of his *Russia and Europe*.[69] During the following year this work was published in *Dawn* (*Zaria*), a new journal which was sponsored by V. V. Kashpirev and edited by Strakhov. *Russia and Europe* did not attract much attention at the time, though it was given a negative appraisal in Katkov's *Russian Messenger* early in 1869. Strakhov immediately came to Danilevskii's defense in three articles which were published in *Dawn* between 1869 and 1871.[70] He was particularly irritated by the *Russian Messenger*'s having dismissed Danilevskii as just another Slavophile who had merely repeated opinions that had often been heard before. Strakhov, giving due credit to the role of the Slavophiles in Russian intellectual life, easily countered this attack by pointing out certain obvious differences between Danilevskii's views and those of the Slavophiles. Danilevskii, for example, did not accept the Slavophile idea that the West was in a state of decay.[71] An even more fundamental difference

was that Danilevskii rejected the notion that the Slavs were predestined to
renew the world and "to find for all of humanity the resolution of the
historical problem."[72] The Slavs had no such predestination quite simply
because a problem that concerned all of humanity was something that did
not exist.[73] Strakhov considered this rejection of the existence of problems
and ideals belonging to all of mankind to be the essence of Danilevskii's
originality:

> Namely, he rejected the *single thread* in the development of humanity, the
> notion that history is the progress of some sort of general idea, of some
> sort of general civilization. There is no such civilization, Danilevskii says,
> but there exist only particular civilizations, there exists the development of
> separate *cultural-historical types*.[74]

Danilevskii's interpretation of history as the development of separate cultural-historical types was a useful theory for Strakhov at that time, because
it provided him with what appeared to be a "strictly scientific" justification
for his own advocacy of Russian cultural independence in the face of the
tremendous authority Western European civilization then had in Russia.[75]

The Slavophiles had long before made this point, which was the reason
for Strakhov's identifying himself with them as early as the beginning of
the 1860's.[76] His Slavophilism was, however, rather arbitrary, and he
definitely did not feel that it was necessary to accept all of the views of the
original Slavophiles, even in regard to questions involving the basic Slavophile philosophy of life and history. Strakhov justified such arbitrariness
in interpreting Slavophilism by pointing to the need for expanding and
broadening the ideas of the Slavophiles instead of merely confirming and
disseminating them in their original form.[77] "Let our views come even into
direct contradiction with known Slavophile opinions. This means, perhaps,
that our views are truer, that they are closer to the true spirit of Slavophilism."[78] With Slavophilism seen in this light, it was, of course, possible
to regard Danilevskii as a variety of Slavophile and his book as a "catechism or codex of Slavophilism."[79] Strakhov, however, also stated that
Russia and Europe was not a direct product of Slavophilism "in the narrow
literary-historical sense of that word" but was broader in scope, including
Slavophilism within itself; it was the culmination of Slavophilism in the
same way Hegelian philosophy was for "Fichte-ism" and "Schellingism."[80]
In other words, it was no more important for Danilevskii to confirm all the
details of Slavophilism than it had been for Hegel to confirm all those of
the philosophies of Fichte and of Schelling. Therefore, it was of relatively
small importance if Danilevskii chose to describe the Slavophile dream of
a Slavic mission to renew mankind as impossible because universal, humanitarian missions simply did not exist. Strakhov, who had long considered himself a Slavophile, greeted this solution as one which eliminated

many difficulties, set limits to "impossible illusions," and established a position based on the "solid ground of reality."[81]

Strakhov, however, never was willing to admit that this "solid ground of reality" had many of the same negative and even immoral implications that he had previously detected in the thinking of the Russian nihilists. Indeed, Danilevskii was, in many respects, just another, to use Jacob Burckhardt's phrase, of the *"terribles simplificateurs"* of the nineteenth century: an extreme nationalist who naïvely believed in the possibility of arbitrarily using the methods and categories of science to study society and history. Vladimir Solov'ev demonstrated this point quite convincingly in his polemics with Strakhov concerning Danilevskii's *Russia and Europe* during the late 1880's and early 1890's. The issues involved in these polemics, however, are only intelligible in their relationship to Danilevskii's theories of Russian society and of historical development. It is therefore preferable to discuss these theories before attempting a final appraisal of Strakhov's conception of organic nationalism as it was reflected in his polemical duel with Solov'ev.

CHAPTER EIGHT

The Theory of Cultural-Historical Types

WHERE Strakhov had been weak, i.e. in the synthesis of ideas, his friend Danilevskii[1] excelled. *Russia and Europe* represents one of the most interesting attempts of the nineteenth century to examine the forces and guiding principles determining the course of universal history. Although Danilevskii's work has seldom been taken seriously by professional scholars, it remains nevertheless an important pioneer venture in the study of social and cultural development. This point has been made rather well by the contemporary student of comparative culture Pitirim Sorokin:

> In commenting on his laws Danilevsky offers several of the most important generalizations of contemporary sociology and anthropology concerning the diffusion, migration, expansion, and mobility of culture. Likewise he clearly sets forth the theory that technology or material culture tends to diffuse universally among all cultures, whereas non-material culture can diffuse only within its own area and cannot spread over various cultures except in its elements. This theory has been reiterated in the twentieth century by Alfred Weber, Louis Weber, R. MacIver, and others. Apparently contemporary representatives of these theories hardly know of Danilevskii's work, for they never refer to it or to the work of several other predecessors.[2]

The role of original pioneer of modern sociological and anthropological theories that Sorokin assigns to Danilevskii is suggestive of some of the difficulties inherent in discussing the genesis of the latter's ideas. One must rely largely on conjecture and inference in tracing the formative influences in his intellectual development.

Danilevskii's early family life during the 1820's, judging by the testimony of his friend P. P. Semenov,[3] was dominated by the traditionally conservative and piously Orthodox spirit characteristic of the Russian service gentry. His father, though he rose to the rank of brigadier general in the Russian army, was apparently a man of modest resources; for after the young Nicho-

102

las Iakovlevich Danilevskii had been given a solid primary and secondary education in private boarding schools and at the Tsarskoe Selo Lyceum, he was obliged to support himself, first as a civil servant and then as a free-lance scientific writer, while a student and, after 1846, candidate for the master's degree at the University of St. Petersburg.[4] At the University, he temporarily departed from the conservative and religious tenets of his youth and became an atheist and an impassioned advocate of Fourier socialism.[5] Like Dostoevskii, Danilevskii belonged to the Petrashevskii circle and was arrested in 1849. Also similar to Dostoevskii, Danilevskii attempted to persuade the special investigating committee that Fourierism was a nonrevolutionary doctrine that aimed to improve society through a gradual and peaceful organization of it along socialist lines. He was more successful than Dostoevskii in this endeavor, for the investigating committee acquitted him of all charges of revolutionary conspiracy against the government. Emperor Nicholas I decided, however, that he was too intelligent and therefore potentially dangerous, so Danilevskii was ordered to Vologda in administrative exile as an assistant to the local provincial governor.[6]

It is interesting to note that the short period Danilevskii passed in prison during his interrogation by the investigating committee had a psychological impact on him similar to that which a much longer and more severe Siberian prison experience had on Fedor Dostoevskii. Danilevskii's imprisonment lasted only a hundred days. At first he was not permitted to read, but later his prison routine was altered and he was allowed to read *Don Quixote* and the Bible. Reading the Bible revived his memory of, as Semenov phrased it, "the pure faith of the first days of youth, and all indications of his long-lived atheism disappeared."[7] At the same time, he acquired a critical attitude toward utopian socialism, although he continued to aspire for improvements in society, particularly for the emancipation of the Russian serfs.[8]

Despite Danilevskii's increasingly critical attitude toward socialism after 1859, his Fourierist period was nevertheless important for his subsequent intellectual development. He was still, for example, generally in favor of the court reforms and of the relaxation of censorship undertaken by Alexander II when he wrote *Russia and Europe* in the late 1860's. He even felt that the new censorship regulations had been too limited in scope and needed further liberalization.[9] Later, it is true, as one can see from the footnotes he prepared for a new edition of *Russia and Europe* in the 1880's, he became disillusioned about Alexander's reforms, particularly the new court system, which he condemned as a caricature of foreign institutions.[10] This disillusionment, however, only seems to have characterized his view of society during the last years of his life, when practically all traces of his earlier liberalism and humanitarianism disappeared from his thinking. But even in this last period of his life, two characteristic features of his world of ideas of the 1840's clearly continued to influence him: his belief in the fundamental unity of things in nature and society as well as within the individual categories of the biological sciences; and his constant search for a system of laws that governed the development and existence of the "phenomena of the external world."[11] In the late 1840's these preoccupations were especially evident in his review articles of Alexander von Humboldt's *Cosmos* and of the writings of the French biologist Henri Dutrochet,[12] as well as in the exposition of Fourier's theories which he prepared for the investigating committee in June, 1849.[13] Nearly twenty years later he was still seeking unity and laws of nature and society when he attempted to demonstrate that each of the ten historical-cultural types he described in *Russia and Europe* had an organic cultural, political, and social individuality that distinguished it in all important respects from other historical-cultural types. He then proposed five laws which allegedly governed the historical development of civilizations and therefore, he believed, had a validity comparable to the laws of the natural sciences.[14]

After the Petrashevskii affair, Danilevskii devoted himself almost entirely to the practical activities of a scientific career. During the next several decades he spent a large part of his time on various scientific expeditions studying the fisheries of the Volga, the Caspian Sea, the White Sea, the Arctic region, Arkhangelsk province, and elsewhere.[15] While on these expeditions Danilevskii was employed primarily as a statistician. He recorded the results of his work in a number of specialized articles on fisheries, climatology, economics, geography, and other similar subjects, which were published periodically during the remainder of his life.[16] These practical activities greatly influenced his general outlook on life. A tendency to think in statistical terms can, for example, be seen particularly well in Chapter VI of *Russia and Europe,* especially where he tabulates statistically the scientific achievements of mankind according to nationality in an attempt to demonstrate the importance of national characteristics in the advancement of scientific knowledge.[17]

Danilevskii's scientific activities were not limited to statistical analysis, for he was equally interested in other branches of science, especially the biological sciences. The last years of his university studies had been devoted to biology, and his major scientific work was a two-volume critical examination of Darwin's theory of natural selection.[18] Danilevskii intended his study of Darwin to be a semipopular work for intelligent nonspecialist readers. The ideas expressed in this work can hardly be considered original, for most of them were based on the arguments of such non-Russian critics of Darwin as Louis Agassiz, Albert Wigand, and Karl Ernst von Baer. Danilevskii was especially influenced by Baer, under whom he had worked between 1853 and 1857 as the statistician of a fisheries expedition in the Volga and Caspian Sea regions. Baer, according to Strakhov, had regarded Danilevskii as his chief assistant on this expedition. Danilevskii, in his turn, referred to Baer more than any other single authority and quoted him extensively in his *Darwinism.*[19]

The implications of Baer's influence are highly suggestive, for it seems to have been especially through him that Danilevskii became imbued with the spirit of German romanticism and idealism as applied to biology. Baer, the discoverer of the mammalian ovum, was a highly significant figure in the development of embryology as a science during the nineteenth century. His point of departure had been the morphological and organic view of development of Goethe and other German idealistic thinkers and writers of the same period. He probably had come into contact with this tradition through his teacher at Würzburg, Ignaz Döllinger, who was a friend of Goethe and had at one time known Schelling rather well.[20] After studying with Döllinger in Würzburg, Baer consistently emphasized the importance of individuality and development in biological life.[21] His important work in embryology and biology was therefore quite in keeping with the general trends of other branches of scholarship in German universities during the early part of the nineteenth century. History, for example, can be cited as one illustration of this point.[22] As Oswei Temkin has pointed out, both history and embryology were developed in Germany around 1800 in connection with the conception that "the ages of man were [to be] reviewed as a 'historical' sequence from conception to death." Temkin emphasized that both history, in the proper sense of the word, and embryology played a decisive role in the formation of this conception and that, likewise, they influenced each other "on the basis of a common idealistic philosophy with religious undercurrents."[23]

Danilevskii's originality consisted in applying to history the methodology and assumptions of the natural sciences. In so doing, he, of course, could hardly restrict himself to German sources of inspiration, for many of the basic concepts of such fields as botany and zoology had been first formulated by Frenchmen such as Antoine de Jussieu and Georges Cuvier around 1800. In *Russia and Europe* Danilevskii mentioned both Jussieu and Cuvier in his discussion concerning the advantages of using a "natural system" in studying history.[24] In such a system the various plants or forms of animal life were classified strictly according to their degree of similarity to other members of the same group and of difference from phenomena of other groups. In each case, Danilevskii wrote, "all objects or phenomena of one group must have between themselves a greater de-

gree of similarity and relationship than with phenomena or objects belonging to another group."[25] Applying these criteria of the "natural system"
of scientific analysis to world history, Danilevskii found ten major civilizations: (1) Egyptian, (2) Chinese, (3) Assyrian-Babylonian-Phoenician,
Chaldean, or ancient Semitic, (4) Indian, (5) Iranian, (6) Jewish, (7) Greek,
(8) Roman, (9) Novo-Semitic or Arabic, and (10) Germano-Romance or
European.[26] Only these peoples or cultural-historical types had, in Danilevskii's opinion, played a positive and leading role in history. He regarded
each of them as a separate and distinct entity with its own cultural ideals
and ultimate ends and its own birth, individual path of historical development, and death.[27] In referring to his ten civilizations in this manner,
Danilevskii obviously went beyond the limits of the "natural" and classi-
ficatory method of analysis that had been developed by botanists and
zoologists like Jussieu and Cuvier. His emphasis on the importance of
individuality and development as well as on birth and death in the history
of civilization is certainly suggestive of the influence of the morphological
and organic interpretation of history and biology so common among German scholars and writers early in the nineteenth century.

On the basis of this application of his "natural system" to history, Danilevskii criticized the traditional division of the entire sweep of history into
the unilinear sequence of ancient, medieval, and modern periods.[28] Such
a division, he argued, did not do justice to history's diversity and complexity. Consequently, he recommended that historians should abandon
this division in writing about world history, for it was only applicable to
the internal development of individual types or civilizations.[29] In other
words, he believed that each civilization independently passed through
the stages of childhood, youth, maturity, and old age; that each civilization had its own spiritual principles, which guided the progress of its development in world history.[30] He was never, however, very successful in
describing or defining the nature of the guiding spiritual principles of the
various historical civilizations. Thus his characterization of violence and
force as the principles of the Germano-Romance cultural-historical type
and the emotional idealization of the Slavic type were certainly rather
arbitrary and hardly any more satisfactory than the conventional treatment
of world history by Western European historians had been.[31] Danilevskii's
failure to give fairly acceptable and convincing characterizations of the
spiritual principles of the major cultural-historical types was an important
one, for without such characterizations there was little reason to believe in
the existence of his ten civilizations.

Danilevskii, however, very definitely did believe in their existence, and,
at the beginning of Chapter V of *Russia and Europe*, he went so far as to

proclaim dogmatically five laws that were supposed to govern the development of the ten cultural-historical types:

Law 1. Every people or family of peoples characterized by a separate language or group of languages whose relationship to one another is close enough to be perceived directly, without profound philological investigations, constitutes an independent cultural-historical type if it is, by virtue of its spiritual qualities, generally capable of historical development and has already passed childhood.

Law 2. In order that the civilization of an independent cultural-historical type may be born and develop, it is necessary that the peoples belonging to it should enjoy political independence.

Law 3. The basic principles of the civilization of one cultural-historical type cannot be transmitted to peoples of another type. Each type works out its own civilization under the greater or lesser influence of preceding or alien civilizations.

Law 4. The civilization belonging to each cultural-historical type only reaches fullness, diversity, and affluence at that time when the different ethnographic elements composing it form a federation, or political system of states, not being swallowed up by one political entity but enjoying political independence.

Law 5. The course of development of cultural-historical types is to be closely likened to that of . . . plants whose period of growth continues indefinitely but whose period of blossoming and fruitbearing is relatively short and exhausts their vital strength once and for all.[32]

In these so-called laws, especially in laws 3 and 4, there is much common sense and accurate observation. Danilevskii's first law, on the other hand, seems to be little more than an attempt on his part to establish the separate identity of the Slavic world as opposed to Western Europe, for even the ten cultural-historical types which he listed do not illustrate any necessary relationship between language and civilization. Ancient Semitic civilization, for example, was originally developed by the non-Semitic Sumerians, whose agglutinative language was radically and fundamentally different from Assyrian, Babylonian, Phoenician, and Chaldean;[33] and Western European civilization has included peoples speaking such diverse languages as Norwegian *landsmål*, Schwyzerdütsch, Finnish, Magyar, Czech, Polish, Croatian, and Slovenian.[34] Danilevskii's second law certainly contains an element of truth, but it is rather doubtful that civilizations are really born and develop in the biological sense of the word. His fifth law merely carries the biological analogy one step farther with its comparison of civilizations to plants. The analogy was, however, undoubtedly made with a special purpose in mind: to demonstrate that Europe was declining and just about ready to be replaced in her role of historical leadership by younger and more vigorous peoples, namely the Slavs.[35]

Despite his conviction that Europe was declining, Danilevskii cautioned his readers in Chapter VI ("Is Europe Decaying?") of *Russia and*

Europe against believing that Europe was already in an advanced stage of decay. He agreed, however, that the idea of European decay, which he associated with the Slavophiles, was at least partly true, but added that it had been formulated in the "heat of battle" and therefore was an exaggeration. Decay, he explained, meant the complete decomposition of organic matter.[36] Europe, in his opinion, had not reached this stage; its civilization was still at a height of vitality and activity. But he considered the very variety of the results of European civilization to be an indication that its creative power was waning, for cultural-historical types, according to Danilevskii, were like plants and therefore grew weaker and tended to decline after they had blossomed.[37] He placed the beginning of the civilization stage of European history in the sixteenth and seventeenth centuries. This chronology had important implications, for Danilevskii had previously maintained that the civilization stage of a cultural-historical type's development, which invariably followed a prolonged gestational period of "unconscious, purely ethnographic forms of life," could usually be expected to last between four and six centuries.[38] This, of course, only allowed Western Europe a few additional centuries of continued existence as a flourishing civilization.

Western Europe, however, was still strong and therefore it was necessary, Danilevskii argued, for Russia and the Slavs to engage in a bitter struggle against Europe's political power and intellectual influence.[39] If he had agreed that Europe was in decay, there would have been little justification for such a struggle because a weakened Europe could only have briefly prevented the Slavic cultural-historical type from assuming a role of historical leadership among the peoples of the world. At the same time, he almost had to reject the notion that Europe was still at the height of her creative power, for this would have allowed the Slavs little hope for success in their struggle with the West.

The Slavs, however, had to make every effort to free themselves from their spiritual slavery to Europe if they were to have any prospect of success in this struggle.[40] They had to realize that Europe was essentially hostile to themselves and that they represented a special cultural-historical type that was distinct from the rest of Europe.[41] In order to demonstrate this point and to indicate what promise the Slavic cultural-historical type held for the future, Danilevskii catalogued the virtues of the Slavs in a number of discussions scattered throughout *Russia and Europe*. There was little original material in these discussions, for in them he repeated and systematized ideas that were commonplace among conservative and nationalistic Russians around the middle of the nineteenth century. Like many other Russian nationalists of the period, he assumed that there were no significant cultural differences between the Russians and the other

Slavs; hence, he seldom paid much attention to the actual customs and beliefs of the Slavs living outside of the Russian-language area.

His views on the ideal relationship between the tsar and his people and on the Orthodox Church, for example, were the usual conventional ones. Thus the tsar was described in *Russia and Europe* as being the "living fulfillment of the political self-awareness and will of the people."[42] He was convinced that autocracy represented "a subject of genuine political faith" for the Russian people and, little more than a decade after *Russia and Europe* was published, wrote that the people would continue to regard the tsar as an omnipotent, unlimited, and autocratic ruler even should he attempt to limit his own authority.[43] As for the Orthodox Church, Danilevskii shared the religious prejudices of other Russians like Dostoevskii and the Slavophiles concerning the spiritual superiority of the Eastern over the Western Church. The Orthodox Church, he insisted, represented Christianity in its pure form. Since the Slavs and the Greeks were the most numerous or influential peoples belonging to the Orthodox Church, they were clearly the peoples "chosen by God" to continue and preserve the true religious tradition of Israel and Byzantium.[44] Western Europe could not be included as a part of this tradition because the Western churches were based on the same violence and force which Danilevskii considered to be the principal characteristics of Western civilization. Thus from the very beginning, Danilevskii averred, Western Catholicism had used force in the name of religion as a means of usurping ecumenical authority for the pope and compelling people to join or stay in the Catholic Church. He alleged that the Inquisition, crusades, and other forcible conversions to Catholicism in Europe over the centuries were examples of such misuse of force.[45]

Protestantism and the European revolutions of the eighteenth and nineteenth centuries were essentially, in Danilevskii's opinion, reactions against the tyranny of Catholicism and feudalism; but they were successful only in dividing the Western Church and in destroying the idea of authority in society and religion without being able to create valid new ideals to replace the false ones of the past.[46] Because of Europe's failure to find such ideals, Europeans could see nothing but lies in their own historical past and therefore, according to Danilevskii, could hardly avoid becoming nihilists.[47]

In regard to nihilism, Danilevskii's views were quite similar to Strakhov's, for they both believed that nihilism in Russia was not an indigenous phenomenon but one that had been imported from Western Europe.[48] Strakhov often spent his vacations on Danilevskii's estate at Mshatka in the Crimea, and the two men were close friends for more than fifteen years. During these years, they must have had a profound intellectual influence on one another, and many of the ideas expressed in their writings during the 1870's and 1880's were probably first formulated in the many conversations they had prior to Danilevskii's death in 1885. Indeed, the very idea of the struggle with the West can well be one that Strakhov borrowed from Danilevskii, for Strakhov's first essays on this theme were written after the publication of *Russia and Europe*. On the other hand, it is likely that Danilevskii was dependent on Strakhov in regard to questions pertaining to philosophy. Thus Danilevskii wrote in 1884 concerning European philosophy of the seventeenth and eighteenth centuries in a manner very reminiscent of many of Strakhov's essays. Danilevskii, in an 1884 essay, singled out Descartes as the one who had introduced the element of doubt into European philosophy. More than a century later Kant's critical philosophy added a finishing touch to what Descartes had begun: "It [Kant's critical philosophy] denies the possibility of the knowledge of things in themselves, in their real essence, *i.e.* metaphysically negates metaphysics, exactly as critical Protestant theology theologically negates all positive theology."[49] Kant's philosophy, Danilevskii concluded, led ultimately to the complete negation of philosophy—to nihilism.[50]

Danilevskii's conviction that nihilism was a crucial and central problem of European social, political, and intellectual life could only reinforce his optimism concerning the future of the Slavs and Russia. In *Russia and Europe* he stated his belief that Russian society altogether lacked the inner contradictions that had placed Europe in a dangerous position between the "Charybdis of Caesarism or military despotism on the one hand and the Scylla of social revolution on the other" (p. 538). In Russia the same classes that threatened Europe with revolution were, Danilevskii asserted, basically conservative because the Russian communal system made the peasants possessors of land. Accordingly, the land in Russia was in the hands of those who cultivated it, so socialist demands for the division of property, Danilevskii somewhat optimistically assumed, could hardly have any application to the special conditions of Russian life. Moreover, the Russian peasant, in contrast to the workers and peasants of Europe, "did not see an enemy in authority" but looked to it with the "fullest confidence," because, Danilevskii wrote, there was a complete absence in Russia of a "historical, internal civil struggle between the various strata of Russian society" (pp. 282, 538–39).

> This very soundness of the socio-economic structure of Russia also constitutes the reason that we may trust in the great socio-economic significance of the Slavic cultural-historical type, which has [the task] of establishing for the first time . . . not only abstract but real and concrete legality in the relations of citizens [p. 539].

The Slavs, however, first had to become fully conscious of their spiritual individuality and to terminate their cultural dependence on Western

Europe before the positive features of the Slavic cultural-historical type could become the basis for a new civilization that would play a leading role in world history (pp. 432, 472–73, 513–15, 555–57). As Danilevskii had stated in his second and fourth laws of historical development, peoples belonging to a given cultural-historical type had to enjoy political independence and to be organized as a federation of states to make it possible for their civilization to be born and to reach an apex of cultural and political development. Accordingly, the Slavs had little prospect of entering into the civilization stage of their development as long as so many of them were deprived of political independence by Austria and the Ottoman Empire. Danilevskii believed that the European great powers, being hostile to the Slavs, were determined to maintain the *status quo* in Eastern Europe. In Chapters XII, XIII, XIV, and XVI of *Russia and Europe* he developed the idea that the Eastern question was therefore the key to the future of the Slavic cultural-historical type: the Slavs had to defeat all Europe militarily so that they could form a federation of states under the leadership of Russia. But such a federation was out of the question as long as Russia continued the foreign policy she had followed since the time of Catherine II, which, according to Danilevskii, ignored her true interests in favor of those of the European powers. In Danilevskii's opinion, Russia could only serve her own interests by joining forces with the other Slavs in a protracted military struggle against the rest of Europe (pp. 355, 482–512).

> Being foreign to the European world in her internal make-up, being besides too strong and powerful to occupy a position as one of the members of the European family, [i.e.] to be [merely] one of the great European powers, Russia can only occupy a place worthy of herself and Slavdom by becoming the head of a special independent system of states and by serving as a counterweight to Europe as a whole. Here are the advantage, utility, and sense of the Pan-Slavic union in relation to Russia [p. 437].

Danilevskii did not deny that war was a great evil. He felt, however, that because of Europe's fundamental hostility to Slavdom, war could not be avoided (pp. 474–75). Indeed, he claimed that it was natural that nations belonging to different cultural-historical types should come into conflict with one another, for each individual cultural-historical type would obviously attempt to extend its influence and sphere of activity to the maximum degree permitted by its strength and resources (p. 330). As he had often done before in other contexts, Danilevskii sought to illustrate his point with an analogy to natural phenomena:

> . . . if tempests and storms are necessary in the physical order of nature, no less necessary are also the direct collisions of peoples, who withdraw their fate from the sphere of the limited, narrowly rational views of political

personalities . . . and place [it] under the immediate guidance of world-governing historical Providence [p. 326].

In regard to the Slavs, the design of Providence was, of course, that they should form a federation of independent states once they had successfully terminated their inevitable conflict with Europe over the Eastern question.

This emphasis on the necessity and even desirability of using naked force in the relations of peoples and nations was especially evident in Danilevskii's discussion of the nature of the Pan-Slavic federation. Although he repeatedly stated that each people had the right to its own government and existence as a state (pp. 95–96, 238), his conception of a Pan-Slavic federation would not allow its non-Russian members the freedom of choice and action necessary for an independent and sovereign state. Danilevskii himself admitted that between twelve and thirteen million hostile Poles and Magyars would have to be forced to become part of his Pan-Slavic federation (p. 447). He did not, it is true, speak the same language concerning such non-Slavic prospective members of the federation as the Greeks and Rumanians, who were given somewhat preferential treatment because of belonging to the Orthodox Church. He realized that the Greeks and Rumanians would most likely have many reservations about membership in a Pan-Slavic federation, but he believed that their geographic position in Eastern Europe and the obvious advantages of membership in the federation would sooner or later convince them that they could not be strong and flourish without the assistance of Russia and the Slavs (pp. 395–96, 438–41). It was, however, highly doubtful that the Greeks and Rumanians would interpret their interests in quite this manner, so in all probability they, too, would have to be forced into partnership with the Slavs. Danilevskii said relatively little concerning the attitudes and interests of the millions of Slavic Catholics, Turks, Albanians, and Germans (especially those in Bohemia) who also would have been included in the federation and who, in most instances, could only have regarded it with the utmost aversion and hostility. Again force would have to be used to bring them into a federation with Russia and the Orthodox Slavs, and only Russia among the members of the Pan-Slavic federation would have been in a position to wield such force.

Russia's relative strength as one of the great powers of Europe assured her a position of hegemony in any union of the Slavic states. Danilevskii justified this leadership in terms of Russia's political experience over many centuries as the only independent Slavic nation and her success in establishing the "most powerful state in the world." He regarded the other Slavic states as too small and weak to play any important role in deciding questions pertaining to the general policies of the federation. Such questions would clearly have to be decided by Russia, the federation's most powerful and experienced member (pp. 420–22). Russia was to be used as the federation's *lingua franca*, and whenever there were any differences in opinion concerning the foreign policy of the federation or the relations between its member states, such differences were to be settled in accordance with Russian wishes. Thus Danilevskii argued that the Greek ambitions for Constantinople could not be recognized because the relatively small area and population of Greece and her insignificance as a power nullified any claim that she might have had as the alleged heir to Byzantium (pp. 402–9, 468–69). For Russia, Constantinople had both strategic and moral importance. Strategically, Russia needed Constantinople in order to be in a position to defend herself to the south by developing her naval and military power in the area of the Black Sea and the Bosphorus (pp. 409–16). Morally, Constantinople was important for Russia as the historical center of Byzantium and of the Orthodox Church.

> . . . [the possession of Constantinople] would give Russia tremendous influence over all the countries of the East. She would take possession of her historical inheritance and appear as the restorer of the Eastern Roman Empire, just as the Kingdom of the Franks once restored the Western Empire, and thus would begin a new Slavic era of world history [p. 416].

Danilevskii denied that Russian leadership represented in any way a threat to the internal independence of the other members of his proposed Slavic federation. He cited Russia's past history, especially her generous treatment of Finland and of the Baltic Germans, as evidence of the unlikelihood that Russia would deprive the Slavic states of their internal political and cultural independence (pp. 443–44). He attempted to demonstrate his own belief in the fact of Russia's magnanimity toward non-Russians by insisting in *Russia and Europe* that Constantinople should not be annexed to the Russian empire once it had been conquered but that, instead, it should be made the capital of the Pan-Slavic federation (pp. 418–20). He reminded his readers that he had referred in a previous discussion (in his treatment of the five laws governing the development of cultural-historical types) to the independence of the members of a political federation as one of the necessary conditions for the full development of the civilization of a cultural-historical type (pp. 95–96, 420). What benefit, he asked, could Russia conceivably derive from oppressing the Slavs living outside of the Russian empire? Union with the Slavs would certainly strengthen Russia, whereas any oppression of the Slavs by Russia could only weaken all of Slavdom in the face of a hostile Europe (pp. 447–48).

Danilevskii also denied that a Slavic union would threaten mankind with a universal monarchy and world domination. He pointed out that Europe's population exceeded that of the Slavic peoples by more than fifty million inhabitants and the Slavs were therefore weak and in no position to threaten Western Europe. A Slavic union, he explained, would have the sole purpose of enabling the Slavs to cooperate with one another so that they could achieve and then defend their freedom and independence. This was the "most sacred duty" of the Slavs, who were only concerned with their own purely Slavic interests and not with "uncertain humanitarian goals" (pp. 448–49). At the same time, he claimed that the political power of the Slavs was a necessary condition for normal and harmonious relations between the nations of the world.

> . . . the political power of Slavdom not only cannot threaten the entire world with enslavement, with universal domination, but also it alone can oppose a sufficient obstacle to the world domination which Europe is attaining more and more all the time (and which [world domination] she has already attained to a significant degree) [p. 449].

Such arguments were scarcely sufficient to reassure those Western Europeans and Slavs who feared Russian domination. For one thing, the European nations did not represent a homogeneous power block and they certainly felt just as hostile to one another as they did to Russia and the Slavs. Because of this division of Europe, any individual European power whose interests conflicted with those of Russia definitely had good reason to fear the establishing of Russian hegemony in Eastern Europe. As for the fears of many Austro-Hungarians and Balkan Slavs concerning the implications of any close association with Russia, there was always the embarrassing Polish question to cause them to be apprehensive about Russia's intentions toward themselves.

The Poles, Danilevskii wrote, were not worthy of political independence because of their repeated intrigues against Russia (pp. 240, 425–31). He defended Russia's role in the partition of Poland as an act completely in consonance with the basic laws of politics. These laws, he declared, had nothing to do with morality but were necessarily based on principles of utility and state interest (p. 32). He felt that Russia had little reason to permit independence or even autonomy to Poland as long as Polish society continued to live under the influence of the Roman Catholic Church and Western Europe (pp. 425–31). If, on the other hand, the Poles would one day realize that Catholicism and European ideas had distorted their "Slavic soul" and if they would demonstrate their willingness to cooperate with the other Slavs, then, Danilevskii suggested, they could hope for at least autonomy in "personal union" with Russia and within the general framework of the Pan-Slavic federation (pp. 431, 530, 538).

Danilevskii's callous and hardheaded attitude toward Poland should certainly not be interpreted as being out of keeping with his general philosophy of life. Danilevskii was a biological determinist who believed in expediency and in the inevitable struggle between peoples as the most important principles of state policy. He rejected universal and humanitarian values and ideas, claiming that each people developed its own values and characteristic ideas. Accordingly, there could hardly be such a thing as morality in regard to the relations of nations to one another. Although Danilevskii did not endorse the ideas of Machiavelli in *Russia and Europe,* he followed Machiavelli's example in separating morality from politics. Having done this, there was no longer any ethical reason why he should not pronounce death sentences over the heads of such nations as Austria-Hungary and the Ottoman Empire, which, in Danilevskii's scheme of things, were destined to disappear from the map of Europe in the course of the military struggle between the Slavs and the West (pp. 394, 495–99). Once the Slavs would have successfully terminated their military struggle with the West, however, there is little reason to believe that morality would then suddenly begin to govern the relations between Russia and the other Slavic states within a Pan-Slavic federation. Danilevskii clearly intended that Russia should dominate the non-Russian Slavs. He also felt that Russia should never sacrifice her own material interests or tolerate "alien" cultural traditions in her relations with the Slavs of the Balkans and of central Europe. In a word, Russian hegemony in Danilevskii's proposed federation would probably have been a nightmare for a substantial proportion of the people living within its frontiers, for their religious and cultural backgrounds, interests, and aspirations were often radically different from those of Russia. It is therefore doubtful that this federation would have been any more satisfactory, in the long run, for the non-Russian Slavs than the existing Austro-Hungarian and Ottoman states had been, whose demise had been proclaimed by Danilevskii in Chapter XIII of *Russia and Europe.*

CHAPTER NINE

Strakhov versus Vladimir Solov'ev

THE CONFLICT of Danilevskii's views with Christian morality was brought out particularly well in a series of polemical articles on the nationality question in Russia written by the philosopher Vladimir Solov'ev during the 1880's and 1890's.[1] Strakhov took Solov'ev's criticism of Danilevskii's theories very seriously, for Solov'ev was an outstanding religious thinker who had once been allied to the Slavophiles and who had also been an intimate friend of Dostoevskii and of Strakhov himself.[2] Moreover, Solov'ev claimed that he was defending Russia's true Christian mission in world history in the face of the threat presented by the national exclusiveness, intolerance, and immorality of the numerous self-styled patriots who were then writing on the national question in Russia.[3] Strakhov certainly had to challenge this claim, especially after Solov'ev, in 1888, singled out for attack Danilevskii's *Darwinism* and *Russia and Europe* as well as Strakhov's own *Struggle with the West*.[4]

Particularly offensive to Strakhov was Solov'ev's contention that *Darwinism* and the *Struggle with the West* did not express any uniquely Russian point of view but were, instead, representative of opinions that had been held and expressed by a number of Western European authors.[5] Danilevskii's study of Darwin's theory of evolution, Solov'ev pointed out quite correctly, was based on the conclusions of Western European anti-Darwinists and therefore could hardly be considered an example of purely Russian scientific thinking.[6] Similarly, in Strakhov's writings, Solov'ev observed, the criticisms made of such European writers as Mill, Strauss, and Renan were ones that any of their European opponents also could have made. Accordingly, Solov'ev reasoned, Strakhov had used much the same method as, for example, someone who attempted to oppose Hegel's philosophical ideas by using Schopenhauer's arguments—such a person would

116

no more be combatting German philosophy as a whole than Strakhov was waging a struggle with the West by merely making pertinent, but not particularly original, critical remarks concerning the philosophies of individual European thinkers.[7]

In regard to *Russia and Europe,* Solov'ev underlined Danilevskii's failure to demonstrate convincingly that Russia could really be described as an entity distinct from the rest of Europe. In neither the fields of science, philosophy, nor literature, he insisted, had Russians been able to give their cultural achievements, which Solov'ev definitely did not minimize, a distinctly Russian or Slavic character. Differences in nuance existed, he admitted, but such traces of the influence of national tastes and characteristics could also be detected in the science, philosophy, and literature of every European nation and did not in themselves prove the existence of Romano-German and Slavic cultural-historical types.[8]

Danilevskii's failure to find adequate evidence to support his arguments concerning the role of nationality in history was not what Solov'ev considered to be the most important shortcoming of *Russia and Europe.* Much more important was Danilevskii's rejection of what Solov'ev considered to be the basic idea of Christianity—the spiritual unity of humanity.[9] In Solov'ev's opinion this rejection was tantamount to disregarding the "highest demands of the Christian religion and returning to a coarsely heathen view, not only pre-Christian but even pre-Roman."[10] Solov'ev, in five articles published in the *Messenger of Europe (Vestnik Evropy)* and *Russian Thought (Russkaia Mysl')* between 1888 and 1890, developed these thoughts with special reference to the political relations between Russia and Western Europe.[11] He paid particular attention to the passages in *Russia and Europe* where Danilevskii spoke of the impending and inevitable struggle between the Slavic and European cultural-historical types. Solov'ev was especially disturbed by Danilevskii's insistence that Slavdom should regard everything pertaining to its relations with Europe strictly in terms of whether it furthered or deterred the special goals of Russia and the Slavs. What stood in the way of the realization of these goals, Solov'ev observed, was to be swept aside whatever the consequences for Europe, humanity, freedom, and civilization.[12] For Solov'ev such a concept of politics could only be described as a form of immoral Machiavellianism.[13] Thus he answered Danilevskii's question, "Why doesn't Europe love Russia?" by pointing out that Europe distrusted Russia above all because of the excesses of Russian nationalists like Danilevskii himself, whose destructive nationalistic ambitions seemed to threaten the very existence of such nations as Germany, Austria, Turkey, and even India.[14]

Solov'ev's polemics against *Russia and Europe* are reminiscent of those of German historians such as Ernst Troeltsch and Friedrich Meinecke against the organic determinism and ardent espousal of immoral power politics on the part of Oswald Spengler and other writers of the post-World War I period in Germany.[15] The analogy is, however, only an approximate one, for the discussions of Troeltsch and Meinecke were much more scholarly and careful in detail than those of Solov'ev. Solov'ev obviously wrote hurriedly and, as D. S. Mirsky has observed, ". . . when disputing with opponents who had no support in public opinion (for example, Strakhov, Rozanov, the Decadents), he preferred to use arguments that were most likely to give him easy victory in the eyes of the reader than to go out of his way to be intellectually fair."[16] But, if his arguments were calculated to give him easy victory in the eyes of readers, their internal weaknesses were not protected from discovery by such a seasoned polemicist as Strakhov, who was determined to avail himself of every conceivable argument in order to defend the historical theories of his friend Danilevskii.

The dispute of Strakhov and Solov'ev over the possible influence of the German writer Heinrich Rückert on Danilevskii is a good illustration of this point. Interestingly enough, it was Strakhov's statement in the preface to the third edition of *Russia and Europe* that Rückert, in his *Lehrbuch der Weltgeschichte in organischer Darstellung* (Leipzig: T. O. Weigel, 1857), had expressed many thoughts similar to Danilevskii's that first suggested to Solov'ev the possibility of such an influence.[17] Solov'ev developed this thought with great skill and made it sound so plausible that Russian and foreign scholars generally came to accept it in their references to Danilevskii's theory of cultural-historical types.[18]

Strakhov, in his time, countered Solov'ev's arguments by showing that there were unmistakable, fundamental differences between the historical theories of Rückert and those of Danilevskii.[19] Above all, he demonstrated Rückert's belief that there was a "single thread" in history as well as goals common to all of humanity. Rückert's historical individualities, if not destroyed by an external force, were permitted to continue their existence throughout history. Therefore they differed radically from Danilevskii's cultural-historical types, which flourished and declined at various times in history and which had definite beginnings and endings within the limits of relatively short historical periods. Also, Rückert's belief that the main thread of history was represented by his own Western European culture suggested a view of world history that was clearly opposed to the very central thesis of *Russia and Europe*.[20]

Nevertheless, as MacMaster has pointed out, many of Rückert's ideas were strikingly similar to those of Danilevskii. This was particularly the case with respect to Rückert's discussions concerning the spiritual individuality of cultures and their development in history.[21] But Solov'ev's

position became weak when he maintained that such similarities necessarily indicated that Rückert had exercised a decisive influence on the
formulation of Danilevskii's theory of cultural-historical types. The mere
fact of similarities can never be interpreted as definite proof of an actual
influence of one thinker on another, for it is clear that two individual
thinkers can independently share a common source of inspiration or arrive at similar conclusions. With regard to Danilevskii and Rückert, this
common inspiration was certainly the tradition of historicism, which had
come to be accepted by the mid-nineteenth century in historical and biological studies in both Russia and Western Europe. More than half a
century later, Oswald Spengler followed this same tradition in developing
his theory of the rise and fall of civilizations. There is, however, little
reason to assume that Spengler was influenced by Danilevskii, despite the
remarkable similarity of their historical views. In the final analysis, both
Danilevskii and Spengler share the rather dubious distinction of having
carried early nineteenth century theories of biological and organic development to their most extreme conclusions. In elaborating the implications of these theories, they contributed many original and even challeng-
ing ideas to modern historiography, but the soundness of these ideas is
highly questionable from the standpoint of both morality and historical
methodology.[22]

Strakhov was therefore quite correct in insisting on the originality of
Danilevskii's theory of cultural-historical types; however, he was unsuccessful in two important respects: (1) he could not demonstrate that there
was anything uniquely Russian in either Danilevskii's theory or in the ideas
expressed in his own *Struggle with the West* and (2) he was not able to
find any valid and convincing arguments to counter Solov'ev's claim that
Danilevskii's political ideas were essentially immoral. In defense of the
uniquely Russian character of *Russia and Europe* and of the *Struggle with
the West,* Strakhov could only repeat his own and Danilevskii's emotional
proclamations of the pressing need for Russia to strive to be herself and
to put an end to her spiritual dependence on the West.[23] This, of course,
missed the point of Solov'ev's arguments. In reply to the charge of immorality in politics, Strakhov merely paraphrased Danilevskii's indirect
statement of the principle that the end justifies the means by referring to
the military and intellectual struggle with the West as the only way for the
Slavs to realize their noble aspirations and to solve the Eastern question.[24]
In other contexts, he tried to justify this struggle as a necessary defense
in the face of what he and Danilevskii regarded to be a hostile West, one
which had, they claimed, always tried to subjugate and oppress the Slavs.[25]
At other times, his arguments were little more than emotional outbursts

that accused Solov'ev of calumny, malicious lying, blindness, and fanaticism.[26]

When viewed in the light of his previous condemnations of so many popularly accepted nineteenth-century ideas, Strakhov's blindness to the weaknesses and immoral implications of Danilevskii's thought is truly surprising. In the 1860's, Strakhov had criticized such writers as Katkov and Pisarev for their denial of the authority of philosophy; but from the early 1870's onward, he championed the theories of Danilevskii, who had disapproved of the use of philosophy as a means of answering important questions concerning the social and intellectual life of society as early as the late 1840's.[27] Throughout his career as a writer Strakhov had been most acute in discerning the various dangers to society implicit in nineteenth-century materialism and skepticism; and he had often been admirably skillful in showing in what ways ideas accepted by the general public in Russia and Europe were contrary to the eternal moral principles which he thought were essential for the continued existence of any organized human group. Indeed, he had even specifically attacked the materialism and political idealism of his time because it aimed at an external, material result, which sooner or later led to the notion that the end justifies the means. Strakhov and Danilevskii, it is true, did not regard their particular Slavic goals as material and external but rather as lofty and sacred. Whether or not these goals actually were lofty and sacred is a matter of interpretation; but they were willing to sanction war, nationalism *à outrance*, and hatred between nations and peoples as the necessary means to assure the material power and greatness of Slavdom in Europe.

Strakhov's inability to see the obvious shortcomings of Danilevskii's *Russia and Europe* and to view it simply as one of the many manifestations of "our sad time" may be explained through an examination of his own ideas before he read Danilevskii's work as well as in terms of his personality. Strakhov made use of organic conceptions from biology and zoology and from German romanticism and idealism to describe the nature of Russian nationality as early as the 1860's. As was the case with Danilevskii, his education had been mainly in the natural sciences, although he supplemented his basic scientific training with the study of such German idealistic philosophers as Kant, Fichte, and Hegel during the late 1850's. His generally conservative, idealistic, and organic view of life brought him almost necessarily into conflict with supporters of materialism such as Pisarev, Dobroliubov, and Chernyshevskii at the very beginning of career as a writer. Thus considerably before he read *Russia and Europe* in the late 1860's, he was already waging a struggle against seemingly Western ideas. When he did read this work, he certainly appreciated it above all as a theoretical justification of his own views on the organic individuality of Russia as opposed to the rest of Europe.

There were also certain personal characteristics proper to Strakhov which help to explain his dogged defense of Danilevskii against the attacks of Solov'ev. Strakhov's inability to synthesize his knowledge and to bring it creatively into new relationships with the life of his own time would seem to be particularly important. It was probably because of this failing that Strakhov was so attracted to strong individuals who excelled in synthesis and who also happened to have ideas on life and society resembling his own. The first such individual in his life was Apollon Grigor'ev, whose organic theory of literary criticism was appropriated by Strakhov and used as a basis for his own endeavors as a literary critic. After the publication of *War and Peace* and *Russia and Europe,* Strakhov stood in a similar relation to Tolstoi and Danilevskii. He adopted and championed their ideas, making them the basis for his own subsequent writings on Russian nationality and on the relationship of Russia to the West. Early in the 1870's he became the personal friend of both Tolstoi and Danilevskii[28] and thereafter spent a good part of the time he was free from the Public Library in St. Petersburg (where he worked until 1885) either at Iasnaia Poliana or at Mshatka, Danilevskii's estate in the Crimea. At St. Petersburg he lived alone in a fifth-floor apartment filled with books. He used his extra money almost exclusively for the expansion of his library.[29] Shortly before Strakhov's death, his friend V. V. Rozanov even likened this apartment to a tomb, because, except for its literary and philosophical treasures and furniture, there was nothing in it. Above all, there was nothing alive in the apartment—no plants or flowers. When Rozanov had jokingly remarked somewhat earlier that the apartment needed the touch of a feminine hand, he received the following reply from Strakhov: "It is necessary to trouble oneself about a *wife*—books are not so demanding and do not require so much fuss."[30]

Strakhov's influence was limited to a small circle of friends and followers. His carefully reasoned, but somewhat unimaginative, articles did not stimulate the minds of young Russian intellectuals who were approaching maturity at the close of the nineteenth century. These articles were definitely out of tune with the needs and spirit of the time. They gave little indication of any awareness of the concrete problems and changing patterns of Russian life and society of the 1880's and 1890's. Thus the rapid industrialization of Russia, the famine of 1891–92, the problem of the urban proletariat, and the plight of the Russian peasant in the countryside —all were completely ignored in Strakhov's writings. At the same time, he stubbornly continued to defend a nationalistic and idealistic conception of life that no longer had much meaning for the average educated reader in

Russia. Earlier in the nineteenth century there had been a real need for insistence on Russia's cultural individuality as a necessary prerequisite for the development of Russian art and literature. By the end of the century, however, Russian artistic achievements had reached a level quite comparable to that of Western Europe. The works of Russian authors, musicians, and artists, it is true, did not possess a uniquely Russian character, but they certainly gave adequate expression to many aspects of Russian society and life. Russian cultural individuality, therefore, no longer seemed to be such a pressing matter to secular-minded, educated Russians, who generally considered keeping Russia in step with the social, economic, and political progress of Western Europe to be a much more urgent question. Strakhov, however, could have made an important contribution to the education of Russian citizens by stressing the ideas of loyalty and patriotism to their country as necessary conditions for national strength and solidarity. Unfortunately, he was exceedingly vague on this matter and never went beyond stating that Russia needed a national form of education that would be fundamentally different from Western European education.[31]

What Strakhov, the other *pochvenniki,* and Danilevskii failed to understand was that at the very same time that they were striving to bring a new conservative and nationalistic Russian philosophy of life into existence, Slavophile and conservative-nationalistic ideas in Russia were undergoing a process of disintegration. More and more, the romantic and idealistic nationalism of the 1840's was being replaced by bombastic chauvinism and religious intolerance in intellectual life, Machiavellianism in political theory, and Great Russian national exclusiveness in internal politics. Danilevskii and the *pochvenniki* made relatively little effort to disassociate themselves from these extremes of Russian nationalism. In fact, their uncritical enthusiasm for all things Russian often led them to express opinions that were not too different from those of the most narrow-minded and reactionary proponents of Russian national exclusiveness. This was true, for example, of Dostoevskii in his anti-Semitism, antiliberalism, and messianic variety of Russian imperialism; of Strakhov in his advocacy of Russification in the name of Russian organic unity; and of Danilevskii in his political Machiavellianism, biological determinism, and (toward the end of his life) condemnation of Alexander II's reforms.

Yet it would be misleading to label the *pochvenniki* and Danilevskii as mere reactionaries, for they were certainly too independent and intellectually honest to associate themselves openly and without reservation with the most extreme forms of nationalism in Russia during the 1860's, 1870's, and 1880's. On the contrary, Dostoevskii and Apollon Grigor'ev had been defenders of artistic and intellectual freedom; Strakhov had insisted on the importance of philosophical and moral principles for the normal and sound development of a society; and Danilevskii had believed in the ideals of religious truth and justice, as well as in the loftiness and nobility of the goals of Slavdom. When he spoke of the necessity of military struggle, he usually justified it as a necessary defense of the freedom and existence of Slavdom in the face of a hostile and powerful Europe. If his condemnation of Poland was merciless and harsh, it should be added that he did not go so far as the established official policy during the 1880's and 1890's, which demanded the Russification of Poland.[32] In other words, the negative sides of Danilevskii's views were frequently implicit rather than explicit. But the secularly oriented Russian reading public of the latter part of the nineteenth century had little interest in such nuances and usually did not bother to carefully differentiate between the *pochvenniki* and Danilevskii on the one hand and the most extreme and unsophisticated advocates of Russian national exclusiveness on the other.

The failure of Danilevskii and the *pochvenniki* to influence the thinking of a substantial part of the Russian reading public must therefore be attributed at least in part to the general vulgarization of Russian conservative and nationalistic thought during the second part of the nineteenth century. Accordingly, the nature and progress of this vulgarization must be examined in order to understand fully the unenthusiastic reception that was accorded to the theories of Danilevskii and Strakhov. This examination should also make clearer the intellectual weaknesses of conservative nationalism in Russia. These weaknesses were surely among the more important reasons for the failure of the Russian government prior to 1905 to make use of patriotism as an effective instrument of the policies of the Russian state.

PART III

*The Dissolution of
Conservative Nationalism*

Introduction

By 1900, historian Paul Miliukov's lecture, "The Dissolution of Slavophilism: Danilevskii, Leont'ev, [and] V. Solov'ev,"[1] interpreted Slavophilism for the Russian reading public. Miliukov believed that the dissolution of Slavophilism resulted from a basic contradiction between its two most important theses: the ideal of Russian nationality on the one hand and the conception of Russia's universal-historical mission on the other. The Slavophiles never admitted such a contradiction, for they considered Russian nationality and Russia's universal-historical mission to be closely related and in essential harmony with one another.[2] Their followers, however, Miliukov argued, did perceive this contradiction and understood that emphasizing Russian nationality could only hinder the full development of a conception of Russia's religious significance for the future world, while the messianic idea could only obscure the true nature of Russian nationality. Because of this difficulty, the followers of the Slavophiles, according to Miliukov, came to be divided into two camps: a Slavophile Right, which further developed the idea of nationality, and a Slavophile Left, which continued to develop the idea of Russia's messianic mission in world history.[3]

Miliukov's Slavophile Right was represented by Nicholas Danilevskii and Constantine Leont'ev. Both Danilevskii and Leont'ev, Miliukov pointed out, rejected the humanitarian elements of Slavophilism. Hence the logical result of their attempts to elaborate organic theories concerning the development of Slavic or Russian historical individuality was national egoism and exclusiveness.[4] This point, already clear in Danilevskii's *Russia and Europe,* became even stronger when Leont'ev adapted Danilevskii's theory of organic cultural growth to Russian society during the 1870's and 1880's. Leont'ev, however, differed with Danilevskii in one important re-

127

spect: he denied that the Slavic peoples outside of the tsarist empire had sufficiently common political and cultural ties with Russia to voluntarily federate with her. His Balkan experiences convinced him that the Slavic peoples looked to Western Europe, not Russia, for political and moral leadership; and, Miliukov emphasized, Leont'ev feared that Russia, too, was in danger of being intellectually overwhelmed by European liberal egalitarianism unless she firmly adhered to her own national and cultural individuality. For Leont'ev, the essence of this individuality was Russia's Byzantine heritage of autocracy in politics, Orthodoxy in religion, and the impossibility of happiness for man in this world.[5] Miliukov labeled Leont'ev's form of Byzantinism "reactionary obscurantism,"[6] since Leont'ev approved the use of governmental force and suppression to preserve and defend "Byzantinism" in Russia.[7]

Because Danilevskii's and Leont'ev's theories proved unsatisfactory, Miliukov reasoned that the Slavophile Left had sought to revive Slavophilism by restoring its original idealistic humanitarianism. But Miliukov was only able to find one thinker belonging to the so-called Slavophile Left —Vladimir Solov'ev. Miliukov apparently assigned Solov'ev to the Slavophile Left because the latter, like the original Slavophiles, considered religion the central problem of human existence and insisted on Russia's moral responsibility for the rest of mankind. For Miliukov, Solov'ev's philosophy was based on a "mystical cosmology" restoring the medieval idea that an ideal relation and unity should exist between secular and religious authority within the framework of a universal Christian monarchy.[8] Such a philosophy, Miliukov wrote, transcended nationality and demanded that the Russian people should sacrifice its own national development to realize its universal-historical mission.[9] Thus Solov'ev envisaged a universal theocracy just as unsatisfactory from the standpoint of the original Slavophile synthesis of nationality and messianism as Leont'ev's obscurantism had been.[10] Miliukov concluded that both the Slavophile Right and the Slavophile Left failed to adapt the original Slavophile doctrines to the needs of a new age. Slavophilism had been the natural product of the early nineteenth-century patriarchal family milieu; but the conditions and needs of Russian society had changed. Slavophilism "had died," and, Miliukov predicted, "it will not be resurrected."[11]

Miliukov's most serious shortcoming was his implicit assumption that all champions of nationalism and of Russia's religious mission were successors of the original Slavophiles. Actually the nationalistic and messianic views expressed in late nineteenth-century Russia resulted from many influences and intellectual crosscurrents and not from any one single source. Even the figures mentioned specifically by Miliukov—Danilevskii, Leont'ev, and Solov'ev—are not too intelligible when viewed primarily in the

Slavophile tradition. Danilevskii based his theory of cultural-historical types on the ideas of French and German biologists and not on those of the Slavophiles. True, he borrowed many Slavophile notions of the positive features of Slavic culture; but such notions were common in Russia even before the Slavophiles publicized their views in the 1840's and 1850's. As for Leont'ev, his views were certainly influenced more by Byzantine-Russian monasticism, Katkov, Danilevskii, Solov'ev, and perhaps even Herzen than they were by the Slavophiles, with whom he differed sharply on Pan-Slavism and internal Russian politics.[12] Finally, Vladimir Solov'ev categorically denied Miliukov's contention that there existed a Slavophile Left headed by himself.[13]

Yet conservative and nationalistic ideas and theories in Russia undoubtedly disintegrated during the second part of the nineteenth century. As Miliukov suggested (and as Dostoevskii, Danilevskii, and Strakhov illustrate), Russian nationalists found it increasingly difficult between 1860 and 1900 to apply the idealistic and humanitarian conceptions of Russian nationality of the 1840's to the concrete problems of Russian society. By the eighties and nineties, continued economic and social progress greatly strengthened the troublesome revolutionary movement of the preceding decades. Many students and even proletarians swelled the ranks of revolutionists in towns. The increasing number of professional people—engineers, statisticians, teachers, agronomists, economists—were prone to criticize the government's paternalistic attitude toward society and often sided openly with the revolutionists. Lawyers, frequently using the legal system established in 1864 to defend the rights of the individual, even the rights of revolutionists, proved particularly irritating to the defenders of government policies.

In the peripheral areas of the empire, economic and social progress also worked against the desires of conservative thinkers and government officials. In these areas new factories, schools, and business opportunities meant additional strength not only for such traditionally dominant groups as the Poles, Swedish Finns, and Baltic Germans but also for the leaders of emerging nationalities. With certain exceptions, the leaders of both the traditionally dominant groups and the emerging nationalities were modern in their outlook, admired Western European progress, and distrusted the nationalism of Russian publicists and the centralizing tendencies of the St. Petersburg bureaucracy. Local leaders regarded aggressive Russian nationalism and vigorous administrative centralization as threats to the position in society they either actually had or aspired to obtain. Defending themselves and promoting their respective causes with every means at their disposal, these leaders were often successful. Their degree of success was an important reason for conservative nationalists' frustration over Russian events near the end of the nineteenth century.

Partially committed to the values of the preceding generation, Dostoevskii and Strakhov felt restraint in giving sanction to authoritarian control or systematic Russification as solutions to such problems as social and revolutionary unrest and nationality in the borderlands of the Russian empire. Danilevskii rejected the values of the 1840's, but he never fully spelled out the logical consequences of his ideas. Other thinkers and public figures, however, such as General Rostislav Fadeev, Constantine Leont'ev, and Constantine Pobedonostsev did not recoil before these consequences. They were prepared to advocate and even justify the use of naked force or suppressive measures to further the interests of the state at home and abroad and to assure social stability inside of Russia. At the same time, these writers continued to emphasize that the development of national feeling and cohesion was one of the most urgent tasks of Russian society. Their writings therefore illustrate the changes in Russian conservative and nationalistic thought toward the end of the nineteenth century.

These same changes can also be detected in the last two true Slavophiles, Iurii Samarin and Ivan Aksakov. It is noteworthy that in Miliukov's attempt to prove his thesis of the dissolution of Slavophilism he analyzed those who, at best, were only vaguely and indirectly connected with Slavophilism and pretty much ignored the last undisputed disciples of the original Slavophiles. It is obvious why Miliukov avoided Ivan Aksakov and Samarin: they were relatively successful in remaining true to the philosophy of life first formulated by the Kireevskii brothers, Khomiakov, and Constantine Aksakov; they never became defenders of "reactionary obscurantism." Hence their writings did not suit Miliukov's purposes as well as did the writings of others, who never properly belonged to the Slavophile school of thought. Yet Ivan Aksakov and Samarin often modified Slavophilism when adapting it to the circumstances and problems of their own time. In modifying, they sometimes distorted its spirit and inadvertently provided convenient arguments for many "reactionary obscurantists," who later claimed to be their followers.

CHAPTER TEN

The Last of the Slavophiles

BOTH Iurii Fedorovich Samarin and Ivan Sergeevich Aksakov dedicated their careers as publicists to furthering the work and popularizing the teachings of the original Slavophiles. Samarin, in contrast to Aksakov who was skeptical about the future of Slavophilism at the beginning of Alexander II's reign,[1] seems to have had few serious doubts about the ultimate triumph of Slavophile principles in Russian society. After the early 1840's he consistently defended the Slavophile view of life in regard to such matters as the peasant commune, religion, education, science, and political authority.[2] Samarin was an unusually effective polemicist whose mind had been disciplined by a thorough basic education as well as by a number of years of research in Russian religious history while a candidate for the Master's degree at the University of Moscow. A man with much imagination and originality, he made a number of important independent contributions to Slavophile theory prior to the late 1850's, especially in his Master's thesis on Stephen Iavorskii and Theophan Prokopovich.[3] As time went on, however, he became increasingly involved in practical administrative work and public debate. He was one of the principal architects of peasant emancipation in Russia, a member of N. A. Miliutin's special mission to Poland in 1863 (which had the task of studying the peasant problem and outlining a program of agrarian reform for Poland), and a determined polemicist against the privileged position of the German nobility in the Baltic provinces. These preoccupations became so central for him that he seems to have had little time or energy during the last decade and a half of his life for original theoretical work on the basic philosophical and religious doctrines of Slavophilism. He was contented with explaining and elucidating the views of the early Slavophiles. Perhaps the best-known example of this is Samarin's excellent, but highly adulatory, introduction to the theological works of Khomiakov.[4] Here he rather uncritically praised Khomiakov as a teacher of the Orthodox Church. Accordingly, Samarin identified himself as one of Khomiakov's pupils—a pupil more interested in preserving his master's exact message than in giving it new meaning through original insights and fundamental reinterpretation.

Ivan Aksakov also assumed the role of faithful disciple of the original Slavophiles after the deaths of his brother Constantine and of Khomiakov in 1860.[5] His skepticism in the mid-1850's concerning the future of Slavophilism lasted only a few years. In the late 1850's he came to participate actively in Slavophile journalism, first as the unofficial editor of the journal *Russian Conversation (Russkaia Beseda)* and then as the editor of the short-lived newspaper *The Sail (Parus)*. With the disappearance from the Russian cultural scene of the original Slavophiles, Ivan Aksakov felt strongly that he had the moral duty and responsibility of continuing their work. For the next twenty-five years he applied the ideas and theories of his brother Constantine, Khomiakov, and the Kireevskii brothers to practically every new problem and event of Russian society. He first did this in a series of successive publications which he edited during the 1860's, then in his capacity as a public leader in the Moscow Slavic Benevolent Committee and other organizations during the 1870's, and finally in his newspaper *Rus'* during the 1880's. He always seemed aware of the spiritual presence of the original Slavophiles, and he frequently quoted from their poetical and prose works. The voices of the original Slavophiles, therefore, were not completely silenced in 1860 but continued to be heard through the media of the journalism and oratory of Ivan Aksakov.

Despite the admiration that both Ivan Aksakov and Samarin had for the opinions of the early Slavophiles, it is abundantly clear that the particular uses they made of Slavophilism gave it new directions and new implications. The application of the idealistic and theoretical ideas of the early Slavophiles to the concrete problems of Russian society during the second part of the nineteenth century brought Slavophilism out of the abstract realm of speculation and into direct contact with the harsh realities of Russian contemporary politics. Once Slavophilism ceased being essentially a speculative and esthetical philosophy, its original idealistic humanitarianism and universalism became increasingly contradictory not only to the elements of chauvinism and national exclusiveness that had always been present in it, but also to the suppressive and sometimes brutal policies Russian autocracy pursued in its attempts to curtail the revolutionary movement in Russia.[6] This dilemma led to an almost inevitable degeneration of Slavophilism in the hands of the last two true representatives of this school of thought in Russia. On the part of Samarin, one can observe the process of degeneration especially in regard to the problem of nationality in Russia; with Aksakov, one can see it in his attempts to preserve autocracy and give Russian society national and social cohesion.

Iurii Samarin's treatment of the nationality question in Russia was in many ways similar to that of Katkov and other advocates of realism in Russian national policy. Although Samarin did engage in polemics with Katkov in 1856 concerning the role of nationality in science and education and in 1863 concerning Russian policy in Poland,[7] he usually stressed Russian state interest rather than Slavophile idealism when writing about the nationality question in Russia's borderlands. Samarin, like Katkov, was convinced that special rights and privileges for Russia's western provinces could only weaken Russia as a state. Therefore he was particularly disturbed about various proposals made during the 1860's to transform Russia into a federation of peoples. Samarin believed that federalism could only make Russia a sort of Hotel Ragatz, frequented by a variety of nationalities who did not know one another and who seated themselves at the same table d'hôte.[8] In other words, he felt that federalism would denationalize Russia; that Germans, Poles, and other peoples in a Russian federation would have little feeling of national attachment to Russia; that Russians would often find themselves foreigners in their own country.[9]

Concern about the national interests of the Russian state had developed gradually in Samarin's mind since his youth and early manhood. The family milieu and general intellectual atmosphere of his formative years taught him early the importance of the governmental order and military strength of Muscovite autocracy in Russian history.[10] These early lessons were reinforced by his experiences in Livonia as a research worker and civil servant during the late 1840's, first as a member of a commission studying Livonian peasant conditions and then as a member of the Khanykov Commission, which had the task of investigating the economy and political institutions of the city of Riga.[11] His contact with the narrow provincial world of the Livonian Germans, especially with their stubborn defense of antiquated privileges and their pride in the German political and cultural heritage of the Baltic provinces, greatly offended the young, nationalistic Muscovite. He also took exception to the manner in which a small minority of Germans completely controlled and exploited the subjugated Latvian and Estonian peasants in Livonia.[12] But the relation of the Livonian Germans to the Russian government irritated him most. Samarin insisted that in the Russian empire all individual, caste, and local rights had to be subordinated to the general welfare of the empire and that the central power should have in its hands the exclusive right to determine just what this general welfare was and what measures were necessary to further it.[13] He felt that it was absurd that the Russian government should allow the Germans of Livonia to reject reforms proposed by St. Petersburg on the ground that such reforms were contrary to the historical privileges of the Livonian nobility. He was equally opposed to the toleration of privileges that reserved governmental and municipal posts in Livonia to Germans and gave the Lutheran Church control of religious affairs in the Baltic provinces. Such privileges and control, Samarin wrote, disenfranchised resident Russians and made the Russian Orthodox Church subordinate to the Lutheran hierarchy in this region. With regard to the religious question, he wholeheartedly approved of the efforts of Russian priests and officials in Livonia in the early 1840's to convert the Estonian and Latvian peasants to Orthodoxy. Samarin thought it natural that so many Livonian peasants wanted to enter the Orthodox Church, because he believed that they could only regard Lutheranism as a religion that had been imposed on them by their German conquerors. He felt that the conversion of the Estonians and Latvians to Orthodoxy definitely needed to be given further encouragement because of its desirability from the standpoint of Russian state interests.[14]

Neither Nicholas I nor Alexander II appreciated Samarin's attempts to defend Russian state interests in Livonia. In 1849 Samarin had been held in the Peter and Paul Fortress at St. Petersburg and then interrogated by Emperor Nicholas himself for having circulated the manuscript of his *Letters from Riga* among friends and acquaintances.[15] Approximately twenty years later, he was obliged to publish his *Borderlands of Russia* in Prague and Berlin because Alexander II shared his father's view that the Baltic Germans, as conservative landowners and loyal servants of the tsar, should not be openly and directly attacked by Russian publicists.[16] After the first part of Samarin's *Borderlands of Russia* had been published at Prague in 1868, Samarin was summoned to the Governor-General's office in Moscow and notified of Alexander II's disapproval of his book.[17] On December 23, 1868, Samarin addressed a special letter to Emperor Alexander in which he defended his work. "My entire book," he wrote, "from the first page to the last, is consecrated to the defense of Russian state interests against the immoderate and ever increasing pretensions of Baltic provincialism."[18] He warned the emperor that defenders of Baltic provincialism such as Woldemar von Bock and Schedo-Ferroti (Baron F. Fircks) were to be equated with figures like Herzen and Ludwig Mieroslawski, the Polish revolutionist-nationalist. According to Samarin, all of them were enemies of Russia who were only waiting for the dissolution and final destruction of the tsarist empire.[19] Alexander II apparently never took Samarin's arguments very seriously, for he continued to follow a conciliatory policy toward the Baltic German nobles until the very end of his reign.

Yet Samarin's polemics against the Baltic Germans were not without influence in official circles. Samarin was closely associated with the Tiutchev sisters, who were influential at the court and regularly corresponded with Constantine Pobedonostsev, then the tutor of the future Alexander III.[20] Through Anna Aksakov (nee Tiutchev) and Pobedonostsev at least two and perhaps all six volumes of Samarin's *Borderlands of Russia* reached the tsarevich.[21] In other words, Samarin's polemical works were obviously used by Pobedonostsev to convince the tsarevich that the Baltic Germans were hostile to Russia and the Orthodox Church and that the Russian government should resolutely pursue a nationalistically Russian policy in the Baltic provinces.[22] Indeed, his success may be seen in Alexander III's policy in this region during the 1880's and 1890's.

Originally Samarin had intended to include historical studies and polemics concerning Belorussia, the Ukraine, and Poland in his *Borderlands of Russia*, but he did not live long enough to complete this task.[23] He did, however, write a number of articles on the Polish question during the 1860's in connection with the Polish uprising. As a Slavophile he necessarily believed that the events of 1863 in Poland represented not merely a rebellion but also a conflict between the Roman Catholic civilization of Poland and the West on the one hand and the Orthodox civilization of the Russian East on the other.[24] Samarin considered the Polish gentry and clergy to be the main bearers of Catholic civilization in Poland and the western provinces. He felt that the best way to weaken the influence of the Polish upper class in these regions was to introduce reforms that would improve the economic and social conditions of the peasantry and thereby strengthen their position in society at the expense of the Polish gentry.[25] As a Slavophile, however, he was relatively tolerant in his attitudes toward Polish nationality and culture and defended Strakhov against Katkov in 1863 concerning the right of the Poles to have their own national and cultural life within the framework of the Russian empire.[26] At the same time, he vigorously attacked the Polish territorial and religious aspirations in Belorussia and the Ukraine and favored firm and even dictatorial control in Poland as long as there was open hostility there to Russia.[27]

In 1863 Samarin took part in N. A. Miliutin's special mission in Poland. Here his views on peasant reform and on the conflict between Catholic and Orthodox civilizations seem to have been of considerable importance for the formulation of Russian policy toward Poland. However, he soon abandoned his work in Poland, apparently because of bad health.[28] In 1865 he again returned to the general question of Poland and the relations between Western Catholic civilization and Russian Orthodox civilization. This time Samarin's polemics were prompted by a letter addressed to Ivan Aksakov's *Day* (*Den'*) by Russian-born Father Martynov, who then lived in Paris as a member of the Society of Jesus. Aksakov, in an editorial written in 1864, had likened the Jesuits to a "gang of cardsharps and thieves" and described them as intriguers against Russia in Poland and the western provinces.[29] Martynov, of course, took exception to Aksakov's editorial and asked him to furnish some sort of proof for his accusations. This Samarin attempted to do in a series of five polemical letters, which were published in *Day* during 1865. In the first three letters Samarin sought to demonstrate historically the conspiratorial and unethical nature of Jesuitism. Here his arguments were based mainly on the old tradition of anti-Jesuit literature in Western Europe and were not particularly original. In 1867 Samarin discovered new materials concerning the Jesuits while in Prague. He added the most important of these materials, the *Monita privata Societatis Iesu*, in the form of new appendices to the second edition of his anti-Jesuit letters and included a Russian translation and explanatory comments. But this document did nothing to reinforce Samarin's dubious polemics concerning the Jesuit conspiracy, for it was later demonstrated to be a forgery. Letters four and five described the anti-Russian and anti-Orthodox activities of the Jesuits in Poland and in Russia during the sixteenth, seventeenth, eighteenth, and early nineteenth centuries. In these two letters Samarin clearly sought to discredit Roman Catholicism and thereby indirectly to strengthen Russian influence in the Ukraine and Belorussia.[30]

One should notice that Samarin almost invariably placed his polemics on the minority groups and nationalities in Russia's borderlands within a historical frame of reference. An early example is his *Letters from Riga*, which was written during the late 1840's. Here he attempted to demonstrate, on the one hand, Russia's historical claim to the Baltic provinces and, on the other, the artificial nature of the privileges of the Baltic German nobility. In discussing the privileges of the Baltic Germans, Samarin stressed that they were not in keeping with the historical development of the modern state. The privileges of corporations and guilds and of the nobility, he argued, belonged to the Middle Ages and had little place in modern society.[31] Commenting on his meaning in the *Letters from Riga* at a later date, in 1864, he wrote: "Everywhere common law and free competition have put an end (*fait justice*) to privilege. One can hardly remember anymore the guild offices and masterships. As for feudal services and seigneurial rights, you will only find them everywhere in a state of ruin, marking the way that nations have followed on the road to progress."[32]

In arguing against the privileges of the Baltic German nobles, Samarin did not appeal to abstract justice and humanity but rather to historical necessity as the final arbiter between conflicting ideas, nations, and nationalities in history. Such reasoning had, of course, been fairly common in Russia since the 1820's—especially as a result of the influence of Hegel's philosophy. In Samarin's case, the historical study he had made in the early 1840's in his Master's dissertation on *Stephen Iavorskii and Theophan Prokopovich* concerning the impact of Catholic and Protestant ideas on Russian society at the time of Peter the Great was certainly of decisive importance in preparing him to take a historicist approach to the problems of his own time. He used this approach again not only in his *Letters from Riga* but also in his *History of Riga, 1200–1845,* which was written under the auspices of the Ministry of the Interior and first published in 1852.[33] Samarin's *History of Riga,* though factual and seldom tendentious, is an interesting and early example of the Russian government's practice of commissioning young officials or scholars to undertake studies that provided historical justification for the centralizing tendencies of the St. Petersburg bureaucracy. Samarin's study was judicious and sober in comparison with official studies made at a later date; nevertheless, his efforts to use history to support the interests of the tsarist state are unmistakable in his treatment of Riga's development.[34] Indeed, this endeavor runs throughout his thinking and writings on the problem of the nationalities in Russia's borderlands. He did not apply such reasoning to only the Poles and Baltic Germans, for while in the Ukraine in 1850 he noted in his diary that the Ukrainians should remember that they had only been able to maintain their religion and identity as a people through their association with Moscow after the seventeenth century. He admitted that the Ukrainians had suffered considerably in one way or another under Moscow but emphasized that it was only through the Russian tsar that they could hope to obtain any improvement of their lot. He felt that this point had been amply demonstrated by the beneficial results obtained by the investigation made by the Bibikov commission (in which Samarin had participated) of the relations between the Ukrainian peasants and their landowners.[35] The Ukrainian people should not forget, he concluded, that "its historical role is within the frontiers of Russia and not outside of her, within the general framework of the Muscovite state. . . ."[36]

Ivan Aksakov did not share Samarin's almost obsessive concern about the defense of the interests of the Russian state. To be sure, Aksakov generally agreed with Samarin concerning questions pertaining to the Baltic Germans, the Poles, and the Ukrainians.[37] But Aksakov's opinions on such matters were the instinctive ones of a Great Russian patriot and seldom the result of any systematic and conscious attempt to defend Russian state interests as such. Ivan Aksakov faithfully followed the example of his brother Constantine in refusing to regard the state as an ultimate goal in itself. Instead, he considered the state as a necessary evil—definitely to be subordinated to man's higher social, religious, and personal ideals.[38] He succinctly expressed this attitude in the mid-1870's in the presence of Constantine Leont'ev. The latter had made some reference to the necessity of the state, to which Aksakov replied: "May the devil take the state if it oppresses and torments its citizens! Let it perish!"[39]

Rather than stressing the importance of state interests in discussing Russian national policy, as Samarin had done, Ivan Aksakov concentrated his attention on the relation of Russian nationality to the Slavic world as a whole. Aksakov was deeply interested in the fate of the Slavs outside of Russia as early as the 1840's.[40] The so-called Slavic question was, in Aksakov's opinion, essentially a Russian question. He believed that Russian participation in Balkan affairs and the liberation of the Orthodox Slavs in Austria and the Ottoman Empire were inextricably associated with Russia's own historical mission as a nation.[41] The popularization in Russia of friendship with the Slavs was probably his chief goal as a publicist. For almost thirty years he did his utmost to establish personal contacts with intellectual leaders in the other Slavic countries and to inform the Russian public more fully concerning the Slavic peoples outside of Russia in his various newspapers and through his activities as a leading figure in the Moscow Slavic Benevolent Committee.

On occasions, Aksakov, like Danilevskii and Dostoevskii, glorified war and displayed unmistakable signs of Great Russian chauvinism and of intolerance toward non-Russian Slavs. Glorification of war was nothing new for the Slavophiles and other varieties of Russian nationalists, who tended to view both the Crimean War and the Russo-Turkish War of 1877–78 as holy wars against either Europe or the infidel Turks.[42] Ivan Aksakov was especially intoxicated with enthusiasm for war during 1877–78. For him this war was more than a struggle on behalf of the Christian religion and for the liberation of the Russians' Slavic brethren in the Balkans: "This war is a historical necessity. This is a people's war, and never has a people turned to a war with such conscious participation."[43] But he did not necessarily need the inspiration of open rebellion on the part of the Slavs to express such thoughts, for as early as 1863 he had approved in principle the idea of war against Austria in order to liberate the Slavs.[44] In his general attitude toward the non-Russian Slavs, Aksakov, again like Danilevskii and Dostoevskii, was often intolerant of the diversity of cultural backgrounds and objectives which have always characterized the Slavic world. In Aksakov's scheme of things, what was good for Russia was also good for the other Slavs. Thus he insisted that Russian should be accepted as the lingua franca of all the Slavs and that the Catholic Slavs should part with the Papacy and join the majority of their Slavic brethren within the fold of the Orthodox Church.[45] One might add that he was most unsympathetic toward the cultural and linguistic aspirations of the Ukrainians.[46] Finally, there is little evidence that he ever raised his voice in protest on behalf of the Poles when Russification was gradually imposed on Poland after 1866.[47]

Such attitudes, however, were never the mainspring of Aksakov's views on the relationship between Russian nationality and the Slavic question. Consciously, the point of departure for his Pan-Slav beliefs and activities was neither Great Russian chauvinism nor the power interests of the Russian state. Instead, it was his lofty ideal of the cultural future of the Slavic world. He therefore, in a sense, continued the work of the early Slavophiles by extending their idealistic and humanitarian conception of Russian nationality to the Slavs who lived outside of Russia. It was precisely this application of the idealized principles of Slavophilism to the Slavic world as a whole that caused difficulties for Aksakov with the Russian government in 1849 and during the Balkan crisis of the 1870's. In 1849 Aksakov was briefly placed under arrest and interrogated by the Third Section. At the time, Nicholas I took particular exception to Aksakov's words concerning the brotherly ties existing between the Orthodox Slavs of Eastern Europe. Such thinking in the opinion of Nicholas, was likely to encourage rebellion against legal authority on the part of the non-Russian Slavs. Nicholas felt that this would be harmful to Russian state interests because such rebellions could only be directed against the governments of Russia and her allies in central Europe, namely Austria and Prussia.[48] In 1877 and 1878 Aksakov's difficulties with the government were caused by his criticisms of official policy in the Balkans. In 1877 he was even critical of his friend Prince Cherkasskii, who was the administrator in charge of civilian affairs in Bulgaria during the Russo-Turkish War, for treating Bulgaria as an occupied province rather than as a liberated country. The government's reaction to such criticism was to increase its control over the activities of Pan-Slavist organizations inside of Russia and to subject the representatives of these organizations in Bulgaria to strict supervision and surveillance.[49] In 1878 Aksakov was greatly incensed about the concessions made by the Russian government to the wishes of the European powers at the Congress of Berlin. He characteristically refused to view Russian policy at the Congress of Berlin as a simple matter of defending Russian interests under the most unfavorable diplomatic circumstances. Instead, the Berlin Congress represented for him a betrayal to the cause of Slavdom. The Russian government was not willing to tolerate such criticism and therefore closed the Moscow Slavic Benevolent Society and sent Aksakov into temporary exile.[50]

If Aksakov's championing of the cause of Slavdom was compatible with the humanitarian idealism of the original Slavophiles, his attempt to apply

Slavophile principles to the political problems of Russian society was much less so. This was strikingly the case after he resumed his activities as a journalist in 1880, when he was granted permission to publish the newspaper *Rus'*. At this time traditional Russian society struggled with such problems as the Jewish question, institutional reform, and the revolutionary movement. The instinctive reaction of conservative nationalists like Dostoevskii, Strakhov, and Aksakov was to cling desperately to the ideal of an Orthodox, autocratic, and nationally awakened Russian society. They earnestly hoped that this society could be kept intact and protected from the influence of the ideas and values of Western European civilization. Aksakov's task was an especially difficult one. He not only had to defend the traditional ideal of Russian society, which was accepted by all Russian conservatives, but also the letter and spirit of Slavophilism as it had been originally conceived during the 1840's and 1850's. Aksakov was not quite up to this task. For one thing, he lacked the philosophical sophistication and training of the other Slavophiles. He had been educated at the School of Jurisprudence, which existed primarily for the purpose of training bureaucrats for government service, rather than in the lecture halls of the University of Moscow. Probably as a result of the deficiencies of this education, little trace of the intellectual refinement and subtlety of the other Slavophiles can be seen in Aksakov's writings. To the contrary, his thinking was often not only banal but even crude.

The Jewish question first attracted Aksakov's serious attention during the early 1860's in connection with various projects of legal and administrative reform that were being discussed in the Russian press. Aksakov definitely opposed granting to the Jews the same legal and administrative rights in Russian society possessed by Christians. He agreed that they should enjoy such rights as cultural autonomy and local self-government but advised against giving them any legislative or administrative powers that might place Christians under their control.[51] In 1867 he urged that emphasis should not be put on emancipating the Jews in Russia but more on emancipating Russians from the Jews. In these writings, he referred particularly to conditions in southwestern Russia, where the Christian peasant population was often economically dependent on Jewish traders and money lenders.[52] The pogroms of 1881 in the Ukraine again called his attention to the Jewish problem. He did not approve of popular justice against the Jews but emphasized that the pogroms dramatically demonstrated that the government should take steps to liberate the common people in the Ukraine from the economic yoke of the Jews.[53] At the same time, Aksakov became increasingly obsessed with the idea that the Jews represented an essentially pernicious and dangerous influence on Christian society.[54] He even gave credence to the idea that there was an international

Jewish conspiracy against Russia that had been organized by the World Israelite Alliance. It was later revealed that the documents used by Aksakov to support his allegations concerning the Israelite alliance were forgeries. But this fact did not affect Aksakov's opinion concerning the nature of the Jewish conspiracy against Russia. As N. V. Riasanovsky has commented: "When he was forced to recognize his mistake, he made the typical comment that the document gave a correct version of the Jews and could have been true, and that therefore it did not matter whether or not it actually was true."[55]

The events of the 1880's produced a similar reaction on the part of Aksakov in regard to the general problem of reform in Russia. As was to be expected, the assassination of Alexander II on March 1, 1881, especially enraged him. Interestingly enough, Aksakov did not direct his fury primarily against the revolutionists who had assassinated the emperor but against the liberal-minded bureaucrats and journalists of St. Petersburg. He firmly believed that such bureaucrats and journalists were responsible more than anyone else for the undermining of the national, religious, and political foundations of Russian life.[56] Almost twenty years before he had written that it was high time for Russia to have social cohesion and spiritual unity based on the Russian people's consciousness of themselves as an independent "national organism."[57] Now he bitterly regretted that Russia was still in the imitative St. Petersburg phase of her development. Russia's salvation, he insisted, was not to be sought in such imitation[58] but in restoring the organic unity between the tsar and his people. Accordingly, Aksakov opposed all reforms that in any way would limit the tsar's autocratic powers, which he considered to be the principal guarantee of the Russian way of life.[59] Writing in this vein during 1881, at the same time that Loris-Melikov was attempting to defend his moderate program of reforms for the Russian government against the attacks of Pobedonostsev, Aksakov by necessity became the close journalistic ally of Katkov in the latter's reactionary campaign against the liberal elements in the Russian bureaucracy. Aksakov was again Katkov's ally in regard to the work of the Kakhanov committee, which was set up in September, 1881 (after Loris-Melikov's resignation as Minister of the Interior) to consider measures to improve the institutions of local self-government in Russia. In a number of articles published between 1882 and 1884, Aksakov not too pertinently condemned the proposals of the Kakhanov committee as being inspired by Western European principles and therefore not applicable to the conditions of Russian life.[60] The proposals of the Kakhanov committee, being the recommendations of a routine, bureaucratic group, unquestionably had many shortcomings. But Aksakov, in his naïve championing of Slavophile principles, failed to understand that in attacking these proposals he was giving indirect support to such people as A. D. Pazukhin and Count Dmitrii Tolstoi (the Minister of the Interior after May, 1882), who advocated the transformation of the Russian zemstvos into institutions that would be under the effective control of the Russian gentry. Pazukhin and Tolstoi were instrumental in terminating the activities of the Kakhanov committee in 1884. This victory paved the way for new legislation that assured the control of the gentry over zemstvo affairs. In a word, Aksakov's agitation against the Kakhanov committee extended a helping hand to the architects of the era of reaction which characterized the policies of the Russian government during the last two decades of the nineteenth century.[61]

Ivan Aksakov himself was never a reactionary. Throughout his career as a journalist he fought for such goals as freedom of speech and religion, independent courts, zemstvo institutions, and the calling of a *zemskii sobor*.[62] His alliance with Katkov in the early 1880's was therefore only a temporary one. He first broke with Katkov early in 1882 when the latter vehemently attacked Count N. P. Ignatiev, then Minister of the Interior, for having proposed the summoning of a *zemskii sobor* and again in 1884 over the question of the position of the courts in Russian society.[63] Aksakov admitted that Russian courts had their shortcomings but compared them favorably with the inequities and inefficiency of the old Russian court system as it had existed during the reign of Nicholas I. In defending the independence of the courts, he commented that courts dependent on the will and caprice of the administration were senseless.[64] Nevertheless, it is clear that Aksakov, during the 1880's, did inadvertently give considerable journalistic assistance to such reactionaries as Pobedonostsev, Katkov, and Dmitrii Tolstoi in their campaign to undo the work of reform of the 1860's and 1870's. This aid was extended above all because Aksakov, like Dostoevskii, was too naïve and uncritical to grasp the possible implications and results of a given idea or press campaign within the frame of reference of the realities and intrigues of Russian political life. In one respect, Aksakov can even be compared unfavorably with Katkov, who was at least consistent in his reaction during the last decade of his activities as a journalist. Aksakov, during this same period, although sincere and nominally faithful to Slavophile principles, was little more than a confused, befuddled, and exceedingly naïve idealist.

Iurii Samarin was much more realistic and sophisticated than Aksakov in dealing with Russian internal affairs. Samarin's thorough education in the humanities gave his thinking discipline and breadth. Just as important for his development as this formal academic training was the extensive practical experience he accumulated as a civil servant in Livonia, the Ukraine, and Poland and as a defender of peasant interests in the Samara provincial committee and the Editorial Commission during the years immediately preceding the emancipation of the Russian serfs. During these years of social and state service, Samarin acquired a realistic understanding of the narrow class interests and ambitions of the Russian gentry as well as of the nature of the social, economic, and political problems confronting Russian society. Because of this understanding, Samarin's approach to such problems was usually much more concrete and less dogmatic than that of the other Slavophiles. A good example of his pragmatic attitude is his treatment of the Russian peasant commune in the late 1850's and early 1860's. As a Slavophile he continued to believe that the commune represented an essential part of the organic unity of Russian life as contrasted with the class antagonisms and social and economic inequities which then troubled and divided Western Europe.[65] But he did not rule out the possibility that the commune might be replaced by the private ownership of farms at some time in the future. He realized that the peasant commune had many economic weaknesses but argued against abandoning it in the immediate future because it was favored by the average peasant and served to maintain social stability in Russia.[66] In other words, his defense of the commune around 1860 was a practical and not a theoretical or dogmatic one.[67]

Samarin, like the other conservative nationalists, identified the advantages of Russian society with the institution of autocracy. He was not unaware that Russia suffered from such evils as inadequate courts, arbitrary police power, and serious encroachments on the freedoms of speech and conscience. But he felt that the remedying of these evils could be best undertaken by the tsar, whose autocratic powers could always be freely used to benefit his subjects. Because of his faith in the positive role of the tsar in Russian society, Samarin was against all attempts to limit the tsar's absolute power. He was therefore inalterably opposed to the proposals for the convocation of a Russian consultative assembly made by the Tver and Moscow gentry during the 1860's. Being a political realist, he saw clearly that such an assembly, at that time, could easily be used by the gentry as a means of establishing their control over the political affairs of the Russian empire. Such control, he wrote in 1862, would drive a wedge between the Russian people and their tsar and could only serve the interests of a small minority and not those of the nation as a whole.[68]

During the 1860's and 1870's Samarin directed a number of polemical articles against the efforts of the Russian gentry to appropriate for themselves a role of leadership and independent political power in Russian society.[69] The last and most significant of these articles was published, together with an article of F. Dmitriev, in book form at Berlin in 1875 (about a year prior to Samarin's death) under the title, *Revolutionary*

Conservatism. He applied the words "revolutionary conservatism" to the variety of conservatism outlined by General Rostislav Andreevich Fadeev in a series of articles which appeared in the *Russian World* (*Russkii Mir*) during 1872.[70] Fadeev had pointed to the chaotic state of Russian public life and had emphasized the need for an elite to take over political and social leadership. He regarded the Russian gentry as the one group in Russia that was suited to play such a role and therefore argued that measures should be taken to strengthen its position in Russian society.[71]

Samarin considered Fadeev's proposals to be a form of social revolution. He defined revolution as "*rationalism in action:* i.e. a formally correct syllogism made use of as a battering ram against the freedom of living tradition."[72] Fadeev, according to Samarin, used the following syllogism in his analysis of Russian society: (a) the strength and vitality of a society depend on its educated elite; (b) in Russia only the gentry possess sufficient education, experience, and maturity to assume a role of elite leadership in society; (c) therefore, it is necessary to strengthen Russia's declining gentry and place them at the head of the Russian state.[73] Samarin agreed with Fadeev that the lack of unifying social ideas and forces was the main illness of Russian society. But he insisted that social unity could not result from the imposition of abstract and external social forms. The forms of social life in Russia, in Samarin's opinion, had to develop naturally and organically and had to correspond to some form of internal unity of belief and conviction within Russian society.[74] Thus, he summarized, Fadeev believed "in the miraculous power of form, in its ability to create spirit from within itself [i.e. from within form]."[75]

Fadeev's desire to impose abstract and formal ideals of social order on Russian society was regarded by Samarin to be particularly dangerous because of the support such notions then seemed to enjoy in official circles. Samarin was especially concerned about the possibility that the zemstvos would soon be deprived of their representative character and placed exclusively under the control of the gentry. He saw confirmation of these fears in the fact that the St. Petersburg gentry had been granted permission in the early 1870's to discuss the new organization of rural districts (*volosti*), which Samarin considered a subject belonging exclusively within the jurisdiction of local zemstvo assemblies.[76] Despite his apprehension that radical surgery along the lines suggested by Fadeev was likely to be performed on Russian society, Samarin was not completely pessimistic about the future:

> [Being] an incorrigible Slavophile, I nevertheless believe that Russia, withdrawing within herself, will also suffer patiently this time and will not perish under the knife. But when will she regain consciousness . . . [and] find

in herself her former faith in the government, in the integrity of its word, in the firmness of its intentions, in the durability and certainty of its works?[77]

Notwithstanding his disapproval of the strong current of aristocratic reaction in Russian official and gentry circles during the 1870's, Samarin shares with Aksakov considerable responsibility for having indirectly given support to certain nationalistic and antiliberal currents in Russian society. Somewhat later these currents culminated in the reactionary policies pursued by the Russian government during the reign of Alexander III. On the credit side of the ledger, Samarin and Aksakov undeniably made an important positive contribution by helping promote the public discussion of significant issues. But the ideas they expressed scarcely represent a contribution to Russian conservative and nationalistic thought that can be compared with Strakhov's analysis of nineteenth-century society or Danilevskii's theory of historical types. Both Samarin and Aksakov were essentially *epigoni* who were primarily important for popularizing and applying the ideas of the original Slavophiles to the concrete problems of Russian society during the decades following the emancipation of the Russian serfs. They were certainly successful in these endeavors, for ideas generally associated with the Slavophiles gained wide acceptance among patriotic writers and government officials during the second part of the nineteenth century. The use that government officials made of Slavophilism, however, tended to be rather questionable, since they often transformed it into a justification for the same sterile and bureaucratic St. Petersburg attitudes and policies that the Slavophiles had previously attacked. As N. Ustrialov wrote in 1925:

> Perhaps the tragedy of St. Petersburg Russia consisted, above all, in the fact that the Russian government itself was too dominated by distorted echoes of its own kind of "Slavophile" prejudices. An analysis of the official ideology of the Russian government of the nineteenth century reveals a series of "romantic" traditions that rendered it [the Russian government] a sad service. Striving to preserve the "old pillars of autocracy" in [a state of] purity, fanatically defending "conservative principles" *quand même*, the Russian tsars little by little placed themselves in sharp contradiction to that . . . basically fruitful principle of the St. Petersburg period—the principle of a great state built on a foundation of justice, which history obliged them to serve.[78]

CHAPTER ELEVEN

Revolutionary Conservatism

═══

AMORAL Machiavellianism became a characteristic feature of the thinking of many Russian intellectuals and St. Petersburg bureaucrats during the latter part of the nineteenth century. Such Machiavellianism was not a uniquely Russian phenomenon, for hardheaded political realism was loudly acclaimed and defended by a vociferous minority of writers and politicians throughout Europe during this period. Danilevskii's *Russia and Europe* was one example of this trend in Russian thought. But Danilevskii never completely outgrew his early infatuation with socialist ideas and the theories of German romanticism and idealism. Thus he continued to believe in scientific progress, the organic development of cultural-historical types, religious truth, and national ideals until the very end of his life. This, despite his rejection of humanitarianism, set him somewhat apart as a man of the 1840's from the new Russian intellectual leaders of the 1860's and 1870's, who usually contemptuously rejected all manifestations of the romanticism and idealism of the preceding generation.

Among Russian conservative thinkers, General Rostislav Andreevich Fadeev was probably the most important popularizer of social and political realism during the 1860's and 1870's. Fadeev, in contrast to most other well-known Russian intellectuals of the mid-nineteenth century, was not a product of the student intellectual circles of Moscow and St. Petersburg. Although his mother, nee Dolgorukaia, had influential friends and relatives among Russia's high aristocracy, Rostislav Fadeev's family spent little time in either of the two Russian capitals. His father, whose family was of the military service gentry, passed most of his adult years as a conscientious and relatively successful civil servant in the Ukraine, the Volga region, and the Caucasus. Rostislav was not sent by his parents to

146

boarding schools in one of the capitals but received his education at home and at gymnasiums located in Ekaterinoslav and Odessa. When he was finally sent to a military school at St. Petersburg in 1837, at the age of thirteen, his stay there was of short duration. Eighteen months after his arrival in St. Petersburg, his tempestuous nature brought him into conflict with the disciplinarian regime of the school. He was expelled and dispatched to Tiraspol in the Ukraine as a cadet in the artillery. Several years later he resigned from the army because of his father's wish that he should enter the civil service. It was not, however, until 1847 that he was able to undertake a trip to St. Petersburg in the hope that he could make use of his family's connections to find a suitable position in the civil service. Luck was again against him in St. Petersburg, for he soon ran into trouble with the Third Section. This time his difficulties arose as a result of his efforts to help a nonpolitical Polish exile whom he had met in Saratov. These efforts took the form of describing his friend's predicament to influential acquaintances of the Fadeev family. D. V. Dubelt, the head of the Third Section, came to hear of these activities, and as a result, Rostislav Fadeev was exiled to Ekaterinoslav for having spread "unallowable gossip." In 1849 friends and his family managed to have him transferred to Tiflis, where his father was a high official in the local administration. In the following year he re-enlisted in the army, being appointed ensign in an artillery battery near the southern border of Daghestan. Here he participated in the final campaigns against Shamil. His service in the Caucasus continued until the mid-1860's. He no longer had difficulties with his superiors because he now enjoyed the support of powerful protectors, especially that of Prince A. I. Bariatinskii, a friend of his father and the commander-in-chief of the Russian army in the Caucasus. By 1864 Fadeev had been promoted to the rank of major general.[1]

The years Fadeev spent in the Caucasus greatly influenced the development of his ideas concerning Russian national policy. Thus he began his career as a military and political writer with a number of articles on the Caucasian wars, which were published in periodicals and in book form in the mid-1850's and during the 1860's.[2] Although primarily concerned in these articles with an analysis and description of the military events of the Caucasian wars, he also contrasted Islamic and Russian civilization and emphasized the importance of the Caucasus for Russia in her diplomatic rivalry with Western Europe. His contact with Mohammedan civilization and religion during these years served to strengthen his faith in Russia and in her mission in Asia. Above all, he regarded Islamic society to be hopelessly stagnant and backward, with little hope for regeneration. In central Asia and the Caucasus, Fadeev reasoned, the weaknesses of Islam clearly made it easy for foreigners to establish their control over the entire area. Russia therefore had to make every effort to maintain and improve her position in the Caucasus, which Fadeev described as both a bridge to Asia and a wall separating central Asia from the outside world.[3]

Fadeev's concern about the defense of Russia's southern frontier soon drew his attention to the general question of Russian military power. In 1867 he published a series of articles in the *Russian Messenger* (*Russkii Vestnik*) on "Russia's Armed Forces," the main point of which was that Russia's military system since Peter the Great had been an imitative one that was not based specifically on Russian needs and conditions. He admitted serfdom had prevented the Ministry of War prior to 1861 from fully utilizing Russia's military potential. But the emancipation of the serfs, he believed, had completely changed this situation. Now Russia could stop acting like a power with a limited 350,000,000-ruble budget, which was surpassed by the incomes of many other states, and begin to develop her army on the basis of a population of 80,000,000, which would place her in the number-one position among the great powers.[4]

Fadeev often stated that force was the final arbiter in deciding every question of international politics. He was considerably more consistent in applying this principle than Danilevskii had been in *Russia and Europe.* When Danilevskii consciously separated morality from politics, he did so in an effort to justify Russia's policies toward Poland. Usually he preferred to blur the distinction between morality and politics, implicitly assuming that whatever Russia did was necessarily moral and just and whatever her opponents did necessarily immoral and bad. Such simplistic reasoning was most apparent in Danilevskii's many vague words on the lofty and sacred aspirations of Slavdom as contrasted with the oppressive and aggressive intentions of the Western European powers toward the Slavs. Fadeev, on the other hand, was much less ambiguous in writing about the role of force in history and politics and thought it superfluous to seek moral justifications for the policies of a powerful state.[5] He had the utmost contempt for such notions as international rights and agreements. These, he averred, were all right for a small country like Switzerland. First-class powers, however, could not allow themselves to be bound by international conventions and treaties but had to depend on their own military strength as the only proper means of furthering their vital interests.[6] The great powers, he explained, were always in competition with one another for military and diplomatic supremacy. Formerly the first power in Western Europe had almost automatically occupied a position of world predominance. But the formation of two new continental nations, the United States and Russia, had changed all of this. Fadeev was convinced that the larger Western European states would soon realize that they were destined to become little more than Switzerlands, Venices, and Swedens in contrast to the increasingly powerful continental states to the east and west. He considered the interests of the United States and of Russia to be essentially compatible. In Europe Russia clearly was to play the leading role. Toward the end of the 1860's he came to interpret this role more and more in terms of the so-called Eastern question. Despite his renown as a Pan-Slavist, he definitely was not interested in allowing the Balkan Slavs to set up sovereign national states that would be fully independent of Russian control, commenting that there was little room in Europe for new small nations, each with its own army and ability to declare war and to make peace and alliances.[7]

The Eastern question was probably first called to Fadeev's attention while he was still in the Caucasus in the early 1860's by Ivan Aksakov's newspaper *Day*. Fadeev, however, had rather mixed feelings toward Slavophilism. In his first serious discussion of this subject in 1873, he condemned the Slavophiles for their utopianism but, at the same time, praised them for having reminded Russians of the importance of nationalism for Russian society.[8] Toward the end of the 1870's he adopted a more positive attitude toward Slavophilism, especially as a result of his appreciation of Ivan Aksakov's effective work as a leader of the Russian Pan-Slavic movement during the Balkan crisis. Between 1874 and 1882 Fadeev sent a number of cordial letters to Aksakov,[9] and at the beginning of the 1880's he marvelled in his *Letters on the Contemporary Situation in Russia* at how successful the Slavophiles had been in popularizing their ideas among a wide reading public in Russia.[10] Another Russian general who had been profoundly influenced by Ivan Aksakov's Pan-Slavic variety of journalism was Michael Grigorovich Cherniaev, who had acquired military fame in the Russian campaigns in central Asia during the 1860's. Like Fadeev, Cherniaev joined the St. Petersburg section of the Moscow Slavic Benevolent Committee. After Cherniaev founded the *Russian World* (*Russkii Mir*) in 1871, the two generals were closely associated because Fadeev became a regular contributor to Cherniaev's journal. They both took an active part in the efforts of the Russian Pan-Slavists to aid their "brother Slavs" during the Balkan crisis of 1875–78. In 1876 Cherniaev became the supreme commander of the Serbian army. Fadeev was only able to arrive in Serbia in 1877 and did not play any major role in the Balkan War. Before his arrival in Serbia he had attempted to cause difficulties for the Ottoman Empire by helping the Khedive of Egypt to organize the Egyptian army, which Fadeev hoped would be used against the Turks in conjunction with an uprising of the Balkan Slavs.[11] Nothing ever came of these schemes, but they illustrate the fantastic lengths to which Fadeev was willing to go in order to further what he considered the military interests of the Russian state.

Fadeev's first published thoughts on the Eastern question may be found toward the end of his series of articles on "Russia's Armed Forces," which was published in the *Russian Messenger* (*Russkii Vestnik*) in 1867. Elsewhere in these articles he had written that the European powers could never be dependable allies of Russia because of their fundamental hostility toward Russia, the Slavs, and the Orthodox religion.[12] In his discussion of the Eastern question, he warned his readers of Western European intrigues to turn the Balkan Slavs against Russia. If these intrigues were successful, he emphasized, a situation would be created that would be against the interests of Russia and of the Slavs in general.[13] He was particularly concerned about the possibility of the Germanization and Catholicization of the Slavs of Eastern Europe. For Fadeev such an eventuality was contrary to Russian interests, both politically and morally. Every great people, he wrote, needed a sympathetic atmosphere around itself. Only Russia was without it; yet the existence of a belt of powers related to Russia by blood and faith provided her with the natural elements for such a sympathetic atmosphere to a greater extent than was the case for any other major power.[14]

Fadeev treated the question of Russia's relations with her southern neighbors in greater detail in his *Opinion on the Eastern Question.* This work was first published serially in the *Stock Exchange News* (*Birzhevyia Vedomosti*) in 1869 and then as a ninety-eight page book in 1870. It appeared in the *Stock Exchange News* during the same year that Danilevskii's *Russia and Europe* made its appearance in Strakhov's *Dawn.* Not only did these two works appear during the same year, but there is also a striking similarity between the general outline of their proposed plans for the organization of a Slavic federation under Russian leadership. They also were in agreement concerning the inevitability of a military struggle between Russia and the Western European states over Eastern Europe. Yet there is no evidence that either of these two writers knew of the other's theories when he wrote his principal work on the Eastern question. The similarity of their ideas may be explained in light of the common inspiration they both undoubtedly found at that time in the many verbose and highly emotional discussions of Russia's importance for the future of the Slavs, which were being conducted by such Russian Pan-Slavic writers as Ivan Aksakov, Prince V. A. Cherkasskii, and Professors Orest Miller and V. I. Lamanskii. These discussions had reached a high point of intensity in connection with the Moscow Slav Congress of 1867.[15]

The principal difference between Fadeev's views and those of other Pan-Slavic thinkers is suggested by Orest Miller's reproach that Fadeev made no effort in his *Opinion on the Eastern Question* to explain the nature of the fundamental task of Slavdom in its struggle with the West.[16]

For most Pan-Slavic thinkers this task was understood in terms of a spiritual and intellectual struggle between two conflicting civilizations and cultural traditions—the older civilization of Western Europe as opposed to the newer and more vital one of the Slavic East. Fadeev shared few such Slavophile preconceptions. To the contrary, he viewed the impending struggle between the Slavs and the West primarily as a military one that could best be understood in terms of such factors as army organization, geographical location, and relative size of populations. Danilevskii, too, had written much about military struggle, but for him war was above all a means of stimulating the creative energies of the Slavs and of making possible future contributions on the part of the Slavic cultural-historical type to civilization. Fadeev was much more concrete and matter-of-fact in regard to war. War was an instrument of national policy that was to be used by a nation to assert its will in crucial areas of political rivalry with other nations. Eastern Europe was such an area. Therefore, in the final analysis, the Slavic question could only be decided by Russian military force, which was to be directed against the principal enemy of the Slavs, namely the Germans.[17]

Once the Slavic question was settled in accordance with the dictates of Russian military force, a new question naturally posed itself: what was to replace the control and predominant influence of the Austro-Germans in Eastern Europe? Fadeev was only willing to accept the idea of a Slavic federation as an answer to this question under certain given conditions. The most important of these was that Eastern Europe should be included within Russia's sphere of predominant influence. Fadeev was much less ambiguous on this particular point than Danilevskii had been in *Russia and Europe*. Where Danilevskii had merely suggested that the members of a Slavic federation would have to follow Russian leadership, Fadeev unequivocally stated that all questions pertaining to the diplomatic and military affairs of the federation would necessarily have to be decided by Russia. He even went so far as to write that the liberation of the Slavs and the formation of a Slavic federation without Russian participation would be worse than German control; for such a federation, being another Pan-Slavic Lithuania of the fourteenth century transposed into the nineteenth, would have a magnetic attraction for all of the non–Great-Russian peoples living within the frontiers of the Russian empire. Like Danilevskii, however, he was willing to permit the members of a Slavic federation formed under Russian leadership to keep their own political institutions and to control their own internal affairs.[18]

This concern about the vital interests of Russia as a great power was also Fadeev's point of departure in his published thoughts on Russian internal affairs. As a military man he naturally believed that Russia had to make full use of her human and material resources so that her military strength would become completely commensurate with her geographical size and population. He soon, however, came to realize that military strength was not dependent on material considerations alone but also on moral ones. For one thing, an army needed popular support. In Russia the censorship of Nicholas I had precluded the possibility of such support prior to 1855. Fadeev himself had been prevented by Russian censors in 1854 from publishing an article on the Caucasian theater of operations of the Crimean War. But even after censorship regulations had been relaxed in the late 1850's, Fadeev found that the Russian public was too badly informed about the Caucasus and military affairs in general to give the army the sort of moral support that it deserved. These reflections caused him to contrast Russia unfavorably with France, where there was a lively and intelligent interest in military affairs.[19] The support that informed public opinion gave to the army in countries such as France, Prussia, and England, he emphasized, was an important source of national strength. In Russia, on the other hand, the reading public usually was disinterested in military affairs and underestimated Russia's military power, which, in Fadeev's opinion, weakened Russia.[20]

During the 1860's Fadeev came to associate the problem of developing a public opinion in Russia informed about military affairs with the task of basing Russian political, cultural, and social life on a firm foundation of Russian nationality. The Slavophiles very likely influenced the development of his thinking on Russian nationality. At a later date he gave them credit for having been the first ones to call the attention of Russian society to the need of terminating the educational and imitative period of Russian history.[21] This same point, without any specific mention of the Slavophiles, had been the main theme of Fadeev's series of articles in 1867 on "Russia's Armed Forces." By the time he wrote these articles, he believed that any successful and viable society had to be based on one dominant nationality. A few years before, in his *Caucasian Letters* of 1864–65, he had been contemptuous of Moslem society because it transcended nationality.[22] In 1867 he was equally disdainful of the military caliber of the Austrian army because of its multinational composition.[23] In contrast to the Moslem world and Austria, he cited England, France, and Prussia as countries whose national spirit had greatly contributed to making them militarily strong.[24] A great people, he explained, had to have faith in itself, in its own fundamental ideas and aspirations.[25]

The specific nature of Russia's fundamental ideas and aspirations was never spelled out by Fadeev. Whenever he did develop his ideas on this subject, the influence of the historicist thinking of Russian conservative nationalists, especially the Slavophiles, is unmistakable, although he hardly ever bothered to identify his sources of intellectual inspiration. Thus he conceived of Russia as having a distinct historical individuality which sharply set her apart from the other nations of Europe.[26] He proclaimed that it was high time for Russians to take a more independent attitude in the realization that a nation of 80,000,000 inhabitants could only flourish in nineteenth-century Europe if its society were based on its own intellectual traditions and nationality.[27] Like Danilevskii, the *pochvenniki*, and the Slavophiles, he spoke of a Russian form of government, religion, social organization, and way of life and described it as being intrinsically different from Western European civilization.[28] Like Danilevskii and Strakhov, he sought the roots of Russian nihilism in Western Europe and asserted that its presence in Russia was the result of European influences.[29] His general emphasis on the need to end the St. Petersburg educational period of Russian history was, of course, completely in keeping with Slavophile ideas.

Fadeev's version of Russian conservatism was also closely related to that of the *pochvenniki*, Danilevskii, and the Slavophiles. Thus he spoke of the need for conservatives in Russia to preserve the basic principles of Russian society: the Orthodox faith, the unity of state, Russian nationality, and the "historical supreme power."[30] He considered the existence of "firm authority" to be particularly fortunate for Russia. He regretted, however, that this satisfactory state of affairs in Russia was restricted to the government and did not extend to Russian society, which was almost completely lacking in cohesion, common ideas, and ideals.[31] One example Fadeev used to illustrate this lack of cohesion should have particularly pleased Samarin. A Russian taking an eight-hour steamboat trip between Pskov and Dorpat, Fadeev pointed out, would not even be able to ask for a glass of water or some bread in his own language once he arrived in Dorpat; yet this town had been within the Russian empire for more than a century. This illustrated, Fadeev concluded, Russia's lack of an inner moral and cultural unity, which a great nation needed in order to win over and assimilate the alien elements contained within itself.[32]

Russian literature and journalism, according to Fadeev, had done little to give Russian society a connecting tie and direction and to provide positive leadership for Russian public opinion. He conceded that the periodic press had gained some influence over society during the 1860's but described this influence as being negative and of little lasting value. He was particularly contemptuous of the radical journals, which he dismissed as being designed for the immature minds of gymnasium students.[33] The numerous terroristic acts committed by young Russian revolutionists toward the end of the 1870's made it impossible for Fadeev to deny the considerable success of radical journalists in influencing young minds in St. Petersburg and Moscow. But he continued to regard the revolutionary movement in Russia as a purely artificial phenomenon that enjoyed no support whatsoever from the mass of the Russian people. He also insisted that educated Russians had relatively little sympathy for the revolutionists. Whatever success the revolutionists had had in causing confusion in Russian society, he argued, was to be attributed to the ineffectual policies of the St. Petersburg bureaucracy and to the artificial obstacles that had been placed in the way of the loyal majority of educated Russians who wanted to assist the government in combating its enemies. Hence the principal task confronting Russia toward the end of the reign of Alexander II was to introduce new reforms that would permit educated Russians to cooperate with the government in putting an end to the prevalent state of confusion in Russian society.[34]

It had been precisely the plans of Fadeev for the reform of Russian society that had alarmed Iurii Samarin in 1875, when he and F. Dmitriev published their *Revolutionary Conservatism* at Berlin. Fadeev's uncomplimentary remarks about the Slavophiles in his essays of 1872 in the *Russian World* had also displeased Samarin. Despite his gradual acceptance of many aspects of the Slavophile analysis of the ills of Russian society, Fadeev always strongly disapproved of the Slavophiles' deification of the Russian people and of their naïve belief in the Russian people's ability to realize the most ambitious national and spiritual goals almost entirely unassisted by the government.[35] Fadeev's own presuppositions and basic objectives were much more concrete and realistic. Above all, he was determined that the internal unity of Russian society should serve as a source of strength for Russia in her external relations with other great powers. In order to further this end, Fadeev wanted to make use of existing social forces in Russian society as a means of developing within it cohesion and effective intellectual and moral leadership. This emphasis on the need for using existing social forces turned Fadeev's attention to the importance of the gentry in Russian society. As late as the 1870's the gentry was still probably the one group in Russia that possessed the educational qualifications and the administrative and political experience required for a role of social and political leadership. Indeed, Fadeev not only noted the importance of the gentry's leadership in Russian society but also described this leadership as being the one logical point of departure for the future reform and development of the Russian nation.[36] Such a recommendation hardly did justice to the increasing importance of the bourgeoisie and the professional intelligentsia in Russian life. It also tended to strengthen the hand of an influential and power-hungry clique among the Russian gentry, which hoped to gain control of Russian society.

It was against the danger of such an aristocratic reaction that Iurii Samarin had warned so eloquently in 1875.

Despite the obvious dangers inherent in Fadeev's argumentation, the political realities of Russian life corresponded, in many ways, more to his proposals than to the Slavophile theories of Samarin. Samarin, like the *pochvenniki*, wanted a nationally awakened Russian intelligentsia that would merge itself into some sort of unity with the tsar and the mass of the Russian people. Within this unity the actual roles of the bureaucracy and the powerful gentry were rather ill-defined. Samarin believed that all initiative and authority had to be concentrated in the hands of the tsar, but he gave little thought to the problem of how the government was to make effective use of the talents of the educated in any nationally-oriented Russian society of the future. Fadeev's service was to concern himself with this very problem.

For Fadeev, the major obstacle to the Russian government's making good use of the talents of educated Russians was the influence that bureaucrats had gained over Russian society. Like Katkov and Ivan Aksakov, Fadeev attributed much of the relative success of nihilism in Russia to the liberal sympathies, incompetence, and lack of practical experience of so many high officials in the bureaucracy.[37] Fadeev's own thinking, however, was in many ways much closer to the mentality of St. Petersburg bureaucrats than to the Moscow Slavophiles. Nevertheless, he repeated the Slavophiles' indictment of St. Petersburg as the non-Russian city of a mechanical administration, which had been imported into Russia from Western Europe. The artificial relationship between people and government resulting from this importation, Fadeev argued, greatly weakened the close ties between tsar and people in Russia and the unquestioning faith of the Russian people in the benevolence of the "supreme power."[38] Fadeev was not willing to go as far as the Slavophiles in denying the necessity of the Petrine period as a stage in Russian historical development. He felt, however, that this stage had already outlived its purpose and usefulness[39] and that its continuance could only have a detrimental effect on Russia's further development. He criticized the St. Petersburg bureaucracy's formal and mechanical view of things, claiming that this outlook paralyzed the initiative of people with independent judgment and practical experience.[40] Thus the bureaucracy used the censorship as a means of silencing honest and loyal Russian subjects, whose criticisms were construed by the bureaucracy as threats to some of its own official rights and prerogatives.[41] Indeed, during the 1860's the bureaucrats had been considerably more tolerant of the destructive teachings of the nihilists than they had been of the nationalistic and conservative ones of the Slavophiles.[42]

The bureaucrats' influence, Fadeev found, was equally negative in regard to local government, the church, and the army in Russia. In local government their control of practically all the important positions prevented the gentry from effectively taking leadership in local affairs; in regard to the church, they had stifled religious life in Russia by making the church a branch of the St. Petersburg bureaucracy;[43] and they had filled the army with non-gentry officials who were no longer able to command the respect of the common soldier. These officials were given high military rank but had little of the dignity and self-assurance of the old Russian officer class. According to Fadeev, their increasingly predominant influence over army affairs had destroyed the former organic organizational unity of the Russian army and discouraged the best and most able representatives of the Russian gentry from becoming career officers.[44]

Fadeev's proposals for the reform of Russian society followed logically from his diagnosis of its shortcomings. First, the bureaucracy had to be cut down in size and influence and its leadership in Russian society had to be replaced with that of the Russian gentry. Such a recommendation, he insisted, was completely in keeping with national tradition. Russia had always been a true people's monarchy whose rulers dispassionately and benevolently looked out for the interests of all their subjects. Thus, Fadeev optimistically predicted that class struggle never could occur in Russian society. Contrary to the situation in Western Europe, there was little place in Russia for castes to develop. The Russian gentry was of the same blood and outlook as the mass of the Russian people and, again unlike the European nobility, did not owe its position in society to some sort of conquest in the dim and distant historical past. Hence the gentry in Russia was merely that part of the Russian people which had been selected by the tsar for governmental service. In other words, the historical role of the gentry in Russian society was to serve as an instrument for the carrying out of the policies of the tsar's government. During the St. Petersburg period of Russian history, the bureaucracy had tended to prevent the gentry from fulfilling the obligations of duty and service they owed traditionally to their country and sovereign. Now, Fadeev admonished, it was urgent for the government to allow the gentry to resume their former position in Russian society as its major instrument in developing civic life and defending public order.[45]

The government therefore needed to continue the work of reform in Russia by gradually allowing the gentry to establish its predominant influence over zemstvo affairs, the local administration, and the army. The practical experience of the gentry on the local level, he explained, would prove invaluable to the government in implementing its policies. The central government, however, was to maintain its prerogatives of political leadership and policy formulation in Fadeev's scheme of things. Thus he did not advocate that the gentry should control the central and provincial administrations. On the provincial level, he felt that the governor and his staff should consult the provincial gentry regarding matters of mutual interest. But he wanted the provincial administration to be controlled by the central government and not by the local gentry. In the early 1870's, he saw no pressing need for the summoning of national conferences of the zemstvos to advise the central government concerning the current crisis of Russian society. Shortly before 1880, however, he changed his mind and recommended that the government should again (as it had once before done in the late 1850's) permit the gentry to send elected representatives to provincial committees. These were to have the task of considering measures to combat the revolutionary movement and to improve the social and economic position of the mass of the Russian peasantry.[46] Around 1880 Fadeev was not alone in making such a recommendation. During these years such figures as P. A. Valuev, Loris-Melikov, Ivan Aksakov, and Count N. P. Ignatiev also urged the summoning of one form or another of consultive assembly to assist the government in coping with the current problems and ailments of Russian society.

The Russian hereditary gentry were not to have exclusive control over Fadeev's ideal society. Their predominant position in this society was justified purely in terms of their long-established tradition of state service. He was quite ready to concede that numerous individuals from the non-gentry strata of the Russian population were highly useful subjects of the tsar. Thus he strongly favored making access to the gentry easier for wealthy merchants. Wealth, however, was not to be the only criterion for admission into the gentry. Fadeev also recommended that scholars, writers, and other professional people should be made "personal" gentry (and under certain circumstances even hereditary gentry) as a form of reward for outstanding achievements and services to society. He considered education an important prerequisite for admission into the gentry but was very much against classifying all people with a completed university education as gentry.[47] Here Fadeev undoubtedly had in mind the many university-educated members of the radical intelligentsia whose parents had belonged to the clergy, lower middle class, or even the peasantry. Such people obviously were not to be included in Fadeev's Russian elite, which was to be similar to England's peerage with its nucleus of hereditary nobles supplemented by select elements from the professions and the business world.

Education was to play a vital role in Fadeev's Russian society of the future. In the past, Fadeev wrote, the Russian government had made the mistake of imitating the educational policies of China instead of those of

Western Europe; Russia had placed much more emphasis on teaching higher knowledge (analogous to the Chinese emphasis on the philosophy of Confucius) than on teaching the practical trades, arts, and sciences. Thus in Russia there were hardly any intermediate educational levels between an intensive classical education and complete illiteracy. In Europe the contrary was the case. Here there were a number of technological and practical schools for every secondary school and institution of higher learning. Russia, for the sake of her own stability and social development, Fadeev argued, clearly needed to follow Europe's example. Indeed, the excesses of the Russian nihilists, who were to a large extent of common origin and had been university trained, were for Fadeev an unmistakable demonstration of the folly of Russia's having followed in China's footsteps. Accordingly, he advocated that education should be further developed in Russia but that everyone should not receive the same education. Thus literacy was the proper goal in educating the mass of the peasantry. In addition to reading and writing, only technological and practical skills were to be taught to the lower middle class and workers. Higher education was to be used chiefly as a means of developing the intellectual independence and cultural cohesion of the Russian gentry. Hence almost all gymnasium and university scholarships at the disposal of the government were to be reserved for children of the poorer members of the hereditary gentry. A small number of such scholarships, he was willing to concede, properly should go to unusually gifted pupils from the lower strata of the population. He also favored giving somewhat preferential treatment to children of priests in regard to scholarships and higher education. He felt that the priests in Russia should be brought closer to the hereditary gentry and that a clear distinction should be made between the children of priests and those of sextons, sacristans, and other church assistants.[48]

Even with such reorganization of Russian education and society, there was still another obstacle in the way of the Russian gentry's playing an effective role of leadership: namely, the restrictions imposed by bureaucratic censorship. Fadeev believed that the existing censorship regulations had served mainly to prevent the best elements in the gentry from assisting the government to develop the social and intellectual cohesion of Russian society.[49] He therefore proposed that the government should permit the zemstvos to publish their own newspapers and also allow well-meaning people to discuss political and religious questions without censorship control. He did not want to abolish censorship altogether, but he was convinced that Russian public life had to be freed of the bureaucratic arbitrariness of the existing censorship practices.[50]

Throughout Fadeev's writings concerning the political and social reorganization of Russia there is the underlying assumption that the gentry represented a creative minority that was capable of providing Russian society with leadership and unifying cultural and national ideals. He realized, however, that in the past the Russian gentry had not been too successful in performing the tasks he assigned to it and that it was still far from being a homogeneous cultured elite.[51] The relative ineffectiveness of the Russian gentry in the past he attributed to the negative influence of the St. Petersburg bureaucracy. Yet there was little in Fadeev's writings that could demonstrate that the gentry was ready to offer Russia creative leadership. Many of his recommendations, in fact, seem bizarre in view of the social and political realities of mid-nineteenth-century Russia. His recommendation, for example, that the predominant influence of the gentry should be assured in local politics, high government offices, and the army would seem superfluous considering the almost exclusive control they already exercised over all phases of Russian life. After all, there were few important branches of the St. Petersburg bureaucracy that were not headed by members of the hereditary Russian gentry. There was good reason for recommending, as Fadeev did,[52] the strengthening of zemstvo institutions of self-government. But why demand that these institutions should be under the control of the gentry? They already were under such control, even though the overwhelming majority of the local gentry apparently were completely uninterested in zemstvo affairs and took no part in them.[53] What reason was there to believe that the Russian gentry was capable of providing Russia with unifying cultural and national ideals? By Fadeev's own admission, Russian gentry society still was internally divided and still lacked social and cultural cohesion. Accordingly, Fadeev was certainly optimistic and even utopian in assuming that the gentry could serve as the main source of unifying social and cultural ideas and of public-spirited leadership in the Russian society of the future. As Samarin wrote in 1875, Fadeev dreamed of an ideal gentry that had no precedent in world history.[54] Inasmuch as Fadeev did not alter his presuppositions before he died in 1883, his unjustified and undemonstrated assumptions concerning the virtues of the Russian gentry can be considered a fundamental weakness underlying all of his proposals for the reform and reorganization of Russian society.

Fadeev's amoral political realism was another good reason for his contemporaries to be suspicious and skeptical in regard to his plans for the future of Russia. He clearly was determined to avoid what he considered the Slavophile error of believing that the Russian people could realize lofty national goals with almost no reference to existing political forces and institutions. Fadeev's own plans for the future were solidly based on the powerful social, economic, and political position of the gentry in Russian life and on the support of influential friends and contacts in the army and government. His supporters included such people as Field Marshall and Prince A. I. Bariatinskii, Loris-Melikov, Count P. A. Shuvalov (chief of the Russian gendarmes during the 1870's), General M. G. Cherniaev, and Count I. I. Vorontsov-Dashkov (a high official at the court who was the organizer of the counterrevolutionary Holy Brotherhood [*Sviashchennaia Druzhina*] of 1881–82).[55] Fadeev was not always too particular in his choice of political and intellectual allies. In the late 1860's, for example, he became a frequent contributor to the newspaper *News (Vest')*,[56] which was notorious for its outspoken espousal of the cause of aristocratic reaction in Russia. In 1874 Fadeev openly acknowledged the similarity of his own program for the reform of Russia to that of the editor of the journal *Citizen (Grazhdanin)*, Prince V. P. Meshcherskii. There was, of course, no way for Fadeev to know in the mid-1870's that Meshcherskii would subsequently acquire a most unsavory reputation as a sexual deviate, court intriguer, and yellow journalist. Fadeev's own comments concerning Meshcherskii's conception of the Russian gentry indicate, however, that Fadeev was quite aware of Meshcherskii's intellectual mediocrity and superficiality.[57] Political opportunism undoubtedly prompted Fadeev to accept Meshcherskii publicly as a fellow champion of the cause of the gentry in Russia.

Perhaps the best example of Fadeev's political opportunism is his *volte-face* of 1876 in regard to the military reforms of D. A. Miliutin. Between 1868 and 1876 Fadeev had persistently and bitterly opposed Miliutin's reforms in a series of articles that appeared in newspapers and journals as well as in book form. In 1876, however, Fadeev hoped to be accepted again for active service in the army (he had been obliged to resign in the late 1860's because of his opposition to Miliutin's reforms) and to be used as a military adviser to the Slavic insurgents in either Bulgaria or Montenegro. But such hopes could scarcely be realized without Miliutin's support. Hence Fadeev ostensibly changed his views on the subject of military reform in Russia and told Miliutin that he now was in favor of the reforms the Ministry of War had introduced in the early 1870's. Miliutin was not at all impressed by Fadeev's alleged change of heart and noted in his diary: "I always had a low opinion of the moral qualities of this chatter-box and intriguer; however, I did not expect that he could disavow everything he had stood for previously with such cynicism."[58] It is interesting to note that Ivan Aksakov and other Pan-Slavist leaders also did not favor Fadeev's designs of 1876. Indeed, they specifically requested that Miliutin should not assign any military duties to Fadeev in the Balkans.[59]

Some of the details of the story of Fadeev's opposition to the reform plans of the Ministry of War between 1868 and 1876 also cast much light on the nature of his activities as a public figure and intellectual leader in Russia. When Fadeev first published his essays on "Russia's Armed Forces" in the *Russian Messenger* during 1867,[60] he still generally favored Miliutin's proposed reforms. Yet, when these same essays were republished in book form in 1868, positive references to Miliutin's reforms were deleted and negative ones introduced.[61] The circumstances and considerations that apparently persuaded him to make these textual revisions cause one to be suspicious of Fadeev's motives.

In the introduction to his book, Fadeev explained these textual changes as being a response to the criticisms high-ranking military figures had privately made of his evaluation of Russia's military problems.[62] Especially important in this connection was Prince Bariatinskii, under whom both Miliutin and Fadeev had served in the Caucasus. Bariatinskii was a good friend of Fadeev's family and had done much to further his military career. Thus it is reasonable to assume that Fadeev accepted Bariatinskii's views on important military issues in the expectation that this would help keep him in Bariatinskii's good graces. At any rate, it is clear that Fadeev was in particularly close contact with Bariatinskii during 1867–68.[63] At the time, Bariatinskii was very much disturbed by Miliutin's insistence that all branches of the army, including the chief of staff, should be strictly subordinated to the control of the Ministry of War. Miliutin's justification for such control was that it would increase the efficiency of the Russian army. Since Bariatinskii then aspired to become chief of staff of the Russian army, he understandably rejected any reform that would place this position under the direct control of the Ministry of War. He opposed such an innovation on the ground that it would undermine the *esprit de corps* of the army. Hence he broke with his former subordinate, Miliutin, and became one of the central figures in the agitation against Miliutin's military reforms.[64]

Another close associate of Fadeev who figured prominently in the agitation against Miliutin was General M. G. Cherniaev. During the 1860's Cherniaev had been one of the principal architects of Russian expansion into central Asia. This expansion had not been carefully planned, but was more the result of the initiative of local commanders like Cherniaev than of the Ministry of War. Miliutin was determined to change this situation. In 1867 he had Cherniaev recalled and placed on leave for having captured Tashkent contrary to orders.[65] Cherniaev never forgave Miliutin for this affront and thereafter attempted to gain revenge by systematically opposing Miliutin's reforms as the editor of the journal *Russian World (Russkii Mir)*.[66] Fadeev, being an unusually intelligent and effective polemicist, was of great assistance to Cherniaev in this endeavor.

In addition to sending a large number of anti-Miliutin memoranda to influential governmental figures, Fadeev participated publicly in the crusade against Miliutin by contributing a series of incisive and well-argued articles to Cherniaev's journal. In 1873 these articles were published in book form under the title *Our Military Question*.[67]

After the official acceptance of Miliutin's reforms in 1874, however, there was little reason for Fadeev to continue his opposition to the Ministry of War. Thus his interest in internal Russian military reforms gradually receded into the background, while plans for aristocratic reform inside of Russia and for the liberation of the Balkan Slavs came to be the guiding motifs of his intellectual and practical activities. Accordingly, it was not difficult for him to assure Miliutin that he no longer opposed the Ministry of War's reforms. This assurance may even have been given in good faith. In any case, Fadeev again clearly had an ulterior purpose in mind—to gain Miliutin's support for his own ambitious projects in the Balkans.

Fadeev's participation in the intrigues of Bariatinskii and Cherniaev against Miliutin indicates how far removed he was from Slavophile idealism in regard to internal Russian politics and Russian nationalism. The historical, national, and social ideas that he had borrowed from the Slavophiles and other historicist writers were shorn of their original spiritual and cultural meaning and used as a means of defending the rights and prerogatives of vested interests inside of Russia as well as the external power interests of the tsarist state in Asia and Europe. It cannot even be said that Fadeev really was an enemy of the bureaucracy, as such, in Russia. His main target was not the bureaucracy as an institution but rather certain individuals within it. Accordingly, he wanted Miliutin and his supporters in the Ministry of War replaced by Bariatinskiis, Cherniaevs, and Fadeevs; and the increasing number of commoners (*raznochintsy*) in the other ministries at St. Petersburg, by bureaucrats from the hereditary gentry. His writings were therefore to a large extent in keeping with the reactionary counterreforms advocated by Katkov and Pazukhin and introduced and implemented by Dmitrii Tolstoi and other bureaucrats of gentry origin during the 1880's. Fadeev's failing health during the years preceding his death in 1883 did not permit him to take any active part in the aristocratic reaction of the era of Alexander III. His published works, however, provided the advocates of counterreform with many forceful and convenient arguments. Hence Fadeev, like Ivan Aksakov, contributed at least indirectly to the victory of Katkov, Pobedonostsev, and Dmitrii Tolstoi over Loris-Melikov and other advocates of moderate reforms in 1881. Since Loris-Melikov was a good friend and even close associate of Fadeev, it is unlikely that the latter was overly pleased about Loris-Melikov's defeat. But it is hardly possible to excuse Fadeev, as one could

Aksakov, on the ground that he was a confused political idealist. This he never was.

Fadeev's role in corrupting conservative and nationalistic ideals in Russia can be viewed as the natural reaction of an intelligent representative of the Russian military service gentry to the rapid and confusing intellectual and social changes of the 1860's and 1870's. In many ways, his place in this process can be considered a peripheral one, for he had little contact during his lifetime with the intellectual circles of St. Petersburg and Moscow. This lack of personal contact made it unlikely that he would share the cultural and intellectual attitudes of the Aksakovs, Danilevskiis, Grigor'evs, and Strakhovs of the two Russian capitals. Nonetheless, the particular use he made of many of the ideas of these and other figures on the Russian intellectual scene was not entirely fortuitous and incidental. In the final analysis, his interpretations of Russian affairs were reconcilable with the main outlines of the theories of such thinkers as Ivan Aksakov and Danilevskii. Moreover, the most significant interpreter and follower of Danilevskii, namely Constantine Leont'ev, came to conclusions that were largely in agreement with and in confirmation of Fadeev's.

CHAPTER TWELVE

Byzantinism

==

ALTHOUGH Constantine Leont'ev, born in 1831, was only three years younger than Strakhov, he belonged intellectually to another generation. The difference in intellectual attitude between Leont'ev and Strakhov and the other *pochvenniki* is certainly not to be seen in terms of differing cultural backgrounds, for Leont'ev belonged to the same Muscovite intellectual world as the *pochvenniki,* Slavophiles, and Westerners. It is clear from his own reminiscences that during the 1850's and early 1860's he shared the liberal and humanitarian idealism of most of his contemporaries. Thus he favored reforms and emancipation for Russian society, admired the virtues and religious experience of the Russian peasant, and romantically exaggerated the prospects of close friendship and understanding between Russia and the Balkan Slavs. As a medical student and author of novels in Moscow, he was often in the company of such Westerners as Turgenev, whom he knew particularly well, Granovskii, Katkov, and V. P. Botkin. He also made the acquaintance of Khomiakov, Pogodin, and such *pochvenniki* as Strakhov and Dmitrii Averkiev. He apparently always had reservations concerning the views of the Slavophiles and the *pochvenniki* but was, at the same time, attracted by their emphasis on the need for an original and national Russian culture. In many ways, his view of life was particularly close to that of Apollon Grigor'ev. Like Grigor'ev, he viewed life as an esthetic and organic process which was the expression of the national and historic existence of a people. Undoubtedly because of the natural affinity of their views, Leont'ev esteemed Grigor'ev very highly and ranked him above Belinskii as a Russian literary critic.[1]

However, Leont'ev had ceased to be an integral part of the Moscow and St. Petersburg intellectual world before chronic alcoholism prematurely ended Apollon Grigor'ev's career as a critic. In 1862 pecuniary diffi-

164

culties obliged Leont'ev to give up his attempts to live as an independent writer and novelist and to embark on a career as a civil servant in the Asian Department of the Ministry of Foreign Affairs. In 1863 the department sent him to the Balkans, where he served in a number of posts during the following decade. In the Balkans, to be sure, he still had indirect contact with the intellectual world of the two Russian capitals through the various literary, historical, scientific, and political journals and newspapers that were sent to him. He also continued to write fiction and essays for publication in Russia. Nonetheless, his decade in the Balkans clearly cut off his day-to-day and personal contacts with the leading figures and currents of Russian intellectual life. Consequently, he increasingly became a stranger among Russian intellectuals. He was first of all estranged from the liberals among the Westerners. Leont'ev rejected their ideas as early as 1862 as a result of the same student and revolutionary disturbances in St. Petersburg that had shocked so many other Russian conservatives at the time. His contact with Bulgarian and Greek liberals in the Balkans only increased his aversion to the defenders of progress and reform in Russia.[2]

But this estrangement from the Russian intellectual scene was not confined to the liberal and radical segments of the intelligentsia. Because of his experiences in the Balkans Leont'ev also became more and more critical of the Slavophiles. What he saw of the Slavic bourgeoisie of the peninsula soon convinced him that Balkan intellectual leaders had little desire to turn to Russia for leadership and inspiration but preferred to reproduce in the Balkans miniature replicas of the liberal-egalitarian society of nineteenth-century Europe. Accordingly, he could only regard the Pan-Slavism of Ivan Aksakov, Danilevskii, and other leaders of the Slavic benevolent committees as based on an untenable and overly optimistic faith in the Balkan Slavs' love and veneration for Russia and the Russian way of life.[3] At a later date, Leont'ev's differences with the Pan-Slavists and the Slavophiles were further accentuated. Above all, he had increasing reservations concerning their favorable attitude toward the reforms of Alexander II. He felt that this attitude greatly detracted from the positive contribution they had made to Russian intellectual life by emphasizing the need for the spiritual and cultural separation of Russia from the West.[4] Toward the end of his life, he even began to doubt the possibility of Russia's ever being able to bring into existence a new civilization that would be both distinct and separate from that of Western Europe.

This further accentuation of the differences between Leont'ev and the other Russian conservative nationalists took place only after he returned to Russia from the Balkans in the mid-1870's. Nevertheless, his Balkan stay was the crucial experience that first separated him spiritually from his contemporaries and enabled him to view the issues and problems of Russian life from a fresh perspective. When he returned to Russia, he, as it were, belonged to another generation. Like a member of a younger generation, he accepted many of the ideas and concepts of the intellectual leaders in Russia at the time to whom he was attracted in one way or another; but he did so with independence of judgment and with little evidence of complete emotional commitment to any school of thought.

Danilevskii's theory of cultural-historical types influenced Leont'ev's thinking during the last two decades of his life more than any other system of ideas developed in nineteenth-century Russia. He had already been prepared for an organic view of historical development before the appearance of *Russia and Europe* in 1869 through his personal and literary contacts with the Slavophiles and the *pochvenniki* during the 1850's and early 1860's. Also, Leont'ev's earlier medical and scientific studies predisposed him to such an approach in examining society and history. It is hardly coincidental that three such outspoken advocates of the theory of organic historical and social development as Danilevskii, Strakhov, and Leont'ev were students of the biological sciences during their formative university years. Leont'ev suggested the importance of his own scientific studies on his development as a thinker in the following words:

> My mind, having been educated from the time of my youth in the spirit of medical empiricism and the impassivity of the natural sciences, was inclined to examine both the entire historical evolution of mankind and, especially, our Russian interests in the East from the standpoint of a particular natural-historical hypothesis, i.e. of the three-in-one process of development which ends shortly before death in confusion and dissolution. . . .[5]

But whatever the importance of Leont'ev's grounding in the medical and natural sciences for the forming of his basic attitudes toward life, it is clear that he was heavily indebted to Danilevskii for his basic philosophy and conception of social and cultural development.

Following the example of Danilevskii, Leont'ev likened the development of nations and societies to the organic growth of plants and animals.[6] Thus nations and societies developed organically in history and invariably passed through the successive stages of "(1) primary simplicity, (2) flowering complexity, and (3) secondary, confused simplicity."[7] Each historical entity, he wrote in the spirit of *Russia and Europe*, had its own individual civilization or culture and its own complicated system of religious, political, moral, and philosophical ideas and principles that had been gradually worked out in the course of its historical development.[8] Leont'ev's theory postulated that historical-cultural entities had a life expectancy of between one thousand and twelve hundred years.[9] Western Europe, in his opinion, was at that time more than one thousand years old and therefore in her final stage of "secondary, confused simplicity." He therefore felt that the period of great cultural achievement for European civilization (which he considered superior to all other civilizations of the past in terms of its cultural accomplishments) was over and that a new period of decline was in the offing for the European West. He saw this decline in Europe's increasing acceptance of the ideas of egalitarianism, material well-being, and democratic progress. He was convinced that similar ideas had characterized the final stage of decline and dissolution of all historical civilizations. Again like Danilevskii, he hoped that Russia and the Orthodox peoples of the Balkans would not be swept into the vortex of general decline and disintegration in Europe. Instead, Russia and the Orthodox peoples of the Balkans were to provide the world with a new Eastern European civilization that would fill the vacuum left by a declining West.[10]

The differences separating Leont'ev from Danilevskii and other conservative nationalists were just as striking as the similarities that linked him to them. For one thing, Leont'ev was the first Russian conservative thinker who fully realized the inherent difficulty involved in any attempt to combine modern nationalism with traditional Eastern European and Muscovite civilization. Modern nationalism for Leont'ev was closely associated with the advance of technology, material progress, the democratization of society, liberalism, and various other changes in the intellectual orientation of society arising out of the French Revolution. He also understood what a threat the social and ideological forces at work in nineteenth-century Europe represented for traditional Russian civilization. It was precisely for this reason that he was so critical of the Slavophiles, the *pochvenniki,* and Danilevskii as advocates of the emancipation and reform of society, the education of the masses, and the liberation of the Balkan Slavs from the yoke of the Turks. He especially reproached them for failing to understand that many of their romantic and humanitarian social ideals were incompatible with their professed faith in autocracy and Orthodoxy as the main pillars of traditional society in Russia.[11]

In many ways, Leont'ev's attitude toward other Russian conservative nationalists resembled that of Rostislav Fadeev. Fadeev, too, criticized the Slavophiles for their liberalism and their deification of the Russian people. Like Leont'ev, Fadeev affirmed the need for force and realism in politics and for the predominance and leadership of the service gentry in Russian society. But Fadeev differed from Leont'ev in his attraction to the ideal of national emancipation for the Balkan Slavs. In addition, Fadeev was greatly impressed by the technology and educational systems of the modern national states of Western Europe. Thus he favored at least literacy for the common people and technological and practical education for the middle strata of the population as a means of strengthening the Russian state. His implicit assumption in this recommendation was, of course, that European technology could be separated from European liberalism, socialism, and philosophy. This was an assumption that Leont'ev refused to make.[12] Leont'ev's rejection of modern European civilization was therefore more fundamental than that of Fadeev or perhaps any other nineteenth-century Russian thinker.

Leont'ev's rejection of European ideas included even the notion of nationalism itself as it was commonly understood in Russia and elsewhere in nineteenth-century Europe. He did not, however, object to cultural nationalism as such. Indeed, at times he expressed almost Slavophile or *pochvennik* sentiments concerning the Russian peasant, monk, and merchant as true representatives of Russian national character. He even urged the Europeanized Russian gentry of his time to imitate the peasants' national style of life.[13] But he did not want the gentry to humble themselves in the presence of the peasants by treating them as equals or accepting popular religious practices and attitudes that offended the critical intelligence of an educated person.[14] He was most emphatic in his disapproval of the egalitarian and liberal nationalism he had encountered in Bulgaria and other parts of the Balkans. In the thinking of Balkan (and also Russian) nationalists he detected a state of mind receptive to the cosmopolitan, democratizing, and emancipatory policies advocated by Napoleon III, Gambetta, Cavour, and other champions of political nationalism in Western Europe. He was convinced that such policies could only produce a destructive leveling of all ranks, classes, and regions within a national society, the result of which could only be confusion and drab uniformity.[15]

In Russia the worst offenders in this respect were, in Leont'ev's opinion, the Pan-Slavists and Russifiers. In contrast to most other Russian conservative nationalists, Leont'ev identified himself with Nicholas I's dynastic interpretation of nationality and Russian foreign policy. Thus he criticized Russian foreign policy after the Crimean War for having been too liberal, too emancipatory, and too pro-Slav.[16] He approved of Nicholas I's reluctance to support Orthodox Christians in any revolt against the legal and legitimate authority of the sultan.[17] For Leont'ev Pan-Slavism was an ideal of modern European inspiration that could only serve to bring Russia into closer contact with the Europeanized Slavic intelligentsia of the Balkans, thereby increasing the influence of European liberal and revolutionary principles in Russia.[18]

The advocates of the Russification of Russia's borderlands, he thought, were also unwitting instruments of Europeanization in Russia. Leont'ev, of course, highly appreciated the patriotic sentiments and intentions of the defenders of alleged Russian interests in Poland, the Baltic region, and elsewhere in the tsarist empire. But he deplored their failure to understand the importance of every conservative religious tradition (whether Catholicism, Protestantism, Buddhism, or Mohammedanism) for the stability and tranquillity of the Russian state.[19] For example, he viewed the Polish Catholics in an entirely different light than most other Russian conservative nationalists did. The conversion of Catholics, he conceded, would be most desirable if it resulted in an increased number of true Orthodox believers. He was, however, skeptical about the profundity and sincerity of such conversions and feared that they would only undermine the religious foundations of society in Russia's southwestern provinces. Such conversions, he concluded, certainly would not serve the interests of the Russian state, for they would tend to uproot the young people in this region and bring them into closer contact with the liberalism and radicalism of the Russian intelligentsia.[20]

He opposed Russification in the Baltic provinces for similar reasons. The Germans in this region, he pointed out, had always been loyal servants of the tsar as well as the mainstays of public order in Baltic society. He had little sympathy for the Estonians and Latvians and considered their national movements to be just another regrettable example of the influence of Western democracy and liberalism in his time. The variety of pro-Estonian, pro-Latvian, and anti-German administrative and linguistic reform advocated by such people as Iurii Samarin and Strakhov was therefore rejected by Leont'ev as being contrary to the interests of Russian conservatism and autocracy. He defended the German nobles' attempts to maintain their traditional rights and privileges as being the best way to preserve conservative society in the Baltic region. The destruction of these rights in the name of administrative uniformity within the tsarist empire would mean, he warned, another step in the direction of transforming Russia in the spirit of the liberal egalitarianism which had dominated French society since the eighteenth century. He agreed that there was good reason to encourage the use of the Russian language in the Baltic provinces but quickly added that language was not always the best test of true Russian national sentiment. Indeed, on one occasion he had commented that many of the articles Herzen wrote in French were much more authentically Russian than any of the articles published in the liberal Russian-language newspaper *Voice* (*Golos*). With specific reference to the Baltic barons, he suggested that they would probably have little objection to the increased of the Russian language if this were not inextricably linked with the destruction of their local aristocratic rights and privileges.[21]

Leont'ev's clear awareness of the difficulty of reconciling many of the vague and emotional teachings of Russian nationalists like Ivan Aksakov and Dostoevskii with the established political and social traditions of the Russian state obliged him to seek his own ideal of Russian culture and civilization. His keen and analytical intelligence told him that the linguistic, administrative, and emancipatory preoccupations of so many Russian conservatives and nationalists were not too different from those of the various national movements of Western Europe and therefore could not serve as a basis for removing Russia from the cultural sphere of Western Europe. Moreover, he had learned from Danilevskii that civilization and culture consisted of complicated philosophical, moral, political, social, and artistic traditions which were the result of the entire life and historical development of peoples and nations. But his thinking was, in many ways, much clearer and more logical than Danilevskii's. He was not willing to follow Danilevskii in accepting the Slavophiles' romantic idealizations of Russian society and history. His own view of the Russian scene was more realistic, being based on a consideration of the actual political and social conditions and philosophical and moral principles that had dominated Russian life for so many centuries.

Byzantinism was the term chosen by Leont'ev to describe his own conception of Russian society and civilization. His stay at Mount Athos in 1871 and 1872, which was a period of personal and religious crisis in his life, was undoubtedly of great importance for this particular choice of terminology.[22] After 1872 the Byzantine ideal of Christian monasticism that Leont'ev had observed at Mount Athos had an almost irresistible attraction for him as a political writer and religious philosopher. His interpretation of Byzantine religion and culture was, however, an individual and subjectively esthetic one and was not reconcilable with any strict interpretation of Byzantine tradition.[23] Leont'ev was a lover of beauty and of harmonious and esthetic forms of life and culture. Thus one reason for his acceptance of Byzantine Christianity was that it appealed to him esthetically. On the other hand, he rejected nineteenth-century European society and technology because he felt that they created a world full of ugliness and mediocrity.[24] His esthetic aversion to nineteenth-century Europe made him all the more determined to preserve in Russia the Byzantine cultural tradition, which he considered to have permeated the "entire Great-Russian social organism."[25]

The tradition Leont'ev hoped to preserve in Russia only superficially resembled the social and national ideals of other Russian conservative thinkers. He shared their belief in the importance of autocracy and Orthodoxy for Russian and Eastern European history; but little agreement was possible between them on the place of nationalism in Russian society, for Leont'ev regarded political nationalism as just another of the ailments of nineteenth-century Europe. Perhaps an even more important source of disagreement was Leont'ev's rejection of humanitarianism and historical and religious optimism. Leont'ev formulated his thoughts on this subject in the following words: "We know that Byzantinism (as Christianity in general) rejects all expectation of general happiness and prosperity . . . ; that it is the strongest antithesis to the idea of humanity in the sense of earthly equality, earthly freedom, earthly perfection, and earthly content-ment."[26] The *pochvenniki,* the Slavophiles, and even Danilevskii and Fadeev had an optimistic conception of life, history, and religion. Leont'ev's view of these subjects was a pessimistic one. For him the individual human being was a helpless and insignificant creature. The true Christian, he believed, had little alternative other than to recognize this fact and to be pessimistic about all earthly things, placing his unqualified faith in the wisdom of Divine Providence.[27]

Leont'ev was particularly scornful of the type of optimistic and humanitarian Christianity preached by Dostoevskii at the Pushkin commemoration at Moscow in 1880. He strongly felt that Dostoevskii's praise of Christian charity and love had little meaning when interpreted freely and dissociated from the traditional context of the teachings of the Orthodox Church.[28] A much better interpretation of these virtues, he argued, was the one made by Constantine Pobedonostsev at the same Pushkin commemoration. In Pobedonostsev's address the need for Russians to love and respect the commands, ceremonies, and traditions of the Orthodox Church had been emphasized.[29] Such a recommendation pleased Leont'ev because it supported his own belief that order could only be maintained in society by virtue of the restraint and moral influence exercised by traditional religion on the mass of the population.[30]

Leont'ev attached special importance to monasticism as a means for the Orthodox Church to exercise its beneficial influence over society in Russia. The Orthodox Church's monasteries, being based on the principle of the renunciation of life, served as a reminder of the ephemeral and inconsequential character of this world and of the Divine Judgment awaiting everyone at the end of his earthly existence. Leont'ev considered the fear of God and the hope for personal salvation to be especially persuasive inducements for the mass of the people in Russia to live in accordance with the precepts of Christianity.[31] Personally, Leont'ev was almost obsessed by thoughts concerning his own sinfulness and salvation. In fact, his concern was so great that the outstanding Orthodox thinker, George Florovskii, has remarked that Leont'ev often seems to be much closer to the teachings of Protestantism than to those of Orthodoxy.[32] In any case, Leont'ev was so strongly drawn to Orthodox monasticism that he spent the last years of his life in the proximity of the Optina Pustyn' monastery and, shortly before his death, was shorn and became a monk at the Trinity-Sergiev Monastery near Moscow.

Leont'ev's view of autocracy also tended to set him apart from most other conservative nationalists in Russia. His conception of Russian autocracy, however, had much in common with Fadeev's, for they both thought of this institution as one directed by an autocratic tsar whose beneficial policies were carried out by a service gentry. Leont'ev developed this idea more fully than Fadeev by making it part of a general authoritarian and pessimistic philosophy of life. Thus he constantly emphasized the need for discipline and severity in the government of any strong and well-ordered society. He could not conceive of such a society as being anything other than a monarchy based on the principle of inequality and on the authority of privileged classes and social institutions such as the family and the peasant commune.[33] For Leont'ev the history of civilization demonstrated that durable forms of public order were only possible in monarchies supported by privileged nobilities. He believed that the true interests of a nation were best served by dividing its society into strictly differentiated class strata so that order could be maintained and anarchy avoided by minimizing the possibilities of social movement and change for the mass of the population. This was precisely what Pazukhin and Dmitrii Tolstoi had attempted to accomplish when they introduced measures in the mid-1880's to strengthen the position of the gentry. Leont'ev only regretted that these measures had been introduced too late to save Russia from the destructive influence of European egalitarian ideas.[34]

Leont'ev denied that the progress of a state had to be liberal and emancipatory. As an example of another type of progress he did not hesitate to point to the gradual enserfment of the Russian peasant, which, he claimed, had at one time represented a form of "salutary progress" for the Russian nation.[35] He did not dispute that the emancipation of the serfs had become necessary by the mid-nineteenth century.[36] His main point was that progress represented whatever might be deemed to be useful by the Russian state at any given stage of its development. Accordingly, Leont'ev heartily approved of Catherine II's having extended serfdom and strengthened the position of the gentry in Russia by legally elevating them above the rest of the population at the end of the eighteenth century. He justified Catherine's policies in the following words:

> For those who do not regard happiness and absolute justice the proper goal for man in this world, there is nothing terrible in the thought that millions of Russians were obliged for many centuries to live under the constraint . . . of the bureaucracy, landowners, and church, because this was necessary so

that Pushkin could write Onegin and Godunov, so that the Kremlin and its cathedrals could be built, so that Suvorov and Kutuzov could gain their national victories.[37]

But Byzantinism was more for Leont'ev than merely an idealization of the *raison d'état* of a well-ordered monarchical and aristocratic society. It was an ideal and a way of life that had once transformed semibarbarian Kievan *Rus'* into a nation and had later given Muscovite and St. Petersburg Russia the spiritual strength to survive Tatar domination and to emerge victorious from military struggles with Poland, Sweden, France, and Turkey.[38] The source of this strength was, in Leont'ev's opinion, the Orthodox and autocratic traditions Russia had inherited from Byzantium. He deplored the ignorance of most Russians concerning the positive sides of Byzantine history, especially their failure to understand the role of Orthodoxy and autocracy in giving the Eastern Roman Empire sufficient inner discipline and spiritual vitality to outlive pagan Rome by more than 1100 years. But Orthodoxy and autocracy were not able to mature fully on the shores of the Bosporus because of the Eastern Roman Empire's exposed geographical position and because of its overly refined and relatively decadent population. Byzantinism in the Eastern Roman Empire, he concluded, therefore remained largely an abstract juridical idea.[39]

In Russia, on the other hand, Byzantinism enjoyed the dual advantages of geographical inaccessibility and of a simple, fresh, and uncomplicated native population. Here, Leont'ev believed, the Byzantine ideal assumed more concrete form in the person of the Russian tsar, whose autocratic powers were not only sanctioned by the authority of the Orthodox Church but also by the reverence of the mass of the people.[40] This ideal had penetrated so deeply into the national mind of Russia, he wrote, that even such leaders of popular revolts in Russia as Stenka Razin and Pugachev were, in a sense, legitimists who never openly dared to challenge the religious and monarchical principles underlying Russian society. Thus Razin was careful to stipulate that he was opposing the boyars and not the tsar; and Pugachev attempted to gain support for himself by telling common Russians that he, and not Catherine, was their legitimate ruler.[41]

As the years passed, however, Leont'ev came to have increasing doubts concerning Russia's ability to preserve and further develop the tradition of Byzantinism she had inherited from East Rome in the face of the growing world-wide influence of Western European applied science, industrialism, and egalitarian liberalism. The origins of these doubts can be traced as far back as the late 1860's. At that time, for example, his discouragement about the prevalence of European ideas and values among Russia's gentry and educated minority caused him to lose faith in the usefulness of obligatory elementary education for the common people. He first seriously developed his ideas on the subject of education for the people in an article that he wrote in 1867.[42] Here his argument was essentially that universal elementary education was undesirable in Russia as long as the upper strata of the population continued to be enamored of European ideas. Until these strata returned to more purely Russian forms of cultural life, he continued, they, as the teachers of the common people, would certainly make use of the schools as a means of disrupting existing cultural patterns and of further disseminating Western European ideas and attitudes throughout Russia.[43]

Opposition to the extension of public education in Russia did not mean that Leont'ev opposed education as such or all forms of progress. This he never did.[44] The type of progress he objected to was the liberal and egalitarian variety, which he associated with nineteenth-century Europe. Europe's progress, Leont'ev averred, was not part of any process of genuine development but, instead, part of that "secondary, confused simplification" which he identified with declining civilizations and peoples.[45] He wanted to avoid having Russia drawn into the orbit of a declining Europe. But he had little confidence in the Russian educated public's ability to save Russia from such a fate, for he regarded them as badly educated, superficial, and empty-headed.[46]

Because of his lack of confidence in the Russian educated public, Leont'ev believed that the Russian government should undertake repressive measures, even some form of new feudalism and despotism, in order to prepare Russia for intellectual and cultural independence at some future date in her history. The measures he advocated included strengthening the ties that kept the peasants bound to their communes, decreasing social mobility in Russian society, curtailing primary schools, and encouraging the adoption of a pessimistic attitude toward science and life in general—all of which were intended as means of saving Russia from the rule of Western individualism and constitutionalism, i.e. from "the total rule of capitalists, bankers, and lawyers."[47] Above all, Leont'ev hoped that the application of these measures would give Russia, as it were, a breathing spell during which she and the Orthodox Christians of the Balkans could work out their own organic culture based on the religious and political traditions of their common Byzantine heritage. He shared Danilevskii's belief that a declining Europe presented Russia and her coreligionists with an excellent opportunity to replace the political and intellectual authority of the West with an Orthodox union organized under the protection of Russian military power and with Constantinople as its capital.[48] Leont'ev's emphasis was, however, always on the disciplining influence of Byzantine Orthodoxy and autocracy rather than on any emancipatory Pan-Slavic nationalism. After the early 1860's he consistently viewed the

Slavic national movements as being essentially liberal and egalitarian rather than Christian and Byzantine. Such a view made him skeptical from the very outset about the prospects for the eventual emergence of a revitalized Orthodox Christian civilization in Eastern Europe.

During the last few years of his life, Leont'ev was haunted by Vladimir Solov'ev's words: "Russian civilization is a European civilization."[49] But he was never willing to accept Solov'ev's thesis that Danilevskii's theory of cultural-historical types was not only incorrect but also misleading and unoriginal. In this respect, Leont'ev clearly sided with Strakhov in the latter's dispute with Solov'ev concerning the significance of Danilevskii's *Russia and Europe*.[50] He also sided with Strakhov in disapproving of Solov'ev's sympathy for Roman Catholicism and for Western European progress. On the other hand, he was attracted by Solov'ev's efforts to formulate the philosophical basis for a theocratic and universal Christian civilization.[51]

Leont'ev's own clear understanding had already inclined him to be pessimistic about the prospects of a new Eastern civilization before he was obliged to come to terms with Solov'ev's polemics against Strakhov and Danilevskii. Leont'ev had preceded Solov'ev by a good number of years in characterizing emancipatory Pan-Slavism as a product of the intellectual life of nineteenth-century Western Europe. Moreover, Leont'ev had long understood the close relationship between European technology and applied science and other aspects of European intellectual and cultural life. He detested this technology and applied science as much as he did all other aspects of modern European civilization; yet, he realized that such things as factories, steam power, and railways were necessary evils if Russia was to be prosperous and strong and to have the requisite military strength to defend the interests of the Russian state and of the Eastern Church.[52] He hoped that Russian scientists could develop their own independent form of science, one which would have "contempt for its own utility."[53] But he never seemed too optimistic that this would ever come to pass.

Even following Danilevskii's line of organic and historical thinking gave Leont'ev little cause for optimism during the last years of his life. This was especially true because he then placed the beginning of the historical development of his Byzantine-Russian civilization at the year A.D. 862[54] instead of at some future historical date, as had been the case for Danilevskii's Slavic cultural-historical type. Beginning Russian civilization's historical development in 862 obviously obliged Leont'ev to accept the commonly-held view that Russia was a thousand years old by the mid-nineteenth century. This, however, left Russian civilization little in the way of a future in terms of the thousand to twelve hundred-year time span allotted by Leont'ev to historical-cultural entities. Following this line of reasoning Leont'ev came to the conclusion that Russia was old—no more than a hundred years younger than Western European nations like France, England, and Germany.[55] Being only slightly younger than the rest of Europe, Russian civilization clearly had passed its peak and had a maximum of several hundred years of historical development before it.[56] Viewing Russia's development in such terms in the late 1880's, Leont'ev could only be pessimistic about the future of Russia and the Slavs. On one occasion he even wrote that it was unlikely that Russia and the Slavs would set up the banners of a new civilization on the ruins of an exhausted Europe; instead, it perhaps would be the recently awakened peoples of Asia who would undertake this task.[57]

Wherever Leont'ev looked during the last few years of his life, he was able to find little encouragement for belief in the flowering of a new and distinctly Russian-Byzantine civilization. Indeed, he followed Chaadaev's example in lamenting that the Russian people had been less original and less creative than practically any other major people in world history. He even denied the Russian people originality in the realm of politics, where Byzantium had been the source of inspiration for the principles and institutions of Russian political life. Although he was proud of the Russian people's feat in bringing into existence a powerful and autocratic state, he qualified praise of this feat by pointing out that a characteristically Russian concept of political order comparable to those of ancient Rome, Byzantium, Great Britain, and pre-revolutionary France had never evolved. Nonetheless, he remained convinced that Russia's Byzantine heritage made her unique in nineteenth-century Europe; and he felt strongly that anarchy and disorder would ensue if Russia did not continue to organize her society in accordance with Byzantine precepts and principles. He could not, however, help but notice that European notions of political and legal order had gradually supplanted Byzantinism and gained the upper hand in Russia after 1861.[58] At one time he had hoped that the Russian peasant would serve as an example for the Europeanized gentry of devotion to the tsar and the traditional Byzantine institutions and way of life of the Russian nation. By the end of the 1880's he was obliged to comment bitterly that the peasants had failed dismally in serving as praiseworthy models of Russian nationality and, instead, had become mere caricatures of the Europeanized Russian gentry.[59]

Leont'ev's early faith in the future of Eastern Orthodox civilization was so shaken toward the end of his life that he came to be increasingly fascinated by the idea that socialism would perhaps eventually triumph everywhere and provide the world with a new form of discipline and a new feudal order. He never seriously believed that the victory of liberalism and capitalism could be a lasting one, for he felt that a society based on social and economic mobility and personal freedom would sooner or later sink into a state of political confusion and anarchy. The socialists and communists, on the other hand, he emphasized, aimed at limiting personal and economic freedom and at establishing new institutions and communes to which the individual would be bound and subordinated.[60] In a letter to A. Aleksandrov he went so far as to toy with the idea that the Russian tsar might place himself at the head of the international socialist movement and imitate the Emperor Constantine in making Constantinople his capital and in establishing a new despotism and a new slavery.[61] He certainly did not advocate this course of action too seriously; and he continued to hope that measures like those championed by Pazukhin and Count Dmitrii Tolstoi would suffice to assure Russia a future of aristocratic and autocratic stability as opposed to one of socialistic despotism. But he became increasingly fatalistc about the prospects of future success for the aristocracy and autocracy in Russia. Around 1890 he no longer spoke so much of a new Eastern European civilization as he did of slowing down the progress of those historical forces that were beginning to produce more and more political anarchy and the leveling of social classes and distinctions in Russia.[62] As much as he disliked and disapproved of these trends, he seemed resigned to the fact that they would eventually prevail.

Leont'ev's gradual disillusionment concerning the future of Russia represents an important stage in the dissolution of Russian conservative and nationalistic ideology. Others had, of course, contributed to this result: Samarin with the convenient arguments he provided for future Russifiers; Ivan Aksakov with his unwitting services to the cause of reaction in the early 1880's; and Fadeev with his deliberate and systematic espousal of amoral power politics and of the vested interests of the Russian gentry. Leont'ev, however, made alterations and additions to the doctrines of the Slavophiles, the *pochvenniki,* and Danilevskii that were much more fundamental than those made by any other Russian thinker.

Of particular importance in this connection was Leont'ev's rejection of nationalism in the sense that it had been understood by most other Russian conservative nationalists. He realized that nineteenth-century Russia had not been successful in creating a uniquely national culture. Consequently, he felt obliged to agree with the substance of Vladimir Solov'ev's critical analysis of the theories of the Slavophiles and Danilevskii. As much as he disapproved of Solov'ev's sympathies for Catholicism and Europe, he accepted his conclusion that nineteenth-century Russia formed an integral part of the intellectual and economic life of Western Europe. He refused to consider such things as a few literary masterpieces, the

Russification of Russia's borderlands, or Pan-Slav idealism as indications of the birth of a new Russo-Slavic civilization, pointing out that similar phenomena were commonplace in nineteenth-century Europe. Unlike so many of his Russian contemporaries, he understood the dilemma in which the economic and technological development of modern Europe placed Russia. He perceived that European technology, science, and economic expansion were inseparable from European parliamentarianism, democracy, liberalism, materialism, and egalitarianism; and he knew that Russia could not isolate herself completely from the rest of Europe, for in order to remain a great power and to defend her way of life and vital interests, Russia would have to move ahead economically and make use of the innovations of modern technology and science.

Leont'ev hoped that Russia could escape this dilemma, or at least slow down the tempo of her Europeanization, through what he once called "rational and enlightened obscurantism."[63] By this he meant that the state should insist on its right of undisputed leadership in society; be ruthless and, if necessary, cruel in order to preserve Byzantinism and make Russia socially and militarily stronger and culturally more productive.[64] Accordingly, he praised Catherine II for having further limited the freedom of the Russian serfs and increased the privileges of the gentry, arguing that this had made possible the military victories of Suvorov and Kutuzov and the cultural achievements of Pushkin. For Leont'ev the bureaucracy was an essential part of Russian autocracy and he had little patience with those who anathemized it. He admitted that the bureaucrats sometimes were arbitrary and oppressive and that they often made mistakes, but he added that they were the "sergeants of the tsar" who loyally carried out the policies of the Russian state.[65] He wanted these bureaucrats to be from the gentry, who were to continue to be a privileged service class having the primary task of assisting the government to maintain order and stability in Russian society. He bitterly opposed social mobility in his Russo-Byzantine state and therefore condemned such modern notions as equality of opportunity and universal and obligatory elementary education. In his scheme the Orthodox Church played an important role in preventing too much mobility and in maintaining traditional social and political order in Russia, for it exercised a restraining moral influence on the mass of the people and taught them fear of God, obedience, and contempt for the things of this world.

There was certainly little Christian love or charity in Leont'ev's Byzantinism. As Nicholas Berdiaev wrote in 1940:

His failure lies in his refusal to understand the dignity of every human personality as an image and likeness of God, despite the fact that he was dominated by the religious sentiment of sin (a feeling which sometimes inspired terror) and the aesthetic feeling of beauty. He had no conception of the dignity and freedom of the spirit, or of the historic sins of the Church on the social plane. Leont'ev's ideas would prove harmful in our day, but his life and history are highly instructive.[66]

In Leont'ev's own day, even those who stood close to him ideologically often were repelled by his strange and paradoxical combination of monastic Byzantinism, romantic estheticism, scientific naturalism, and political reaction. Moreover, the sharp criticisms Leont'ev had made of the inconsistencies of Pan-Slavic and Slavophile Russian conservatism hardly endeared him to other conservative nationalists. Leont'ev's criticism of the Slavophiles, for example, very much offended Ivan Aksakov, who also disapproved of Leont'ev's sympathetic attitude toward Vladimir Solov'ev's dream of a universal Christian Church centered outside of Russia.[67] Strakhov, who had been the principal defender of Danilevskii in the controversy over the significance and originality of *Russia and Europe*, could only share Aksakov's disapproval of Leont'ev as a close friend of Vladimir Solov'ev. But Strakhov's attitude toward Leont'ev seems to have been a mixture of admiration and antipathy. He undoubtedly respected Leont'ev for his ability and brilliance as a conservative writer, but Strakhov's orderly and scholarly mind was disturbed by Leont'ev's esthetical and almost demoniacal form of monastic and Byzantine Christianity. Strakhov, as V. V. Rozanov once wrote, "disliked and almost feared Leont'ev."[68]

Another conservative nationalist, Constantine Pobedonostsev, also shared these mixed feelings in regard to Leont'ev. Pobedonostsev highly appreciated Leont'ev as a thinker and even purchased copies of his three-volume work *The East, Russia, and Slavdom* for use in Russian seminaries. He also must have felt himself to be much closer to Leont'ev's disciplinarian and pessimistic form of Christianity than to the Christian humanitarianism of Dostoevskii, for he apparently approved of the criticisms Leont'ev made of Dostoevskii's speech at the Pushkin commemoration at Moscow in 1880.[69] At the same time, Pobedonostsev was certainly displeased with Leont'ev's support of the Greek clergy in their efforts to prevent the Balkan Slavs from becoming more independent of the Greek-dominated Patriarchate of Constantinople. After all, Leont'ev was a close friend of Tertii Filippov, the State Comptroller, whose support for the Patriarchate at Constantinople had long been a source of great irritation for Pobedonostsev, who regarded Filippov as a personal enemy. Leont'ev's friendship with Filippov therefore doubtless contributed to keep a certain distance between Leont'ev and the Over Procurator of the Holy Synod.[70]

The differences separating Leont'ev from such people as Ivan Aksakov, Strakhov, and Pobedonostsev did not alter the fact that Leont'ev was the most brilliant and most gifted continuer of the traditions of the Slavophiles, the *pochvenniki,* and Danilevskii in the Russia of the 1880's and early 1890's. The last of the true Slavophiles, Ivan Aksakov, to be sure, considered Leont'ev's influence to be a negative and harmful one. But, as the renegade socialist L. A. Tikhomirov remarked in 1894, the Slavophiles had not necessarily said the last word on the subject of nationality in Russia.[71]

There was good reason for Aksakov's alarm about the possible influence of Leont'ev's ideas because Leont'ev's "obscurantism" definitely represented a form of intellectual betrayal. For centuries the role of the churchman and the intellectual, as Julien Benda has pointed out,[72] had been to oppose a realm of abstract moral, philosophical, and religious principles to the passions, power interests, and violence of the material world. Leont'ev, like so many other intellectual leaders of the nineteenth and twentieth centuries, was not in the least interested in abstract philosophical and moral principles and had the utmost scorn for those who preached in the name of humanity and justice. He refused to associate himself with the philosophers, poets, and peasants in Russia but unequivocally placed himself on the side of the generals, administrators, and landowners. Above all, he sought a society that would be characterized by hierarchical order and stability and ruled by a privileged, disciplined, and creative minority. For this end he was ready to sanction social injustice, political repression, and, if necessary, autocratic despotism.

Other Russian conservative nationalists, it is true, did not always sympathize with Leont'ev's political, social, and religious views. But they, too, were prone to one form or another of intellectual betrayal. Dostoevskii, who had been very much offended by Leont'ev's criticism of his Pushkin address,[73] had glorified war and justified power politics and Russian conquest in the Balkans. Danilevskii had preached a similar variety of Russian imperialism; but he refused to believe in Dostoevskii's dream of a worldwide, civilizing mission for Russia and based his own ideas concerning Russian leadership in Eastern Europe on amoral Machiavellianism and a biological form of historical determinism. Strakhov, despite his insistence on the importance of moral and philosophical principles, defended Danilevskii as a thinker and Pan-Slavist and emphasized the need for Russification in Russia's borderlands as a means of furthering organic unity and national uniformity within Russia. In the case of Rostislav Fadeev, it is not surprising that he should not be true to the intellectual's proper calling of providing society with new and disinterested artistic, religious, and philosophical truths. After all, he was a military man who had spent most of his adult life in the armed forces of his country. But the minds of such figures as Ivan Aksakov and Iurii Samarin had been nurtured by the debates and teachings of the intellectual circles of Moscow. Hence it is more difficult to excuse Aksakov's vociferous and bombastic antiliberalism, anti-Semitism, and Great Russian chauvinism. It is equally difficult to excuse Samarin's almost obsessive concern about the interests of the Russian state and his elaboration of many of the historical arguments that were later used to justify the administrative, religious, and linguistic Russification of Russia's borderlands.

By the 1890's it was clear that the Slavophiles, the *pochvenniki*, Danilevskii, and Fadeev had failed in their self-appointed task of creating ideals of Russian national life that would serve to bring together the Russian state, the mass of the people, and the intelligentsia in some form of harmonious and organic unity. This failure resulted partly from shortcomings in their own thinking about Russian society and partly from circumstances over which they had no control. They certainly were not very successful in reconciling traditional Russian conservatism with such conflicting ideas and movements as Pan-Slavism, German romanticism, freedom of conscience, Russification, Great Russian chauvinism, anti-Semitism, and idealistic humanitarianism. Both Vladimir Solov'ev and Leont'ev trenchantly analyzed these contradictions in the tradition of conservative nationalism in Russia. After the publication of Solov'ev's and Leont'ev's essays on this subject around 1890, there was, with the notable exception of L. A. Tikhomirov, no first-rate Russian thinker who still sought to harmonize nationalism and conservatism in the manner of the Slavophiles, the *pochvenniki*, and Danilevskii. To be sure, there were many Russian writers at the beginning of the twentieth century such as Nicholas Berdiaev and V. V. Rozanov[74] who admired them for their religious and organic view of life. But such writers were too sophisticated and well-informed to subscribe to the contradictory social, political, and nationalistic teachings of Russian conservative nationalism. Tikhomirov, on the other hand, was more interested in the stability and authority of the Russian autocratic state than he was in the flowering of a new Russian civilization.[75]

There were also circumstances over which Russian conservative nationalists had little or no control. They were, for example, in no way responsible for the Polish uprising of 1863; yet the Polish problem obliged them to approve policies which, in many ways, were incompatible with their basic philosophy of life. The development of the Russian revolutionary movement placed them between the horns of another dilemma. Although they championed the cause of freedom for the individual in society, they felt obligated to defend, at one time or another, the government's use of repressive or preventive measures to curtail a movement that threatened the conservative foundations of Russian society. Though they did not give unqualified support to the government in its struggle with the revolutionary movement, the support they did give tended to identify them with unpopular and repressive governmental policies. Such support could only lose friends for them in nineteenth-century educated society, which, as a whole, strongly believed in freedom, liberty, equality, and economic and social progress.

Moreover, the nature of Russia's economic development was unfavorable for the cause of those who, like the populists and the conservative nationalists, believed that Russia's historical development was *sui generis* and intrinsically different from that of Western Europe. As Leont'ev realized, Russia had to accept and use Western scientific and technological innovations if she were to maintain her standing as a great power. But Western technology, science, and economic progress could not be separated from European ideas. As Russian society was gradually transformed economically, it came more and more to have the same problems and to face the same issues as Western European society. This naturally affected the thinking of educated Russians. In the course of time, they therefore became increasingly critical of the theories of the conservative nationalists concerning the unique historical destiny of the Russian nation.

The failure of Russian conservative nationalists to convert a majority of thinking Russians to their organic view of Russian life did not preclude all possibility of success for conservative nationalism in Russia. It is, after all, doubtful that there ever has been a society in which intellectuals have determined the nature of basic social and governmental policies. The determination of such policies is usually the responsibility of rulers, statesmen, and administrators. In a word, it is always possible for effective governmental leadership to introduce and implement a wide variety of social and national policies irrespective of the shortcomings of a given society's intellectuals.

In nineteenth-century Russia, unfortunately, there was no conservative leader like Bismarck or Stolypin to firmly and imaginatively take over the direction of Russian national and social policy. Russia did not lack a substantial number of bureaucrats who spoke out loudly in the name of firm government and Russian national interests and who praised the Slavophiles, Dostoevskii, and Danilevskii for their services in awakening a feeling of nationalism in the minds of Russians; but such bureaucrats in nineteenth-century Russia were almost invariably men without flexibility, imagination, and creative intelligence. The most famous and influential representative of the nationalistic and conservative bureaucracy in Russia was Constantine Petrovich Pobedonostsev, whose career is a particularly good illustration of some of the reasons for the St. Petersburg bureaucracy's ineffectiveness in furthering the cause of conservative nationalism in Russia.

CHAPTER THIRTEEN

Bureaucratic Nationalism

In 1841 young Constantine Petrovich Pobedonostsev, the grandson of a priest and the son of a pious, patriotic, and industrious professor of Russian literature at the University of Moscow, was sent to the School of Jurisprudence in St. Petersburg. This school had the special task of preparing young Russians from gentry families for service in courts and in the judicial and legal branches of the imperial bureaucracy. It was one example of the Russian government's constant efforts during the nineteenth century to train qualified civil servants.[1] In 1846 Pobedonostsev returned to his native Moscow, where he was attached to the Eighth Department of the Senate. His duties there were apparently not too onerous, for they permitted him to conduct extensive historical research on Russian civil law and legal institutions. In the late 1850's and early 1860's, he published a number of articles on these subjects and took part in the deliberations concerning the reform of Russia's legal system. Between 1859 and 1865, while continuing his service in the Eighth Department of the Senate, he was also a lecturer on Russian law at the University of Moscow, which brought him into contact with many of the leading figures of Russian scholarship at the time.[2]

Nevertheless these activities were to separate Pobedonostsev permanently from his native Moscow, for they singled him out as an unusually promising young scholar, teacher, and administrator. In 1861 he was asked to come to St. Petersburg for a year to give lectures on jurisprudence to the heir to the throne, Nicholas Aleksandrovich. In 1863 he accompanied Nicholas on his traditional circuit tour of European Russia. After the death of Nicholas Aleksandrovich in 1865, Pobedonostsev was invited to move to St. Petersburg in order to serve as tutor for the new heir to the throne, the future Alexander III. In 1866 he settled permanently in St.

Petersburg. Thereafter, he rose rapidly in the official world of the Russian capital: in 1868 he was made a member of the Ruling Senate; in 1872, a member of the State Council; and in 1880, the Over Procurator of the Holy Synod.[3]

Pobedonostsev's position as the former tutor of the Russian emperor and the role he played in the intrigues against Loris-Melikov in 1881 gave him a special place among the advisers of Alexander III. During the months following his father's assassination, Alexander was deeply impressed by Pobedonostsev's emotional diatribes against the alleged danger liberalism presented to the principles of autocratic government in Russia. These months were exciting and exhilarating ones for Pobedonostsev, who again and again imposed himself on the emperor—even in the middle of the night—with his unending admonishments about the need to punish severely the murderers of Alexander II and to rule Russia with a firm hand.[4] In so doing, he not only believed that he was acting in accordance with the interests of traditional order in Russia but also in accordance with the unexpressed and unformulated will of the Russian people. The people, he felt, wanted the same things that he, Pobedonostsev, did: i.e. the tsar was to protect Russia from the projects of constitutional reform associated with the names of such people as Loris-Melikov and the Grand Duke Constantine Nikolaevich.[5] Pobedonostsev's professed closeness to the common people in Russia must have given him additional stature in the eyes of Alexander III. In any case, it was Pobedonostsev who drafted the famous imperial manifesto of April 29, 1881,[6] which marked the point of departure for the postponement of all serious consideration of political reform in Russia for the duration of an entire generation.

This success in the governmental circles of St. Petersburg had an effect on Pobedonostsev's thinking that was similar to the influence ten years of service in the Balkans had on the thinking of Constantine Leont'ev. Like Leont'ev, Pobedonostsev came to view the social, political, and philosophical theories of his former associates in Moscow with increasing distrust and skepticism. He now took the hardheaded, practical, and official view of Russian affairs of a member of the State Council, an intimate adviser of the emperor, and the chief administrative officer of one of the more important branches of the imperial bureaucracy.[7]

Nonetheless, Pobedonostsev's formative years in Moscow left many lasting traces on his way of thinking and viewing the world. In his later years, for example, he was a confirmed historicist who considered the institutions and norms of any given society to be the necessary product of its historical development and of the national spirit of its people.[8] This historicist approach to society and culture, as has already been pointed out, was a commonplace in the Moscow of the 1850's. But Pobedonostsev probably did not learn his historicism from literary and philosophical writers such as Grigor'ev and Strakhov. To the contrary, it was obviously the historical and legal research conducted by Pobedonostsev while working for the Eighth Department of the Senate in Moscow that taught him to take a historicist view of practically all political and social phenomena. He did so, however, in an unimaginative and pedantic fashion, for the articles he published during these years are characterized by the painstaking and critical analysis he made of a multitude of facts concerning Russian laws, statutes, and legal institutions rather than by his insight and originality in formulating new ideas and generalizations. This was also the case in his major work, *Course in Civil Law*, the first volume of which was published in 1868. When he did generalize and make interpretations of Russian law and history, he almost invariably compared Russian law with Latin, German, English, and French law or described Russian laws and institutions as the unique product of Russian historical development. Here, of course, the influence of the German historical school, especially as represented by Savigny, is unmistakable.[9]

Another probable source of Pobedonostsev's historicism and nationalism may be seen in his association with Ivan Aksakov. He and Aksakov had been good friends since the early 1840's, when they both attended the School of Jurisprudence in St. Petersburg.[10] They had also worked at the same time in departments of the Senate in Moscow during the late 1840's. Their paths parted subsequently, but they were brought together again during the 1860's, 1870's, and 1880's through Anna and Catherine Tiutchev. Both Anna and Catherine were ladies-in-waiting at the court and personal friends and correspondents of Pobedonostsev. Anna married Ivan Aksakov and moved to Moscow in 1865, after which rather close contact was maintained with Pobedonostsev through Anna's sister in St. Petersburg. Pobedonostsev, himself, addressed a number of personal letters to Aksakov. The tone of these letters is cordial, although often somewhat condescending. Pobedonostsev clearly appreciated Aksakov's patriotic services as a journalist and public leader and he was determined that key figures in the government and at the court be exposed to the influence of Aksakov and other Slavophiles and conservative nationalists. During the 1860's and 1870's he was particularly eager that the future Alexander III should become familiar with Samarin's writings on the Baltic question.[11] This was an important part of his efforts to use the arguments of the Moscow Slavophiles to impress on young Alexander the need for more emphasis on nationality and the Orthodox traditions of the Russian past in the formulation and conduct of governmental policies. He was aided in these efforts by the Tiutchev sisters. In his speech on Alexander III before the Russian Historical Society in 1895, he gave Anna Tiutchev, Aksakov's wife, credit for having first brought to the attention of the tsarevich the ideas of the Slavophiles on the close relationship between Russian nationality and the Orthodox Church.[12]

Pobedonostsev's use of Slavophile ideas was, however, highly arbitrary and selective, for he consistently refused to accept many of the basic tenets of the Slavophile philosophy of life. He was, for example, more than once most disturbed by the appeals Ivan Aksakov made in his speeches and publications for more justice in Russian courts and more freedom for the press and the Orthodox Church.[13] He also did not sympathize very much with Slavophile theories concerning the peasant commune. He felt that it would be dangerous to introduce too suddenly the principle of economic freedom into the affairs of the Russian countryside and that the peasant commune would remain for some time the most practical means of protecting the peasants from proletarianization and the designs of unscrupulous kulaks and capitalists; but he did not consider the commune to be an integral part of the Russian way of life or an institution that could be justified economically. To the contrary, he dismissed the arguments of such Slavophiles as Khomiakov and Constantine Aksakov (though without mentioning their names) on behalf of the peasant commune as a distinctly Russian institution by simply stating that communal institutions could not be considered as an exclusively Slavic historical phenomenon because modern scholarship had demonstrated that communal ownership of land had preceded private ownership in the history of practically every major nation. He assumed that it would be just a matter of time until the Russian peasant would have enough capital and be sufficiently productive and efficient to justify the abolition of the peasant commune in Russia.[14]

Pobedonostsev was also much more pessimistic and circumspect in his attitude toward Russian nationalism and society than the Slavophiles were. Like Constantine Leont'ev, Pobedonostsev rejected all forms of modern political and cultural nationalism that accorded to each nationality such rights as self-determination and political autonomy. Indeed, he considered such a concept of nationalism to be incompatible with the interests of social order and political stability in multinational states like Russia and Austria-Hungary;[15] and he concurred with Leont'ev in regarding the Russian people as backward, ignorant, and incapable of advancement and progress without the constant guidance of church and state. Although Pobedonostsev often praised the Great Russian people for their instinctive love of the tsar as the preserver of the Orthodox faith and of the national unity of Russia,[16] he clearly considered them to be a passive element that only gained national and historical significance through identification with the religious, social, and political traditions and institutions of the Russian nation. For Pobedonostsev these traditions and institutions were the product of the Russian national spirit and of Russia's historical development. They therefore contained the essence of important civic virtues and national moral values that the mass of the people, who were allegedly incapable of rational thought, could only understand symbolically in the person of national heroes and the tsar and as a part of the ceremonies and teachings of the Orthodox Church.[17] Thus Pobedonostsev, although he considered himself to be close to the Slavophiles and never attacked them openly in print, was just as far from their idealistic humanitarianism as Constantine Leont'ev was, for both he and Leont'ev attached primary importance to the power and authority of the Russian state supported by the official church and bureaucracy. Neither of them shared the Slavophiles' belief that the profound religious feelings and spontaneous national creativity of the Russian people had been the main source of progress and national well-being in the course of Russian history.

Such extreme pessimism did not come to characterize Pobedonostsev's view of Russian society until after the early 1860's. In his earliest years his views do not seem to have differed greatly from those of other young intellectuals in Moscow toward the end of the reign of Nicholas I. Pobedonostsev recalled, in his recollections concerning his chief at the Eighth Section of the Senate in Moscow, that, in 1848, he and his friends were excited by the February Revolution in France and avidly read French newspapers so that they could find out as much as possible about the revolutionary events in Paris.[18] During the early years of the reign of Alexander II, Pobedonostsev was generally in sympathy with the reforms that were then being discussed and considered in government committees and in newspapers and journals. He was particularly interested in the reform of the Russian legal system and participated in the work of the jurists who prepared the court reforms of 1864.[19] But even during these years Pobedonostsev insisted that Russia's vastness and inadequate political and economic development made it mandatory for the government to control and supervise the functioning of the Russian court system.[20] In contrast to most other leading Russian jurists at the time, he opposed borrowing legal theories and institutions from neighboring states, arguing that laws and legal institutions should always conform strictly to the national traditions and needs of a given society.[21]

The Polish uprising and the revolutionary ferment and nihilism in Russia's major cities and towns in the early 1860's seem to have shocked Pobedonostsev just as much as they did Katkov, Dostoevskii, and so many other conservative-minded contemporaries. Like Katkov, Pobedonostsev believed that Russia was threatened by enemies almost everywhere. But he lost faith in the feasibility of reform in Russia much sooner than Katkov did. As early as December, 1864, he expressed, in a letter to Anna Tiutchev, his disgust with the reforms and the "bazaar of projects" in St. Petersburg.[22] Since a good proportion of educated Russians in the two capitals continued to believe in reform and occasionally (e.g. at the time of the Zasulich affair) even openly sympathized with the revolutionary movement, Pobedonostsev became increasingly pessimistic about human nature and disenchanted with Russian educated society. His feelings of pessimism about Russia and humanity in general were particularly aroused by such issues as court reform, constitutionalism, censorship, and education. The success of many revolutionists and lawyers in making use of the court system established in 1864 both as a public forum and as a means of preventing the government from taking punitive action against terrorists convinced Pobedonostsev that the court reforms of 1864 had been a serious mistake. He granted that many of the ideas contained in these reforms worked quite well in a country like England, where legal and political institutions had been firmly established in the course of history and where there was generally high respect for law and order. But Russia, according to Pobedonostsev, lacked maturity, respect for law, and serious intellectual interests; it had neither the same highly developed judicial procedures and systematized laws and legislation nor the corps of experienced lawyers that the Western European countries did. Hence he contended that the court reforms of 1864 had given too much independence and influence to relatively inexperienced Russian judges, lawyers, and juries. In Russia, he concluded, more governmental control and supervision of the courts were needed. He recommended that the government should gradually modify the 1864 court reforms so that it could again effectively use the courts as instruments of autocratic and legal governmental authority.[23]

Much the same arguments were made by Pobedonostsev in regard to constitutionalism, censorship, and education. The tremendous size of Russia, the complex national composition of her population, the ignorance and economic backwardness of the Russian peasants, the irresponsibility and triviality of the intelligentsia, and even the essential inertia, laziness, and lack of initiative that Pobedonostsev associated with Slavic character[24]—all were among the facts and circumstances of Russian life he adduced to demonstrate the folly of introducing into Russia representative government, freedom of the press, secular education, and laissez-faire economics. As for representative government, he, of course, opposed it in principle, arguing that party strife, patronage, demagoguery, corruption, and a general decline of political authority were the necessary products of modern parliamentary democracy. He did not deny that the parliamentary system had been fairly successful in England, but he attributed this success to representative government's having been an integral part of English historical development and national life. He cautioned, however, that this had never been the case for the nations on the European continent, where representative government allegedly had invariably led to political chaos and confusion. He felt that this applied particularly to the Slavs and warned that representative government in Russia would serve primarily to paralyze governmental initiative and authority, separate the people from the tsar, and lead to the ruin of the Russian nation.[25] What Russia needed, Pobedonostsev emphasized again and again, was firm authority and resolute governmental action. She needed energetic and dedicated public servants who would formulate sound policies and who would control and supervise Russian society.[26] Pobedonostsev bitterly regretted that Russian officialdom was so often lax in exercising such control over society during the second part of the nineteenth century. He was especially disturbed about laxity in the censorship of the press and literature. Thus he frequently used his personal influence to persuade the censorship authorities to forbid the publication or performance of the works of such writers as Leo Tolstoi, Ibsen, Leskov, and Vladimir Solov'ev; and he repeatedly cautioned both Alexander III and Nicholas II that irresponsible writers, journalists, and intellectuals might succeed in influencing the common people to lose faith in the Orthodox Church and to oppose the political authority of the Russian state.[27]

Pobedonostsev's conception of conservative nationalism was not, however, entirely a negative one, for he understood that the Russian government could only be effective in furthering the cause of conservative nationalism in Russia if it concentrated its attention and resources on two highly important positive objectives: (1) the education of the Russian masses in the spirit of patriotism and loyalty to their country, the tsar, and the Orthodox Church; and (2) the promotion of values and ideas that would bring the non-Russian nationalities of the tsarist empire spiritually into more intimate contact with the Russian people and government. Here Pobedonostsev's task was essentially the same one that faced political and educational leaders in such countries as France and Germany during this period. In both these countries the government and nationalistic educators and writers largely succeeded in creating a national ideology that profoundly influenced the thinking of young Germans and Frenchmen educated in elementary and secondary schools during the decades preceding World War I. Thus education made an important contribution to the national solidarity and cohesion of both German and French societies, although the German government was not overly successful in convincing Poles, Danes, and even Alsatians of the intrinsic merits of the German way of life.

Many Russians agreed that education should also be used in Russia to promote national unity and social cohesion. But the question remained: how was this to be done and what was to be the content of Russian national education? Pobedonostsev's answer was not acceptable to many of his contemporaries, but it was strictly in keeping with traditional Russian beliefs and practices.

Traditionally, the education of the common people in Russia had always been entrusted to the care of parish priests. Beginning with the reign of Peter I, the Russian government had officially supported religious education for the people by establishing village parish schools.[28] Although these efforts were continued by the rulers who followed Peter, and in particular by Nicholas I, parish schools made only an insignificant contribution to the cause of increasing literacy and disseminating religious education among the common people. This was the case primarily because the social structure of pre-1861 Russia did not permit the rapid expansion of any form of education for the masses. The priests themselves, lacking knowledge and living under almost intolerable material conditions, were very poor teachers.[29] Nevertheless, there was a general feeling in governmental circles, especially in the Holy Synod, that elementary education in Russia should be developed on the basis of the parish schools that were already in existence. Thus the initial expansion of elementary education in the early 1860's was pretty much limited to parish schools, which increased in number from 2,270 in 1857 to 21,420 in 1865.[30]

After 1865, however, church schools underwent a rapid decline. From the very beginning there had been many people who had felt that elementary education in Russia would be best administered by the Ministry of Public Instruction, and not by the Holy Synod. The educational reform of 1864 did not recognize any special right on the part of the church to control elementary education, for it permitted the Ministry of Public Instruction, the zemstvos, and various other institutions and groups in Russia to found elementary schools. It was also a blow to the cause of church education in Russia when Count Dmitrii Tolstoi, who was also Over Procurator of the Holy Synod between 1865 and 1880, was made Minister of Public Instruction in 1866. Thereafter, Tolstoi, an able and ambitious bureaucrat, lost much of his previous interest in the affairs of the Holy Synod. He ceased giving active support to church schools and concentrated on bringing all schools within the tsarist empire under the jurisdiction of the Ministry of Public Instruction.[31] Moreover, various deficiencies in the parish schools won them little popularity on the local level. Their instruction was of a routine nature and the clergy generally lacked the requisite pedagogical training, interest, and spare time to devote themselves seriously and whole-heartedly to the tasks of public education. These deficiencies were often admitted by the ecclesiastical journals and the priests themselves, and secular writers on pedagogical subjects were even more unsparing in their criticisms of the priests as teachers.[32] As a result of public hostility to the parish schools, as well as insufficient financial support from the government, the number of these schools in Russia fell to 9,059 as early as 1872;[33] and by 1880, to 4,348.[34] By 1880 schools supported by the zemstvos or peasant communes had increased in number to 17,782 out of a total of 22,770 elementary schools in European Russia.[35]

In other words, church schools had ceased being the main instrument of elementary education in Russia by the time that Pobedonostsev undertook his campaign on their behalf in the early 1880's. The expansion of education that did take place in Russia during the preceding decades had been largely the result of the initiative and the efforts of the zemstvos, peasant communes, and municipalities. Such schools, to be sure, still educated but a small part of the Russian population. They were, however, the only form of elementary education that had evolved naturally out of the conditions of Russian society at the time and therefore represented a logical and reasonable point of departure for the further expansion of elementary education in Russia. Hence Pobedonostsev's arbitrary efforts to replace these schools with the unpopular and unsuccessful parish schools were essentially incompatible with his own belief that viable social institutions could never be the artificial and synthetic product of abstract theory but necessarily had to arise out of the historical conditions and experiences of a given people.

But Pobedonostsev was not alone in recommending the parish school as the form of education best suited to serve the interests of stability and order in Russia. There were, in fact, many people in governmental circles and elsewhere who were alarmed by the decline of church education during the 1870's and who, in one way or another, associated the increasing popularity of revolutionary ideas in Russian society with the influence the zemstvos had won over elementary education. Indeed, Pobedonostsev had not initiated serious discussion of this matter on the governmental level, for it had been brought up in the Council of Ministers as early as 1879,[36] a year before Pobedonostsev became the Over Procurator of the Holy Synod. Also, Pobedonostsev had little to do with the isolated attempts made during the 1870's to revitalize instruction in parish schools. Particularly noteworthy in this connection were the efforts of S. A. Rachinskii, an admirer of the Slavophiles and friend of Katkov who had resigned from his post as professor of botany at the University of Moscow in 1868 in order to devote himself to the cause of education among the peasants. He believed that elementary education for the peasants had to be mainly religious and practical and he therefore emphasized such subjects as church singing, Old Church Slavonic, study of the Bible, the three "R's," and agricultural instruction in his village school at Tatevo. He realized that the indifference of the clergy and the hostility of the intelligentsia to religion represented serious obstacles to the success of his pedagogical ideas in Russia; but he was determined to demonstrate their soundness through his own practical activities.[37] Since he was an intelligent, energetic, and dedicated teacher, he inspired many of his pupils with his ideas and persuaded them to become elementary school teachers in a number of schools in the vicinity of Smolensk.[38] Rachinskii's activities soon came to the attention of Pobedonostsev. The Over Procurator of the Synod, in a number of letters addressed to Alexander III, praised Rachinskii for being one of many Russians who were working quietly and courageously in the obscurity of the provinces for the good of their country.[39] Having stressed the role of the Orthodox Church in teaching the Russian people to love their tsar as early as 1864,[40] Pobedonostsev's ideas on elementary education in Russia had always been similar to those of Rachinskii. It seems, however, that he gave little serious thought to this subject until around 1880, so Rachinskii's experiment at Tatevo must have had an important influence on Pobedonostsev's pedagogical theories and educational policies as Over Procurator of the Holy Synod. In 1901, it is interesting to note, Pobedonostsev published part of Rachinskii's pedagogical work *Absit omen* in the fifth edition of his *Reflections of a Russian Statesman (Moskovskii sbornik)*.[41]

As is well known, Pobedonostsev succeeded brilliantly in persuading the Russian government to allot increasingly large sums of money to the Holy Synod for the purpose of making parish schools the principal form of elementary education in Russia.[42] In 1885 the government had given the Synod only 55,000 rubles for the support of church schools; by 1902, this amount had been increased to 10,338,916 rubles, which was twice the amount received by the Ministry of Public Instruction for elementary schools that same year. In 1905 the Holy Synod had jurisdiction over 46.5 per cent of the elementary schools in Russia.[43]

Despite the statistical success of the parish schools, it is doubtful whether they served the purpose for which they were intended. As officially announced, they were supposed to disseminate useful knowledge among the people and to "inspire in their hearts love for the Holy Church and devotion to Tsar and Fatherland."[44] The government understood that the Russian masses had to become at least literate if Russia was to survive in an age of industrialization and technology. Pobedonostsev, himself,

noted in his report for 1888–89 that an educated population was an un-
avoidable necessity at a time when railroads, steam power, and factory
production were being rapidly developed in Russia.[45] The parish schools,
however, were unsuited to meet the demands of an industrial society. As
Pobedonostsev realized, the priests were inadequate as teachers, and the
main emphasis of the two-year and four-year schools and of the make-
shift "schools of literacy" of the Holy Synod was not on subjects that would
prepare the common people for a productive role in an industrialized society. Instead, it was on Bible reading, church singing, religious history,
and the learning of prayers and the Orthodox liturgy and catechism.[46]

Pobedonostsev resembled Leont'ev in opposing too much mobility in
society. Accordingly, he cautioned against any form of education that
would uproot the child from the milieu to which he was accustomed.[47]
He not only wanted to limit elementary education to religion plus the
three "R's" and patriotism, but he also approved of the efforts of Count
I. D. Delianov, the Minister of Public Instruction between 1882 and 1897,
to close the doors of secondary schools to children from the lower strata
of the Russian population.[48] Delianov's most famous pronouncement on
this subject was his circular letter of June 18, 1887, which is commonly
known as the "circular on cooks' children." Needless to say, an educational policy that excluded (with only rare exceptions) the children of
cooks and like people from gymnasiums and universities scarcely served
the interests of Russia as a great power at the end of the nineteenth and
beginning of the twentieth centuries.

One may also question whether Pobedonostsev's parish schools even
succeeded in teaching patriotism and good citizenship. The effective
teaching of nationalism and loyalty to a particular form of government
demands the imaginative use of historical myths and patriotic symbols.
In such a country as France this purpose was accomplished rather well
after 1871, whether one approves of the results or not, through the ex-
ploitation of such concepts, symbols, and myths as France's civilizing
mission, Jeanne d'Arc, German barbarism, the Marseillaise, the tricolor,
and *liberté, egalité,* and *fraternité.*[49] There was little of a comparable nature in Pobedonostsev's parish schools. Certainly, church singing, Bible
reading, and the learning of prayers did not represent the best way for a
modern society to mold the minds and influence the hearts of its young
citizens in the spirit of nationalism and political loyalty. The likelihood of
success for such an endeavor in Russia toward the end of the nineteenth
century was further diminished by the absence of a large number of truly
dedicated priests interested in carrying out Pobedonostsev's program.[50]

Pobedonostsev's schools did not even make effective use of history.
Pobedonostsev, himself, had praised historical legend as a means of teach-

ing the people the national ideals and traditions of the Russian nation.[51] In the parish schools, however, formal instruction in history was limited to two or three hours a week during the third and fourth years of the curriculum of four-year schools, which constituted but a small percentage of the schools under the administration of the Synod.[52] The factual and monotonously political treatment of history in the textbooks used in the church schools is suggestive of how ineffectually tedious and boring history instruction must have been.[53] Of course, it would have been possible for priests and teachers in the parish schools to have aroused feelings of nationalism in their pupils by dramatically recreating for them some of the deeds performed by the national heroes and saints of the Russian Orthodox Church. But the strict bureaucratic supervision and the bad material conditions in the Russian parish schools obviously discouraged such dramatic pedagogy. What is more, the inculcation of Christian principles and virtues in the mind of a child may not be the best way to teach him nationalism, for religion tends to transcend and even to be in conflict with nationalism. This point is illustrated in nineteenth-century Russia by the difficulty honest thinkers like Vladimir Solov'ev and Leont'ev had in reconciling nationalism with many of the traditional teachings of Orthodox Christianity.

The support that the peasantry gave to the forces of disorder in Russia during the Revolution of 1905 indicates the negligible effect of Pobedonostsev's church schools on the thinking and conduct of the Russian masses. This lack of success is not surprising in view of the bureaucratic nature and the many shortcomings of the parish schools. From the very beginning they tended to have a negative rather than a positive purpose: i.e. to isolate the common people from the liberal ideas of many zemstvo teachers and from the revolutionary ideas of the radical intelligentsia. Pobedonostsev realized that the parish schools were inadequate, but he considered it preferable to entrust the education of the peasants to priests, however poor they might be as teachers, rather than to the "obstinate fools and visionaries"[54] of the zemstvos. He was certain that the mass of the people were on his side rather than on the side of the zemstvos in regard to education. In his estimation, church and school had always been inextricably linked in the mind of the people, who were long accustomed to learning to read and write from prayer-books and psalters.[55] But he chose to ignore that the church had played a minor role in educating the people in Russia and that the zemstvo schools had been primarily responsible for most of the progress in the dissemination of elementary education in Russia during the 1860's and 1870's. True, the number of parish schools rapidly increased during the 1880's and 1890's; but the type of progress represented by the spread of these schools was more convincing on paper than in fact. The statistics concerning this progress were impressive; and they enabled Pobedonostsev, as a master bureaucrat, to compile detailed statistical tabulations on the parish schools in his periodic reports to the emperor. Such reports undoubtedly served to persuade the emperor that Pobedonostsev was performing his job well as the chief administrative officer of the Holy Synod. They did not, however, alter the fact that the parish schools were ineffectual as a means of teaching the masses in Russia useful knowledge, patriotism, and loyalty to the tsarist state.

Just as important as the parish schools in Pobedonostsev's efforts to promote nationality and political stability in Russia were his activities in regard to the borderlands and the non-Orthodox religious groups of the tsarist empire. Here again his point of departure was the premise that Russia's strength and unity as a nation were based on the close collaboration of the Orthodox Church with the Russian state.[56] He believed that through the spiritual influence of Orthodoxy the non-Russian nationalities in the empire could be made a more integral part of Russian national and political life.[57] Similarly, he regarded the continued existence of the Uniate Church and of various schismatic forms of Orthodox Christianity to be an anomalous situation that artificially separated the tsar from millions of his subjects and morally weakened Russia as a nation; he therefore supported all sorts of missionary and propagandistic activities, legal sanctions, and administrative and police pressures to bring the Uniates and schismatics (*raskol'niki*) back into the official Orthodox Church.[58]

Despite his great influence, Pobedonostsev cannot be given credit for having conceived the nationality and religious policies pursued by the government of Alexander III. The policies championed by Pobedonostsev had been worked out in principle and largely implemented long before he had any important influence on governmental decision-making in St. Petersburg. In regard to the Poles, Baltic Germans, Uniates, and *raskol'niki*, for example, the basic line of firmness, Russification, and support for the special interests of the Orthodox Church had already been established under Nicholas I.[59] Under Alexander II, to be sure, the measures against the *raskol'niki* were not always vigorously enforced, and the pressure on the Baltic Germans to conform to Russian usages and to accept the Orthodox Church as a privileged institution in the Baltic provinces was somewhat relaxed. But it was also under Alexander II that the Russian government undertook systematic measures to diminish the Polish and Catholic influence and to Russify the peasant population in the western Ukraine.[60] These policies were even extended to Poland proper, where Count Dmitrii Tolstoi, as Minister of Public Instruction and Over Procurator of the Holy Synod, proceeded to Russify the entire Polish educational system and to force the Uniates in the Chelm region (who had not been affected by Nicholas I's abolition of the Uniate Church in the western Ukraine and White Russia in 1839) to sever their ties with Rome and become Orthodox Christians.[61] Tolstoi also gave official sanction and support to the efforts of Professor N. I. Il'minskii in Kazan to found church schools and to train teachers conversant in oriental languages as a means of attracting the non-Russian peoples of eastern European Russia and Siberia to Russian nationality and Orthodox Christianity.[62]

Pobedonostsev could only approve of the measures and activities of such figures as Nicholas I, Dmitrii Tolstoi, and N. I. Il'minskii to further the cause of Orthodoxy and Russian nationality among the non-Russian peoples of the tsarist empire. One of his major concerns was always to prevent liberal-minded bureaucrats in St. Petersburg from influencing the government to abandon a firm nationalistic policy both at home and abroad. During the 1860's and 1870's he became convinced that Alexander II had definitely failed to provide Russia with firm leadership.[63] Thus he did his utmost to expose the future Alexander III to the influence of the ideas of those who advocated a more aggressively nationalistic conduct of Russian policy in the borderlands of the empire and in Eastern Europe.[64]

After 1881 Pobedonostsev's authority and influence in the Russian government enabled him to give either financial or moral support to the professors, priests, and nationalistic officials who labored zealously in many corners of the empire and abroad to advance the interests of Orthodoxy and Russian nationality. Through his extensive correspondence with such professors, priests, and officials, Pobedonostsev not only encouraged their work but also obtained information that was highly useful to him in deciding how best to allocate funds placed at the disposal of the Synod. Such information helped him in his efforts to persuade the tsar to make appointments and follow policies deemed by Pobedonostsev to be in conformance with the interests of the Orthodox Church and Russian nationalism.

Pobedonostsev was particularly grateful to Professor Il'minskii for his assistance in carrying out tasks that lay completely within the jurisdiction of the Holy Synod. Il'minskii had worked indefatigably since the late 1840's to strengthen the position of the Orthodox Church among the non-Russian peoples of the Volga region.[65] In 1864 he founded his school for Tatar converts, which trained thousands of Tatar boys and girls and hundreds of teachers for native schools in the spirit of Orthodoxy and Russian nationality.[66] After Pobedonostsev became Over Procurator of the Holy Synod, Il'minskii provided him with detailed information concerning the aggressive tactics used by Tatar village officials and religious leaders to return Tatar converts to the Mohammedanism of their fore-fathers.[67] Pobedonostsev used this information and other data provided by Il'minskii to justify requests for more money from the tsar. He pointed out that the Synod needed more financial support so that it could better meet the danger of the Mohammedan offensive against Orthodoxy by building more churches, creating more parish schools, and sending out a larger number of missionaries throughout the Volga-Ural region and Siberia.[68]

The accomplishments and needs of individual missionaries, priests, and officials engaged in the struggle against Islam, Roman Catholicism, and Lutheranism were described in ample detail by Pobedonostsev in his letters and reports to Alexander III and Nicholas II. He had always felt that Russia urgently needed more people who actively pursued positive goals and who had a strong sense of duty and belief in their calling as patriotic servants of the Russian state.[69] Thus the future homogeneous and unified Russian society envisaged by Pobedonostsev was to be based on the foundation laid in the obscurity of Russia's provinces by conscientious officials and ordinary priests and teachers. These were to spread civilization and true Orthodox enlightenment among the Moslems, Buddhists, heathens, and *raskol'niki* of the Volga, the Urals, and Siberia[70] and to defend Russian national and religious interests against the alleged intrigues of the Catholic Poles and Austrians and Lutheran Germans to the west.[71]

Pobedonostsev considered the modest efforts of unknown individuals in Russia's provinces important enough to be brought to the personal attention of the tsar. In 1883, for example, he wrote to Alexander III concerning a certain Ianushkevich, a priest near Grodno who had opened a school for forty girls. Pobedonostsev requested that the tsar should make Ianushkevich a personal gift of an icon of the Virgin as a symbol of imperial approval of his work on the behalf of Orthodoxy and Russian nationality in the Grodno area. He also proposed that the tsar should aid Ianushkevich materially by making 200 rubles available for the purpose of purchasing school books.[72] This type of request was frequently made by Pobedonostsev. It illustrates his tendency to lose himself in petty detail, which was one of his chief weaknesses as an administrator.[73]

This preoccupation with petty detail is closely related to Pobedonostsev's inability to formulate policies toward Russia's national and religious minorities that were based on an understanding of the actual social and political conditions and climate of public opinion in Russia's borderlands. Pobedonostsev was so taken up with writing reports concerning the piety and patriotic zeal of isolated priests and the firmness of unimaginative and inflexible officials in outlying posts of the tsarist empire that he lost sight of the inherent difficulties involved in Russifying and converting to Orthodoxy tens of millions of people living in areas that culturally and religiously had long been separate and distinct from the rest of Russia.

There was a basic inconsistency underlying all of Pobedonostsev's thinking concerning Russia's minority peoples and religions. On the one hand, he had always insisted that man was the product of historical tradition; on the other, he refused to Russia's minorities the right to defend their cultural and historical forms of life against the encroachments and bureaucratic enactments of the Russian state. When Polish Catholics, Chelm Uniates, and Baltic Lutherans did attempt to defend their traditional ways of life, Pobedonostsev condemned their actions as part of the intrigues and conspiracy of the Baltic Germans, the Austrian government, the Polish Jesuits and revolutionists, the Papacy, and international Protestantism against Russia.[74] Accordingly, he repeatedly urged the tsar to send to and keep in Russia's western borderlands officials who were Russian in spirit, firm in their convictions, and zealous in their defense of the interests of Orthodoxy and Russian nationality.[75] In the context of the 1880's and 1890's, this meant support for those officials who worked for the Russification of all levels of education in Poland and the Baltic provinces, who sought to force the Chelm Uniates back into the Orthodox Church, who exercised the strictest administrative controls over the activities of Catholic priests, Jesuits, and Lutheran pastors, and who vigorously promoted conversions to Orthodoxy and the construction of Orthodox churches and parish schools everywhere in this region.[76]

A typical example of the sort of provincial bureaucrat supported by Pobedonostsev was Prince S. V. Shakhovskoi, the Governor of Estonia between 1885 and 1894. During the seventies Shakhovskoi had been one of the many Russian officials who took an active part in Slavic affairs, first as a Pan-Slavic Russian consul in Ragusa and later as a member of the St. Petersburg Slavic Benevolent Society, official in Odessa, and Red Cross worker in Bulgaria. His participation in Slavic affairs brought him into close contact with Ivan Aksakov, whose Russian nationalism and Pan-Slavism had a profound effect on Shakhovskoi's general outlook on life. In 1881 Shakhovskoi was sent to Chernigov to investigate the Jewish pogroms that had taken place there shortly before. After investigating the problem, he characteristically reported that the Jews' economic oppression of the local inhabitants of the Chernigov region was the principal cause of the pogroms. His report so pleased his superiors that he was placed in charge of the administration of the Chernigov *guberniia*.[77] In April, 1885, he was transferred to Estonia, where he thenceforth worked energetically to accelerate the Russification of the entire bureaucracy and all levels of education as well as to encourage the Estonian masses to abandon Lutheranism and enter into the Orthodox Church. He considered the conversion of the Estonians to be an objective of vital political importance for the Russian state.[78] As he wrote in a letter of 1877:

> We shall not be blind. The entire so-called *Ostsee* question will be only and exclusively decided by the way of the union of the local population with Orthodoxy. Lutheranism is the only connection between the Germans and the native population. Cut off this connection, and all that is alien and hostile to Russia will float to the surface. Do not forget that Russia and Orthodoxy are synonymous.[79]

Shakhovskoi came close to being Pobedonostsev's ideal representative of Russian national and religious interests in the western provinces of the tsarist empire. The anti-Semitism Shakhovskoi displayed while in the Ukraine could only serve to make him more acceptable to Pobedonostsev, who had always been unrelenting in his denunciations of the Jews as enemies of the Orthodox faith and exploiters of helpless and economically dependent Russian peasants.[80] After all, it was Pobedonostsev who proposed the classical and well-known solution to the Jewish question: "One-third will die out, one-third will become assimilated with the Orthodox population, and the rest will wander out."[81] In regard to the Baltic question, Pobedonostsev was again in complete agreement with Shakhovskoi. The Over Procurator of the Holy Synod had long since believed that the interests of Orthodoxy and of the Russian state were synonymous in the Baltic region. Hence Pobedonostsev was most disturbed in 1892 when rumor had it that Prince Shakhovskoi was about to be transferred to Kursk. He warned Alexander III that Shakhovskoi's transfer would have unfortunate consequences for Russian policy in the Baltic region, above all because the Germans regarded Shakhovskoi to be the embodiment of the "firm principles of the new Russian policy."[82] Pobedonostsev therefore felt that Shakhovskoi's transfer would be considered by the Germans as a turning point in the government's Baltic policy and as a victory over Russian nationalism. This, Pobedonostsev maintained, would clearly not be in keeping with the government's avowed interest in establishing institutions in the Baltic provinces that would influence the local population to accept Russian Orthodoxy and national culture.[83]

Ostensibly, Pobedonostsev, Shakhovskoi, and other like-minded officials were eminently successful in bringing Russia's borderlands and religious minorities into more intimate contact with Russian nationality and Orthodoxy. A new type of narrow-minded, inflexible, but firmly nationalistic and conservative official now occupied key positions in Poland, the Ukraine, the Baltic provinces, and other outlying areas. As a result, the non–Great-Russian provinces of the empire came to be treated as though they were in the heart of Russia, but a few miles from Moscow. Pobedonostsev was especially interested in having the government support the efforts of zealous officials in these provinces by making generous appropriations for the construction of churches and the establishment of parish schools.[84] He illustrated the need for new churches and parish schools in the non-Russian parts of the empire by reporting to the tsar in the minutest detail concerning the success the Synod had had in bringing thousands of converts yearly into the Orthodox Church. For the fifteen-year period 1891–1905, the Holy Synod reported 267,768 conversions to Orthodoxy—a yearly average of 17,841.[85] Each year these statistics were broken down according to province and former religions of the converts. In 1889 even such a trivial and insignificant detail as the conversion of one Mohammedan living in Minsk *guberniia* was carefully recorded.[86]

Pobedonostsev's belief that the conversion of less than 20,000 individuals to Orthodoxy each year served to unify Russia politically and spiritually was obviously both unrealistic and naïve. According to his own statistics, more than thirty million of the Russian empire's one hundred million inhabitants in 1889 were not members of the Orthodox Church.[87] In fact, 20,000 converts not only represented an infinitesimally small part of the thirty million non-Orthodox subjects of the tsar but also a meager 4 per cent of their probable annual natural population increase.[88] In addition, there is good reason to believe that a substantial proportion of these converts did not accept Orthodoxy because of sincere conviction but, instead, because of either opportunism or coercion. After freedom of religion in Russia was proclaimed in April, 1905, hundreds of thousands of such opportunistic or coerced converts returned to the faith of their fathers.[89] In the Chelm region alone, according to A. L. Pogodin, almost 200,000 former Uniates became Roman Catholics, which meant the effective Polonization of the entire area.[90] Tens of thousands of others reverted to Mohammedanism, Lutheranism, and Buddhism during the years immediately following 1905.

Conversion to Orthodoxy proved to be superficial even among a people as primitive as the Buriat Mongols. In October, 1913, Archbishop Seraphim of Irkutsk reported that practically all the Buriat converts had returned to Buddhism after 1905. He explained the failure of Orthodox Christianity to win genuine support among the Buriats in terms of the external pressures employed by priests, government officials, and the police during the nineteenth century to bring the Buriats into the Orthodox Church and to force Buriat converts to baptize their children.[91] Considering that Archbishop Seraphim's words concerning the Buriats also could be used to characterize the high-handed tactics resorted to by Russian state and church officials to convert Uniates, Old Believers, Catholics, Moslems, and Lutherans,[92] it is not surprising that the Orthodox religion commanded so little respect among both converts and non-Orthodox believers at the beginning of the twentieth century.

These consequences of Russification and forced conversions to Orthodoxy, as has already been pointed out, had been accurately foreseen by Constantine Leont'ev. Leont'ev had much more insight than Pobedonostsev into the fundamental conflict in Russia between modern progress, technology, and nationalism and traditional social and political order. Russification, Pan-Slavism, administrative and religious uniformity, and education for the masses, Leont'ev realized, represented ideas or policies that could only move Russia away from her traditional cultural, political, and social moorings and bring her closer to the technological and egalitarian society of nineteenth-century Europe. Pobedonostsev, in contrast to Leont'ev, naïvely believed that it was possible to introduce Western technology and to extend education in Russia without weakening the childlike faith of the Russian masses in the tsar and the teachings of the Orthodox Church; to deprive the Baltic Germans of their special privileges without strengthening the democratic Latvian and Estonian national movements at the expense of conservative social order in the Baltic provinces;[93] and to convert Catholics, Mohammedans, Buddhists, and Lutherans to Orthodoxy without undermining the hold traditional religion had over the minds of millions of people in the non-Russian regions of the tsarist empire.

Such naïveté is particularly serious in the thinking of a man who criticized others for being impractical idealists and dreamers and who prided himself on being a statesman. Pobedonostsev's thinking revealed many of the same weaknesses and inconsistencies that the rather confused ideas of such people as Dostoevskii, Danilevskii, and Ivan Aksakov did. But Pobedonostsev never seems to have been aware of his own shortcomings as a thinker. Indeed, for someone who wrote or translated an impressive number of books and essays on such varied subjects as religion, law, politics, education, and the family, he displayed remarkably little genuine intellectual curiosity. In effect, he was more a pedant turned propagandist than a thinker.

Pobedonostsev was admittedly a well-educated man who knew a variety of languages and had read widely. But his training at the School of Jurisprudence and his research had been of a one-sided and narrowly specialized nature. Subsequently, it is true, he broadened his interests and wrote essays on a wide range of subjects. The ideas he developed so tendentiously in these essays were, however, far from original. To a large extent, they were notions he had uncritically absorbed from his elders during the years of his youth; and he often borrowed and even plagiarized the ideas of others. Thus Boris Chicherin relates how Pobedonostsev had his wife copy parts of A. N. Bakhmeteva's history of the Orthodox Church and then published his wife's notes as a manual on Orthodox church history under his own name and with no mention of Bakhmeteva.[94] He also borrowed liberally—and again often without acknowledgments—from the ideas of such Western European writers as Frederic Le Play and Max Nordau.[95] But he always used these ideas in his own way and for his own purposes. At times he even deliberately distorted the meaning of books he had translated or made use of in his writings, which Byrnes has referred to as Pobedonostsev's intellectual dishonesty.[96]

Truth for Pobedonostsev was inseparable from the interests of the Russian Orthodox Church and of the Russian autocratic state. It never seems to have occurred to him that there could be a conflict between truth and morality and the interests of established order in Russia. He also seems never to have seriously experienced any need to give new meaning to traditional Russian ideas or to devise new theories of social and cultural development. As Constantine Leont'ev once described Pobedonostsev:

> He is a very useful person. But how? He is like a frost that hinders further decay, but he will never get anything to grow. He not only is not a creator but is not even a reactionary, not a regenerator, not even a restorer. He is only a conservative in the narrowest sense of the word. He is, I say, a frost, a watchman, an unventilated tomb, an "innocent" old maid and nothing more.[97]

In short, he lacked sophistication as a thinker and contributed little to conservative nationalism in Russia as an intellectual phenomenon. There is nothing in Pobedonostsev's writings comparable to Strakhov's efforts to base Russian conservative nationalism on sound philosophical principles and reasoning. Nor is there a suggestion of the artistic or intellectual originality of such writers as Apollon Grigor'ev, the Slavophiles, Dostoevskii, Danilevskii, and Leont'ev. Even the social, political, and military theories of General Rostislav Fadeev, whose amoral glorification of the power of the Russian state closely resembled Pobedonostsev's, seem exciting and original when compared with the heavy, dull, and ponderous thinking of Constantine Pobedonostsev.

Lack of originality also characterized Pobedonostsev as a bureaucrat. He was most effective in criticizing the projects of others and least effective in proposing practical measures and policies that would enable the government to deal with the manifold problems associated with Russia's emergence as a major industrial power.[98] He was, of course, quite right in insisting that Russia needed firm authority and resolute governmental action; but he failed to spell out satisfactorily for the tsar exactly how the government could firmly and imaginatively take into its hands the direction of Russian national and social policy.

The policy recommendations Pobedonostsev did make to Alexander III and Nicholas II represented mainly a continuation of policies established prior to 1881, especially by Count Dmitrii Tolstoi, his predecessor in the office of Over Procurator. But he endeavored to apply these policies with a consistency and a doctrinaire rigidity that had seldom been known previously in Russia. He believed that the Russian empire could be united morally and nationally through the introduction and enforcement of bureaucratic norms by zealous and nationalistic provincial officials. Like General Fadeev, he wanted to impose external and abstract social forms on Russian society. Samarin had criticized Fadeev for suggesting that such forms could be forced on Russian society irrespective of whether they were based on an already existing internal unity of belief and conviction among the tsar's subjects. Pobedonostsev, though his ideas lacked the originality of Fadeev's, can be similarly criticized, because he attempted to impose on millions of the tsar's subjects a way and view of life to which they were either indifferent or hostile. Thus Pobedonostsev was, to borrow the term Samarin used in his polemics with Fadeev, a "revolutionary conservative" who aspired to force tsarist society, *nolens volens*, to fit into the mold prescribed for it by a handful of nationalistic thinkers and bureaucrats.

The forces opposing Pobedonostsev's "revolutionary conservatism" were too strong at the beginning of the twentieth century to permit it much chance of success. Its most impressive accomplishment was the assistance it gave to the multiplication of officials, priests, and professors who, in numerous public addresses, books, and articles, indiscriminately praised the Slavophiles, Dostoevskii, Katkov, Danilevskii, and even Strakhov as defenders of Russian national culture and who talked and wrote endlessly about the "brother Slavs" and the national and religious interests of the Russian state.[99] They were, however, a minority among educated Russians; and their public statements, as those of Pobedonostsev, served chiefly to discredit further the ideas of the original Russian conservative nationalists in the eyes of the generation that reached maturity during the years preceding the Revolution of 1905.

CHAPTER FOURTEEN

Conclusion

NATIONAL and spiritual unity and historical continuity are ideas that have been cherished and praised by all modern conservatives. Among themselves they have often disagreed on fundamental political and philosophical ideas. Some of them, like Edmund Burke, Alexis de Tocqueville, and the Slavophiles, approached moderate liberalism in treating the problems of modern society. Others, like Maurice Barrès, Friedrich Nietzsche, Leont'ev, and Pobedonostsev, were in many ways the intellectual precursors of twentieth-century totalitarianism. But they all instinctively would have applauded Joseph de Maistre's exclamation that France consists not of thirty million Frenchmen but of the billion or so people who for centuries have lived between the Pyrenees and the Rhine. That is, the dead count more than the living, and it is our memory of past generations that gives patriotism continuity and makes nations more than mere associations of isolated individuals thrown together by the ephemeral interests and contingencies of day-to-day living.[1]

Important though this message is, conservatives, confronted by the kaleidoscopic and rapidly changing world of the past several hundred years, have occupied a defensive position. Conservative governments controlled the greater part of Europe during much of this period. Their leaders, however, seldom directed change or mastered the problems of modern society. Otto von Bismarck perhaps partly succeeded in doing this; but the German neoconservatives, who followed Bismarck and attempted to give new dimensions and meaning to conservatism, were only a vociferous minority that did much to prepare Germany intellectually for Hitler.[2]

Russia's conservative nationalists had their share of difficulties, although one form or another of their ideas enjoyed the official support of the gov-

204

ernment for a number of decades during the nineteenth century. With the notable exceptions of Leont'ev and Pobedonostsev, all of the major conservative nationalists who have been discussed were briefly imprisoned, exiled, or at least harassed by censorship authorities. Even a journalist as influential, loyal, and hardheaded as Katkov, on several occasions barely managed to save his *Russian Messenger* and *Moscow News* from the attacks of offended bureaucrats. Under Alexander III nationalists and conservatives fared somewhat better than before. But it was under this same ruler that the Russian government gave more support than ever before to the task of hastening the industrial development of Russia. The industrial upsurge of the 1890's, made possible by protective tariffs, state encouragement of railway construction, and foreign loans, destroyed the dream that Russia could avoid the evils of modern European bourgeois and capitalist society. In the new Russia that emerged around 1900 neither the populist ideal of agrarian socialism based on the peasant commune nor the conservative nationalists' idealized and harmonious society ruled by the tsar, administered by the service gentry, and inspired by the Orthodox Church was a reasonable or likely alternative for Russia.

The official sanction and approval that conservative nationalists enjoyed under Alexander III and Nicholas II often did them more harm than good. Official approval led contemporaries to associate them with such heavy-handed bureaucrats as Pobedonostsev and Prince Shakhovskoi, who utilized the most questionable and weakest elements of conservative nationalism to justify unpopular governmental policies. Thus conservative nationalism became inextricably linked with the twentieth-century debacle of Russian tsarism. The last outstanding Russian conservative nationalist, the former *narodnik* and terrorist L. A. Tikhomirov, witnessed the Revolution of 1917 from the sanctuary of the Trinity Sergiev monastery and died, unmolested by the Bolsheviks, in 1923. His was the dubious distinction of being hailed in the early 1930's as the father of Russian fascism.[3]

Conservative nationalism is, however, more than a prelude to an abortive Russian fascism. Such thinkers as Apollon Grigor'ev, Samarin, Strakhov, Danilevskii, and Leont'ev made important contributions to the intellectual life of nineteenth-century Russia. Their search for the origins and foundations of Russian culture and society revealed truths about Russia that often escaped their more liberal or radical compatriots. They realized, for example, that Russia's thousand-year development in semi-isolation from the rest of Europe, her vastness, and her complex population made it ill-advised to remodel Russia in the image of smaller European countries or in accordance with some scheme of utopian reform. They undeniably imputed more harmonious and organic unity to traditional Russian society than it ever possessed; but they were correct that firm tsarist authority, especially assisted by the serving gentry, had long been a *sine qua non* of Russian progress. They were aware of various shortcomings and deficiencies in Russian society but thought these could best be remedied by a powerful autocratic ruler promoting the welfare of his subjects. They were disturbed most by the alienation since the eighteenth century of the upper strata of the Russian population from the mass of the people. They hoped that this alienation could be overcome through the encouragement and development of Russian nationalism. It is clear, however, that tsarist Russia was not able to use nationalism effectively as an instrument of state policy. This failure does not necessarily mean that the cure Russian conservative nationalists prescribed for the ills of Russian society was altogether incorrect and outdated. Indeed, they comprehended one of modern Russia's most urgent tasks: the need for national cohesion and unifying social ideas.

Notes

PART I: INTRODUCTION

1. Karl Mannheim, *Essays on Sociology and Social Psychology* (London: Routledge and K. Paul, 1953), p. 82.

2. The basic work on early German historicism is Friedrich Meinecke's *Die Entstehung des Historismus* (2nd ed.; Munich: Leibniz Verlag, 1946). The influence of Burke on German conservatism is examined by Jacques Droz, *L'Allemagne et la Révolution française* (Paris: Presses Universitaires de France, 1949), pp. 348–92, 465–67. See also G. Rexius, "Studien und Staatslehre der historischen Schule," *Historische Zeitschrift*, CVII (1911), 496–539; and E. Rothacker, "Savigny, Grimm, Ranke: Ein Beitrag zur Frage nach dem Zusammenhang der historischen Schule," *Historische Zeitschrift*, CXXVIII (1923), 415–55.

3. Cf. Edward C. Thaden, "The Beginnings of Romantic Nationalism in Russia," *American Slavic and East European Review*, XIII (December, 1954), 515–17.

4. Karamzin's articles include: "Strannost'," *Sochineniia* (3d ed.; Moscow: S. Selivanskii, 1820), IX, 135–40; "O liubvi k otechestvu i narodnoi gordosti," *ibid.*, VII, 126–39; "O sluchaiakh i kharakterakh v rossiiskoi istorii, kotorye mogut byt' predmetom khudozhestv," *ibid.*, VII, 247–65; and "O novom obrazovanii narodnago prosveshcheniia v Rossii," *ibid.*, VIII, 254–65.

5. Cf. Thaden, "The Beginnings . . . ," *American Slavic . . . Review*, XIII, 509.

6. Karamzin, *Sochineniia*, VII, 265.

7. *Ibid.*, pp. 247–48.

8. N. N. Strakhov, *Kriticheskiia stat'i, 1861–1894 gg.*, ed. I. P. Matchenko (Kiev: Izdanie I. P. Matchenko, 1902), p. 158; Strakhov, "Zhizn' i trudy N. Ia. Danilevskago," introductory article to N. Ia. Danilevskii, *Rossiia i Evropa: Vzgliad na kul'turnyia i politicheskiia otnosheniia slavianskago mira k germano-romanskomu* (5th ed.; St. Petersburg: Tipografiia Brat. Panteleevykh, 1895).

CHAPTER ONE

1. V. O. Kliuchevskii, "Istoriia soslovii v Rossii," *Sochineniia* (Moscow: Gospolitizdat, 1956–59), VI, 372, 462; S. A. Korf, *Dvorianstvo i ego soslovnoe*

upravlenie za stoletie 1762–1855 godov (St. Petersburg: Trenke and Fiusno, 1906), pp. 2–3; A. Romanovich-Slavatinskii, *Dvorianstvo v Rossii ot nachala XVIII veka do otmeny krepostnago prava* (St. Petersburg: Tipografiia Ministerstva Vnutrennikh Del, 1870), p. 2; G. Vernadsky, *The Mongols and Russia* (New Haven, Conn.: Yale University Press, 1953), pp. 367–72.

2. Vernadsky, *The Mongols and Russia*, p. 337; N. Runovskii, *Tserkovno-grahdanskiia zakono-polozheniia otnostil'no pravoslavnago dukhovenstva v tsarstvovanie Imperatora Aleksandra II* (Kazan: Imperatorskii Universitet, 1898), pp. 5–30.

3. P. V. Miliukov, *Ocherki po istorii russkoi kul'tury* (Jubilee ed.; Paris: Izdatel'stvo "Sovremennyia Zapiski," 1930–37), III, chaps. 1–3; Kliuchevskii, "Kurs russkoi istorii," *Sochineniia*, II, 117–18, 126–27, 137; D. S. Likhachev, *Natsional'noe samosoznanie drevnei Rusi* (Moscow–Leningrad: Akademiia Nauk, 1945), chaps. 5–6; W. K. Medlin, *Moscow and East Rome: A Political Study of the Relations of Church and State in Muscovite Russia* (Geneva: E. Droz, 1952), chaps. 4–5; Michael Cherniavsky, *Tsar and People: Studies in Russian Myths* (New Haven, Conn.: Yale University Press, 1961), chaps. 2–4.

4. *Svod zakonov Rossiiskoi Imperii* (2nd ed.; St. Petersburg: V. tipografii Vtorago otdeleniia Sobstvennoi Ego Imperatorskago Velichestva Kantseliarii, 1842), I, 3.

5. *Ibid.*, p. 11.

6. M. Korff, *The Accession of Nicholas I* (London: J. Murray, 1857), pp. 276–77.

7. Korf, *Dvorianstvo i ego soslovnoe upravlenie* . . . , pp. 354–57; Romanovich-Slavatinskii, *Dvorianstvo v Rossii* . . . , pp. 494–95.

8. P. N. Sakulin, *Iz istorii russkago idealizma: Kniaz' V. Odoevskii, myslitel'-pisatel'* (Moscow: Izdanie M. i S. Sabashnikovykh, 1913), I, Part 2, 174.

9. The initial Russian responses to the Revolution are described by M. M. Shtrange, *Russkoe obshchestvo i frantsuzskaia revoliutsiia 1789–1794 gg.* (Moscow: Akademiia Nauk, 1956).

10. This is now available with helpful notes in Richard Pipes (trans.), *Karamzin's Memoir on Ancient and Modern Russia* (Cambridge, Mass.: Harvard University Press, 1959).

11. Speranskii's reforms and the attitude of the gentry toward them are best analyzed in Marc Raeff, *Michael Speransky: Statesman of Imperial Russia 1772–1839* (The Hague: Martinus Nijhoff, 1957), chaps. 3–6.

12. A competent general discussion of these and other aspects of Nicholas I's reign is given in Nicholas V. Riasanovsky, *Nicholas I and Official Nationality in Russia, 1825–1855* (Berkeley and Los Angeles: University of California Press, 1959). The best account in English of the activities of the Third Section is Sidney Monas' *The Third Section: Police and Society in Russia under Nicholas I* (Cambridge, Mass.: Harvard University Press, 1961). Also useful is M. K. Lemke's *Nikolaevskie zhandarmy i literatura 1826–1855 gg.* (2nd ed.; St. Petersburg: S. V. Bunin, 1909). On the restrictive nature of education in Russia during the first part of the nineteenth century, see S. V. Rozhdestvenskii, *Istoricheskii obzor deiatel'nosti ministerstva narodnago prosveshcheniia, 1802–1902* (St. Petersburg: Izdanie Ministerstva Narodnago Prosveshcheniia, 1902), pp. 166, 256.

13. Korf, *Dvorianstvo i ego soslovnoe upravlenie* . . . , pp. 456–57.

14. A convenient analysis, though hostile to the church, of the influence

and role of the church in Muscovite society is given in V. V. Titlinov's *Pravoslavie na sluzhbe samoderzhaviia v russkom gosudarstve* (Leningrad: Gosizdat, 1924).

15. For a detailed description of the position of the church in eighteenth-century Russia, see A. V. Kartashev, *Ocherki po istorii russkoi tserkvi* (Paris: Y.M.C.A. Press, 1959), II, 378–557.

16. N. F. Dubrovin, "Nashi mystiki-sektanty: Aleksandr Fedorovich Labzin i ego zhurnal 'Sionskii Vestnik,'" *Russkaia Starina*, LXXXII (September, 1894), 145–203, (October) 101–26, (November) 58–91, (December) 98–132, and LXXXIII (February, 1895), 35–52; N. K. Schilder, *Imperator Aleksandr Pervyi, ego zhizn' i tsarstvovanie* (St. Petersburg: A. S. Suvorin, 1897–1904), III, 321–28, 344–46; A. M. Ammann, *Abriss der ostslawischen Kirchengeschichte* (Vienna: Verlag Herder, 1950), p. 464; S. R. Tompkins, "The Russian Bible Society: A Case of Religious Xenophobia," *American Slavic and East European Review*, VII (October, 1948), 255–56.

17. See Schilder, *Imperator Aleksandr Pervyi* . . . , IV, 246–51, 316–21; Tompkins, "The Russian Bible Society . . . ," pp. 265–67; Avtobiografiia iurevskago arkhimandrita Fotiia," *Russkaia Starina*, LXXXI (May, 1894), 91–114, LXXXII (July, 1894), 195–230, (September) 204–33, (October) 127–42, and LXXXIII (February, 1895), 174–216; S. I. Miropol'skii, "Fotii Spaskii, iurevskii arkhimandrit: Istoriko-biograficheskii ocherk," *Vestnik Evropy*, LXXIV (December, 1878), 587–636.

18. F. V. Blagovidov, *Ober-prokurory sviateishago sinoda v XVIII i v pervoi polovine XIX stoletiia* (Kazan: Imperatorskii Universitet, 1899), pp. 381–424.

19. Filaret, *Slova i rechi sinodal'nago chlena Filareta mitropolita moskovskago* (Moscow: Tipografiia A. Semena, 1844–45), III, 5–11, 107–14.

20. *Ibid.*, p. 114.

21. Filaret, *Mneniia, otzyvy i pis'ma Filareta mitropolita moskovskago i kolomenskago po raznym voprosam za 1821–1867 gg.* (Moscow: Sinodal'naia Tipografiia, 1905), pp. 60–63, 322–24; *idem, Sobranie mnenii i otzyvov Filareta, mitropolita moskovskago i kolomenskago, po uchebnym i tserkovno-gosudarstvennym voprosam* (St. Petersburg: Sinodal'naia Tipografiia, 1885–88), IV, 296–97, 565–67.

22. Filaret, *Sobranie* . . . , IV, 296–97 and Vol. V, Part 1, 67, 184–86.

23. *Ibid.*, Vol. V, Part 1, 5–17.

24. Filaret's draft of the emancipation proclamation is to be found in *ibid.*, Vol. V, Part 1, 9–15.

CHAPTER TWO

1. See *Povesti o Kulikovskoi bytve*, ed. M. N. Tikhomirov, V. F. Rzhiga, and L. A. Dmitriev (Moscow: Akademiia Nauk, 1959), for various laudatory accounts of the Battle of Kulikovo Field written by churchmen in the fifteenth, sixteenth, and seventeenth centuries.

2. This description of Ivan is given in *Istoriia russkogo iskusstva*, ed. I. E. Grabar', V. N. Lazarev, and V. S. Kemenov (Moscow: Akademiia Nauk, 1953–), III, 572–78.

3. D. S. Likhachev, *Natsional'noe samosoznanie drevnei Rusi* (Moscow–Leningrad: Akademiia Nauk, 1945), pp. 98–101; N. Andreyev, "Filofey and his Epistle to Ivan Vasil'yevich," *Slavonic and East European Review*, XXXVIII

(December, 1959), 1–2. They did, however, associate themselves indirectly with the heritage of the Rome of the Caesars by making use of a false genealogy of the early sixteenth century which traced the ancestry of the Muscovite rulers back to the Roman emperors through Augustus' fictitious brother, Prus.

4. See Pierre Pascal, *Avvakum et les débuts du Raskol: La crise réligieuse au XVIIe siècle en Russie* (Paris: Honoré Champion, 1938), pp. 1–8; A. Brückner, *Die Europäisierung Russlands Land und Volk* (Gotha: F. A. Perthes, 1888), pp. 276–80; Likhachev, *Natsional'noe* . . . , pp. 111–18.

5. Brückner, *Die Europäisierung* . . . , pp. 338–40.

6. A recent Roman Catholic account of Catherine II's efforts to bring the Ukrainian Uniates back into the Orthodox Church is given by A. M. Ammann, *Abriss der ostslawische Kirchengeschichte* (Vienna: Verlag Herder, 1950), pp. 441–47.

7. Richard Pipes (trans.), *Karamzin's Memoir on Ancient and Modern Russia* (Cambridge, Mass.: Harvard University Press, 1959), p. 124.

8. *Ibid.*, p. 121.

9. *Ibid.*, p. 122.

10. *Ibid.*, p. 123.

11. See A. S. Shishkov, *Razsuzhdenie o starom i novom sloge rossiiskago iazyka* (St. Petersburg: Imperatorskaia Tipografiia, 1803), pp. 1–13, 91–92; *idem*, "Pis'ma A. S. Shishkova Grafu Dmitriiu Ivanovichu Khvostovu," *Russkaia Starina*, LXXXVI (April, 1896), 33–38; N. A. Palitsyn, "Manifesty napisannye Shishkovym v otechestvennuiu voinu i patroticheskoe ikh znachenie," *Russkaia Starina*, CL (June, 1912), 477–91; V. V. Vinogradov, *Ocherki po istorii russkoi literaturnago iazyka XVII–XIX vekov* (2nd ed.; Leiden: E. J. Brill, 1949), pp. 195–99; A. Brückner, *A Literary History of Russia* (London and Leipzig: T. F. Unwin, 1908), pp. 143–44.

12. N. K. Schilder, *Imperator Aleksandr Pervyi ego zhizn' i tsarstvovanie* (St. Petersburg: A. S. Suvorin, 1897–1904), III, 259–60.

13. S. I. Miropol'skii, "Fotii Spaskii, iurevskii arkhimandrit: Istoriko-biograficheskii ocherk," *Vestnik Evropy*, LXXIV (December, 1878), 587–617; "Avtobiografiia iurevskago arkhimandrita Fotiia," *Russkaia Starina*, LXXXIV (August, 1895), 169–200, (November) 207–36, (December) 189–203, LXXXVII (July, 1896), 163–99, and (August) 423–43; Schilder, *Imperator Aleksandr Pervyi* . . . , IV, 246–51 and 316–21; S. R. Tompkins, "The Russian Bible Society: A Case of Religious Xenophobia," *American Slavic and East European Review*, VII (October, 1948), 263–67.

14. Miropol'skii, "Fotii Spaskii . . . ," pp. 614–17; Tompkins, "The Russian Bible Society . . . ," p. 267.

15. S. V. Rozhdestvenskii, *Istoricheskii obzor deiatel'nosti ministerstva narodnago prosveshcheniia, 1802–1902* (St. Petersburg: Izdanie Ministerstva Narodnago Prosveshcheniia, 1902), pp. 176–77.

16. For a more detailed and comprehensive discussion of official nationality, see N. V. Riasanovsky's study, *Nicholas I and Official Nationality in Russia, 1825–1855* (Berkeley and Los Angeles: University of California Press, 1959).

17. N. P. Barsukov, *Zhizn' i trudy M. P. Pogodina* (St. Petersburg: M. M. Stasiulevich, 1888–1910), IV, 83–85.

18. S. S.Uvarov, *Desiatiletie ministerstva narodnago prosveshcheniia, 1833–1843* (St. Petersburg: Imperatorskaia Akademiia Nauk, 1864), p. 106; Rozhdestvenskii, *Istoricheskii Obzor* . . . , pp. 244–45.

19. Uvarov, *Desiatiletie* . . . , p. 107.

20. Cf. N. V. Riasanovsky, "'Nationality' in the State Ideology during the Reign of Nicholas I," *Russian Review*, XIX (January, 1960), 38–46; A. Koyré, *La philosophie et le problème national en Russie au début du XIXe siècle* (Paris: Honoré Champion, 1929), pp. 201–7.

21. Uvarov, *Desiatiletie* . . . , pp. 11–12; Riasanovsky, *Nicholas I and Official Nationality in Russia*, pp. 140–41.

22. *Zhurnal Ministerstva Narodnago Prosveshcheniia*, I (1834), vi.

23. Uvarov, *Desiatiletie* . . . , pp. 36–47; Rozhdestvenskii, *Istoricheskii Obzor* . . . , pp. 212–13, 296–308, 383.

24. See [I. Semashko], *Zapiski Iosifa mitropolita litovskago* (St. Petersburg: Imperatorskaia Akademiia Nauk, 1883), 3 vols.; E. Orlovskii, *Sud'by pravo-slaviia v sviazi s istorieiu latinstva i unii v grodnenskoi gubernii v XIX stoletii, 1794–1900 gg.* (Grodno: Gubernskaia Tipografiia, 1903), pp. 53–109.

25. Uvarov, *Desiatiletie* . . . , pp. 48–61.

26. W. Kahle, *Die Begegnung des baltischen Protestantismus mit der Russisch-orthodoxen Kirche* (Leiden: E. J. Brill, 1959), p. 127.

27. Studies of the conversion movement usually have been made from either a partisan German or Russian point of view. See M. Stephany, *Konversion und Rekonversion in Livland* (*Abhandlungen der Herder-Gesellschaft und des Herder-Instituts zu Riga*, Vol. IV, No. 8 [Riga, 1931]); R. Stupperich, "Motive und Massnahmen der livländischen Bauernbewegung der Jahre 1845–47," *Kyrios*, IV (1939–40), 39–56; Iu. F. Samarin, "Pravoslavnye Latyshi," *Sochineniia Iu. F. Samarina* (Moscow: A. I. Mamontov, 1877–1911), VIII, 419–622 and X, 409–80; *Istoriia Latviiskoi SSSR*, ed. Ia. Ia. Zutis, K. Ia. Strazdin', *et al.* (Riga: Akademiia Nauk Latviiskoi SSR, 1952–58), I, 517–18. The most famous example of Nicholas I's restraining the zeal of Russian patriots in the Baltic region was his brief imprisonment and reprimanding of Iurii Samarin. See B. E. Nol'de, *Iurii Samarin i ego vremia* (Paris: Imprimerie de Navarre, 1926), pp. 47–49.

28. Riasanovsky, *Nicholas I and Official Nationality in Russia*, pp. 137–67; *idem.*, "Some Comments on the Role of the Intelligentsia in the Reign of Nicholas I of Russia, 1825–1855," *Slavic and East European Journal*, V (1957), 163–73.

29. For Nicholas I's reaction to Aksakov's Pan-Slavism, see I. S. Aksakov, *Ivan Sergeevich Aksakov v ego pis'makh* (Moscow: M. G. Volchaninov, 1888–92), II, 154–55.

30. On the connection between Burachek and Shishkov, see Apollon A. Grigor'ev, "Razvitie idei narodnosti v nashei literature so smerti Pushkina," *Sobranie sochinenii Apollona Grigor'eva*, ed. V. F. Savodnik (Moscow: I. N. Kushnerev, 1915–16), Vypusk III, p. 118.

31. S. Burachek, "Kabinet izbrannykh proizvedenii," *Maiak*, 1840, Part IV, chap. 4, p. 185.

32. S. Burachek, review of Lermontov's *Geroi nashego vremeni*, in *Maiak*, 1840, Part IV, chap. 4, pp. 210–19.

33. S. Burachek, "Russkaia narodnost'," *Maiak*, 1842, Parts XVII and XVIII, chap. 4, p. 20

34. A. N. Pypin, *Istoriia russkoi etnografii* (St. Petersburg: M. M. Stasiulevich, 1890–92), I, 360–62.

35. S. Burachek, "Leitenant Ventsov," *Maiak*, 1840, Part I, chap. 2 (Prose), p. 48.

36. A. G. Dement'ev, *Ocherki po istorii russkoi zhurnalistiki 1840–1850 gg.* (Leningrad: Goslitizdat, 1951), p. 90.

37. See S. A. Vengerov, "Molodaia redaktsiia *Moskvitianina*," *Vestnik Evropy*, CXVII (February, 1886), 581–612; A. G. Dement'ev, "Granovskii i Shevyrev," *Uchenye Zapiski* of the Leningrad State University, Philological Series, No. 46, Vypusk III (Leningrad, 1939), pp. 341–47; letter of T. I. Filippov to S. P. Shevyrev, January 19, 1860, Shevyrev Papers, Manuscript Division, Saltykov-Shchedrin Public Library, Leningrad.

CHAPTER THREE

1. Much of this chapter is based on my article "The Beginnings of Romantic Nationalism in Russia," *American Slavic and East European Review*, XIII (December, 1954), 500–21.

2. H. Rogger, "The Russian National Character: Some Eighteenth-Century Views," *Harvard Slavic Studies*, IV (1957), 17–34. Cf. Rogger, *National Consciousness in Eighteenth-Century Russia* (Cambridge, Mass.: Harvard University Press, 1960), pp. 73–84, 262–75.

3. Rogger, "The 'Nationalism' of Ivan Nikitich Boltin," in *For Roman Jakobson: Essays on the Occasion of His Sixteenth Birthday 11 October 1956* (The Hague: Mouton, 1956), pp. 423–29; Rogger, *National Consciousness* . . . , pp. 228–38; N. L. Rubinshtein, *Russkaia istoriografiia* (Moscow: Gospolitizdat, 1941), pp. 138–50.

4. Rogger, "The 'Nationalism' . . . ," p. 428. Cf. Rogger, *National Consciousness* . . . , p. 237.

5. N. M. Karamzin, "Natal'ia, boiarskaia doch'," *Sochineniia* (3rd ed.; Moscow: S. Selivanskii, 1820), VI, 100.

6. Karamzin's concern about the unity and power interests of Russia vis-à-vis Poland is especially evident in his essay "Mnenie russkago grazhdanina," *Neizdannyia sochineniia i perepiska Nikolaia Mikhailovicha Karamzina* (St. Petersburg, N. Tiblen, 1862), pp. 3–8. Cf. Karamzin, "Istoricheskoe pokhval'noe slovo Ekaterine II," *Sochineniia*, VIII, 22, 30–32.

7. F. Meinecke, *Die Entstehung des Historismus* (2nd ed.; Munich: Leibniz Verlag, 1946), p. 5.

8. See Thaden, "The Beginnings . . . ," pp. 500–501.

9. Concerning their influence, see A. Koyré, *La philosophie et le problème national en Russie au début du XIXe siècle* (Paris: Honoré Champion, 1929), pp. 113–36; D. I. Chizhevskii, *Gegel' v Rossii* (Paris: "Dom Knigi" and "Sovremennyia Zapiski," 1939), pp. 37–38; N. K. Koz'min, *Nikolai Nikolaevich Nadezhdin: Zhizn' i nauchno-literaturnaia deiatel'nost' (1804–1836)* (St. Petersburg: M. A. Aleksandrov, 1912).

10. P. N. Sakulin, *Iz istorii russkago idealizma: Kniaz' V. Odoevskii, myslitel'-pisatel'* (Moscow: Izdanie M. i S. Sabashnikovykh, 1913), I, Part 1, 104.

11. D. V. Venevitinov, *Polnoe sobranie sochinenii* (Moscow–Leningrad: "Academia," 1934), pp. 216–20; Koyré, *La philosophie* . . . , pp. 150–52. Cf. Thaden, "The Beginnings of Romantic Nationalism in Russia," *American Slavic and East European Review*, XIII (December, 1954), 516–17.

12. The Stankevich circle has been described by E. J. Brown, "The Circle

of Stankevich," *American Slavic and East European Review,* XVI (October, 1957), 349–68. Cf. Chizhevskii, *Gegel' v Rossii,* pp. 50–52, 69–83, 237–43.

13. A. N. Pypin, *Istoriia russkoi etnografii* (St. Petersburg: M. M. Stasiulevich, 1890–92), I, 390.

14. See A. I. Herzen, "Byloe i dumy," *Sobranie sochinenii* (Moscow: Akademiia Nauk, 1954–), IX, 148, 153, 162–63.

15. E. V. Bobrov, *Filosofiia v Rossii: Materialy i izsledovaniia* (Kazan: Imperatorskii Universitet, 1901–3), Vypusk IV, p. 206.

16. S. A——ev, "Katkov," *Russkii biograficheskii slovar'* (St. Petersburg–Petrograd: Izdanie Imperatorskago Russkago Istoricheskago Obshchestva, 1896–1918), VIII, 548–49; S. Nevedenskii, "Katkov i Belinskii," *Russkii Vestnik,* CXCVI (June, 1888), 16–54.

17. M. N. Katkov, review of *Pesni russkago naroda,* ed. I. Sakharov (St. Petersburg, 1838–39), in *Otechestvennyia Zapiski,* IV (1839), Section VI, pp. 8, 11–15, 30–34.

18. *Ibid.,* p. 36.

19. P. V. Miliukov, *Glavnyia techeniia russkoi istoricheskoi mysli* (3d ed.; St. Petersburg: M. V. Aver'ianov, 1913), pp. 282–83, 299; V. Setschkareff, *Schellings Einfluss in der russichen Literatur der 20er und 30er Jahre des XIX Jahrhunderts* (Berlin University, Slavisches Institut. Veröffentlichungen, Vol. 22 [Leipzig: Kommissionsverlag O. Harrassowitz, 1939]), pp. 66–74; Thaden, "The Beginnings . . . ," pp. 517–19.

20. N. A. Polevoi, *Istoriia russkago naroda* (2nd ed.; Moscow: Tipografiia A. Semena, 1830–33), II, 141.

21. N. P. Barsukov, *Zhizn' i trudy M. P. Pogodina* (St. Petersburg: M. M. Stasiulevich, 1888–1910), II, 140–48, 153; IV, 360–62. These aphorisms were originally published in the *Moskovskii Vestnik,* which Pogodin edited. In 1836 they were published in book form at Moscow (*Istoricheskie aforizmy*).

22. See Herzen, *Sobranie sochinenii,* II, 134–37, 194–98, and IX, 165.

23. "Parallel' russkoi istorii s istoriei evropeiskihk gosudarstv otnositel'no nachala," *Moskvitianin,* 1845, Part I, No. 1 (Science section), pp. 1–18.

24. *Ibid.,* pp. 1–3.

25. *Ibid.,* pp. 4–13.

26. *Ibid.,* pp. 13–18.

27. He experienced, for example, such feelings in the Uspenskii Sobor of the Kremlin during a festival of the Virgin on October 3, 1843. See "Zhurnal S. P. Shevyreva: Zapiski i zametki 1843–1852," Shevyrev Papers, Manuscript Division, Saltykov–Shchedrin Public Library, Leningrad.

28. S. P. Shevyrev, *Istoriia russkoi slovesnosti* (Moscow: Universitetskaia Tipografiia, 1846–60), I, 11.

29. *Ibid.*

30. S. P. Shevyrev, "Vzgliad russkago no sovremennoe obrazovanie Evropy," *Moskvitianin,* 1841, Part I, No. 1, pp. 295–96.

31. *Ibid.,* p. 296.

32. E. Benz, *Die abendländische Sendung der östlich-orthodoxen Kirche* (Mainz: Verlag der Akademie der Wissenschaften und der Literatur, 1950), p. 272.

33. V. F. Odoevskii, *Russkiia nochi* (Moscow: Pechatnia A. Snegirevoi, 1913), pp. 341–46, 416–23; Sakulin, *Iz istorii russkago idealizma . . . ,* pp. 271–72; Thaden, "The Beginnings . . . ," pp. 519–20.

34. Cf. N. V. Riasanovsky's discussion of the Slavophiles' treatment of the theme of the decline of Europe in his *Russia and the West in the Teaching of the Slavophiles* (Cambridge, Mass.: Harvard University Press, 1952), pp. 117–19.

35. See B. M. Sokolov, *Sobrateli narodnykh pesen: P. V. Kireevskii, P. I. Iakushkin i P. V. Shein* (Moscow: V. V. Dumnov, 1923), pp. 16–21.

36. See S. Chetverikov, *Optina Pustyn'* (Paris: Y.M.C.A. Press, 1926), pp. 44–50.

37. Constantine Aksakov's historical articles are collected in Volume I of *Polnoe sobranie sochinenii Konstantina Sergeevicha Aksakova* (Moscow: P. Bakhmetev, 1861). Cf. N. Kostomarov, "O znachenii kriticheskikh trudov Konstantina Aksakova po russkoi istorii," *Russkoe Slovo* (February, 1861), pp. 1–28. Khomiakov wrote a number of theological and polemical articles, usually in French, on the Orthodox Church and the differences between it and Western Catholicism and Protestantism. On Khomiakov, see A. Gratieux, *A. Khomiakov et le mouvement slavophile* (Paris: Éditions du Cerf, 1939), 2 volumes.

38. See, for example, Aksakov, *Polnoe sobranie sochinenii K. S. Aksakova*, I, 311–18 and 415–23.

39. See volumes II, III, and IV of *Sochineniia Iu. F. Samarina* (Moscow: A. I. Mamontov, 1877–1911).

40. See *Polnoe sobranie sochinenii K. S. Aksakova*, I, 10–15 and 294–97.

41. Constantine Aksakov, "Dopolnenie k zapiske o vnutrennem sostoianii Rossii," in *Rannie slavianofily*, ed. N. L. Brodskii (Moscow: I. D. Sytin, 1910), p. 98.

42. "Zapiska K. S. Aksakova 'O vnutrennem sostoianii Rossii,' predstavlennaia Gosudariu Imperatoru Aleksandru II v 1855 g.," *Rannie slavianofily*, pp. 92–93 and 96.

43. "Dopolnenie k zapiske . . . ," p. 97.

44. *Ibid.*

45. *Ibid.*, p. 98.

46. See I. S. Aksakov, "K chemu vedet vzgliad na Tserkov' kak na gosudarstvennoe uchrezhdenie," *Sochineniia* (Moscow: M. G. Volchaninov, 1886–87), IV, 124–26.

47. The concept of *sobornost'* is discussed by Riasanovsky, "Khomiakov on Sobornost'," in *Continuity and Change in Russian and Soviet Thought*, ed. E. J. Simmons (Cambridge, Mass.: Harvard University Press, 1955), pp. 183–96; and by Peter K. Christoff, *An Introduction to Nineteenth-Century Slavophilism: A Study in Ideas;* Vol. 1: *A. S. Khomiakov* ('S-Gravenhage: Mouton, 1961), pp. 137–71. Cf. A. S. Khomiakov, "Pis'ma redaktoru 'L'Union Chrétienne' o znachenii slov: 'Kafolicheskii' i 'sobornyi,' po povodu rechi Iezuita ottsa Gagarina," *Polnoe sobranie sochinenii* (3d ed., Moscow: Universitetskaia Tipografiia, 1900–1907), II, 307–14.

48. Khomiakov, *Polnoe sobranie sochinenii*, II, 53–57, 67, and 312–13.

49. Franco Venturi, *Roots of Revolution: A History of the Populist and Socialist Movements in Nineteenth Century Russia*, trans. Francis Haskell (New York: Knopf, 1960), pp. 4–8, 20, 71–72; N. M. Druzhinin, *Gosudarstvennye krest'iane i reforma P. D. Kiseleva* (Moscow: Akademiia Nauk, 1946–58), I, 480–81.

50. C. Aksakov, "Kratkii istoricheskii ocherk zemskikh soborov," *Polnoe sobranie sochinenii*, I, 291–92.

51. See Khomiakov, *Polnoe sobranie sochinenii*, III, 288–90, 462.

52. Letter of V. I. Nazimov to A. S. Norov, December, 1855, in "Khoda-taistvo slavianofilov i otsenka ikh znacheniia v russkom obshchestve: Pis'mo V. I. Nazimova," *Russkaia Starina*, XXXIII (February, 1882), 485.

53. *Ibid.*, pp. 485–86.

54. *Ibid.*, p. 487.

55. *Ibid.*, pp. 487–88.

56. *Ibid.*, p. 488.

57. *Ibid.*, p. 489.

58. *Ibid.*, p. 484.

59. Letter of Ivan Aksakov to his parents, October 9, 1856, *Ivan Sergeevich Aksakov v ego pis'makh* (Moscow: M. G. Volchaninov, 1888–92), III, 290–91.

60. A. G. Dement'ev, *Ocherki po istorii russkoi zhurnalistiki 1840–1850 gg.* (Leningrad: Goslitizdat, 1951), pp. 392–97.

61. M. N. Katkov, "Vopros a narodnosti v nauke," *Russkii Vestnik*, III (1856), "Sovremennaia letopis'" section, Book II (June, 1856), pp. 312–14 and 318.

62. N. N. Strakhov, "Vospominaniia o Fedore Mikhailoviche Dostoevskom," in *Biografiia, pis'ma i zametki iz zapisnoi knizhki F. M. Dostoevskago* (St. Petersburg: A. S. Suvorin, 1883), pp. 204–7. Hereafter cited as "Vospominaniia . . . ," *Biografiia* . . . .

63. F. M. Dostoevskii, "Dnevnik pisatelia za 1873 god," *Polnoe sobranie sochinenii* (8th ed.; St. Petersburg: Tovarischestvo "Prosveshchenie," 1911–18), XIX, 142.

64. *Ibid.*, p. 209.

65. *Ibid.*, p. 141.

66. See Riasanovsky, *Russia and the West* . . . , pp. 53–54; and A. F. Tiutcheva, *Pri dvore dvukh imperatorov: Vospominaniia-dnevnik* (Moscow: Izdanie M. i S. Sabashnikovykh, 1928–29), II, 225–27.

CHAPTER FOUR

1. For evidence of Katkov's opportunism and high-handed editorial practices, see the following: N. A. Liubimov, *Mikhail Nikiforovich Katkov i ego istoricheskaia zasluga* (St. Petersburg: Tipografiia "Obshchestvennaia Pol'za," 1889), pp. 122–23; R. I. Sementkovskii, *M. N. Katkov, ego zhizn' i publitsisticheskaia deiatel'nost'* (St. Petersburg: Iu. N. Erlikh, 1892), p. 51; *Dnevnik D. A. Miliutin*, ed. P. A. Zaionchkovskii (Moscow: Lenin Public Library, 1947–50), I, 34; *F. M. Dostoevskii: Pis'ma*, ed. A. S. Dolinin (Moscow–Leningrad: Goslitizdat, 1928–59), I, 445–46; I. S. Turgenev, *Lettres à Madame Viardot*, ed. E. Halperine-Kaminsky (Paris: E. Fusquelle, 1907), p. 225; *Turgenev's Letters: A Selection*, ed. and trans. E. H. Lehrman (New York: Knopf, 1961), pp. 163–64, 325–26, 333; W. B. Edgerton, "Nikolai Leskov: The Intellectual Development of a Literary Nonconformist" (unpublished doctoral dissertation, Columbia University, 1954), pp. 313–14.

2. A. F. Koni, *Na zhiznennom puti* (St. Petersburg: Tovarishchestvo "Trud," 1912), II, 91–92; S. Nevedenskii, *Katkov i ego vremia* (St. Petersburg: A. S. Suvorin, 1888), p. 533.

3. Koni, *Na zhiznennom puti*, II, 91.

4. *Dnevnik A. V. Nikitenko*, ed. I. Ia. Aizenshtok (Leningrad: Goslitizdat, 1955–56), II, 354, 400.

5. P. Miliukov, C. Seignobos, and L. Eisenmann, *Histoire de Russie* (Paris: E. Leroux, 1932–33), III, 918.

6. V. I. Lenin, *Sochineniia* (4th ed.; Moscow–Leningrad: Gospolitizdat, 1948–60), XVIII, 250.

7. I. A., "Katkov," *Entsiklopedicheskii slovar'* (St. Petersburg: Brockhaus-Efron edition, 1890–1904), XIV, 734; Sementkovskii, *M. N. Katkov . . .*, pp. 74–80.

8. See F. M. Dostoevskii: *Pis'ma*, III, 145, 337–38, for Dostoevskii's irritation about the high rate paid to Tolstoi by Katkov for *Anna Karenina*.

9. Liubimov, *M. N. Katkov i ego istoricheskaia zasluga*, pp. 47–48.

10. *Ibid.*, p. 48.

11. *Ibid.*, p. 53

12. *Russkii Vestnik*, I (January, 1856), "Sovremennaia letopis'" section, pp. 1–2.

13. Liubimov, *M. N. Katkov . . .*, p. 118.

14. Katkov, "Vopros o narodnosti v nauke," *Russkii Vestnik*, III (1856), "Sovremennaia letopis'" section, Book II (June, 1856), pp. 312–19.

15. B. N. Chicherin, "Eshche o sel'skoi obshchine," *ibid.*, III (June, 1856), 773–94, and IV (July, 1856), 129–66; S. M. Solov'ev, "Schlözer i anti-istoricheskoe napravlenie," *ibid.*, VIII (April, 1857), 431–80.

16. A. I. Butovskii, "Obshchinnoe vladenie i sobstvennost'," *ibid.*, XVI (July, 1858), 5–59; D. D. Neelov, "O lichnom i obshchinnom vladenii zemleiu," *ibid.*, XVI (July and August, 1858), 197–240, 389–440; S. S. Ivanov, "Lichnaia zavisimost' krest'ian i ustroistvo otnoshenii ikh k pomeshchikam," *ibid.*, XVII (September, 1858), 311–37; editorial, "Krest'ianskii vopros," *ibid.*, XVI (July, 1858), "Sovremennaia letopis'" section pp. 77–103.

17. "Politicheskoe obozrenie," *Russkii Vestnik*, XV (June, 1958), 383.

18. *Ibid.*, p. 384.

19. Liubimov, *M. N. Katkov . . .*, pp. 192–93.

20. "Vidy na *entente cordiale* s Sovremennikom," *Russkii Vestnik*, XXXIV (July, 1861), "Literaturnoe obozrenie i zametki" section, pp. 60–95; "Zametki dlia izdatelia *Kolokola*," *ibid.*, XXXIX (June, 1862), 834–52.

21. M. N. Katkov, "O nashem nigilizme po povodu romana Turgeneva," *Russkii Vestnik*, XL (July, 1862), 410.

22. Nevedenskii demonstrated this point with numerous references to Katkov's editorials in the *Moskovskiia Vedomosti* as early as 1888 (see chaps. 9–12 of *Katkov i ego vremia*). Cf. A. A. Kornilov, "Mikhail Nikiforovich Katkov," in *Istoriia russkoi literatury XIX veka*, ed. D. N. Ovsianko-Kulikovskii (Moscow: Tovarishchestvo "Mir," 1908–10), V, 124–30; and Marc Raeff, "A Reactionary Liberal: M. N. Katkov," *Russian Review*, II (July, 1952), 157–67.

23. M. N. Katkov, *Nasha uchebnaia reforma* (Moscow: M. G. Volchaninov, 1890), pp. 7–12 and 126–27 (originally in *Moskovskiia Vedomosti*, No. 205, September 19, 1864, and No. 156, July 18, 1871).

24. Editorial of November 14, 1862, *Sovremennaia Letopis'*, No. 46, 1862, p. 10.

25. *Moskovskiia Vedomosti*, Nos. 82 and 220, April 17 and October 11, 1863.

26. Editorial of December 20, 1861, *Sovremennaia Letopis'*, No. 51, 1861, p. 17.

27. *Moskovskiia Vedomosti*, Nos. 37, 105, and 215, February 18, May 13, and October 3, 1865.

28. A. A. Kornilov, *Obshchestvennoe dvizhenie pri Aleksandre II* (Moscow: A. I. Mamontov, 1909), pp. 171–74.

29. *Moskovskiia Vedomosti*, No. 251, November 16, 1865; *ibid.*, No. 217, September 1, 1874. In regard to the inkstand presented to Katkov in 1865 by the Moscow gentry, see the frontispiece of the *Sobranie peredovykh statei Moskovskikh Vedomostei. 1866 god* (Moscow: V. V. Chicherin, 1897).

30. A. D. Pazukhin, "Sovremennoe sostoianie Rossii i soslovnyi vopros," *Russkii Vestnik*, CLXXVI (January, 1885), 5–58.

31. *Moskovskiia Vedomosti*, No. 27, February 2, 1864.

32. "Bor'ba protiv pol'skoi propagandy v iugo-zapadnoi Rossii," *Sovremennaia Letopis'*, 1863, No. 1 (January), pp. 9–12.

33. "Otzyvy i zametki: Pol'skii vopros," *Russkii Vestnik*, XLIV (January, 1863), 447–48.

34. Nevedenskii, *Katkov i ego vremia*, pp. 257–58.

35. *Moskovskiia Vedomosti*, Nos. 128, 139, 155, and 161, June 13 and 26, July 16 and 24, 1863.

36. *Ibid.*, Nos. 187 and 195, August 28 and September 8, 1863; Katkov, "Po povodu stat'i 'Rokovoi vopros,'" *Russkii Vestnik*, XLV (May, 1863), 398–418. Cf. Iu. F. Samarin, *Sochineniia*, (2nd ed.; Moscow: A. I. Mamontov, 1900), I, 261–84; I. S. Aksakov, *Sochineniia* (Moscow: M. G. Volchaninov, 1886–87), III, 3–22.

37. "Mikhail Nikiforovich Katkov i Graf Petr Aleksandrovich Valuev v ikh perepiske, 1863–1879," ed. V. Mustafin *Russkaia Starina*, CLXIII (August, 1915), 297–98. Cf. A. Kizevetter, "Pis'ma M. N. Katkova k P. A. Valuevu," *Russkii Istoricheskii Arkhiv* (Prague: Izdanie Russkogo Zagranichnogo Istoricheskogo Arkhiva v Prage, 1929), I, 287.

38. *Moskovskiia Vedomosti*, No. 180, August 18, 1863.

39. E. M. Feoktistov, *Vospominaniia E. M. Feoktistova: Za kulisami politiki i literatury 1846–1896 gg.* (Leningrad: "Priboi," 1929), pp. 130–31.

40. *Ibid.*, p. 131.

41. *Moskovskiia Vedomosti*, Nos. 73, 180, 181, and 202, April 8, August 26 and 28, and September 28, 1866.

42. Nevedenskii, *Katkov i ego vremia*, chap. VI.

43. *Moskovskiia Vedomosti*, No. 254, November 19, 1864.

44. *Ibid.*, No. 109, May 17, 1864, and No. 181, August 18, 1867.

45. *Ibid.*, No. 109, 1864.

46. See M. N. Katkov, review of *Pesni russkago naroda*, in *Otechestvennyia Zapiski*, IV (1839), Section 6, pp. 6, 24, and 28.

47. See Liubimov, *M. N. Katkov . . .*, pp. 76–97.

48. Nil Popov, *Kratkii otchet a desiatiletnei deiatel'nosti slavianskago blagotvoritel'nago komiteta v Moskve* (Moscow: Universitetskaia Tipografiia, 1868), pp. 1–2.

49. See, for example, N. F. Dubrovin, "Serbskii vopros v tsarstvovanie Aleksandra I," *Russkii Vestnik*, XLVI (July and August, 1863), 89–167, 525–70; N. P. V-v., "Obshchii kharakter pritiazanii pol'skoi partii v zapadnom krae," *ibid.*, XLVI (August, 1863), 833–51; P. K. Shchebal'skii, "Prezhnii i nyneshnii panslavizm," *ibid.*, LXVIII (April, 1867), 830–41; *Moskovskiia Vedomosti*, No. 222, October 22, 1866.

50. *Moskovskiia Vedomosti*, Nos. 112 and 128, May 23 and June 23, 1867.

51. *Ibid.*, No. 247, November 10, 1867.

52. *Ibid.; ibid.,* No. 111, May 25, 1868, and No. 273, December 14, 1871.

53. See Nevedenskii, *Katkov i ego vremia,* p. 285.

54. *Moskovskiia Vedomosti,* No. 87, April 13, 1877.

55. *Ibid.,* No. 252, November 17, 1864, and No. 182, August 20, 1865.

56. *Ibid.,* No. 105, May 14, 1867.

57. Nevedenskii, *Katkov i ego vremia,* chap. VI; "M. N. Katkov i Aleksandr III v 1886–1887 gg.: dokladnye zapiski M. N. Katkova Tsariu Aleksandru III," *Krasnyi Arkhiv,* LVIII (1933), 58–85.

58. See B. H. Sumner, *Russia and the Balkans, 1870–1880* (Oxford: The Clarendon Press, 1937), pp. 19–23, 69, 80–90, 147, 153–54, 158.

59. *Moskovskiia Vedomosti,* No. 2, January 3, 1865. Cf. Charles de Mazade, "La Russie sous l'Empereur Alexandre II," *Revue des deux Mondes,* LXII (March, 1866), 273–311.

60. *Moskovskiia Vedomosti,* No. 151, July 19, 1866.

61. *Ibid.,* No. 341, December 10, 1886.

62. *Ibid.,* Nos. 85 and 95, April 2 and 12, 1878.

63. *Ibid.,* Nos. 83 and 85, April 4 and 6, 1879.

64. *Ibid.,* Nos. 128 and 203, May 23 and August 9, 1879; *ibid.,* No. 213, August 2, 1880.

65. *Ibid.,* No. 213, August 2, 1880; *ibid.,* No. 291, October 20, 1884.

66. "Nasha konstitutsiia," *Russkii Vestnik,* CLIX (June, 1882), 930 (reprinted from the *Moskovskiia Vedomosti,* No. 130, May 12, 1882).

67. Katkov's words here are reminiscent of Article I of the *Collected Laws of the Russian Empire* (see *Svod zakonov Rossiiskoi Imperii* [St. Petersburg, 1842], I, 3).

68. *Moskovskiia Vedomosti,* No. 47, February 17, 1880; *ibid.,* No. 315, November 13, 1882; *ibid.,* Nos. 12, 70, and 291, January 12, March 11, and October 20, 1884; *ibid.,* No. 75, March 17, 1885; *ibid.,* No. 274, October 4, 1886.

69. Pazukhin, "Sovremennoe sostoianie Rossii i soslovnyi vopros."

70. *Moskovskiia Vedomosti,* Nos. 136 and 242, May 31 and September 23, 1879; *ibid.,* No. 125, May 7, 1880.

71. See, for example, *ibid.,* No. 139, June 26, 1865.

72. *Ibid.,* No. 217, August 24, 1879; *ibid.,* No. 35, February 5, 1880; L. Voronov, "Finansovo-ekonomicheskaia deiatel'nost' M. N. Katkova," in *Pamiati Mikhaila Nikiforovicha Katkova* (Moscow: V. Chicherin, 1897), pp. 108–9; Irene Grüning, *Die russische öffentliche Meinung und ihre Stellung zu den Grossmächten, 1878–1894* (Berlin–Königsberg: Ost-Europa Verlag, 1929), pp. 93–98.

73. Nevedenskii, *Katkov i ego vremia,* pp. 554–57.

74. "Tserkov' i narodnaia shkola," *Russkii Vestnik,* CLXI (October, 1882), 956 (reprinted from the *Moskovskiia Vedomosti,* No. 290, October 19, 1882).

75. Nevedenskii, *Katkov i ego vremia,* pp. 135, 565–67.

76. "K kakoi prinadlezhim my partii?" *Russkii Vestnik* XXXVII (February, 1862), 843.

77. "Tserkov' i narodnaia shkola," *Russkii Vestnik,* CLXI, 953.

78. R. I. Sementkovskii, *M. N. Katkov . . . ,* p. 33.

79. *Ibid.,* p. 51; *Dnevnik D. A. Miliutina,* I, 34; *Dnevnik A. V. Nikitenko,* III, 32, 34, 417–18; V. P. Meshcherskii, *Moi vospominaniia* (St. Petersburg: V. P. Meshcherskii, 1897–1912), II, 47–53; N. A. Liubimov, *M. N. Katkov*

. . . , pp. 341–46; S. S. Tatishchev, *Imperator Aleksandr II, ego zhizn' i tsarstvovanie* (2nd ed.; St. Petersburg: A. S. Suvorin, 1911), II, 10–11.

80. Feoktistov, *Za kulisami politiki i literatury,* p. 240.

PART II: INTRODUCTION

1. F. M. Dostoevskii, "Dnevnik pisatelia za 1873 god," *Polnoe sobranie sochinenii* (8th ed.; St. Petersburg: Tovarishchestvo "Prosveshchenie, 1911–18), XIX, 14 (originally published in *Vremia,* I (1861), 1–34).

2. *Ibid.,* pp. 33–34.

3. *Ibid.,* p. 14.

4. "Ob"iavlenie o podpiske na zhurnal *Vremia* 1863 g.," *Biografiia, pis'ma i zametki iz zapisnoi knizhki F. M. Dostoevskago* (St. Petersburg: A. S. Suvorin, 1883), appendix, p. 32.

5. Dostoevskii, "Dnevnik pisatelia za 1873," pp. 141–42.

6. N. N. Strakhov, "Vospominaniia . . . ," *Biografiia* . . . , p. 229.

7. *Ibid.*

8. "Ob"iavlenie o podpiske na zhurnal *Vremia* 1863 g.," and "Ob"iavlenie o podpiske na zhurnal *Epokha* 1865 g.," *ibid.,* appendix, pp. 33 and 37–38.

9. Strakhov, "Vospominaniia . . . ," *Biografiia* . . . , p. 180; Dostoevskii, "Dnevnik pisatelia za 1873 god," p. 34.

10. *Epokha,* July, 1864, Part XI, "Nashi domashniia dela" section, pp. 10–11; *ibid.,* September, 1864, Part XIII, "Nashi domashniia dela," section, pp. 10–18.

11. Solomon Schwarz, "Populism and Early Russian Marxism on Ways of Economic Development of Russia (The 1880's and 1890's)," in *Continuity and Change in Russian and Soviet Thought,* ed. Ernest J. Simmons (Cambridge, Mass.: Harvard University Press, 1955), pp. 46–47, 61.

CHAPTER FIVE

1. Apollon A. Grigor'ev, "Moi literaturnyia i nravstvennyia skital'chestva," in *Polnoe sobranie sochinenii i pisem Apollona Grigor'eva,* ed. V. Spiridonov (Petrograd: P. P. Ivanov, 1918), I, 31–32, 37–43; A. Fet, *Rannie gody moei zhizni* (Moscow: A. I. Mamontov, 1893), pp. 153–54; D. I. Chizhevskii, *Gegel' v. Rossii* (Paris: "Dom Knigi" and "Sovremennyia Zapiski," 1939), pp. 53–54.

2. See Grigor'ev's letter to Pogodin of 1845 to N. P. Barsukov, *Zhizn' i trudy M. P. Pogodina* (St. Petersburg: M. M. Stasiulevich, 1888–1910), VIII, 38–39.

3. See Grigor'ev's letter to Pogodin of 1860, *ibid.,* XVIII, 429.

4. A. A. Grigor'ev, "Belinskii i otritsatel'nyi vzgliad v literature," in *Sobranie sochinenii Apollona Grigor'eva,* ed. V. F. Savodnik (Moscow: I. N. Kushnerev, 1915–16), Vypusk III: *Razvitie idei narodnosti v nashei literature so smerti Pushkina,* pp. 103–9; Grigor'ev, "Paradoksy organicheskoi kritiki," *ibid.,* Vypusk II: *Osnovaniia organicheskoi kritiki,* p. 163.

5. "Belinskii i otritsatel'nyi vzgliad v literature," p. 109.

6. V. Spiridonov, "Apollon Grigor'ev," *Polnoe sobranie sochinenii* . . . , I, lv–lvi.

7. See *ibid.,* pp. lviii–lxi. The Slavophile articles probably read by Grigor'ev at the time, according to Spiridonov, include the following: A. S. Khomiakov, "Pis'mo v Peterburg," *Moskvitianin,* 1845, Part I, Book II, pp. 71–86; Khomiakov, "Mnenie inostrantsev o Rossii," *ibid.,* Part II, Book IV, pp. 21–48; I. V. Kireevskii, "Obozrenie sovremennago sostoianiia slovesnosti," *ibid.,* Part

I, Book I, Review section, pp. 1–28; P. V. Kireevskii, "O drevnei russkoi istorii," *ibid.*, Part II, Book III, Science section, pp. 11–46.

8. Spiridonov, "Apollon Grigor'ev," *Polnoe sobranie sochinenii* . . . , I, lx–lxi.

9. Grigor'ev, review of "*Rukovodstvo k poznaniiu zakonov*. Sochinenie Grafa Speranskago, S.P.B. V tipografii Vtorago Otdeleniia Sobstvennoi E. I. V. Kantseliarii, 1845," *Finskii Vestnik*, Vol. IX (1846), Section V, pp. 1–12. A second reference of Spiridonov to pages 55–56 of the same issue of the *Finskii Vestnik* concerns the works of Zagoskin and has little connection with the Slavophiles.

10. *Ibid.*, p. 6.

11. Grigor'ev, *Sobranie sochinenii* . . . , Vypusk XII: *Rannie proizvedeniia Grafa L. N. Tolstogo*, p. 13. Cf. *ibid.*, Vypusk III: *Razvitie idei* . . . , pp. 6–7.

12. A. G. Dement'ev, *Ocherki po istorii russkoi zhurnalistiki 1840–1850 gg.* (Leningrad: Goslitizdat, 1951), p. 216.

13. *Ibid.*, pp. 221–22.

14. Concerning the narrowly Orthodox and nationalistic views of Filippov, see N. Barsukov, *Zhizn' i trudy M. P. Pogodina*, XI, 79–82.

15. Dement'ev, *Ocherki* . . . , p. 221. In 1850 the number of subscribers rose from three or four hundred to five hundred; in 1851, to eleven hundred.

16. "Russkaia literatura v 1851 godu," *Moskvitianin*, 1852, Vol. 1, Section V, No. 1, pp. 1–9, No. 2, pp. 13–28, No. 3, pp. 53–68, and No. 4, pp. 95–108. This article was first republished by N. N. Strakhov, *Sochineniia Apollona Grigor'eva* (St. Petersburg: Tovarishchestvo "Obshchestvennaia Pol'za," 1876), I, 1–44. It also appeared in the later editions of Savodnik and Spiridonov.

17. "Russkaia literatura v 1851 godu," *Polnoe sobranie sochinenii i pisem Apollona Grigor'eva*, ed. V. Spiridonov, I, 96–99.

18. *Ibid.*, pp. 99–100.

19. *Ibid.*, p. 100.

20. *Ibid.*, p. 101.

21. *Ibid.* Grigor'ev apparently had the following two works of Georg Gottfried Gervinus in mind: *Geschichte der poetischen Nationalliteratur der Deutschen* (5 vols.; Leipzig: W. Engelmann, 1835–42), and *Shakespeare* (4 vols.; Leipzig: W. Engelmann, 1849–50).

22. *Ibid.*, p. 102.

23. *Ibid.*

24. *Ibid.*, pp. 103–16, 141–67. See also *Sobranie sochinenii* . . . , Vypusk VI: *Vzgliad na russkuiu literaturu so smerti Pushkina*, pp. 6–75; Vypusk VII: *Lermontov i ego napravlenie;* Vypusk XI: *O natsional'nom znachenii tvorchestva A. I. Ostrovskago.*

25. *Ibid.*, Vypusk VI: *Vzgliad na russkuiu literaturu*, p. 10.

26. *Ibid.*, pp. 20–21 and 26–27.

27. *Ibid.*, Vypusk VII: *Lermontov i ego napravlenie*, pp. 1–19, 94–96; *ibid.*, Vypusk XII: *Rannie proizvedeniia Grafa L. N. Tolstogo*, pp. 48–50.

28. "Russkaia literatura v 1851 godu," *Polnoe sobranie sochinenii A. A. Grigor'eva*, I, 103–16; "Russkaia iziashchnaia literatura v 1852 godu," *ibid.*, pp. 141–46; *Sobranie sochinenii*, Vypusk VIII: *N. V. Gogol' i ego "Perepiska s druz'iami,"* p. 10.

29. *Sobranie sochinenii*, Vypusk XI: *Posle "Grozy" Ostrovskago*, pp. 54, 58–59.

30. Dement'ev, *Ocherki* . . . , pp. 234–39; S. A. Vengerov, "*Molodaia redaktsiia Moskvitianina,*" *Vestnik Evropy,* CXVII (February, 1886), 611–12.

31. Barsukov, *Zhizn' i trudy M. P. Pogodina,* XVIII, 429–32.

32. *Ibid.,* p. 429. In referring to Tushino Fourierism, Grigor'ev apparently wished to associate Fourierism with various antinational tendencies centered in the village of Tushino during the Time of Troubles at the beginning of the seventeenth century.

33. *Ibid.,* XV, 360–61.

34. *Apollon Aleksandrovich Grigor'ev: Materialy dlia biografii,* ed. V. Kniaznin (Petrograd: Izdanie Pushkinskago Doma pri Akademii Nauk, 1917), p. 273.

35. Barsukov, *Zhizn' i trudy M. P. Pogodina,* XVIII, 432.

36. These articles were the following: "O pravde i iskrennosti v iskusstve," *Russkaia Beseda,* 1856, No. 3; "Kriticheskii vzgliad na osnovy, znachenie i priemy sovremennoi kritiki iskusstva," *Biblioteka dlia Chteniia,* CXLVII (1858); "Neskol'ko slov o zakonakh i terminakh organicheskoi kritiki," *Russkoe Slovo,* 1859, No. 5; "Paradoksy organicheskoi kritiki," *Epokha,* 1864, No. 5. These articles were republished in *Sobranie sochinenii, Vypusk II: Osnovy organicheskoi kritiki.*

37. A. A. Grigor'ev, "Odinokii kritik," *Knizhki Nedeli,* September, 1895, pp. 61–80.

38. *Ibid.,* p. 70.

39. "Kriticheskii vzgliad na osnovy, znachenie i priemy sovremennoi kritiki iskusstva," *Sobranie sochinenii, Vypuski II: Osnovy organicheskoi kritiki,* p. 90.

40. *Ibid.,* pp. 90–91.

41. *Ibid.,* p. 101.

42. "Paradoksy organicheskoi kritiki," *ibid.,* p. 143.

43. L. Grossman, *Tri sovremennika: Tiutchev, Dostoevskii, Apollon Grigor'ev* (Moscow: Tovarishchestvo "Knigoizdatel'stvo Pisatelei v Moskve," 1922), pp. 56–58.

44. "Moi literaturnyia i nravstvennyia skital'chestva," *Polnoe sobranie sochinenii A. Grigor'eva,* I, 50–51.

45. Armand Coquart, *Dmitri Pisarev et l'idéologie du nihilisme russe* (Paris: Institut d'Études Slaves de l'Université de Paris, 1946), pp. 293–95.

46. N. N. Strakhov, "Vospominaniia . . . ," *Biografiia* . . . , p. 212.

47. Strakhov, "Vospominaniia ob Apollone Aleksandroviche Grigor'eve," *Epokha,* September, 1864, eighth article, p. 7.

48. *Ibid.,* pp. 43–44. Cf. Strakhov, "Novyia pis'ma Apollona Grigor'eva," *Epokha,* February, 1865, p. 182.

49. D. Averkiev, "Apollon Aleksandrovich Grigor'ev," *Epokha* (August, 1864), eighth article in issue, pp. 4–7.

CHAPTER SIX

1. Strakhov, "Vospominaniia . . . ," *Biografiia* . . . , p. 204.

2. G. Florovskii, *Puti russkogo bogosloviia* (Paris: Y.M.C.A. Press, 1937), p. 299.

3. V. V. Zenkovskii, *A History of Russian Philosophy,* trans. G. L. Kline (New York: Columbia University Press, 1953), I, 428–30.

4. Cf. R. Lauth, *Die Philosophie Dostojewskis* (Munich: R. Piper, 1950), p. 21.

5. See the letter of Dostoevskii to M. V. Belinskaia, January 5, 1863, *F. M. Dostoevskii: Pis'ma*, I, 313–14 and note 161, p. 559; V. Belinskii, "Vzgliad na russkuiu literaturu 1846 goda," *Polne sobranie sochinenii* (Moscow: Akademiia Nauk, 1953–59), X, 28–32.

6. Strakhov, "Vospominaniia . . . ," *Biografiia* . . . , pp. 225, 238.

7. Dostoevskii, "Dnevnik pisatelia za 1873 god," *Polnoe sobranie sochinenii,* XIX, 309.

8. N. Lossky, *Dostoevskii i ego khristianskoe miroponimanie* (New York: Chekhov Publishing House, 1953), pp. 59–64; S. D. Ianovskii, "Vospominaniia o Dostoevskom," *Russkii Vestnik,* CLXXVI (April, 1885), 796–819.

9. See Peter Scheibert, *Von Bakunin zu Lenin: Geschichte der russischen revolutionären Ideologien 1840–1895* (Leiden: E. J. Brill, 1956——), I, 307–12.

10. N. F. Bel'chikov, *Dostoevskii v protsesse Petrashevtsev* (Moscow–Leningrad: Akademiia Nauk, 1936), p. 80.

11. *Ibid.,* p. 81.

12. *Ibid.,* p. 80.

13. *Ibid.,* p. 92.

14. Dostoevskii, "Dnevnik pisatelia za 1873 god," p. 162.

15. Letter of Dostoevskii to N. D. Fonvizina, February 20, 1854, *F. M. Dostoevskii: Pis'ma,* I, 142.

16. Sofiia Kovalevskaia, "Vospominaniia detstva," *Vestnik Evropy,* XXV (August, 1890), 624; N. Lossky, *Dostoevskii i ego khristianskoe miroponimanie,* pp. 73–74.

17. Dostoevskii, "Dnevnik pisatelia za 1873 god," pp. 308–9.

18. K. Mochul'skii, *Dostoevskii: Zhizn' i tvorchestvo* (Paris: Y.M.C.A. Press, 1947), pp. 136–38.

19. Letter of Dostoevskii to E. I. Todleben, March 24, 1856, *Pis'ma,* I, 178.

20. Dostoevskii to Alexander II, October 10–18, 1859, *ibid.,* p. 267.

21. *Biografiia, pis'ma i zametki iz zapisnoi knizhki F. M. Dostoevskago,* appendix, p. 58, footnote.

22. Dostoevskii, "Dnevnik pisatelia za 1873 god," p. 77.

23. *Ibid.,* p. 78.

24. See, for example, Ernest J. Simmons, *Dostoevski: The Making of a Novelist* (New York: Oxford University Press, 1940) pp. 131–32; Mochul'skii, *Dostoevskii,* p. 215.

25. Strakhov, "Vospominaniia . . . ," *Biografiia* . . . , pp. 232–33.

26. Dostoevskii, "Dnevnik pisatelia za 1873 god," p. 177.

27. *Ibid.,* p. 178.

28. Strakhov's article, "Rokovoi vopros," was republished, together with other pertinent materials, in his *Bor'ba s zapadom v nashei literature* (2nd ed.; St. Petersburg: Tipografiia Brat. Panteleevykh, 1887–96), II, 111–46, hereafter cited as *Bor'ba s zapadom.* Cf. Strakhov, "Vospominaniia . . . ," *Biografiia* . . . , pp. 245–69; *Dnevnik A. V. Nikitenko,* II, 340–41 (June 10, 1863).

29. Strakhov, "Vospominaniia . . . ," *Biografiia* . . . , pp. 269–84.

30. A. P. Miliukov, *Literaturnyia vstrechi i znakomstva* (St. Petersburg: A. S. Suvorin, 1890), p. 223.

31. Letter of Dostoevskii to A. N. Maikov, August 16/28, 1867, *Pis'ma,* II, 32.

32. *Ibid.,* p. 31.

33. Letters of Dostoevskii to Maikov, February 18/March 1, 1868, December

11/23, 1868, May 15/27, 1869, March 25/April 6, 1870, October 9/21, 1870, *ibid.*, pp. 77–83, 148–51, 189–94, 263–65, 290–93.

34. Dostoevskii to Maikov, March 20/April 2, 1868, *ibid.*, p. 100.

35. *Ibid.*

36. "Uchastie i pominki F. M. Dostoevskago v Slavianskom Blagot-voritel'nom Obshchestve," in *Biografiia, pis'ma i zametki iz zapisnoi knizhki F. M. Dostoevskago*, appendix, p. 49.

37. Dostoevskii, "Dnevnik pisatelia za 1877, 80 i 81 gg.," *Polnoe sobranie sochinenii*, XXI, 497.

38. *Ibid.*, p. 502.

39. *Ibid.*, p. 503.

40. *Ibid.*

41. Letter of F. M. Dostoevskii to M. M. Dostoevskii, February 22, 1854, *Pis'ma*, I, 139.

42. Dostoevskii to A. N. Maikov, January 18, 1856, *ibid.*, p. 165.

43. This trend of thought was not, however, completely absent from his writings in the early sixties. See "Dnevnik pisatelia za 1873 god," pp. 19–21 and 38.

44. These opinions are particularly evident in Chapter VI ("Opyt o burzhua") of Dostoevskii's *Zimnie zametki o letnikh vpechatleniiakh*.

45. Dostoevskii to A. N. Maikov, February 18/March 1, 1868, *Pis'ma*, II, 81.

46. Dostoevskii to Maikov, December 11/23, 1868, *ibid.*, p. 149.

47. Dostoevskii to N. N. Strakhov, March 18/30, 1869, *ibid.*, p. 181.

48. Dostoevskii to Maikov, October 9/21, 1870, *ibid.*, p. 293.

49. Dostoevskii, *Sobranie sochinenii* (Moscow: Goslitizdat, 1956–58), VII, 267.

50. *Ibid.*

51. Dostoevskii, "Dnevnik pisatelia za 1877, 80 i 81 gg.," *Polnoe sobranie sochinenii*, XXI, 18.

52. *Ibid.*

53. R. Lauth, *Die Philosophie Dostojewskis*, p. 492.

54. Dostoevskii, "Dnevnik pisatelia za 1877, 80 i 81 gg.," pp. 114–17.

55. *Ibid.*, p. 364.

56. *Ibid.*, pp. 364–69, 372–74.

57. Leonid Grossman, in his *Tri sovremennika: Tiutchev, Dostoevskii, Apollon Grigor'ev*, pp. 92–97, shows that Dostoevskii had already acquired his pro-German sentiments by 1873, when he was the editor of *Grazhdanin*. Concerning his attitude at the time of the Franco-Prussian War, see the letters of Dostoevskii to Maikov, December 30, 1870/January 10, 1871, and January 26/February 5, 1871, *Pis'ma*, II, 308, 324–25.

58. Dostoevskii, "Dnevnik pisatelia za 1877, 80 i 81 gg.," pp. 372–73.

59. *Ibid.*, p. 373.

60. *Ibid.*, p. 367.

61. See, especially, Dostoevskii, *Sobranie sochinenii*, IX, 394–96.

62. Dostoevskii, "Dnevnik pisatelia za 1877, 80 i 81 gg.," p. 446.

63. Concerning Dostoevskii's views on the Jewish problem, see the following: "Dnevnik pisatelia za 1877, 80 i 81 gg.," pp. 82–96; "Iz zapisnoi knizhki F. M. Dostoevskago," in *Biografiia, pis'ma i zametki iz zapisnoi knizhki F. M. Dostoevskago*, Section containing letters, p. 358; letter of Dostoevskii to G. A. Kovner, February 14, 1877, *Pis'ma*, III, 256–58. The Grand Inquisitor scene in

The Brothers Karamazov is, of course, the most famous example of Dostoevskii's anti-Catholic bias. Others are scattered throughout his *Diary of a Writer*.

64. Dostoevskii, "Dnevnik pisatelia za 1877, 80 i 81 gg.," p. 514.

65. *Ibid.*, pp. 519–21.

66. *Ibid.*, p. 523.

67. L. P. Grossman, "Materialy k biografii F. M. Dostoevskogo," in F. M. Dostoevskii, *Sobranie sochinenii*, X, 595–97.

68. R. F. Byrnes, "Dostoevsky and Pobedonostsev," *Jahrbücher für Geschichte Osteuropas*, N.S., IX (June, 1961), 57–71; "Dostoevskii i Pobedonostsev: Pis'ma F. M. Dostoevskogo," ed. N. F. Bel'chikov, *Krasnyi Arkhiv*, II (1922), 240–55; "Dostoevskii i pravitel'stvennye krugi 1870-kh godov," ed. L. P. Grossman, *Literaturnoe Nasledstvo*, No. 15 (1934), pp. 83–162.

69. "Dostoevskii i pravitel'stvennye krugi," p. 89.

70. See the letter of Dostoevskii to A. N. Maikov, March 25/April 6, 1870, *Pis'ma*, II 263–64. Cf. Byrnes, pp. 63–64.

71. See Dostoevskii, "Dnevnik pisatelia za 1876 god," *Polnoe sobranie sochinenii*, XX, 205–7; "Dnevnik pisatelia za 1877, 80 i 81 gg.," *Polnoe sobr. soch.*, XXI, 398–417; "Iz zapisnoi knizhki F. M. Dostoevskago," *Biografiia*, pp. 364–65.

72. "Dostoevskii i Pobedonostsev: Pis'ma F. M. Dostoevskogo," *Krasnyi Arkhiv*, II, 252.

CHAPTER SEVEN

1. S. A. Vengerov, "Strakhov," *Entsiklopedicheskii Slovar'*, XXXa, 783.

2. N. N. Strakhov, "Gosudarstvennyia uchrezhdeniia Rossiiskoi Imperii," 1844, Manuscript Division of the Institute of Russian Literature (Pushkinskii Dom), Academy of Sciences of the USSR, Leningrad, 258 pages.

3. *Ibid.*, p. 1.

4. *Ibid.*

5. *Ibid.*, p. 16.

6. *Entsiklopedicheskii Slovar'*, XXXIa, 783.

7. *Sochineniia Apollona Grigor'eva* (St. Petersburg: Tovarishchestvo "Obshchestvennaia Pol'za," 1876).

8. A. S. Dolinin, "F. M. Dostoevskii i N. N. Strakhov," in *Shestidesiatye gody*, ed. N. K. Piksanov and O. V. Tsekhovitser (Moscow–Leningrad: Akademiia Nauk, 1940), pp. 239–42 and 252–53.

9. Letter of N. N. Strakhov to L. N. Tolstoi, November 28, 1883, *Tolstovskii Muzei*, Vol. II: *Perepiska L. N. Tolstogo s N. N. Strakhovym, 1870–1894*, ed. B. L. Modzalevskii (St. Petersburg: Izdanie Obshchestva Tolstovskago Muzeia, 1914), pp. 307–8.

10. Ia. Kolubovskii, "Materialy dlia istorii filosofii v Rossii 1855–1888, IX: N. N. Strakhov," *Voprosy Filosofii i Psikhologii*, Vol. VII (March, 1891), criticism and bibliographical section, pp. 99–100. Kolubovskii's article consists mainly of a most useful analytical bibliography of Strakhov's works.

11. Strakhov, "Vospominaniia o F. M. Dostoevskom," *Biografiia*, p. 183.

12. *Ibid.*, p. 184.

13. Strakhov, "Znachenie gegelevskoi filosofii v nastoiashchee vremia," *Filosofskie ocherki* (2nd ed.; Kiev: Izdanie I. P. Matchenko, 1906), pp. 1–39; Chizhevskii, *Gegel' v Rossii*, pp. 270–72; A. Vvedenskii, "Znachenie filosofskoi deiatel'nosti N. N. Strakhova," *Obrazovanie*, March, 1896, 2nd section, pp. 1–8.

14. Strakhov, *Kriticheskiia stat'i ob I. S. Turgeneve i L. N. Tolstom, 1862–1885* (St. Petersburg: Tipografiia Brat. Panteleevykh, 1885), pp. 1–49, 225–392.

15. Probably the best discussions of Strakhov as a literary critic are those of V. Gol'tsev and A. S. Dolinin. Gol'tsev, although he praised several of Strakhov's literary interpretations, was essentially hostile to Strakhov both as a critic and a thinker. Dolinin spoke highly of Strakhov's erudition and some of his insights but was mainly interested in his relationship to Dostoevskii. See V. Gol'tsev, "N. N. Strakhov kak khudozhestvennyi kritik," *Voprosy Filosofii i Psikhologii*, Vol. XXXIII (May–June. 1896). 431–40; and A. S. Dolinin, "F. M. Dostoevskii i N. N. Strakhov," *Shestidesiatye gody*, pp. 239–53. Examples of Strakhov's literary criticism are to be found in the following collections of his articles: *Bednost' nashei literatury: Kriticheskii i istoricheskii ocherk* (St. Petersburg: Tipografiia Nekliudova, 1868); *Zametki o Pushkine i drugikh poetakh* (St. Petersburg: Tipografiia Brat. Panteleevykh, 1888); *Iz istorii literaturnago nigilizma, 1861–1865* (St. Petersburg: Tipografiia Brat. Panteleevykh, 1890); *Kriticheskiia stat'i, 1861–1894* (Kiev: Izdanie I. P. Matchenko, 1902); *Kriticheskiia stat'i ob I. S. Turgeneve i L. N. Tolstom, 1862–1865.*

16. N. N. Strakhov, *Bor'ba s zapadom*. Specialized articles written by Strakhov concerning such fields as philosophy, psychology, embryology, physiology, and zoology also can be considered as part of his struggle against the West. See the following collections of Strakhov's writings for examples of such articles: *Ob osnovnykh poniatiiakh psikhologii i fiziologii* (St. Petersburg: Tipografiia Brat. Panteleevykh, 1886); *O vechnykh istinakh: Moi spor o spiritizme* (St. Petersburg: Tipografiia Brat. Panteleevykh, 1887); *Mir kak tseloe: Cherty iz nauki o prirode* (2nd ed.; St. Petersburg: Tipografiia Brat. Panteleevykh, 1892); *Filosofskie ocherki.*

17. *Perepiska L. N. Tolstogo s N. N. Strakhovym, 1870–1894*, pp. 6–8.

18. Letter of L. N. Tolstoi to Strakhov, March 14, 1882, *ibid.*, p. 291.

19. Letter of Strakhov to Tolstoi, March 31, 1882, *ibid.*, p. 292.

20. *Ibid.*

21. *Ibid.*, p. 293.

22. *Ibid.*, p. 292.

23. Strakhov, *Bor'ba s zapadom*, I, 288, 356, 375–77.

24. Strakhov, *Kriticheskiia stat'i, 1861–1894*, pp. 202–3.

25. *Ibid.*, p. 206. Pypin's work was later published as a separate book in a number of editions under the title of *Obshchestvennoe dvizhenie v Rossii pri Aleksandre I.*

26. *Ibid.*, pp. 218–19.

27. *Ibid.*, p. 219.

28. *Ibid.*, p. 226.

29. Strakhov, *Bor'ba s zapadom*, I, 288, 356, and 375.

30. *Ibid.*, pp. 376–77.

31. V. V. Rozanov, "O bor'be s zapadom v sviazi s literaturnoi deiatel'-nost'iu odnogo iz slavianofilov," *Voprosy Filosofii i psikhologii*, Vol. IV (1890), criticism and bibliography section, pp. 32–35; Rozanov, *Literaturnye Izgnan-niki* (St. Petersburg: A. S. Suvorin, 1913), I, 480–83.

32. Letter of Strakhov to I. S. Aksakov, December 12, 1884, Arkhiv Aksakovykh, Manuscript Division of the Institute of Russian Literature (Pushkinskii Dom), Academy of Sciences of the USSR, Leningrad; letters of Strakhov to

Tolstoi, December 12, 1877, March 25, 1880, June 20, 1884, May 20, 1887, and October–November, 1887, *Perepiska L. N. Tolstogo s N. N. Strakhovym,* pp. 135–37, 250–51, 314, 351–52, 357–58.

33. Strakhov, *Bor'ba s zapadom,* I, 452.

34. *Ibid.,* pp. 449–50.

35. Such negative, conservative views concerning French society and civilization of the nineteenth century were expressed particularly often in Katkov's *Russkii Vestnik.* See, for example, V. P. Bezobrazov, "Voina i revoliutsiia," *Russkii Vestnik,* CXVI (March, 1875), 35.

36. Strakhov, *Bor'ba s zapadom,* I, 356 and 440–50.

37. Renan's *La réforme intellectuelle et morale* has recently been republished in *Oeuvres complètes de Ernest Renan* (Paris: Calmann-Lévy, 1947———), I, 325–407.

38. Strakhov, *Bor'ba s zapadom,* I, 85–86, and II, 93–94.

39. *Ibid.,* II, xviii.

40. *Ibid.,* pp. xvii–xviii.

41. *Ibid.,* pp. 84–85, 91–92, 96.

42. *Ibid.,* p. 98.

43. *Ibid.,* pp. 80–84.

44. *Ibid.,* pp. 61–110.

45. See N. N. Strakhov, *Iz istorii literaturnago nigilizma, 1861–1865,* pp. 240–57, 448–49. Two rather friendly letters of Strakhov to Katkov, however, apparently written in the 1860's, were published in the *Russkii Vestnik,* CCLXXIII (June, 1901), 460–62.

46. Letter of Strakhov to Tolstoi, July 27, 1887, *Perepiska L. N. Tolstogo s N. N. Strakhovym,* p. 356.

47. Letter of Strakhov to N. Ia, Danilevskii, March 21, 1883, *Russkii Vestnik,* CCLXXI (February, 1901), 464.

48. Strakhov, *Bor'ba s zapadom,* II, viii–ix.

49. *Ibid.,* p. xxiii.

50. *Ibid.,* II, xxiii–xxiv, and III, 45–46; Strakhov, *Mir kak tseloe: Cherty iz nauki o prirode,* p. vi. Cf. Chizhevskii, *Gegel' v Rossii,* pp. 270–72.

51. Strakhov, *Bor'ba s zapadom,* I, 170.

52. "Znachenie gegelevskoi filosofii v nastoiashchee vremia."

53. Strakhov, *Bor'ba s zapadom,* I, 185–87.

54. *Ibid.,* pp. 210–15.

55. *Ibid.,* p. 178.

56. *Ibid.,* p. 187.

57. *Ibid.,* pp. 175–78.

58. *Ibid.,* pp. 178–79.

59. Strakhov, *Iz istorii literaturnago nigilizma, 1861–1865,* p. 411.

60. *Ibid.,* pp. 561–62.

61. *Ibid.,* p. 492; *Bor'ba s zapadom,* II, 160–61.

62. *Bor'ba,* II, ix.

63. Strakhov, *Kriticheskiia stat'i ob I. S. Turgeneve i L. N. Tolstom,* p. 296.

64. *Ibid.,* p. 306. The italics are those of Strakhov.

65. *Ibid.,* pp. 311–12.

66. *Ibid.,* pp. 354–55.

67. *Ibid.,* pp. 360–61.

68. Strakhov, *Bor'ba,* II, xxviii–xxix.

69. Strakhov, "Zhizn' i trudy N. Ia. Danilevskago," in N. Ia. Danilevskii, *Rossiia i Evropa: Vzgliad na kul'turnyia i politicheskiia otnosheniia slavianskago mira k germano-romanskomu* (5th ed.; St. Petersburg: Tipografiia Brat. Panteleevykh, 1895), pp. xiv–xv, xxiii. This work will hereafter be cited as *Rossiia i Evropa*.

70. These three articles (which appeared originally in *Zaria*, Nos. 7 and 11, 1869, and No. 3, 1871) were republished in Strakhov, *Kriticheskiia stat'i 1861–1894*. The third article also appeared in somewhat modified form as part of the introduction to several editions of *Russia and Europe* (3rd, 4th, and 5th) and was read by Strakhov before the St. Petersburg Slavic Welfare Society in November, 1886. A short introduction was then added which contained Strakhovs' famous remark about *Russia and Europe*'s being a "catechism or codex of Slavophilism."

71. Strakhov, *Kriticheskiia stat'i 1861–1894*, pp. 146, 150–51.

72. *Ibid.*, p. 165.

73. *Ibid.*, pp. 164–65.

74. *Ibid.*, p. 163.

75. See *ibid.*, p. 157; Danilevskii, *Rossiia i Evropa*, p. xxvi.

76. Strakhov, "Vospominaniia . . . ," *Biografiia* . . . , pp. 203–5.

77. Strakhov, *Kriticheskiia stat'i, 1861–94*, pp. 158–67.

78. *Ibid.*, p. 167.

79. *Ibid.*, p. 158.

80. *Ibid.*, p. 161.

81. *Ibid.*, p. 165.

CHAPTER EIGHT

1. Danilevskii's ability as a synthesizer of ideas is closely related to his activities as a natural scientist. This point is especially well developed by Professor Robert E. MacMaster's unpublished doctoral dissertation, "Danilevskii, Scientist and Panslavist" (Harvard University, 1952).

2. P. A. Sorokin, *Social Philosophies in an Age of Crisis* (Boston: Beacon Press, 1951), pp. 327–28.

3. *Memuary P. P. Semenova-Tian-Shanskago*, Vol. I: *Detstvo i iunost', 1827–1855* (Izdanie sem'i; Petrograd: M. M. Stasiulevich, 1915–17), pp. 180, 218.

4. *Ibid.*, pp. 194–95, 210; Danilevskii, *Rossiia i Evropa*, pp. xi–xii.

5. P. P. Semenov, *Detstvo i iunost'*, pp. 180, 218.

6. *Ibid.*, pp. 206–12; *Delo Petrashevtsev*, ed. V. A. Desnitskii (Moscow–Leningrad; Akademiia Nauk, 1937–51), II, 285–335.

7. Semenov, p. 218.

8. *Ibid.*

9. Danilevskii, *Rossiia i Evropa*, pp. 300–310

10. See *ibid.*, notes to pp. 300–301 and 314.

11. Danilevskii, Review of the Russian translation of Alexander von Humboldt's *Kosmos* (St. Petersburg, 1848), in *Otechestvennyia Zapiski*, LIX (1848), Section V, p. 23.

12. *Ibid.*, Danilevskii, "Diutroshe," *Otechestvennyia Zapiski*, LVIII (1848), Section II, pp. 1–48, 99–127 (see, especially, p. 127).

13. *Delo Petrashevtsev*, II, 290–94.

14. See Danilevskii, *Rossiia i Evropa*, pp. 77–118.

15. *Ibid.*, pp. xiv–xx.

16. See *ibid.*, pp. xxxiv–xxxviii for Strakhov's bibliography of Danilevskii's writings.

17. Cf. MacMaster, "Danilevskii, Scientist and Panslavist," Chapter IV: "The Statistician"; Danilevskii, *Rossiia i Evropa*, pp. 162–71.

18. Danilevskii, *Darvinism: Kriticheskoe izsledovanie* (St. Petersburg: M. E. Komarov, 1885–89), Vol. I, Parts 1 and 2.

19. G. L. Kline, "Darwinism and the Russian Orthodox Church," in *Continuity and Change in Russian and Soviet Thought*, ed. E. J. Simmons (Cambridge, Mass.: Harvard University Press, 1955), pp. 314–20; MacMaster, pp. 257–58; *Rossiia i Evropa*, pp. xiv–xv; *Darvinizm*, Vol. I, Part 1, pp. 1–2, 26–28.

20. MacMaster, pp. 257–67; Oswei Temkin, "German Concepts on Ontogeny and History around 1800," *Bulletin of the History of Medicine*, XXIV (1950), pp. 232–34. See also K. M. Ber (Karl Ernst van Baer), *Avtobiografiia* (Russian trans.; Leningrad: Akademiia Nauk, 1950), pp. 162–404 for Baer's own account of the twenty years he spent in Germany.

21. Temkin, p. 234.

22. Cf. F. Meinecke, *Die Entstehung des Historismus* (2nd ed.; Munich: Leibniz Verlag, 1946).

23. Temkin, p. 246.

24. *Rossiia i Evropa*, pp. 78–88.

25. *Ibid.*, p. 81.

26. *Ibid.*, p. 91.

27. *Ibid.*, pp. 91–97, 111–18.

28. *Ibid.*, pp. 82–88.

29. *Ibid.*, pp. 88–91.

30. *Ibid.*, pp. 90–97.

31. See *ibid.*, pp. 191–211.

32. *Ibid.*, pp. 95–96.

33. The existence of the Sumerian language was, of course, still a debated hypothesis when Danilevskii wrote *Russia and Europe* in 1867. He was apparently completely unaware of the philological and historical research on this question until the time of his death in 1885.

34. Danilevskii regarded the Finns (and perhaps also the Magyars) as "ethnographic material" and not as a historical people. He considered the western and southern Slavs, who belonged to the cultural sphere of Western Europe, to have been brought within Western civilization through force and conquest. Nevertheless, even if one is willing to admit that Danilevskii was partly correct in his statements concerning the forcible Westernization of many of the Slavs, the course of their historical development and their cultural heritage undeniably made them an integral part of the Western world. (See *Rossiia i Evropa*, pp. 93, 131–33, 199–200, 376–81.) One might also ask whether the relationship between two Germanic languages such as the Norwegian *landsmål* and Schwyzerdütsch can be "perceived directly without profound philological investigations."

35. See, especially, *Rossiia i Evropa*, pp. 181–83, 555–57. For a more detailed discussion of Danilevskii's "laws," see P. A. Sorokin, *Social Philosophies in an Age of Crisis*, pp. 60–71, 205–43.

36. *Ibid.*, p. 175.

37. *Ibid.*, pp. 181–82.

38. *Ibid.*, pp. 111–12, 181.
39. *Ibid.*, pp. 181–83, 323–24, 355, 472–512.
40. *Ibid.*, pp. 472–73.
41. *Ibid.*, pp. 432–38, 513–14.
42. *Ibid.*, pp. 501–2.
43. Danilevskii, "Neskol'ko slov po povodu konstitutsionnykh vozhdelenii nashei 'liberal'noi pressy,' " in *Sbornik politicheskikh i ekonomicheskikh statei* (St. Petersburg: Tipografiia Brat. Panteleevykh, 1890), p. 227.
44. Danilevskii, "G. Vladimir Solov'ev o pravoslavii i katolitsizme," *ibid.*, p. 272; *Rossiia i Evropa*, pp. 192, 525.
45. *Rossiia i Evropa*, pp. 191–98.
46. Danilevskii, "Proiskhozhdenie nashego nigilizma: Po povodu stat'i 'Etiudy gospodstvuiushchago mirovozzreniia,' " *Sbornik politicheskikh i ekonomicheskikh statei*, pp. 246–48.
47. *Ibid.*, p. 249.
48. *Ibid.*, p. 256; *Rossiia i Evropa*, pp. 314–15.
49. Danilevskii, *Sbornik*, p. 252.
50. *Ibid.*

CHAPTER NINE

1. These articles were first republished in 1891 under the title *Natsional'-nyi vopros v Rossii* and then (with the inclusion of additional articles) in Volume V of *Sobranie sochinenii Vladimira Sergeevicha Solov'eva*. All footnote citations that follow will be made from the first edition of E. L. Radlov (St. Petersburg: Tovarishchestvo "Obshchestvennaia Pol'za," 1901–7).
2. D. Strémooukhoff, *Vladimir Soloviev et son oeuvre messianique* (Publications de la Faculté des Lettres de l'Université de Strasbourg, fasc. 69 [Paris: Société d'édition Les Belles Lettres, 1935]), pp. 30–38, 64–66, 200–202).
3. See Solov'ev, *Sobranie sochinenii*, V, i–iv, 33–34, 50–52, 71, 137, 141–43, 246–49, 276–78, 463–512.
4. Solov'ev, "Rossiia i Evropa," *ibid.*, pp. 76–137.
5. *Ibid.*, pp. 129–32; Strakhov, *Bor'ba s zapadom*, II, 274–82.
6. Solov'ev, *Sobranie sochinenii*, V, 129–30, 263–64. Cf. G. L. Kline, "Darwinism and the Russian Church," in *Continuity and Change in Russian and Soviet Thought* (Cambridge, Mass.: Harvard University Press, 1955), pp. 315–19.
7. Solov'ev, *Sobranie sochinenii*, V, 131–32.
8. *Ibid.*, pp. 91–102, 134–37.
9. *Ibid.*, p. 123.
10. *Ibid.*, pp. 101–2.
11. All five of these articles were republished in Volume V of *Sobranie sochinenii V. S. Solov'eva*. Their titles and location in the fifth volume of Solov'ev's collected works are as follows: "Rossiia i Evropa," pp. 76–137; "O grekhakh i bolezniakh," pp. 243–61; "Mnimaia bor'ba s zapadom," pp. 262–84; "Shchastlivyia mysli N. N. Strakhova," pp. 285–92; and "Nemetskii podlinnik i russkii spisok," pp. 293–322.
12. *Ibid.*, pp. 274–75.
13. *Ibid.*, pp. 273–75.
14. *Ibid.*, p. 137.

15. Cf. E. C. Thaden, "Natural Law and Historicism in the Social Sciences," *Social Science,* XXXII–1 (January, 1957), 32–33.

16. D. S. Mirsky, *A History of Russian Literature* (London: Routledge and K. Paul, 1949), p. 351.

17. Danilevskii, *Rossiia i Evropa,* p. xxxi. Cf. *ibid.,* fifth edition, pp. xxvii–xxviii.

18. R. E. MacMaster, "The Question of Heinrich Rückert's Influence on Danilevskij," *American Slavic and Eastern European Review,* XIV (February, 1955), pp. 60–61.

19. Strakhov, *Bor'ba s zapadom,* III, 169–71, 199–244.

20. *Ibid.,* pp. 209–10, 218–22. MacMaster is in general agreement with these arguments of Strakhov, though he concludes: "The question remains open and probably will continue to do so." (MacMaster, "The Question of Heinrich Rückert's Influence on Danilevskij," pp. 63–66.)

21. MacMaster, pp. 61–63.

22. Cf. R. E. MacMaster, "Danilevsky and Spengler: A New Interpretation," *Journal of Modern History,* XXVI (June, 1954), 154–61; Konrad Pfalzgraf, "Die Politisierung und Radikalisierung des Problems Russland und Europa bei N. J. Danilevskij," *Forschungen zur Osteuropäischen Geschichte,* I (1954), 199–201. Spengler's general view of history is to be found in the first several chapters of his *Decline of the West.* See, especially, O. Spengler, *The Decline of the West* (New York: Knopf, 1946), I, 25–26, 103–13.

23. Strakhov, *Bor'ba s zapadom,* II, 281–82, and III, 196–97.

24. *Ibid.,* II, 291–92.

25. *Ibid.,* II, 297, and III, 192.

26. *Ibid.,* III, 194–95. The emotional nature of Strakhov's reaction to Solov'ev's polemics can also be observed in Strakhov's correspondence with L. N. Tolstoi, V. V. Rozanov, and K. N. Bestuzhev-Riumin. See, especially, the following letters: Strakhov to Tolstoi, August 22 and September 20, 1890, *Perepiska L. N. Tolstogo s N. N. Strakhovym, 1870–1894,* pp. 409 and 414–15; Strakhov to Rozanov, September 13 and December 12, 1890, in V. V Rozanov, *Literaturnye izgnanniki,* I, 245–46 and 260; Strakhov to Bestuzhev-Riumin, March 21, 1888, Archive of Bestuzhev-Riumin, Manuscript Division of the Institute of Russian Literature (Pushkinskii Dom), Academy of Sciences of the USSR, Leningrad.

27. See *Petrashevtsy, sbornik materialov,* ed. P. E. Shchegolev (Moscow: Gosizdat, 1926–28), II, 120; and Danilevskii, *Sbornik politicheskikh i eko-nomicheskikh statei* (St. Petersburg: Tipografiia Brat. Panteleevykh, 1890), p. 274.

28. The close friendship between Strakhov and Danilevskii is also evidenced by their published correspondence. See "Pis'ma N. N. Strakhova k N. Ia. Danilevskomu," *Russkii Vestnik,* CCLXXI (January and February, 1901), 127–42, 453–69; *ibid.,* CCLXXII (March, 1901), 125–41.

29. Nikolai Grot, "Pamiati N. N. Strakhova: K kharateristike ego filo-sofskago mirosozertsaniia," *Voprosy Filosofii i Psikhologii,* XXXII (March–April, 1896), 306.

30. Rozanov, *Literaturnye izgnanniki,* I, 511.

31. Strakhov devoted a special article in 1863 (which was published in the October, 1863, issue of the *Biblioteka dlia Chteniia*) to the problem of educa-

tion in Russia. See N. N. Strakhov, *Iz istorii literaturnago nigilizma 1861–1865*, pp. 271–91.

32. See Danilevskii, *Rossiia i Evropa*, p. 428.

PART III: INTRODUCTION

1. This lecture was read in the auditorium of the Historical Museum at Moscow on January 22, 1893. It first appeared in print in *Voprosy Filosofii i Psikhologii*, XVIII (May, 1893), 46–96, and was republished in P. Miliukov, *Iz istorii russkoi intelligentsii* (2nd ed.; St. Petersburg: Tipografiia Montvida, 1903), pp. 266–306.

2. Miliukov, *Iz istorii russkoi intelligentsii*, pp. 267–70, 303.

3. *Ibid.*, pp. 267, 303.

4. *Ibid.*, pp. 279, 291–92.

5. *Ibid.*, pp. 280–84.

6. *Ibid.*, p. 290.

7. *Ibid.*, pp. 285–90.

8. *Ibid.*, pp. 296–300.

9. *Ibid.*, p. 299.

10. *Ibid.*, p. 303.

11. *Ibid.*, pp. 305–6.

12. See Constantine N. Leont'ev, *Sobranie sochinenii* (Moscow: V. M. Sablin, 1912–13), VI, 335–36; " 'Moia literaturnaia sud'ba': Avtobiografiia Konstantina Leont'eva," ed. N. Mesheriakov and S. Durlyn, *Literaturnoe Nasledstvo*, Nos. 22–24 (1935), pp. 451–57; N. A. Berdiaev, *Konstantin Leont'ev: Ocherk iz istorii russkoi religioznoi mysli* (Paris: Y.M.C.A. Press, 1926), pp. 125–41; 152–61; V. S. Solov'ev, *Sobranie sochinenii*, V, 461.

13. Solov'ev, *Sobranie sochinenii*, V, 458–59.

CHAPTER TEN

1. Ivan Aksakov's changes of attitude from naive, youthful Slavophilism to skepticism and then back to Slavophilism can best be followed in volumes II, III, and IV of his collected letters. See *Ivan Sergeevich Aksakov v ego pis'makh* (Moscow: M. G. Volchaninov, 1888–92), II, 149–63; III, 243–512 and appendix, pp. 107–53; IV, 1–68, 180–83.

2. The best study of Samarin's life and works is still that of Baron B. E. Nol'de, *Iurii Samarin i ego vremia* (Paris: Imprimerie de Navarre, 1926).

3. Samarin's thesis is to be found in Volume V of his collected works: *Sochineniia Iu. F. Samarina* (Moscow: A. I. Mamontov, 1877–1911), V, 3–464.

4. *Ibid.*, VI, 329–70.

5. The most convenient sources of information concerning Ivan Aksakov's career as a journalist and public figure are the following: *I. S. Aksakov v ego pis'makh* (4 vols.); A. A. Kornilov, "Ivan Sergeevich Aksakov," in *Istoriia russkoi literatury XIX veka*, ed. D. N. Ovsianiko-Kulikovskii (Moscow, 1910), V, 101–18; V. Smirnov, *Aksakovy, ikh zhizn' i literaturnaia deiatel'nost'* (St. Petersburg: "Obshchestvennaia Pol'za," 1895); and S. Trubachev, "Ivan Sergeevich Aksakov," *Russkii Biograficheskii Slovar'*, I, 97–100. See also N. V. Riasanovsky, *Russia and the West in the Teaching of the Slavophiles* (Cambridge, Mass.: Harvard University Press, 1952), pp. 52–55.

6. Cf. Riasanovsky, pp. 173–74, 180–82; Vladimir Solov'ev, "Slavianofil'stvo i ego vyrozhdenie," *Sochineniia*, V, 161–222, esp. 174–75.

7. See Samarin, *Sochineniia* (2nd ed.; Moscow: A. I. Mamontov, 1900), I, 144–57, 321–22, 337–39.

8. Letter of Samarin to Baroness Edith Rahden, October 3/14, 1864, *Perepiska Iu. F. Samarina s Baronessoiu E. F. Raden, 1861–1876* (Moscow: A. I. Mamontov, 1893), p. 27.

9. *Ibid.*, pp. 26–29.

10. See Samarin's letter to the French politician Mauguin for an early expression of Samarin's political views (Samarin, *Sochineniia*, XII, 60–69).

11. D. Samarin, "Iu. F. Samarin," *Russkii Biograficheskii Slovar'*, XVIII, 137.

12. Letter of Samarin to Constantine Aksakov, April, 1848, *Sochineniia*, XII, 200; Samarin to M. P. Pogodin, October 9, 1847, *ibid.*, p. 264; Samarin to Const. Aksakov, July 19–20, 1846, *ibid.*, p. 177; Samarin, "Pis'ma iz Rigi," *ibid.*, VII, 6–7; letter of Samarin to E. Rahden, September–October 28/16, 1864, *Perepiska Iu. F. Samarina s Baronessoiu E. F. Raden*, pp. 14–18.

13. Letter of Samarin to M. P. Pogodin, April, 1848, *Sochineniia*, XII, 264; Samarin, "Pis'ma iz Rigi," *ibid.*, VII, 132.

14. Letter of Samarin to Const. Aksakov, July 19–20, 1846, *ibid.*, XII, 178; Samarin to M. P. Pogodin, April, 1848, *ibid.*, pp. 261–64; Samarin, "Pis'ma iz Rigi," *ibid.*, VII, 134–58; "Pravoslavnye Latyshi," *ibid.*, VIII, 482, 487, 504–5, 519–21, 524–29.

15. Nol'de, *Iurii Samarin i ego vremia*, pp. 46–49.

16. *Ibid.*, pp. 198–201; Samarin, *Okrainy Rossii. Seriia pervaia: Russkoe Baltiiskoe pomorie*, I and II (Prague: Tipografiiia Dra. F. Sreishovskago and Tipografiia Dr. E. Gregra, 1868); III–VI (Berlin: B. Behr's Buchhandlung, 1871–76).

17. Nol'de, p. 203.

18. Samarin, *Sochineniia*, VIII, xiv.

19. *Ibid.* Von Bock was one of the principal targets for Samarin's polemics on the Baltic question. Baron Firck's best-known work was *Que fera-t-on de la Pologne*, in which he defended the advisability of permitting the Poles to have their own laws and autonomy within the Russian empire. Mieroslawski was briefly dictator of Poland during the Polish uprising of 1863.

20. Iu. V. Got'e, "K. P. Pobedonostsev i naslednik Aleksandr Aleksandrovich, 1865–1881," in *Sbornik*, published by the Publichnaia Biblioteka SSSR imeni Lenina, II (Moscow, 1928), 108–9.

21. Letter of A. F. Aksakova to Pobedonostsev, March 2, 1867, Correspondence of Constantine P. Pobedonostsev with A. F. Aksakova and E. F. Tiutcheva, Manuscript Division, Lenin Library, Moscow (cf. Got'e, p. 116); letter of Alexander Aleksandrovich to Pobedonostsev, March 23, 1876, *K. P. Pobedonostsev i ego korrespondenty: Pis'ma i zapiski* (Moscow: Gosizdat, 1923), Vol. I, Part 2, p. 1015.

22. For Pobedonostsev on the Baltic Germans, see the following letters: Pobedonostsev to Alexander III, March 3, 1884, February 28 and December 21, 1887, and May 5, 1892, *Pis'ma Pobedonostseva k Aleksandru III* (Moscow: "Novaia Moskva," 1925–26), II, 51, 137–38, 165–67, 259; Pobedonostsev to Edouard Naville, March, 1888, in Friedrich Steinmann and Elias Hurwicz, *Konstantin Petrowitsch Pobjedonoszew, der Staatsmann der Reaktion unter Alexander III* (Königsberg-Berlin: Ost-Europa Verlag, 1933), pp. 78–79.

23. Nol'de, pp. 202–3.

24. Samarin, *Sochineniia*, I (2nd ed.), 329–43.

25. *Ibid.* Cf. Stanley J. Zyzniewski, "Miljutin and the Polish Question," in *Harvard Slavic Studies*, IV, (1957), 240–41; and Anatole Leroy-Beaulieu, *Un homme d'État russe (Nicholas Milutine) d'après sa correspondance inédite: Étude sur la Russie et la Pologne pendant le règne d'Alexandre II (1855–1872)* (Paris: Hachette, 1884), pp. 204–7, 215–23, 263–71, 276–84.

26. Samarin, *Sochineniia.* I, 261–84.

27. *Ibid.*, pp. 338–43. Cf. Michael B. Petrovich, "Russian Pan-Slavists and the Polish Uprising of 1863," in *Harvard Slavic Studies*, I (1953), 219–47.

28. Nol'de, pp. 169–71, 179.

29. Samarin, *Sochineniia*, VI. 6–9.

30. Nol'de, pp. 191–92, 200; Samarin. *Sochineniia*, VI, 3–4. Samarin's "Otvet iezuitu otsu Martynovu" was republished on a number of occasions: in 1866, 1868, 1870, and finally in 1887 in Volume VI of his *Sochineniia*, pp. 1–326.

31. Samarin, "Pis'ma iz Rigi," *Sochineniia*, VII, 21–57, 106–33.

32. Letter of Samarin to Rahden, September 28, 1864, *Perepiska Iu. F. Samarina s Baronessoiu E. F. Raden*, p. 18.

33. Samarin's *Istoriia Rigi, 1200–1845* was republished in Vol. VII of his *Sochineniia*, pp. 161–633.

34. See, for example, *ibid.*, pp. 252–53, 271–72.

35. "Iz dnevnika vedennago Iu. F. Samarinym v Kieve v 1850 godu," *Russkii Arkhiv*, XV (February, 1877), 229–32.

36. *Ibid.*, p. 232.

37. *I. S. Aksakov v ego pis'makh*, II, 157–59; letter of Aksakov to N. I. Kostomarov, October 30, 1861, *ibid.*, IV, 257–63; *Sochineniia I. S. Aksakova, 1860–1868* (Moscow: M. G. Volchaninov, 1886–87), I, 71, III, 208, 324–33, 405–13.

38. See Aksakov, *Sochineniia*, II, 19 (*Den'* editorial of November 11, 1861).

39. " 'Moia literaturnaia sud'ba': Avtobiografiia Konstantina Leont'eva," ed. S. Durylin and N. Meshcheriakov, *Literaturnoe Nasledstvo*, Nos. 22–24 (1935), p. 457.

40. See *I. S. Aksakov v ego pis'makh*, II, 154–55.

41. Cf. A. N. Pypin, "Slavianskii vopros po vzgliadam I. Aksakova," *Vestnik Evropy*, CXX (August, 1886), 766; Aksakov, *Sochineniia*, I, 248.

42. Khomiakov, for example, referred to the Crimean War as a "holy war." See N. Ustrialov, "Natsional'naia problema u pervykh Slavianofilov," *Russkaia Mysl'*, October, 1916, Section II, pp. 19–20; A. S. Khomiakov, *Polnoe sobranie sochinenii* (3d ed.; Moscow: Universitetskaia Tipografiia, 1900–1907), III, 195.

43. Aksakov, *Sochineniia*, I, 271. Cf. *ibid.*, pp. 251–53.

44. Orest Miller, "Ivan Sergeevich Aksakov," *Russkaia Starina*, XLIX (March, 1886), 756.

45. Aksakov, *Sochineniia*, I, 163–65, 173–78.

46. See the letter of Aksakov to N. I. Kostomarov, October 30, 1861, *I. S. Aksakov v ego pis'makh*, IV, 257–63.

47. To be sure, he did occasionally disapprove of certain abuses of bureaucratic power in Poland, as for example the use of force in returning the Chelm Uniates to the Orthodox Church (*Sochineniia*, I, 580). Such admissions were, however, rare and he was generally blind to the encroachments of the Russian bureaucracy on Polish nationality. For Aksakov's views on Poland during the 1880's, see especially *Sochineniia*, I, 568–83, 622–35, 648–66.

48. *I. S. Aksakov v ego pis'makh*, II, 154–55, 159–60.

49. "Perepiska I. S. Aksakova s Kn. V. A. Cherkasskim (1875–78)," in *Slavianskii sbornik: Slavianskii vopros i russkoe obshchestvo v 1867–1878*, ed. N. M. Druzhinin (Moscow: Lenin Public Library, 1948), pp. 136–38, 176–78.

50. A. A. Kornilov, "Ivan Sergeevich Aksakov," *Istoriia russkoi literatury XIX veka*, V, 114–15. Aksakov criticized the Russian government's policy at the Berlin Congress in a speech before the Moscow Slavic Benevolent Society (the former Moscow Slavic Benevolent Committee was officially made a society in 1877) on June 22, 1878. This speech is to be found in Aksakov's *Sochineniia*, I, 297–308.

51. Aksakov, *Sochineniia*, III, 693–98.

52. *Ibid.*, pp. 711–14.

53. *Ibid.*, pp. 717–25.

54. *Ibid.*, pp. 731, 790, 825–26.

55. Riasanovsky, *Russia and the West in the Teaching of the Slavophiles*, p. 184. Aksakov's views on the World Israelite Alliance were published in *Rus'* on November 1, 1883, and December 15, 1883 (*Sochineniia*, III, 819–43).

56. Aksakov, *Sochineniia*, V, 618, 622–28.

57. *Ibid.*, II, 32–33, 35, 40.

58. *Ibid.*, V, 612.

59. *Ibid.*, pp. 31–35.

60. *Ibid.*, pp. 518, 523, 554–59, 568, 588–96.

61. For discussions of the intrigues of Pazukhin and Tolstoi against the Kakhanov committee, see the following two articles: S. Ia. Tseitlin, "Zemskoe samoupravlenie i reforma 1890 g.," in *Istoriia XIX veka* (St. Petersburg: A. I. Granat and Co., n.d.), V, 120–27; and S. M. Bleklov, "Krest'ianskoe obshchest-vennoe upravlenie," *ibid.*, pp. 162–64.

62. Aksakov's views on such matters as freedom of speech and religion, the zemstvos, and the *zemskii sobor* are to be found especially in Vols. IV and V of his *Sochineniia*.

63. A. A. Kornilov, "Ivan Sergeevich Aksakov," *Istoriia russkoi literatury XIX veka*, V, 116–17.

64. Aksakov, *Sochineniia*, IV, 654–56, 662–63.

65. Samarin first expressed such views in an unpublished article of 1842 or 1843, which is now to be found in the Manuscript Division of the Lenin Library in Moscow. See S. S. Dmitriev, "Ekonomicheskie vozzreniia slaviano-filov, 1840–1850 gg.," (Candidate's dissertation, Moscow University, 1940), pp. 91–96. Cf. Nol'de, p. 34.

66. Samarin, *Sochineniia*, II, 163, 166–71, III, 168–70, and IV, 501–2, 510–13.

67. Cf. Marc Raeff, "Georges Samarin et la commune paysanne après 1861," *Revue des Études Slaves*, XXIX (1952), 77–81.

68. Nol'de, pp. 176–79, 189–90; A. A. Kornilov, *Obshchestvennoe dvizhenie pri Aleksandre II, 1855–1881* (Moscow, 1909), pp. 120–21.

69. These articles were prepared for publication in Volume XI of Samarin's *Sochineniia*. This volume, however, was unfortunately never published. The articles are listed on pp. 234–35 of Nol'de's study of Samarin.

70. These articles were originally published under the title of "Chem nam byt'" and subsequently as a separate book, *Russkoe obshchestvo v nastoiashchem*

i budushchem, in 1874 and in Volume III, Part 2 of Fadeev's *Sobranie sochinenii* in 1889.

71. R. A. Fadeev, *Sobranie sochinenii* (St. Petersburg: V. V. Komarov, 1889), Vol. III, Part 1, pp. 4–5, 62–68, 89–95, 107–8.

72. Iu. Samarin and F. Dmitriev, *Revoliutsionnyi konservatizm* (Berlin: B. Behr's Buchhandlung, 1875), p. 10.

73. *Ibid.*, p. 11.

74. *Ibid.*, p. 47.

75. *Ibid.*, p. 48.

76. *Ibid.*, p. 72. Cf. *Russkii administrator noveishei shkoly: Zapiska Pskovskago Gubernatora B. Obukhova i otvet na nee*, ed. Iurii F. Samarin (Berlin: B. Behr's Buchhandlung, 1868).

77. Samarin and Dmitriev, *Revoliutsionnyi konservatizm*, p. 72.

78. N. V. Ustrialov, "Politicheskaia doktrina slavianofil'stva (ideia samoderzhaviia v slavianofil'skoi postanovke)," *Izvestiia Iuridicheskogo Fakulteta* of the Vysshaia Shkola in Harbin, Manchuria, I (1925), 71.

CHAPTER ELEVEN

1. There are two basic, but rather inadequate, accounts of Fadeev's life: N. A. F[adeev]a, "Vospominaniia o Rostislave Fadeeve," in R. A. Fadeev, *Sobranie sochinenii* (St. Petersburg: V. V. Komarov, 1889), Vol. I, Part 1, pp. 1–68; and S. Trubachev, "Rostislav Andreevich Fadeev," *Russkii Biograficheskii Slovar'*, XXI, 6–10. The two articles in the *Russkii Vestnik* in 1891 and 1892 ("R. A. Fadeev i ego sochineniia, *Russkii Vestnik*, CCXVI [September, 1891], 117–41, and CCXVII [November, 1891], 281–99; and "R. A. Fadeev kak voennyi deiatel' i pisatel'," *ibid.*, CCXIX [April, 1892], 90–122, and CCXX [May, 1892], 124–65) contribute little of interest. See also Trubachev's biographical sketches concerning Fadeev's father and mother: "Andrei Mikhailovich Fadeev" and "Elena Pavlovna Fadeeva," *Russkii Biogr. Slovar'*, XXI, 4–6.

2. His first essays on the Caucasian wars were published in *Severnaia Pchela* and *Journal de St. Petersbourg* at the beginning of Alexander II's reign. In 1860 he published an official history of these wars (*Shest'desiat let kavkazskoi voiny*). And in 1864–65 his *Pis'ma s Kavkaza* appeared in Katkov's *Moskovskiia Vedomosti*. The latter two works were republished in Volume I of Fadeev's *Sobranie sochinenii*.

3. Fadeev, "Shest'desiat let kavkazskoi voiny," *Sobranie sochinenii*, Vol. I, Part 1, pp. 8–10; "Pis'ma s Kavkaza," *ibid.*, pp. 239–40, 245–50.

4. Fadeev, "Vooruzhennyia sily Rossii," *ibid.*, Vol. II, Part 1, pp. 23, 196.

5. See *ibid.*, pp. 5, 36–37.

6. *Ibid.*, pp. 197–98.

7. "Mnenie o vostochnom voprose," *ibid.*, Vol. II, Part 2, pp. 296 and 316–19.

8. "Russkoe obshchestvo v nastoiashchem i budushchem," *ibid.*, Vol. III, Part 1, pp. 12–14.

9. Six of these letters are to be found in the Aksakov family Archive in the Manuscript Division of the Institute of Russian Literature (Pushkinskii Dom) of the Academy of Sciences of the USSR, Leningrad.

10. Fadeev, "Pis'ma o sovremennom sostoianii Rossii," *Sobranie sochinenii*, Vol. III, Part 2, p. 36.

11. B. H. Sumner, *Russia and the Balkans, 1870–1880* (Oxford: The Clarendon Press, 1937), pp. 70–71, 184–85, 328; M. B. Petrovich, *The Emergence*

of Russian Panslavism, 1856–1857 (New York: Columbia University Press, 1956), p. 142; P. S. Usov, "Vospominaniia o R. A. Fadeeve," *Istoricheskii Vestnik*, XV (February, 1884), 378.

12. Fadeev, "Vooruzhennyia sily Rossii," *Sobranie sochinenii*, Vol. II, Part 1, pp. 34–35.

13. *Ibid.*, pp. 205–6.

14. *Ibid.*, pp. 207–8.

15. The best account of these discussions is given by M. B. Petrovich, *The Emergence of Russian Panslavism*, especially in Chapters VIII and IX.

16. Orest Miller, *Slavianstvo i Evropa* (St. Petersburg: G. E. Blagosvetlov, 1877), pp. 95–97.

17. Fadeev, "Mnenie o vostochnom voprose," *Sobranie sochinenii*, Vol. II, Part 2, pp. 296, 301–2, 316–19.

18. *Ibid.*, pp. 300, 313.

19. P. S. Usov, "Vospominaniia o R. A. Fadeeve," *Istoricheskii Vestnik*, XV (February, 1884), 375.

20. Fadeev, "Vooruzhennyia sily Rossii," *Sobranie sochinenii*, Vol. II, Part 1, pp. 10–11.

21. "Russkoe obshchestvo v nastoiashchem i budushchem," *Sobranie sochinenii*, Vol. III, Part 1, pp. 4–12; "Pis'ma o sovremennom sostoianni Rossii," *ibid.*, Vol. III, Part 2, p. 36.

22. "Pis'ma s Kavkaza," *ibid.*, Vol. I, Part 1, pp. 243–47.

23. "Vooruzhennyia sily," *ibid.*, Vol. II, Part 1, pp. 21–23.

24. *Ibid.*, pp. 11–21.

25. *Ibid.*, p. 203.

26. See *ibid.*, pp. 203, 207, 215; Vol. III, Part 1, pp. 10–12, 144–45.

27. "Russkoe obshchestvo v nastoiashchem i budushchem," *ibid.*, Vol. III, Part 1, p. 97.

28. See *ibid.*, pp. 10, 62–66, 144–45; Vol. III, Part 2, pp. 25, 48.

29. *Ibid.*, Vol. III, Part 1, p. 38; Vol. III, Part 2, pp. 13–24.

30. *Ibid.*, Vol. III, Part 1, p. 165.

31. *Ibid.*, pp. 4–5.

32. *Ibid.*, pp. 56–57.

33. *Ibid.*, pp. 6–8.

34. "Pis'ma o sovremennom sostoianii Rossii," *ibid.*, Vol. III, Part 2, pp. 13–22; "Zapiska o bor'be s revoliutsionnym dvizheniem putem sozyva gubernskikh zemskikh komitetov s predstaviteliami krest'ian dlia obsuzhdeniia neobkhodimykh reform," December, 1879, R. A. Fadeev Papers, Manuscript Division, Lenin Public Library, Moscow, pp. 1–6.

35. See Fadeev, *Sobranie sochinenii*, Vol. III, Part 1, pp. 13–14, for views on the Slavophiles expressed by Fadeev which Samarin must have found particularly objectionable.

36. See *ibid.*, Vol. II, Part 1, pp. 10–11, 203, 215; Vol. III, Part 1, pp. 50, 68, 108, 162–63, 177–79.

37. "Pis'ma o sovremennom sostoianii Rossii," *ibid.*, Vol. III, Part 2, pp. 3–6.

38. *Ibid.*, pp. 21–22, 23, 111–13.

39. *Ibid.*, p. 60; "Russkoe obshchestvo v nastoiashchem i budushchem," *ibid.*, Vol. III, Part 1, pp. 45–46.

40. *Ibid.*, Vol. III, Part 1, pp. 107–8; Vol. III, Part 2, pp. 5–6.

41. *Ibid.*, Vol. III, Part 2, pp. 6, 37–38.

42. *Ibid.*, pp. 35–36.

43. *Ibid.*, Vol. III, Part 1, pp. 89 and 107–8; Vol. III, Part 2, pp. 45–46.

44. This point of view was expressed by Fadeev particularly forcefully in his memorandum of 1872 "O merakh dlia vosstanovleniia armii," which is now to be found in the Central State Historical Archive in Moscow. This document is quoted by P. A. Zaionchkovskii, *Voennye reformy 1860–1870 godov v Rossii* (Moscow: Izdatel'stvo Moskovskogo Universiteta, 1952), pp. 290–91. The same point of view is expressed throughout Fadeev's "Nash voennyi vopros," *Sobranie sochinenii,* Vol. II, Part 2.

45. Fadeev. *Sobranie sochinenii,* Vol. III, Part 1, pp. 62–63, 68, 82, 89, 96, 103, 107–8, 144–45.

46. *Ibid.*, pp. 93–95, 102–3. 108, 140; "Zapiska o bor'be s revoliutsionnym dvizheniem . . . , Manuscript Division, Lenin Library, Moscow, pp. 3, 6.

47. *Sobranie sochinenii,* Vol. III, Part 1, pp. 70–74.

48. *Ibid.*, pp. 97–101; Vol. III, Part 2, p. 2.

49. *Ibid.*, Vol. III, Part 2, pp. 35–38.

50. *Ibid.*, pp. 38–39.

51. See *ibid.*, Vol. III, Part 1, pp. 5–10, 138–39, 211–13.

52. See *ibid.*, pp. 102–3, 206; Vol. III, Part 2, pp. 70–79.

53. For a good, though antigentry, account of the nature of gentry participation in zemstvo affairs, see the two articles of S. Ia. Tseitlin, "Zemskaia reforma" and "Zemskoe samoupravlenie i reforma 1890 g.," in *Istoriia Rossii v XIX veke* (St. Petersburg: Granat and Co., n.d.), III, 179–231, and V, 79–138 (especially III, 194–96, 212–13; V, 84–91).

54. Samarin, *Revoliutsionnyi konservatizm,* p. 48.

55. P. A. Zaionchkovskii, *Voennye reformy 1860–1870 godov v Rossii,* pp. 127–32, 289; *Dnevnik D. A. Miliutina 1873–1882,* I, 38, 40, IV, 148–49, 173; S. Iu. Witte, *Vospominaniia* (Moscow–Petrograd–Leningrad: Gosizdat, 1923–24), III, 20–24, 127 (Witte was Fadeev's nephew); S. Trubachev, "Rostislav Andreevich Fadeev," *Russkii Biogr. Slovar',* XXI, 10. Concerning the Holy Brotherhood, see Stephen Lukashevich, "The Holy Brotherhood: 1881–1883," *American Slavic and East European Review,* XVIII (December, 1959), 491–509.

56. Zaionchkovskii, p. 130; *Dnevnik D. A. Miliutina,* I, 38.

57. Fadeev, *Sobranie sochinenii,* Vol. III, Part 1, pp. 211–13.

58. *Dnevnik D. A. Miliutina,* II, 108.

59. *Ibid.*

60. Fadeev, "Vooruzhennyia sily Rossii," *Russkii Vestnik,* LXVII (February, 1867), 723–87, LXVIII (March and April, 1867), 161–210, 411–505, LXIX (May and June, 1867), 61–107, 536–64, LXX (July, 1867), 65–88.

61. Zaionchkovskii, p. 128. Cf. Fadeev, *Vooruzhennyia sily Rossii* (Moscow: Universitetskaia Tipografiia, 1868), p. 244.

62. Fadeev, *Vooruzhennyia sily Rossii,* p. iii.

63. See Witte, *Vospominaniia,* III, 20; Fadeev, *Sobranie sochinenii,* Vol. I, Part 1, pp. 42–44.

64. Zaionchkovskii, pp. 21, 51–59, 127, 132; Witte, *Vospominaniia,* III, 22–24.

65. B. H. Sumner, *Russia and the Balkans,* pp. 47–50 and 184–85.

66. P. S. Usov, "Vospominaniia o R. A. Fadeeve," *Istoricheskii Vestnik,* XV, 378.

67. "Nash voennyi vopros" was included in Vol. II, Part 2 of Fadeev's *Sobranie sochinenii*, pp. 1–85.

CHAPTER TWELVE

1. See Constantine N. Leont'ev, *Sobranie sochinenii* (Moscow: V. M. Sablin, 1912–13), V, 362, VI, 335–36, VII, 26–27, 265, VIII, 102, and IX, 30–34. Also: Leont'ev, "Neskol'ko vospominanii i myslei o pokoinom Ap. Grigor'eve: Pis'mo k Nik. Nik. Strakhovu," in Apollon Grigor'ev, *Vospominaniia*, ed. Ivanov-Razumnik (Moscow–Leningrad: "Academia," 1930), pp. 528–56 (written in June, 1869, and first published in *Russkaia Mysl'*, September, 1915, pp. 109–24). A good general account of Leont'ev's life and activities is given by A. Konopliantsev, "Zhizn' K. N. Leont'eva," in *Pamiati Konstantina Nikolaevicha Leont'eva* (St. Petersburg: Tipografiia "Sirius," 1911), pp. 3–141. Cf. Konopliantsev, "Konstantin Nikolaevich Leont'ev," *Russkii Biograficheskii Slovar'*, X, 229–49. The most complete bibliography of works by and about Leont'ev is contained in *Pamiati K. N. Leont'eva*, pp. 405–24. For later references to works on Leont'ev, see the bibliographies at the end of the following two studies: Nicholas Berdiaev, *Konstantin Leont'ev: Ocherk iz istorii russkoi religioznoi mysli* (Paris: Y.M.C.A. Press, 1926), and Jordon Kurland, "The History and Destiny of Russia according to Konstantin Leont'ev" (Columbia University Master's thesis, 1952). Berdiaev's study of Leont'ev has been translated into both English and French. Another good biographical and analytical account of Leont'ev's life and thought is Iwan von Kologriwof's book, *Von Hellas zum Mönchtum; Leben und Denken Konstantin Leontjews, 1831–1891* (Regensburg: Gregorius Verlag, 1948).

2. Leont'ev, "Dva grafa: Aleksei Vronskii i Lev Tolstoi," *Sobranie sochinenii*, VII, 266–67. Leont'ev's essay on "Gramotnost' i narodnost'," which was written in the late 1860's and published in *Zaria* in 1870, is a good example of his antiliberal stand while still in the Balkans. See *ibid.*, pp. 13–55.

3. These arguments are developed throughout Leont'ev's three volumes, "The East, Russia, and Slavdom" ("Vostok, Rossiia i slavianstvo," *Sobranie sochinenii*, V, VI, and VII), especially V, 108; VI, 189; VII, 88–89, 241. Leont'ev also gives an amusing account of his differences with the Slavophiles in "'Moia literaturnaia sud'ba': Avtobiografiia Konstantina Leont'eva," ed. N. Meshcheriakov and S. Durylin, *Literaturnoe Nasledstvo*, Nos. 22–24 (1935), pp. 442–58.

4. Leont'ev, "Pis'ma k Vladimiru Sergeevichu Solov'evu (o natsionalizme politicheskom i kul'turnom)," *Sobranie sochinenii*, VI, 335–36; "Vladimir Solov'ev protiv Danilevskago," *ibid.*, VII, 324.

5. "Pis'ma k Vladimiru Sergeevichu Solov'evu (o natsionalizme politicheskom i kul'turnom)," *ibid.*, VI, 340. Cf. "Vizantizm i slavianstvo," *ibid.*, V. 187–97.

6. "Vizantizm i slavianstvo," *ibid.*, V, 188–89.

7. *Ibid.*, p. 197.

8. *Ibid.*, p. 250.

9. *Ibid.*, p. 210.

10. "Dopolnenie k dvum stat'iam o panslavizme, *ibid.*, V, 107–8; "Khram i tserkov'," *ibid.*, p. 347; "Pis'ma o vostochnykh delakh," *ibid.*, p. 455.

11. See "Slavianofil'stvo teorii i slavianofil'stvo zhizni," *ibid.*, VII, 431–34.

12. "Vladimir Solov'ev protiv Danilevskago," *ibid.*, VII, 367–68.

13. *Ibid.*

14. "Kak nado ponimat' sblizhenie s narodom," *ibid.*, p. 227; "Moe obrashchenie i zhizn' na sv. afonskoi gore," *ibid.*, IX, 31–34.

15. "Vizantizm i slavianstvo," *ibid.*, V, 147; "Pis'ma otshel'nika," *ibid.*, p. 376; "Plody natsional'nykh dvizhenii na pravoslavnom vostoke," *ibid.*, VI, 240.

16. "Plody natsional'nykh dvizhenii . . . ," *ibid.*, VI, 250.

17. *Ibid.*, p. 217.

18. "Plemennaia politika, kak orudie vsemirnoi revoliutsii," *ibid.*, VI 189; "Peredovyia stat'i 'Varshavskago Dnevnika' 1880 g.," *ibid.*, VII, 96–98; " 'Moia literaturnaia sud'ba': Avtobiografiia Konstantina Leont'eva," *Literaturnoe Nasledstvo*, Nos. 22–24, p. 445.

19. "Nashi okrainy," *ibid.*, VII, 224–25.

20. *Ibid.*, pp. 249–52.

21. *Ibid.*, pp. 256–61. For Leont'ev's comments on Herzen and language, see "Vizantizm i slavianstvo," *ibid.*, V, 146–47.

22. The importance of Leont'ev's stay at Athos is suggested best by his article "Moe obrashchenie i zhizn' na sv. Afonskoi gore," *ibid.*, IX, 11–34.

23. For views on Leont'ev by Orthodox scholars, see K. Aggeev, *Khristianstvo i ego otnoshenie k blagoustroeniiu zemnoi zhizni: Opyt kriticheskago izucheniia i bogoslovskoi otsenki raskrytago K. N. Leont'evym ponimaniia khristianstva* (Kiev: Tipografiia "Petr Barskii," 1909); and G. Florovskii, *Puti russkogo bogosloviia* (Paris: Y.M.C.A. Press, 1937), pp. 302–5. One example of Leont'ev's subjective and esthetic view of Christianity can be seen in his novel "Egipetskii golub'," *Sobranie sochinenii*, III, 375.

24. Leont'ev, "Dva predstavitelia industrii," *Sobranie sochinenii*, VII, 467–70; "Srednii evropeets, kak ideal i orudie vsemirnago razrusheniia," *ibid.*, VI, 63; letter of Leont'ev to V. V. Rozanov, August 13, 1891, "Iz perepiski K. N. Leont'eva," ed. V. V. Rozanov, *Russkii Vestnik*, CCLXXXV (June, 1903), 417.

25. "Vizantizm i slavianstvo," *Sobranie sochinenii*, V, 139.

26. *Ibid.*, p. 114.

27. "Peredovyia stat'i 'Varshavskago Dnevnika' 1880 g.," *ibid.*, VII, 134.

28. "O vsemirnoi liubvi: Rech' F. M. Dostoevskago na pushkinskom prazdnike," *ibid.*, VIII, 200–8.

29. *Ibid.*, pp. 207–8. It is interesting to note that Pobedonostsev sent a copy of Leont'ev's article to Dostoevskii. See *F. M. Dostoevskii: Pis'ma*, IV, 433–34.

30. "Peredovyia stat'i 'Varshavskago Dnevnika' 1880 g.," *Sobranie sochinenii*, VII, 68, 73–74. See also "O vsemirnoi liubvi . . . ," *ibid.*, VIII, 197; and "Vladimir Solov'ev protiv Danilevskago," *ibid.*, VII, 374–75.

31. "Dobryia vesti," *ibid.*, VII, 383–84.

32. G. Florovskii, *Puti russkogo bogosloviia*, p. 302.

33. "Vizantizm i slavianstvo," *Sobranie sochinenii*, V, 132–34, 136–37, 186, 252–53; "Pis'ma o vostochnykh delakh," *ibid.*, p. 441; "Koshelev i obshchina," *ibid.*, VII, 170; "Nad mogiloi Pazukhina," *ibid.*, pp. 420–21; A. M. Konopliantsev, "Zhizn' K. N. Leont'eva v sviazi s razvitiem ego mirosozertsaniia," *Pamiati Konstantina Leont'eva*, p. 111.

34. "Nad mogiloi Pazukhina," *Sobranie sochinenii*, VII, 420–24.

35. "Peredovyia stat'i 'Varshavskago Dnevnika' 1880 g.," *ibid.*, p. 76.

36. "Chem i kak liberalizm nash vreden?" *ibid.*, p. 195.

37. "Peredovyia stat'i . . . ," *ibid.*, pp. 76–77. See also "Vizantizm i slavianstvo," *ibid.*, V, 134.

38. "Vizantizm i slavianstvo," *ibid.*, V, 137.

39. *Ibid.*, pp. 120–22, 126–27. It should be noted that Leont'ev also criticized Danilevskii for not having included Byzantine civilization among his cultural-historical types. See "Pis'ma k Vladimiru Sergeevichu Solov'evu (o natsionalizme politicheskom i kul'turnom)," *ibid.*, VI, 339.

40. "Vizantizm i slavianstvo," *ibid.*, V, 126–27.

41. *Ibid.*, pp. 139–40.

42. A. Konopliantsev, "Konstantin Nikolaevich Leont'ev," *Russkii Biograficheskii Slovar'*, X, 235–36. This article was published three years later in *Zaria* and is to be found in Volume VII, pp. 13–55, of Leont'ev's *Sobranie sochinenii*.

43. "Gramotnost' i narodnost'," *Sobranie sochinenii*, VII, 43–55.

44. See, for example, *ibid.*; and "Chem i kak liberalizm nash vreden?" *ibid.*, pp. 186–87.

45. "Vizantizm i slavianstvo," *ibid.*, V, 229; "Eshche o 'Dikarke,'" *ibid.*, VIII, 95.

46. "Chem i kak liberalizm nash vreden?" *ibid.*, VII, 196.

47. "Pis'ma o vostochnykh delakh," *ibid.*, V. 441–44; "Srednii evropeets, kak ideal i orudie vsemirnago razrusheniia," *ibid.*, VI, 50–51; "Pis'ma k Vladimiru Sergeevichu Solov'evu," *ibid.*, p. 294; "Koshelev i obshchina," *ibid.*, VII, 168–70; "Chem i kak liberalizm nash vreden?" *ibid.*, pp. 186–87, 196–97; "Zapiska o neobkhodimosti novoi bol'shoi gazety v S.-Peterburge," *ibid.*, p. 502.

48. "Dopolnenie k dvum stat'iam o panslavizme," *ibid.*, V, 107–8; "Khram i tserkov'," *ibid.*, p. 347; "Vizantizm i slavianstvo," *ibid.*, p. 165; "Srednii evropeets, kak ideal i orudie vsemirnago razrusheniia," *ibid.*, VI, 67.

49. "'Moskovskiia Vedomosti' o dvoevlastii," *ibid.*, VII, 519.

50. Leont'ev discussed the Strakhov–Solov'ev controversy in a series of articles appearing in *Grazhdanin* during 1888 (See "Vladimir Solov'ev protiv Danilevskago," *ibid.*, VII, 285–379).

51. "Vladimir Solov'ev protiv Danilevskago," *ibid.*, VII, 287; "'Moskovskiia Vedomosti' o dvoevlastii," *ibid.*, pp. 519, 523; letter of Leont'ev to V. V. Rozanov, May 24, 1891, "Iz perepiski K. N. Leont'eva," *Russkii Vestnik* CCLXXXV (May, 1903), 158.

52. "Vladimir Solov'ev protiv Danilevskago," *Sobranie sochinenii*, VII, 367–68; "Dva predstavitelia industrii," *ibid.*, pp. 468–69.

53. I. Fudel', "Kul'turnyi ideal K. N. Leont'eva," *Russkoe Obozrenie*, XXXI (January, 1895), 268.

54. See "Pis'ma o vostochnykh delakh," *Sobranie sochinenii*, V, 424–25.

55. "Nad mogiloi Pazukhina," *ibid.*, VII, 416.

56. "Pis'ma o vostochnykh delakh," *ibid.*, V, 425; "Plody natsional'nykh dvizhenii na pravoslavnom Vostoke," *ibid.*, VI, 233.

57. "Kak nado ponimat' sblizhenie s narodom," *ibid.*, VII, 241.

58. "Pis'ma k Vladimiru Sergeevichu Solov'evu," *ibid.*, VI, 342–43; "Chem i kak liberalizm nash vreden?" *ibid.*, VII, 188–92.

59. "Plody natsional'nykh dvizhenii no pravoslavnom Vostoke," *ibid.*, VI, 245–46. Cf. "Vizantizm i slavianstvo," *ibid.*, V, 137–40; and "Peredovyia stat'i 'Varshavskago Dnevnika' 1880 g.," *ibid.*, VII, 75. Even the literary masterpieces produced by such writers as Turgenev, Tolstoi, and Dostoevskii did little to alter Leont'ev's gloomy thoughts about the future of Russia. Generally speaking

(with the exceptions of such works as *War and Peace* and *Anna Karenina*), he regarded Russian literature since Gogol, especially because of its prosaic themes, subject matter, and heroes, to be merely another example of the general cultural decline and vulgarization of Russian life. See Jordan Kurland, "Leont'ev's Views on the Course of Russian Literature," *American Slavic and East European Review*, XVI (October, 1957), 260–74.

60. "Pis'ma o vostochnykh delakh," *Sobranie sochinenii*, V, 451–53; "Srednii evropeets, kak ideal i orudie vsemirnago razrushennia," *ibid.*, VI, 59–61; "Nad mogiloi Pazukhina," *ibid.*, pp. 414–17; " 'Moskovskiia Vedomosti' o dvoevlastii," *ibid.*, VII, 525–27.

61. Letter of Leont'ev to A. Aleksandrov, May 3, 1890, *Pamiati K. N. Leont'eva: Pis'ma K. N. Leont'eva k Anatoliu Aleksandrovu*, ed. A. A. Aleksandrov (Sergiev Posad: Tipografiia Sv.-Tr. Sergievoi Lavry, 1915), pp. 94–95..

62. "Nad mogiloi Pazukhina," *Sobranie sochinenii*, VII, 416, 425–26.

63. "Ne kstati i kstati," *ibid.*, p. 489.

64. "Peredovyia stat'i 'Varshavkago Dnevnika' 1880 g.," *ibid.*, p. 66.

65. "Zapiska o neobkhodimosti novoi bol'shoi gazety v S.-Peterburge," *ibid.*, p. 505.

66. N. Berdiaev, *Leontiev* (London: G. Bles, The Centenary Press, 1940), p. ix.

67. Konopliantsev, "Zhizn' K. N. Leont'eva," *Pamiati K. N. Leont'eva* (St. Petersburg, 1911), pp. 123–24; letter of I. S. Aksakov to K. P. Pobedonostsev, February 15, 1884, in "Pis'ma I. S. Aksakova k K. P. Pobedonostsevu," *Russkii Arkhiv*, XLV (1907), Part 3, pp. 175–76.

68. V. V. Rozanov, "Neuznannyi fenomen," *Pamiati K. N. Leont'eva*, pp. 180–81; letter of Leont'ev to Rozanov, May 24, 1891, "Iz perepiski K. N. Leont'eva," *Russkii Vestnik*, CCLXXXV (May, 1903), 158–60. Leont'ev also had mixed feelings toward Strakhov. He esteemed Strakhov for his conservatism but disapproved of his systematic learning and pedantic and philosophical approach to life.

69. See *F. M. Dostoevskii: Pis'ma*, IV, 433–34.

70. Konopliantsev, "Zhizn' K. N. Leont'eva," *Pamiati*, p. 124; S. Iu. Witte, *Vospominaniia*, III, 250–51; V. P. Meshcherskii, *Moi vospominaniia*, III, 338; letter of Pobedonostsev to Alexander III, August 4, 1888, *Pis'ma Pobedonostseva k Aleksandru III* (Moscow, 1925–26), II, 190.

71. L. A. Tikhomirov, "Russkie idealy i K. N. Leont'ev," *Russkoe Obozrenie*, XXIX (October, 1894), 871–73.

72. Benda's *Trahison des clercs* has recently been republished by Beacon Press: *The Betrayal of the Intellectuals* (Boston, 1955). Leont'ev, it is true, was not an ardent political nationalist, as was the case for most of the other intellectuals described by Benda. However, Leont'ev's apotheosis of an all-powerful Russian state represents a similar type of intellectual betrayal.

73. *Biografiia, pis'ma i zametki iz zapisnoi knizhki F. M. Dostoevskago*, 2nd section, p. 369.

74. For a recent analysis of Rozanov, see Richard Hare, *Portraits of Russian Personalities between Reform and Revolution* (London: Oxford University Press, 1959), pp. 285–93.

75. Tikhomirov's views are most fully developed in his four-volume work *Monarkhicheskaia gosudarstvennost'* (Moscow: Universitetskaia Tipografiia, 1905).

CHAPTER THIRTEEN

1. Concerning the School of Jurisprudence, see *Ko dniu LXXV iubileia Imperatorskago Uchilishcha Pravovedeniia 1835–1910 gg.*, ed. G. Siuzor (St. Petersburg: Gosudarstvennaia Tipografiia, 1910); K. P. Pobedonostsev, "Vospominaniia o Zubkove," *Russkii Arkhiv*, XLII (1904), Part 1, p. 301; and *K. P. Pobedonostsev i ego korrespondenty: Pis'ma i zapiski* (Moscow: Gosizdat, 1923), pp. 519–20.

2. Professor Boris Chicherin's remarks concerning Pobedonostsev during the years he lectured at Moscow University are of particular interest. See B. N. Chicherin, *Vospominaniia Borisa Nikolaevicha Chicherina: Zemstvo i moskovskaia duma* (Moscow: Kooperativnoe Izdatel'stvo "Sever," 1934), pp. 102–3.

3. There is no satisfactory biographical and analytical study of Pobedonostsev's life and activities. Professor R. F. Byrnes is, however, presently working on such a study. Pobedonostsev, himself, provides such information in his letter of March 21, 1901, to Nicholas II, *Pis'ma Pobedonostseva k Aleksandru III* (Moscow: "Novaia Moskva," 1925–26), II, 329–35. He also published excerpts from his school diary while at the School of Jurisprudence in a limited edition intended for friends: *Dlia nemnogikh: Otryvki iz shkol'nago dnevnika, 1842–1845 gg.* (St. Petersburg: Tipografiia Ministerstva Putei Soobshcheniia, 1885). This diary was republished, though with omissions, and edited by Peter Bartenev in 1907: "Iz dnevnika K. P. Pobedonostseva," *Russkii Arkhiv*, XLV (1907), Part 1, pp. 636–52. Four articles written by Professor Byrnes also contain useful biographical data: "Pobedonostsev's Conception of the Good Society: An Analysis of His Thought after 1880," *Review of Politics*, XIII (1951), 169–90; "Pobedonostsev as a Historian," in *Teachers of History: Essays in Honor of Laurence Bradford Packard*, ed. H. Stuart Hughes (Ithaca: Cornell University Press, 1954), pp. 105–21; "Pobedonostsev on the Instruments of Russian Government," in *Continuity and Change in Russian and Soviet Thought*, ed. Ernest J. Simmons (Cambridge, Mass.: Harvard University Press, 1955), pp. 113–28; and "The Pobedonostsev Family," in *Indiana Slavic Studies*, II (1958), 63–78. Many valuable biographical facts are provided by Iu. V. Got'e in his article (which is based on the Lenin-Library collection of letters written by Pobedonostsev to the Tiutchev sisters) "K. P. Pobedonostsev i naslednik Aleksandr Aleksandrovich, 1865–1881," in *Sbornik*, published by Publichnaia Biblioteka SSSR imeni Lenina (Moscow, 1928), II, 107–34. Part of Got'e's article has appeared in English translation (though with no mention of Got'e's name): "Pobedonostsev and Alexander III," *Slavonic and East European Review*, VII (June, 1928), 30–54. Background materials concerning Pobedonostsev are also to be found in the first chapter of a somewhat inaccessible Moscow-University Candidate's thesis: S. L. Evenchik, "Reaktsionnaia deiatel'nost' Pobedonostseva v 80-kh gg. XIX veka" (Moscow: 1939). Views expressed in the Russian press concerning Pobedonostsev at the time of his death have been collected by an admirer: I. V. Preobrazhenskii, *K. P. Pobedonostsev, ego lichnost' i deiatel'nost' v predstavlenii sovremennikov ego konchiny* (St. Petersburg: Tipografiia "Kolokol," 1912). See also *K. P. Pobedonostsev i ego korrespondenty;* B. B. Glinskii, "Konstantin Petrovich Pobedonostsev: Materialy dlia biografii," *Istoricheskii Vestnik*, CVIII (1907), 246–74; and Friedrich Steinmann and Elias Hurwicz, *Konstantin Petrovitsch Pobjedonoszew der Staatsmann der Reaktion unter Alexander III* (Königsberg-Berlin: Ost-Europa Verlag, 1933).

4. Letters of Pobedonostsev to Catherine Tiutchev, March 3 and 26 and December 9 and 20, 1881, Manuscript Division, Lenin Library, Moscow (the letter of March 3, 1881, has been published in the article "Pervyia nedeli tsarstvovaniia Imperatora Aleksandra Tret'iago: Pis'ma K. P. Pobedonostseva iz Peterburga v Moskvu k E. F. Tiutchevoi," *Russkii Arkhiv*, XLV [1907], Part II, pp. 89–102); letter of Pobedonostsev to Alexander III, March 30, 1881, *K. P. Pobedonostsev i ego korrespondenty*, pp. 47–48; note of Alexander III to Pobedonostsev, early March, 1881, *ibid.*, p. 43.

5. See the letters of Pobedonostsev to Alexander III, April 2, 1879, March 3 and 16, 1881, *Pis'ma Pobedonostseva k Aleksandru III*, I, 194, 314–16. Cf. draft letter of Pobedonostsev to Alexander III, March 1, 1881, *K. P. Pobedonostsev i ego korrespondenty*, pp. 45–46.

6. Pobedonostsev's draft of the imperial manifesto of April 29, 1881, is to be found in *K. P. Pobedonostsev i ego korrespondenty*, pp. 51–52.

7. Chicherin comments in his memoirs concerning the change that took place in Pobedonostsev's character and personality after he moved to St. Petersburg. See *Vospominaniia Borisa Nikolaevicha Chicherina: Zemstvo i moskovskaia duma*, pp. 104–6.

8. See, for example, K. P. Pobedonostsev, *Moskovskii sbornik* (4th augmented ed.; Moscow: Sinodal'naia Tipografiia, 1897), pp. 223–24; and "Gosudar' Imperator Aleksandr Aleksandrovich: Rech' o nem K. P. Pobedonostseva v zasedanii Imperatorskago Istoricheskago Obshchestva," *Russkii Arkhiv*, XLIV (1906), Part I, p. 619.

9. Of particular importance in this context are the articles Pobedonostsev published in the *Russkii Vestnik* between 1858 and 1861 on Russian serfdom and legal reform: "Zametki dlia istorii krepostnago prava v Rossii," *Russkii Vestnik*, XV (June and July, 1858), 209–48, 459–98, XVI (August, 1858), 537–82; "O reformakh v grazhdanskom sudoproizvodstve," *ibid.*, XXI (June, 1859), 541–80, XXII (July, 1859), 5–34, 153–90; "Utverzhdenie krepostnago prava v Rossii v XVIII stoletii," *ibid.*, XXXV (September, 1861), 223–53. It is especially in Vols. I and II of his *Kurs grazhdanskago prava* (2nd ed.; St. Petersburg: Sinodal'naia Tipografiia, 1896) that Pobedonostsev displays historicist reasoning; Vol. III has a more formal and juridical character (it discusses contracts and obligations). The best analysis of Pobedonostsev as a historian is to be found in the article written by Professor Byrnes in the *Festschrift* in honor of Laurence B. Packard.

10. Iu. V. Got'e, "K. P. Pobedonostsev i naslednik Aleksandr Aleksandrovich, 1865–1881," *Sbornik*, II, 109.

11. Letters of Pobedonostsev to Alexander III, November or December, 1867, March 10, 1875, and March 22, 1876, *Pis'ma Pobedonostseva k Aleksandru III*, I, 6, 36, 43; letters of Alexander III to Pobedonostsev (no date given for first letter—apparently written in 1868 or 1869), April 6, 1875, and March 23, 1876, *K. P. Pobedonostsev i ego korrespondenty*, pp. 1007, 1014–15.

12. "Gosudar' Imperator Aleksandr Aleksandrovich," *Russkii Arkhiv*, XLIV, Part I, p. 623. Cf. Iu. V. Got'e, "K. P. Pobedonostsev i naslednik Aleksandr Aleksandrovich, 1865–1881," *Sbornik*, II, 115–16.

13. Pobedonostsev, "Aksakovy," in *Vechnaia pamiat'* (2nd ed.; Moscow: Sinodal'naia Tipografiia, 1899), pp. 63–73; letter of Pobedonostsev to I. S. Aksakov, December 18, 1870, "Moskovskii adres Aleksandru II v 1870 g.: Iz perepiski K. P. Pobedonostseva s I. S. Aksakovym," *Krasnyi Arkhiv*, XXXI

(1928), 152–53; letter of Pobedonostsev to N. N. Subbotin, November 13, 1881, in V. S. Markov, *K istorii raskola-staroobriadchestva vtoroi poloviny XIX stoletiia* [*Chteniia v Imperatorskom Obshchestve Istorii i Drevnostei Rossiiskikh pri Moskovskom Universitete*, CCLII, Book 1] (Moscow, 1915), p. 219; letter of Pobedonostsev to A. N. Shakhov, March 10, 1884, *K. P. Pobedonostsev i ego korrespondenty*, pp. 485–86.

14. Pobedonostsev, *Kurs grazhdanskago prava*, I, 542–47 and 553–57.

15. Pobedonostsev, *Moskovskii sbornik*, pp. 46–47.

16. I. Babst and K. Pobedonostsev, *Pis'ma o puteshestvii gosudaria naslednika tsarevicha po Rossii ot Peterburga do Kryma* (Moscow: Tipografiia Gracheva i komp., 1864), pp. 185–86, 192–93; letters of Pobedonostsev to Alexander III, November 24, 1867, and March 3, 1881, *Pis'ma Pobedonostseva k Aleksandru III*, I, 4–6, 314–15; Russia, Sviateishii Sinod, *Vsepoddanneishii otchet ober-prokurora Sviateishago Sinoda K. Pobedonostseva po vedomstve pravoslavnago ispovedanniia za 1888 i 1889 gody* (St. Petersburg: Sinodal'naia Tipografiia, 1891), pp. 1–3.

17. Pobedonostsev, *Moskovskii sbornik*, pp. 110, 150–51, 193–95; Pobedonostsev, "Gosudar' Imperator Aleksandr Aleksandrovich," *Russkii Arkhiv*, XLIV, Part 1, pp. 619–20.

18. Pobedonostsev, "Vospominaniia o Zubkove," *Russkii Arkhiv*, XLII (1904), Part 1, p. 305.

19. G. A. Dzhanshiev, *Epokha velikikh reform* (8th ed.; Moscow: I. N. Kushnerev, 1900), pp. 366, 552; *Istoriia pravitel'stvuiushchago senata za dvesti let, 1711–1911 gg.* (St. Petersburg: Senatskaia Tipografiia, 1911), IV, 468–72.

20. A. E. Nol'de, *K. P. Pobedonostsev i sudebnaia reforma* (Petrograd: Tipografiia Tovarishchestva "Obshchestvennaia Pol'za," 1915), p. 30.

21. Pobedonostsev, "O reforme v grazhdanskom sudoproizvodstve," *Russkii Vestnik*, XXI, 546–47.

22. Letter of Pobedonostsev to Anna F. Tiutchev, December 14, 1864, Manuscript Division, Lenin Library, Moscow; Babst and Pobedonostsev, *Pis'ma o puteshestvii gosudaria naslednika tsarevicha po Rossii ot Peterburga do Kryma*, p. 87.

23. Letter of Pobedonostsev to Alexander III, April 8, 1878, *Pis'ma Pobedonostseva k Aleksandru III*, I, 116–20; comments of Pobedonostsev concerning the reform of Russian courts, 1885, *K. P. Pobedonostsev i ego korrespondenty*, pp. 508–14; P. P. Schilovsky, "Reminiscences of K. P. Pobedonostsev," *Slavonic and East European Review*, XXX (June, 1952), 364–65; Pobedonostsev, *Moskovskii sbornik*, pp. 58–59 and 95–96.

24. Letters of Pobedonostsev to Alexander III, May 4, 1882, and December 12, 1889, *Pis'ma Pobedonostseva k Aleksandru III*, I, 381, and II, 226; Pobedonostsev to Nicholas II, May 22, 1899, *ibid.*, II, 319; Pobedonostsev, *Kurs grazhdanskago prava*, I, 554–56; letter of Pobedonostsev to Bishop Nikanor, July 30, 1884, "Perepiska K. P. Pobedonostseva s Episkopom Nikanorom," *Russkii Arkhiv* LIII (1915), Part 2, p. 369; Babst and Pobedonostsev, *Pis'ma o puteshestvii gosudaria*, p. 91.

25. Pobedonostsev, *Moskovskii sbornik*, pp. 25–30, 47–55; "Rech' K. P. Pobedonostseva o konstitutsii (proiznesena 3 marta 1881 goda v zimnem dvortse)," *Russkii Arkhiv*, XLV (1907), Part 2, p. 104; *Dnevnik E. A. Perettsa (1880–1883)*, ed. A. E. Presniakov and A. A. Sergeev (Moscow–Leningrad:

Gosizdat, 1927), pp. 38–40; letter of Pobedonostsev to Alexander II, May 4, 1882, *Pis'ma K. P. Pobedonostsev k Aleksandru III*, I, 381.

26. Letters of Pobedonostsev to Alexander III, October 12, 1876, May 4, 1882, and May 22, 1899, *Pis'ma Pobedonostseva*, I, 52–53, 381, and II, 319. Cf. A. E. Adams, "Pobedonostsev and the Rule of Firmness," *Slavic and East European Review*, XXXII (December, 1953), 132–39.

27. Letters of Pobedonostsev to E. M. Feoktistov, February 19, 1887, June 12, 1888, February 6, 1890, and May 5 and November 17, 1891, "Pis'ma K. P. Pobedonostseva k E. M. Feoktistovu," ed. B. Gorev and I. Aizenshtok, *Literaturnoe Nsaledstvo*, Nos. 22–24 (1935), pp. 524, 537, 540–41, 545, 549; letters of Pobedonostsev to Alexander III and Nicholas II, February 18 and June 23, 1887, January 11, 1889, November 1, 1891, and May 22, 1899, *Pis'ma Pobedonostseva*, II, 131–32, 157, 212–13, 252–53, 319; letter of Pobedonostsev to S. Iu. Witte, December 24, 1904, *Krasnyi Arkhiv*, XXX (1928), 106.

28. "O merakh k privedeniiu v blagoustroistvo sel'skikh prikhodskikh uchilishch v kazennykh seleniiakh," November 23, 1842, *Polnoe sobranie zakonov Rossiiskoi Imperii*, Sobranie vtoroe, Vol. XVII, Otdelenie vtoroe, 1842, No. 16,248, pp. 152–53.

29. F. V. Blagovidov, *Deiatel'nost' russkago dukhovenstva v otnoshenii k narodnomu obrazovaniiu v tsarstvovanie Aleksandra II* (Kazan: Imperatorskii Universitet, 1891), pp. 4–6.

30. *Ibid.*, pp. 13–25, 29–33, and 72–74; V. I. Charnoluskii, "Nachal'noe obrazovanie vo vtoroi polovine XIX stoletiia," *Istoriia Rossii v XIX veke* (St. Petersburg: Granat and Co., n.d.), VII, 126–28. An interesting example of the attitude within the Holy Synod toward education at the beginning of the 1860's is the memorandum prepared by T. Filippov in 1862: "Zapiska o narodnykh uchilishchakh," *Sbornik T. Filippova* (St. Petersburg: Tipografiia Glavnago Upravleniia Udelov, 1896), pp. 128–65.

31. Blagovidov, pp. 113–14.

32. *Ibid.*, pp. 247, 254–55, 265, 276–77, 283, 320, 328–29.

33. *Ibid.*, p. 141.

34. Charnoluskii, p. 127.

35. P. Miliukov, C. Seignobos, and L. Eisenmann, *Histoire de Russie* (Paris: E. Leroux, 1932–33), III, 879.

36. *Istoricheskii obzor deiatel'nosti komiteta ministrov*, ed. S. M. Seredonin (St. Petersburg: Gosudarstvennaia Tipografiia, 1902), Vol. III, Part 2, pp. 191–92, Vol. IV, p. 417; S. S. Tatishchev, *Imperator Aleksandr II, ego zhizn' i tsarstvovanie* (2nd ed.; St. Petersburg: A. S. Suvorin, 1911), II, 560–68.

37. S. A. Rachinskii, *Sel'skaia shkola: Sbornik statei* (5th ed.; St. Petersburg: Sinodal'naia Tipografiia, 1902), pp. 2–9, 90.

38. E. N. Medynskii, *Istoriia russkoi pedagogiki do velikoi oktiabrskoi sotsialisticheskoi revoliutsii* (2nd ed.; Gos. Uchebno-pedagogicheskoe Izdatel'stvo Narkomprosa RSFSR, 1938), pp. 323–24; letter of O. A. Novikova to Rachinskii, October 19, 1890, Rachinskii Archive, Manuscript Division, Saltykov-Shchedrin Public Library, Leningrad.

39. Letters of Pobedonostsev to Alexander III, March 10, 1880, December 21, 1881, and February 9, 1883, *Pis'ma Pobedonostseva*, I, 275, 361, II, 5–6. Cf. *Vsepoddanneishii otchet ober-prokurora . . . za 1890–1891*, p. 469.

40. Babst and Pobedonostsev, *Pis'ma o puteshestvii gosudaria*, pp. 54–55.

41. Medynskii, p. 328. Rachinskii's work, *Absit omen: Po povodu preo-brazovaniia srednei shkoly,* was published at St. Petersburg in 1901.

42. For Pobedonostsev's views on the need to make church schools the principal form of elementary education, see, especially, the letter of Pobedonostsev to Alexander III, March 28, 1883, *Pis'ma Pobedonostseva,* II, 27–28.

43. Comparative figures on money allotted to the Holy Synod and the Ministry of Public Instruction for educational purposes are conveniently tabulated by Medynskii, *op. cit.,* p. 321.

44. *Pravila i programmy dlia tserkovno-prikhodskikh shkol i shkol gramoty* (2nd ed.; St. Petersburg: Sinodal'naia Tipografiia, 1894), p. 10; *Polnoe sobranie zakonov Rossiiskoi Imperii,* Sobranie tretie, Vol. IV, 1884, No. 2318, pp. 372–73.

45. *Vsepoddanneishii otchet ober-prokurora . . . za 1888–1889 gg.,* p. 383.

46. Letters of Pobedonostsev to S. A. Rachinskii, September 24 and October 5, 1883, Rachinskii Archive, Manuscript Division, Saltykov-Shchedrin Library, Leningrad; J. S. Curtiss, *Church and State in Russia: The Last Years of the Empire, 1900–1917* (New York: Columbia University Press, 1940), pp. 184–85.

47. Letter of Pobedonostsev to Alexander III, March 22, 1881, *Pis'ma Pobedonostseva,* I, 323–24; *Moskovskii sbornik,* p. 76.

48. Medynskii, pp. 338–39; M. N. Kovalevskii, "sredniaia shkola," *Istoriia Rossii v XIX veke,* VII, 190–92.

49. The best account of the uses of nationalism in modern France is Carlton J. H. Hayes' *France: A Nation of Patriots* (New York: Columbia University Press, 1930).

50. Pobedonostsev attempted to answer arguments similar to the ones made in the preceding paragraphs in his article "Russia and Popular Education: A Reply to Prince Kropotkin," *North American Review,* CLXXIII (September, 1901), 349–54. His best argument—namely that Russia's vastness and cultural backwardness made it difficult to provide her with regular schools—is somewhat weakened by the fact that he seemed more interested in curtailing the zemstvo schools than in teaching the common people literacy and elementary knowledge.

51. Pobedonostsev, "Gosudar' Imperator Aleksandr Aleksandrovich," *Russkii Arkhiv,* XLIV (1906), Part 1, p. 620; *Moskovskii sbornik,* pp. 149–50.

52. *Pravila i programmy dlia tserkovno-prikhodskikh shkol i shkol gramoty,* pp. 109–12; Curtiss, *Church and State in Russia,* pp. 183–84.

53. This observation can be confirmed by examining some of the history texts used in the parish schools. See D. Ilovaiskii, *Kratkie ocherki russkoi istorii* (11th ed.; Moscow: Tipografiia Gracheva i komp., 1870); and P. K. Shchebal'skii, *Chtenie iz russkoi istorii s iskhoda XVII veka* (2nd ed.; St. Peters-burg–Moscow: Tipografiia Riumina i komp. and Universitetskaia Tipografiia, 1864–71), 5 vols. Cf. Blagovidov, *Deiatel'nost' russkago dukhovenstva,* pp. 238, 247.

54. Letter of Pobedonostsev to S. A. Rachinskii, October 5, 1883, Rachinskii Archive, Manuscript Division, Saltykov-Shchedrin Library, Leningrad.

55. *Vsepoddanneishii otchet ober-prokurora . . . za 1890–1891 gg.* (St. Petersburg, 1893), p. 468.

56. *Vsepoddanneishii otchet ober-prokurora . . . za 1888–1889,* p. 32.

57. Draft of Pobedonostsev report to Nicholas II, March, 1905, "Iz chernovykh bumag K. P. Pobedonostseva," *Krasnyi Arkhiv,* XVIII (1926), 204–5; *Moskovskii sbornik,* pp. 1–6, 224–26, 266–67; "Rech' K. P. Pobedonostseva o konstitutsii," *Russkii Arkhiv,* XLV (1907), Part 2, p. 104

58. Letter of Pobedonostsev to Alexander III, July 30, 1883, *K. P. Pobedonostsev i ego korrespondenty*, p. 313; draft of letter written by Pobedonostsev to Alexander III, January 5, 1886, *ibid.*, pp. 580–82; letters of Pobedonostsev to Alexander III and Nicholas II, March 28, 1883, April 1, 1886, January 21 and June 23, 1887, and May 15, 1896, *Pis'ma Pobedonostseva*, II, 27–28, 102–4, 128–30, 157, 316; *Vsepoddanneishii otchet ober-prokurora . . . za 1888–1889*, pp. 169–70; *Vsepoddanneishii otchet . . . za 1890–1891*, pp. 172, 188–98, 210, 225, 236.

59. Cf. Uvarov, *Desiatiletie ministerstva narodnago prosveshcheniia, 1833–1843*, pp. 35–70; Markov, *K istorii raskola-staroobriadchestva vtoroi poloviny XIX stoletii*, pp. 110–11; E. Orlovskii, *Sud'by pravoslaviia v sviazi s istorieiu latinstva i unii v grodnenskoi gubernii v XIX stoletii, 1794–1900 gg.* (Grodno: Gubernskaia Tipografiia, 1903), pp. 53–56, 109; [I. Semashko], *Zapiski Iosifa Metropolita Litovskago* (St. Petersburg: Imperatorskaia Akademiia Nauk, 1883), I, 23–44.

60. Rozhdestvenskii, *Istoricheskii obzor deiatel'nosti ministerstva narodnago prosveshcheniia*, pp. 463–68, 581–85; I. P. Kornilov, *Pamiati Grafa Mikhaila Nikolaevicha Murav'eva: K istorii vil'enskago uchebnago okruga za 1863–1868 gg.* (St. Petersburg: V. V. Komarov, 1898), pp. 77, 105; A. A. Sidorov, *Pol'skoe vozstanie 1863 goda* (St. Petersburg: N. P. Karbasnikov, 1903), pp. 232–34.

61. A. L. Pogodin, *Glavnyia techeniia pol'skoi politicheskoi mysli* (St. Petersburg: "Prosveshchenie," 1907), pp. 21–23.

62. N. I. Il'minskii, *Izbrannye mesta iz pedagogicheskikh sochinenii* (Kazan: Universitetskaia Tipografiia, 1892), pp. 16–23, 41–45; P. Znamenskii, *Na pamiat' o Nikolae Ivanoviche Il'minskom* (Kazan: Izdanie Bratstva Sviatitelia Guriia, 1892), pp. 195–96, 221; letter of Il'minskii to Pobedonostsev, October 9, 1884, *Pis'ma N. I. Il'minskago k ober-prokuroru sinoda Konstantinu Petrovichu Pobedonostsevu* (Kazan: Imperatorskii Universitet, 1895), pp. 116–18; Medynskii, *Istoriia russkoi pedagogii*, pp. 352–57.

63. Letters of Pobedonostsev to A. F. and E. F. Tiutchev, December 14, 1864, September 24, 1877, and February 25, 1880, Manuscript Division, Lenin Library, Moscow.

64. See the letters of Pobedonostsev to Alexander III, October 28, 1869, December 1, 1875, and October 18, 1876, *Pis'ma Pobedonostseva*, I, 9–10, 40, 55–57; letters of Alexander III to Pobedonostsev, March 13 and December 1, 1875, *K. P. Pobedonostsev i ego korrespondenty*, pp. 1014–15; letter of Pobedonostsev to E. F. Tiutchev, May 25, 1876, Manuscript Division, Lenin Library, Moscow.

65. Znamenskii, *Na pamiat' o N. I. Il'minskom*, pp. 21–81.

66. *Ibid.*, p. 165; Medynskii, *Istoriia russkoi pedagogii*, pp. 353–55.

67. Letter of Il'minskii to Pobedonostsev, March 9, 1882, *Pis'ma Nikolaia Ivanovicha Il'minskago k ober-prokuroru . . .*, pp. 6–10.

68. Letters of Pobedonostsev to Alexander III, October 4, 1883 and June 19, 1885, *Pis'ma Pobedonostseva*, II, 42–48, 80–81; *Vsepoddanneishii otchet . . . za 1890–1891*, pp. 79–104; draft report of Pobedonostsev to Nicholas II, February, 1905, "Iz chernovykh bumag K. P. Pobedonostseva," *Krasnyi Arkhiv*, XVIII (1926), 204–5.

69. See Babst and Pobedonostsev, *Pis'ma o puteshestvii gosudaria*, pp. 95–96.

70. Letters of Pobedonostsev to Alexander III and Nicholas II, October 4,

1883, June 19, 1885, April 1 and June 6, 1886, and February, 1891, *Pis'ma Pobedonostseva*, II, 42–43, 79–81, 103, 108–9, and 296–301.

71. Letters of Pobedonostsev to Alexander III and Nicholas II, October 18, 1876, November 11, 1881, February 12, 1882, and September 21, 1899, *ibid.*, I, 55–57, 355–56, and 373, II, 324; A. E. Adams, "Pobedonostsev's Religious Policies," *Church History*, XXII (1953), 315–17; Steinmann and Hurwicz, *Konstantin Petrovitsch Pobjedonoszew der Staatsmann der Reaktion unter Alexander III*, pp. 78–79.

72. Letters of Pobedonostsev to Alexander III, March 28, 1883, *Pis'ma Pobedonostseva*, II, 26–27.

73. See E. M. Feoktistov, *Vospominaniia E. M. Feoktistova: Za kulisami politiki i literatury 1846–1896 gg.* (Leningrad: "Priboi," 1929), p. 221.

74. Letters of Pobedonostsev to Alexander III and Nicholas II, November 11, 1881, February 15, 1882, May 24, 1882, March 3, 1884, February 28 and December 21, 1887, and September 21, 1899, *Pis'ma Pobedonostseva*, I, 355, 373, 385, and II, 51, 137–38 165–67, 324; *Vsepoddanneishii otchet . . . za 1888–1889*, pp. 138–43, 169–70; *Vsepoddanneishii otchet . . . za 1890–1891*, pp. 111–13, 117; Steinmann and Hurwicz, p. 79.

75. Letters of Pobedonostsev to Alexander III, June 23, 1887, and September 23, 1888, *Pis'ma Pobedonostseva*, II, 154–57, 199–200; draft of Pobedonostsev' letter to Alexander III, May 30, 1885, *K. P. Pobedonostsev i ego korrespondenty*, pp. 505–6. Cf. Pobedonostsev to D. A. Tolstoi, September 5, 1883, *ibid.*, p. 314.

76. A. L. Pogodin, *Glavnyia techeniia pol'skoi politicheskoi mysli*, pp. 23–33, 41–48; Medynskii, *Istoriia russkoi pedagogii*, pp. 347–50; Rozhdestvenskii, *Istoricheskii obzor deiatel'nosti ministerstva narodnago prosveshcheniia*, pp. 463–68, 581–85, 688–90.

77. *Iz arkhiva Kniazia S. V. Shakhovskago: Materialy dlia istorii nedavniago proshlago pribaltiiskoi okrainy, 1885–1894 gg.* (St. Petersburg: V. Eriks, 1909–10), I, vi–xxii.

78. Letter of S. V. Shakhovskoi to Pobedonostsev, February 18, 1887, *ibid.*, III, 32.

79. *Ibid.*, III, v.

80. Letters of Pobedonostsev to Alexander III, June 23, 1887, and May 20, 1889, *Pis'ma*, II, 154, 220; Pobedonostsev to F. M. Dostoevskii, August 19, 1879, "Dostoevskii i pravitel'stvennye krugi 1870-kh godov," ed. L. Grossman, *Literaturnoe Nasledstvo*, No. 15 (1934), p. 142; Alexander III to Pobedonostsev, May 15, 1876, *K. P. Pobedonostsev i ego korrespondenty*, p. 1016; *Vsepoddanneishii otchet . . . za 1890–1891*, pp. 125–26.

81. A. S. Rappoport, "Pobiedonostzev, the Apostle of Absolutism and Orthodoxy," *The Fortnightly Review*, New Series, LXXXI (May 1, 1907), 871. Pobedonostsev made this remark in the course of a conversation with Alexander Zederbaum, the editor of the Jewish journal *Hamelitz*. Pobedonostsev did not, however, favor pogroms, for he strongly disapproved of all forms of popular disorder and mass passion (cf. letter of Pobedonostsev to Alexander III, June 6, 1881, *Pis'ma*, I, 344).

82. Letter of Pobedonostsev to Alexander III, May 5, 1892, *Pis'ma*, II, 258.

83. *Ibid.*

84. See, for example, *Vsepoddanneishii otchet . . . za 1890–1891*, p. 102.

85. These figures have been obtained by adding up the number of converts reported by the Holy Synod annually between 1891 and 1905, and then by

dividing the total by fifteen. The largest number of converts reported was 21,522 in 1892 (see *Vsepoddanneishii otchet . . . za 1892 i 1893 gody* [St. Petersburg, 1895], p. 47 of appendix); the smallest number, 11,416 in 1905 (see *Vsepoddanneishii otchet . . . za 1905–1907 gody* [St. Petersburg, 1910], p. 59 of appendix). The annual figures for this fifteen-year period are as follows: 1891, 19,472; 1892, 21,522; 1893, 19,486; 1894, 19,548; 1895, 19,306; 1896, 17,824; 1897, 18,802; 1898, 17,236; 1899, 18,739; 1900, 17,004; 1901, 17,894; 1902, 18,003; 1903, 14,790; 1904, 16,726; 1905, 11,416.

86. *Vsepoddanneishii otchet . . . za 1890–1891* p. 186.

87. *Vsepoddanneishii otchet . . . za 1888–1889* p. 7.

88. Pobedonostsev reported that the population of the tsarist empire increased by 1,500,000 yearly (*ibid.*, p. 383). If one assumes that the rate of increase was approximately the same for all religious groups in the empire, its 30,000,000 non-Orthodox inhabitants in 1889 should have been increasing at the rate about 450,000 each year.

89. J. S. Curtiss, *Church and State in Russia*, p. 228.

90. Pogodin, *Glavnyia techeniia pol'skoi politicheskoi mysli*, p. 33.

91. "Tserkov' i russifikatsiia buriato-mongol pri tsarizme," ed. I Shpitsberg, *Krasnyi Arkhiv*, LIII (1932), 105–6, 111–12, 123–24.

92. One particularly striking account of the methods used by Russian officialdom on behalf of Orthodoxy is quoted by Wilhelm Kahle, *Die Begegnung des baltischen Protestantismus mit der russisch-orthodoxen Kirche*, pp. 215–16.

93. The vehemence and violence of the Revolution of 1905 in the Baltic provinces illustrates tht accuracy of Leont'ev's observations on the subjects of conversion to Orthodoxy and Russification. See "Pribaltiiskii krai v 1905 godu," ed. A. S., *Krasnyi Arkhiv*, XI–XII (1925), 263–88; and C. L. Lundin, "The Road from Tsar to Kaiser: Changing Loyalties of the Baltic Germans, 1905–14," *Journal of Central European Affairs*, X (October, 1950), 231–35.

94. *Vospominaniia Borisa Nikolaevicha Chicherina: Zemstvo i moskovskaia duma*, pp. 105–6.

95. Rappoport, "Pobiedonostzev, the Apostle of Absolutism and Orthodoxy," *Fortnightly Review*, New Series, LXXXI, 870.

96. "Pobedonostsev's Conception of the Good Society: An Analysis of his Thought after 1880," *Review of Politics*, XIII, 173.

97. A. Konopliantsev, "Zhizn' K. N. Leont'eva," *Pamiati Konstantina Nikolaevicha Leont'eva* (St. Petersburg: Tipografiia "Sirius," 1911), p. 124.

98. Such public figures as Prince V. P. Meshcherskii, V. I. Gurko, and S. Iu. Witte, who were in basic disagreement on a number of matters, concurred in regarding Pobedonostsev to be ineffective as an innovator and originator of positive governmental policies. See V. P. Meshcherskii, *Moi vospominaniia*, III, 334–35; V. I. Gurko, *Features and Figures of the Past: Government and Opinion in the Reign of Nicholas II* (Stanford: Stanford University Press, 1939), p. 54; and S. Iu. Witte, *Vospominaniia*, I, 271–72, III, 250, 301–2.

99. For examples of such sentiment other than those already given, see the following: P. N. Batiushkov, *Podoliia: Istoricheskoe opisanie* (St. Petersburg: Izdanie pri Ministerstve Vnutrennikh Del, 1891); M. M. Borodkin, *Slavianofil'stvo Tiutcheva i Gertsena* (St. Petersburg: S.-Peterburgskaia Elektropechatnia, 1902); Borodkin, *Pamiati finliandskago general-gubernatora Nikolaia Ivanovicha Bobrikova* (Kharkov: Tipografiia Gubernskago Upravleniia, 1905); Borodkin, "Zapadnye okrainy i russkaia gosudarstvennost'," *Russkii Vestnik*,

CCLXXXVIII (November, 1903), 104–20, and (December, 1903), 568–88; I. Fudel', "Kul'turnyi ideal K. N. Leont'eva," *Russkoe Obozrenie*, XXXI (January, 1895), 257–80; I. P. Kornilov, *Zadachi russkago prosveshcheniia v ego proshlom i nastoiashchem: Sobranie statei* (St. Petersburg: A. P. Lopukhin, 1902); S. Levitskii, *Pravoslavie i narodnost'* (Moscow: Tipografiia A. i L. Snegirevykh, 1888); A. P. Liprandi, *Pol'sha i pol'skii vopros* (St. Petersburg: E. E. Kittel'berger, 1901); I. V. Preobrazhenskii, *Za brat'ev-slavian: Po povodu 25-letiia sviashchennoi voiny 1877–1878 gg.* (St. Petersburg: P. Soikin, 1903); S. L., "Idealy budushchago nabrosanny v romane 'Brat'ia Karamozovy,'" *Pravoslavnoe Obozrenie*, III (September and October, 1880), 29–67, 215–44.

CHAPTER FOURTEEN

1. Émile Faguet, "Joseph de Maistre," *Revue des deux Mondes*, XC (December, 1888), 818.

2. German neoconservatism has been recently analyzed by Klemens von Klemperer, *Germany's New Conservatism: Its History and Dilemma in the Twentieth Century* (Princeton: Princeton University Press, 1957).

3. V. A. Maevskii, *Revoliutsioner-monarkhist: Pamiati L'va Tikhomirova* (Novi Sad, Yugoslavia: S. Filonov, 1934), pp. 9–10, 75–85.

Selected Bibliography

MANUSCRIPTS

In the Manuscript Division of the Lenin Public Library, Moscow:

R. A. Fadeev Papers.
Correspondence of K. P. Pobedonostsev with Anna and Catherine Tiutchev.

In the Manuscript Division of the Institute of Russian Literature (Pushkinskii dom), Academy of Sciences of the USSR, Leningrad:

Aksakov Family Papers.
K. N. Bestuzhev-Riumin Papers.
N. N. Strakhov Papers.

In the Manuscript Division of the Saltykov-Shchedrin Public Library, Leningrad:

S. A. Rachinskii Papers.
S. P. Shevyrev Papers.

PERIODICALS AND NEWSPAPERS

Epokha. St. Petersburg, 1864–65. Edited by M. M. Dostoevskii until June 10, 1864; then, unofficially by F. M. Dostoevskii.
Maiak (full title after 1842: *Maiak, zhurnal sovremennago prosveshcheniia, iskusstva i obrazovaniia v dukhe narodnosti russkoi*). St. Petersburg, 1840–45. Edited by S. Burachek and P. Korsakov.
Moskovskiia Vedomosti. Published after 1756 by Moscow University. Edited by M. N. Katkov between 1850 and 1855; by Katkov and P. M. Leont'ev between 1863 and 1875; and by Katkov alone between 1875 and 1887.
Moskvitianin. Moscow, 1841–57. Edited by M. P. Pogodin.
Russkaia Beseda. Moscow, 1856–60. Edited by T. I. Filippov, A. I. Koshelev, and I. S. Aksakov.
Russkii Vestnik. Moscow, 1856–1906. Edited by Katkov between 1856 and 1887.

Sovremennaia Letopis'. Moscow, 1861–71. Published by Katkov as a weekly supplement to the *Russkii Vestnik* between 1861 and 1862 and to the *Moskovskiia Vedomosti* between 1863 and 1871.

Vremia. St. Petersburg, 1861–63. Edited by M. M. Dostoevskii.

Zaria. St. Petersburg, 1869–72. Published by V. V. Kashpirev and edited mainly by N. N. Strakhov.

BOOK AND ARTICLES

Adams, A. E. "Pobedonostsev and the Rule of Firmness," *Slavic and East European Review*, XXX (June, 1952), 132–39.

——. "Pobedonostsev's Religious Policies," *Church History*, XXII (1953), 315–26.

Aggeev, K. *Khristianstvo i ego otnoshenie k blagoustroeniiu zhizni: Opyt kriticheskago izucheniia i bogoslovskoi otsenki raskrytago K. N. Leont'evym ponimaniia khristianstva*. Kiev: Tipografiia "Petr Barskii," 1909.

Aksakov, I. S. *Ivan Sergeevich Aksakov v ego pis'makh*. Moscow: M. G. Volchaninov, 1888–92. 4 vols.

——. "Perepiska I. S. Aksakova s Kn. V. A. Cherkasskim (1875–1878)," in *Slavianskii sbornik: Slavianskii vopros i russkoe obshchestvo v 1876–1878 gg.*, ed. N. M. Druzhinin. Moscow: Lenin Public Library, 1948.

——. "Pis'ma I. S. Aksakova k K. P. Pobedonostsevu," *Russkii Arkhiv*, XLV (1907), Part 3, pp. 163–92.

——. *Sochineniia*. Moscow: M. G. Volchaninov, 1886–87. 7 vols.

Aksakov, K. S. *Polnoe sobranie sochinenii*. Vol. I, Moscow: P. Bakhmetev, 1861–80. Vols. II–III, Moscow: Universitetskaia Tipografiia, 1875–80.

Averkiev, D. V. "Apollon Aleksandrovich Grigor'ev," *Epokha*, No. 8 (August, 1864) eighth article in issue, pp. 1–16.

Barsukov. N. P. *Zhizn' i trudy M. P. Pogodina*. St. Petersburg: M. M. Stasiulevich, 1888–1910. 22 vols.

Bel'chikov, N. F. *Dostoevskii v protsesse Petrashevtsev*. Moscow–Leningard: Akademiia Nauk, 1936.

Benz, E. *Die abendländische Sendung der östlich-orthodoxen Kirche*. Mainz: Verlag der Akademie der Wissenschaften und der Literatur, 1950.

Berdiaev, N. A. *Konstantin Leont'ev: Ocherk iz istorii russkoi religioznoi mysli*. Paris: Y.M.C.A. Press, 1926.

Blagovidov, F. V. *Deiatel'nost' russkago dukhovensta v otnoshenii k narodnomu obrazovaniiu v tsarstvovanie Aleksandra II*. Kazan: Imperatorskii Universitet, 1891.

——. *Ober-prokurory sviateishago sinoda v XVIII i v pervoi polovine XIX stoletiia*. Kazan: Imperatorskii Universitet, 1899.

Brodskii, N. L. (ed.). *Rannie slavianofily*. Moscow: I. D. Sytin, 1910.

Byrnes, R. F. "Dostoevsky and Pobedonostsev," *Jahrbücher für Geschichte Osteuropas*, N. S., IX (June, 1961), 57–71.

——. "Pobedonostsev's Conception of the Good Society: An Analysis of His Thought after 1800," *Review of Politics*, XIII (1951), 169–90.

——. "Pobedonostsev as a Historian," in *Teachers of History: Essays in Honor of Laurence Bradford Packard*, ed. H. S. Hughes. Ithaca: Cornell University Press, 1954, pp. 105–21.

——. "Pobedonostsev on the Instruments of Russian Government," in *Con-*

tinuity and Change in Russian and Soviet Thought, ed. E. J. Simmons. Cambridge, Mass.: Harvard University Press, 1955, pp. 113–28.

————. "The Pobedonostsev Family," *Indiana Slavic Studies*, II (1958), 63–78.

Cherniavsky, Michael. *Tsar and People: Studies in Russian Myths*. New Haven and London: Yale University Press, 1961.

Chizhevskii, I. I. *Gegel' v Rossii*. Paris: "Dom Knigi" and "Sovremennyia Zapiski," 1939.

Chmielewski, Edward. *Tribune of the Slavophiles: Konstantin Aksakov*. (University of Florida Monographs, Social Sciences, XII.) Gainsville: University of Florida Press, 1962.

Christoff, P. K. *An Introduction to Nineteenth-Century Russian Slavophilism: A Study in Ideas*. Vol. I: *A. S. Khomiakov*. S-Gravenhage: Mouton, 1961.

Curtiss, J. S. *Church and State in Russia: The Last Years of the Empire, 1900–1917*. New York: Columbia University Press, 1940.

Danilevskii, N. Ia. *Darvinizm: Kriticheskoe izsledovanie*. St. Petersburg: M. E. Komarov, 1885–89. 2 vols.

————. *Rossiia i Evropa: Vzgliad na kul'turnyia i politicheskiia otnosheniia slavianskago mira k germano-romanskomu*. 5th ed.; St. Petersburg: Tipografiia Brat. Panteleevykh, 1895.

————. *Sbornik politicheskikh i ekonomicheskikh statei*. St. Petersburg: Tipografiia Brat. Panteleevykh, 1890.

Dement'ev, A. G. "Granovskii i Shevyrev," *Uchenye Zapiski* of the Leningrad State University, Philological Series, No. 46, Vypusk III (Leningrad, 1939), 321–54.

————. *Ocherki po istorii russkoi zhurnalistiki, 1840–1850 gg.* Leningrad: Goslitizdat, 1951.

Desnitskii, V. A. (ed.). *Delo Petrashevtsev*. Moscow–Leningrad: Akademiia Nauk, 1937–51. 3 vols.

Dmitriev, S. S. Ekonomicheskie vozzreniia slavianofilov, 1840–1850 gg. Candidate's dissertation; Moscow University, 1940.

Dostoevskii, F. M. *Biografiia, pis'ma i zametki iz zapisnoi knizhki F. M. Dostoevskago*, eds. O. F. Miller and N. N. Strakhov. St. Petersburg: A. S. Suvorin, 1883.

————. "Dostoevskii i Pobedonostsev: Pis'ma F. M. Dostoevskogo," ed. N. F. Bel'chikov, *Krasnyi Arkhiv*, II (1922), 240–55.

————. *F. M. Dostoevskii: Pis'ma*, ed. A. S. Dolinin. Moscow–Leningrad: Goslitizdat, 1928–59. 4 vols.

————. *Polnoe sobranie sochinenii*. 8th ed.; St. Petersburg: Tovarishchestvo "Prosveshchenie," 1911–18. 23 vols.

————. *Sobranie sochinenii*. Moscow: Goslitizdat, 1956–58. 10 vols.

Evenchik, S. L. Reaktsionnaia deiatel'nost' K. P. Pobedonostseva v 80-kh gg. XIX-go veka. Candidate's dissertation; Moscow University, 1939.

Fadeev, R. A. *Sobranie sochinenii*. St. Petersburg. V. V. Komarov, 1889. 3 vols.

Fadner, Frank. *Seventy Years of Pan-Slavism in Russia: Karazin to Danilevskii 1800–1870*. Washington, D.C.: Georgetown University Press, 1962.

Feoktistov, E. M. *Vospominaniia E. M. Feoktistova: Za kulisami politiki i literatury, 1846–1896 gg.* Leningrad: "Priboi," 1929.

Fet, A. A. *Rannie gody moei zhizni*. Moscow: A. I. Mamontov, 1893.

Filaret, Metropolitan of Moscow. *Mneniia, otzyvy i pis'ma Filareta Mitropolita*

Moskovskago i Kolomenskago po raznym voprosam za 1821–1867 gg., ed. L. Brodskii. Moscow: Sinodal'naia Tipografiia, 1905.

————. *Slova i rechi sinodal'nago chlena Filareta, Mitropolita Moskovskago.* Moscow: Tipografiia A. Semena, 1844–45. 3 vols.

————. *Sobranie mnenii i otzyvov Filareta, Mitropolita Moskovskago, po uchebnym i tserkovno-gosudarstvennym voprosam*, ed. Savva, Archbishop of Tver. St. Petersburg: Sinodal'naia Tipografiia, 1885–88. 5 vols.

Filippov, T. I. *Sbornik T. Filippova.* St. Petersburg: Tipografiia Glavnago Upravleniia Udelov, 1896.

Florovskii, G. *Puti russkogo bogosloviia.* Paris: Y.M.C.A. Press, 1937.

Fudel', I. "Kul'turnyi ideal K. N. Leont'eva," *Russkoe Obozrenie,* XXXI (January, 1895), 257–80.

Glinskii, B. B. "Konstantin Petrovich Pobedonostsev: Materialy dlia biografii," *Istoricheskii Vestnik,* CVIII (1907), 246–74.

Got'e, Iu. V. "K. P. Pobedonostsev i naslednik Aleksandr Aleksandrovich, 1865–1881 gg.," in *Sbornik*, published by Lenin Public Library, II (Moscow, 1929), 107–34.

————. "Pobedonostsev and Alexander III," *Slavonic and East European Review,* VII (June, 1928), 30–54.

Gratieux, A. *A. Khomiakov et le mouvement slavophile.* Paris: Éditions du Cerf, 1939. 2 vols.

Grigor'ev, Aleksandr Apollonovich. "Odinokii kritik," *Knizhki Nedeli,* August, 1895, pp. 5–23; September, 1895, pp. 52–81.

Grigor'ev Apollon A. *Apollon Aleksandrovich Grigor'ev: Materialy dlia biografii*, ed. V. Kniazhnin. Petrograd: Izdanie Pushkinskogo Doma pri Akademii Nauk, 1917.

————. *Polnoe sobranie sochinenii i pisem*, ed. V. Spiridonov. Petrograd: P. P. Ivanov, 1918. Only Vol. I published.

————. *Sobranie sochinenii Apollona Grigor'eva*, ed. V. F. Savodnik. Moscow: I. N. Kushnerev, 1915–16. 14 vols.

————. *Sochineniia Apollona Grigor'eva*, ed. N. N. Strakhov. St. Petersburg: Tovarishchestvo "Obshchestvennaia Pol'za," 1876. Only Vol. I published.

————. *Vospominaniia*, ed. Ivanov-Razumnik. Moscow–Leningrad: "Academia," 1930.

Grossman, L. P. (ed.). "Dostoevskii i pravitel'stvennye krugi 1870-kh godov," *Literaturnoe Nasledstvo,* No. 15 (1934), pp. 83–162.

————. *Tri sovremennika: Tiutchev, Dostoevskii, Apollon Grigor'ev.* Moscow: Tovarishchestvo "Knigoizdatel'stvo Pisatelei v Moske," 1922.

Il'minskii, N. I. *Izbrannye mesta iz pedagogicheskikh sochinenii.* Kazan: Universitetskaia Tipografiia, 1892.

————. *Pis'ma Nikolaia Ivanovicha Il'minskago k Ober-Prokuroru sviateishchago sinoda Konstantinu Petrovichu Pobedonostsevu.* Kazan: Imperatorskii Universitet, 1895.

Istoriia XIX veka. St. Petersburg: Edition of A. I. Granat and Co., n.d. 9 vols.

Istoriia russkoi literatury XIX veka, ed. D. N. Ovsianiko-Kulikovskii. Moscow: Tovarishchestvo "Mir," 1908–10. 5 vols.

Karamzin, N. M. *Karamzin's Memoir on Ancient and Modern Russia*, ed. and trans. Richard Pipes. Cambridge, Mass.: Harvard University Press, 1959.

————. *Neizdannyia sochineniia i perepiska.* St. Petersburg: N. Tiblen, 1862.

————. *Sochineniia.* 3d ed.; Moscow: S. Selivanskii, 1820. 9 vols.

Katkov, M. N. "Mikhail Nikiforovich Katkov i Graf Petr Aleksandrovich Valuev v ikh perepiske," *Russkaia Starina*, CLXIII (August, 1915), 279–300, (September) 403–13; CLXIV (October, 1895) 91–95, (November) 247–51, (December) 416–30; and CLXVI (June, 1916), 346–65.

———. *Nasha uchebnaia reforma*. Moscow: M. G. Volchaninov, 1890.

———. "Pis'ma M. N. Katkova k P. A. Valuevu," ed. A. Kizevetter, *Russkii Istoricheskii Arkhiv*, I (Prague, 1929), 283–300.

———. *Sobranie peredovykh statei Moskovskikh Vedomostei, 1863–1887 gg.* Moscow: V. V. Chicherin, 1897–98. 25 vols.

Khomiakov, A. S. *Polnoe sobranie sochinenii*. 3d ed.; Moscow: Universitetskaia Tipografiia, 1900–1907. 8 vols.

Kohn, Hans. *Pan-Slavism: Its History and Ideology*. 2nd ed.; New York: Vintage Books, 1960.

Kologriwof, I. *Von Hellas zum Mönchtum: Leben und Denken Konstantin Leontjews, 1831–1891*. Regensburg: Gregorius Verlag, 1948.

Kolubovskii, Ia. "Materialy dlia istorii filosofii v Rossii 1855–1888 gg., IX: N. N. Strakhov," *Voprosy Filosofii i Psikhologii*, Vol. VII (March, 1891), Criticism and bibliography section, 99–121.

Korf, S. A. *Dvorianstvo i ego soslovnoe upravlenie za stoletie 1762–1855 godov*. St. Petersburg: Trenke and Fiusno, 1906.

Kornilov, A. A. *Obshchestvennoe dvizhenie pri Aleksandre II*. Moscow: A. I. Mamontov, 1909.

Kovalevskii, M. M. "Filosofskoe ponimanie sudeb russkago proshlago mysliteliami i pisateliami 30-kh i 40-kh godov," *Vestnik Evropy*, December, 1915, pp. 163–210.

Koyré, A. *La philosophie et le problème national en Russie au début du XIXe siècle*. Paris: Honoré Champion, 1929.

Kudriavtsev, I. A. "*Istoriia gosudarstva rossiiskogo* N. M. Karamzina v russkoi istoriografii." Candidate's dissertation; Moscow University, 1955.

Kurland, J. "Leont'ev's Views on the Course of Russian Literature," *American Slavic and East European Review*, XVI (October, 1957), 260–74.

———. "The History and Destiny of Russia according to Konstantin Leont'ev." Master's dissertation; Columbia University, 1952.

Lauth, R. *Die Philosophie Dostojewskis*. Munich: R. Piper, 1950.

Leont'ev, K. N. "Iz perepiski K. N. Leont'eva," ed. V. V. Rozanov, *Russkii Vestnik*, CCLXXXIV (April, 1903), 633–52, CCLXXXV (May, 1903), 155–82, (June) 409–38.

———. " 'Moia literaturnaia sud'ba': Avtobiografiia Konstantina Leont'eva," *Literaturnoe Nasledstvo*, Nos. 22–24 (1935), pp. 427–96.

———. *Sobranie sochinenii*. Moscow: V. M. Sablin, 1912–13. 9 vols.

———. *Pamiati Konstantina Leont'eva: Literaturnyi sbornik*. St. Petersburg: Tipografiia "Sirius," 1911.

———. *Pamiati K. N. Leont'eva: Pis'ma K. N. Leont'eva k Anatoliu Aleksandrovu*, ed. A. Aleksandrov. Sergiev Posad: Tipografiia Sv.-Tr. Sergievoi Lavry, 1915.

Leroy-Beaulieu, A. *Un homme d'état russe (Nicolas Milutine)*. Paris: Hachette, 1884.

Likhachev, D. S. *Natsional'noe samosoznanie drevnei Rusi*. Moscow–Leningrad: Akademiia Nauk, 1945.

Liubimov, N. A. *Mikhail Nikiforovich Katkov i ego istoricheskaia zasluga*. St. Petersburg: Tipografiia "Obshchesvennaia Pol'za," 1889.

Lossky, N. *Dostoevskii i ego khristianskoe miroponimanie*. New York: Chekhov Publishing House, 1953.

MacMaster, R. E. "Danilevsky and Spengler: A New Interpretation," *Journal of Modern History*, XXVI (June, 1954), 154–61.

———. "Danilevsky, Scientist and Panslavist." PhD. dissertation; Harvard University, 1952.

———. "The Question of Heinrich Rückert's Influence on Danilevskij," *American Slavic and East European Review*, XIV (February, 1955), 59–66.

Maevskii, V. A. *Revoliutsioner-monarkhist: Pamiati L'va Tikhomirova*. Novi Sad, Yugoslavia: S. Filonov, 1934.

Markov, V. S. *K istorii raskola-staroobriadchestva vtoroi poloviny XIX stoletiia: Perepiska Prof. N. I. Subbotina*. (*Chteniia v Imperatorskom Obshchestve Istorii i Drevnostei Rossiiskikh pri Moskovskom Universitete*, CCLII, Book 1.) Moscow, 1915.

Medynskii, E. N. *Istoriia russkoi pedagogii do velikoi oktiabrskoi sotsialisticheskoi revoliutsii*. 2nd ed.; Moscow: Gos. Uchebno-pedagogicheskoe Izdatel'stvo Narkomprosa RSFSR, 1938.

Meinecke, F. *Die Entstehung des Historismus*. 2nd ed.; Munich: Leibniz Verlag, 1946.

Meshcherskii, V. P. *Moi vospominaniia*. St. Petersburg: V. P. Meshcherskii, 1897–1912. 3 vols.

Miliukov. P. N. *Glavnyia techeniia russkoi istoricheskoi mysli*. 3d ed.; St. Petersburg: M. V. Aver'ianov, 1913.

———. *Iz istorii russkoi intelligentsii*. 2nd ed.; St. Petersburg: Tipografiia Montvida, 1903.

———. *Ocherki po istorii russkoi kul'tury*. Jubilee ed.; Paris: Izdatel'stvo "Sovremennyia Zapiski," 1930–37. 3 vols.

Miliukov, P., Seignobos, C., and Eisenmann, L. *Histoire de Russie*. Paris: E. Leroux, 1932–33. 3 vols.

Miliutin, D. A. *Dnevnik D. A. Miliutina*, ed. P. A. Zaionchkovskii. Moscow: Lenin Public Library, 1947–50. 4 vols.

Miller, O. F. "Ivan Sergeevich Aksakov," *Russkaia Starina*, XLIX (March, 1886), 745–59.

———. *Slavianstvo i Evropa: Stat'i i rechi Oresta Millera, 1865–1877 gg*. St. Petersburg. G. E. Blagosvetlov, 1877.

Mochul'skii, K. *Dostoevskii: Zhizn' i tvorchestvo*. Paris: Y.M.C.A. Press, 1947.

Monas, S. "Shishkov, Bulgarin, and the Russian Censorship," *Harvard Slavic Studies*, IV (1957), 127–47.

———. *The Third Section: Police and Society in Russia under Nicholas I*. Cambridge, Mass.: Harvard University Press, 1961.

Nazimov, V. I. "Khodataistvo slavianofilov i otsenka ikh znacheniia v russkom obshchestve: Pis'mo V. I. Nazimova," ed. M. N. Pokhvisnev, *Russkaia Starina*, XXXIII (February, 1882), 484–90.

Nevedenskii, S. "Katkov i Belinskii," *Russkii Vestnik*, CXCVI (June, 1888), 16–54.

———. *Katkov i ego vremia*. St. Petersburg: A. S. Suvorin, 1888.

Nikitenko, A. V. *Dnevnik A. V. Nikitenko*, ed. I. I. Aizenshtok. Leningrad: Goslitizdat, 1955–56. 3 vols.

Nol'de, A. E. *K. P. Pobedonostsev i sudebnaia reforma*. Petrograd: Tipografiia Tovarishchestva "Obshchestvennaia Pol'za," 1915.

Nol'de, B. E. *Iurii Samarin i ego vremia*. Paris: Imprimerie de Navarre, 1926.

Odoevskii, V. F. *Russkiia nochi.* 2nd ed.; Moscow: Pechatnia A. Snegirevoi, 1913.

Pazukhin, A. D. "Sovremennoe sostvianie Russii i soslovnyi vopros," *Russkii Vestnik,* CLXXV (January, 1885), 5–58.

Petrovich, M. B. "Russian Pan-Slavists and the Polish Uprising of 1863," *Harvard Slavic Studies,* I (1953), 219–47.

———. *The Emergence of Russian Panslavism 1856–1870.* New York: Columbia University Press, 1956.

Pfalzgraf, Konrad. "Die Politisierung und Radikalisierung des Problems Russland und Europa bei N. J. Danilevskij," *Forschungen zur Osteuropäischen Geschichte,* I (1954), 55–204.

Piksanov, N. K., and Tsekhovitser, O. V. (eds.) *Shestidesiatye gody.* Moscow–Leningrad: Akademiia Nauk, 1940.

Pipes, Richard. "Karamzin's Conception of Monarchy," *Harvard Slavic Studies,* IV (1957), 35–58.

Pobedonostsev, K. P. *Dlia nemnogikh: Otryvki iz shkol'nago dnevnika, 1842–1845 gg.* St. Petersburg: Tipografiia Ministerstva Putei Soobshcheniia, 1885.

———. "Gosudar' Imperator Aleksandr Aleksandrovich: Rech' o nem K. P. Pobedonostseva v zasedanii Imperatorskago Russkago Istoricheskago Obshchestve, 6 aprelia 1895," *Russkii Arkhiv,* XLIV (1906), Part 1, pp. 619–24.

———. "Iz chernovykh bumag K. P. Pobedonostseva," *Krasnyi Arkhiv,* XVIII (1926), 203–7.

———. "Iz dnevnika K. P. Pobedonostseva," ed. P. Bartenev, *Russkii Arkhiv,* XLV (1907), Part 1, pp. 636–52.

———. *K. P. Pobedonostsev i ego korrespondenty: Pis'ma i zapiski.* Moscow: Gosizdat, 1923. Only Vol. I, Parts 1 and 2 published.

———. *Kurs grazhdanskago prava.* 2nd ed.; St. Petersburg: Sinodal'naia Tipografiia, 1896. 3 vols.

———. "Moskovskii adres Aleksandru II v 1870 g. (iz perepiski K. P. Pobedonostseva s I. S. Aksakovym)," *Krasnyi Arkhiv,* XXXI (1928), 144–54.

———. *Moskovskii sbornik.* 4th augmented edition; Moscow: Sinodal'naia Tipografiia, 1897.

———. "Perepiska K. P. Pobedonostseva s Episkopom Nikanorom," *Russkii Arkhiv,* LIII (1915), Part 1, pp. 458–73; Part 2, pp. 68–111, 244–56, 335–84, 501–28; Part 3, pp. 81–108, 249–68.

———. "Perepiska Vitte i Pobedonostseva (1895–1905 gg.)," *Krasnyi Arkhiv,* XXX (1928), 89–116.

———. "Pervyia nedeli tsarstvovaniia Imperatora Aleksandra Tret'iago: Pis'ma K. P. Pobedonostseva iz Peterburga v Moskvu k E. F. Tiutchevoi," *Russkii Arkhiv,* XLV (1907), Part 2, pp. 89–102.

———. "Pis'ma K. P. Pobedonostseva k E. M. Feoktistovu," ed. B. Gorev and I. Aizenshtok, *Literaturnoe Nasledstvo,* Nos. 22–24 (1935), pp. 497–560.

———. *Pis'ma Pobedonostseva k Aleksandru III.* Moscow: "Novaia Moskva," 1925–26. 2 vols.

———. "Rech' K. P. Pobedonostseva o konstitutsii (proiznesena 8 marta 1881 goda v zimnem dvortse)," *Russkii Arkhiv,* XLV (1907), Part 2, pp. 103–5.

———. *Vechnaia pamiat'.* 2nd ed. Moscow: Sinodal'naia Tipografiia, 1899.

———. "Vospominaniia o Zubkove," *Russkii Arkhiv,* XLII (1904), Part 1, pp. 301–5.

Pobedonostsev, K., and Babst, I. *Pis'ma o puteshestvii gosudaria naslednika tsarevicha po Rossii ot Peterburga do Kryma.* Moscow: Tipografiia Gracheva i komp., 1864.

Pogodin, A. L. *Glavnyia techeniia pol'skoi politicheskoi mysli 1863–1907 gg.* St. Petersburg: Tipografiia "Prosveshchenie," 1907.

Pogodin, M. P. *Istoricheskie aforizmy.* Moscow: Universitetskaia Tipografiia, 1836.

———. "Parallel' russkoi istorii s istoriei evropeiskikh gosudarstv, otnositel'no nachala," *Moskvitianin,* 1845, Part I, No. 1 (Science section), pp. 1–18.

Pravila i programmy dlia tserkovno-prikhodskikh shkol i shkol gramoty. 2nd ed.; St. Petersburg: Sinodal'naia Tipografiia, 1894.

Preobrazhenskii, I. V. *Konstantin Petrovich Pobedonostsev, ego lichnost' i deiatel'nost' v predstavlenii sovremennikov ego konchiny.* St. Petersburg: Tipografiia "Kolokol," 1912.

Pypin, A. N. "Slavianskii vopros po vzgliadam Iv. Aksakova," *Vestnik Evropy,* CXX (August, 1886), 763–807.

———. *Istoriia russkoi etnografii.* St. Petersburg: M. M. Stasiulevich, 1890–92. 4 vols.

Rachinskii, S. A. *Sel'skaia shkola: Sbornik statei.* 5th ed.; St. Petersburg: Sinodal'naia Tipografiia, 1902.

Raeff, Marc. "A Reactionary Liberal: M. N. Katkov," *Russian Review,* II (July, 1952), 157–67.

———. "Georges Samarin et la commune paysanne après 1861," *Révue des Études Slaves,* XXIX (1952), 71–81.

———. *Michael Speransky: Statesman of Imperial Russia 1772–1839.* The Hague: Martinus Nijhoff, 1957.

Rappoport, A. S. "Pobiedonostzev, the Apostle of Absolutism and Orthodoxy," *Fortnightly Review,* N.S., LXXXI (1907), 868–78.

Riasanovsky, N. V. "Khomiakov on *Sobornost'*," in *Continuity and Change in Russian and Soviet Thought,* ed. E. J. Simmons. Cambridge, Mass.: Harvard University Press, 1955, pp. 183–96.

———. " 'Nationality' in the State Ideology during the Reign of Nicholas I," *Russian Review,* XIX (January, 1960), 38–46.

———. *Nicholas I and Official Nationality in Russia, 1825–1855.* Berkeley and Los Angeles: University of California Press, 1959.

———. "Pogodin and Shevyrev in Russian Intellectual History," *Harvard Slavic Studies,* IV (1957), 149–67.

———. *Russia and the West in the Teaching of the Slavophiles.* Cambridge, Mass.: Harvard University Press, 1952.

———. "Some Comments on the Role of the Intelligentsia in the Reign of Nicholas I of Russia, 1825–1855," *Slavic and East European Journal,* XV (Fall, 1957), 163–76.

Rogger, H. *National Consciousness in Eighteenth-Century Russia.* Cambridge, Mass.: Harvard University Press, 1960.

———. "The 'Nationalism' of Ivan Nikitich Boltin," in *For Roman Jakobson: Essays on the Occasion of His Sixtieth Birthday, 11 October 1956.* The Hague: Mouton, 1956, pp. 423–29.

Romanovich-Slavatinskii, A. *Dvorianstvo v Rossii ot nachala XVIII veka do otmeny krepostnago prava.* St. Petersburg: Tipografiia Ministerstva Vnutrennikh Del, 1870.

Rozanov, V. V. *Literaturnye izgnanniki.* St. Petersburg: A. S. Suvorin, 1913.

Rozhdestvenskii, S. V. *Istoricheskii obzor deiatel'nosti ministerstva narodnago prosveshcheniia.* St. Petersburg: Izdanie Ministerstva Narodnago Prosvesh-cheniia, 1902.

Sakulin, P. N. *Iz istorii russkago idealizma: Kniaz' V. P. Odoevskii, myslitel'-pisatel'.* Moscow: Izdanie M. i S. Sabashnikovykh, 1913. Only Vol. I, Parts 1 and 2 published.

Samarin, Iu. F. *Perepiska Iu. F. Samarina s Baronessoiu E. F. Raden, 1861–1876 gg.* Moscow: A. I. Mamontov, 1893.

———— (ed.). *Russkii administrator noveishei shkoly: Zapiska Pskovskago Gubernatora B. Obucheva i otvet na nee.* Berlin: B. Behr's Buchhandlung, 1868.

————. *Sochineniia.* Moscow: A. I. Mamontov, 1877–1911. Vols. I–X and XII published. The second edition of Volume I (Moscow, 1900) has been used in this study.

Samarin, Iu. F., and Dmitriev, F. *Revoliutsionnyi konservatizm.* Berlin: B. Behr's Buchhandlung, 1875.

[Semashko, I. I.]. *Zapiski Iosifa Mitropolita Litovskago.* St. Petersburg: Tipografiia Imperatorskoi Akademii Nauk, 1883. 3 vols.

Sementkovskii, R. I. *M. N. Katkov, ego zhizn' i literaturnaia deitel'nost'.* St. Petersburg: Iu. N. Erlikh, 1892.

Seredonin, S. M. *Istoricheskii obzor deiatel'nosti komiteta ministrov.* St. Petersburg: Gosudarstvennaia Tipografiia, 1902. 4 vols.

Setschkareff, W. *Schellings Einfluss in der russischen Literatur der 20er und 30er Jahre des XIX Jahrhunderts.* (Berlin University, Slavisches Institut. Veröffentlichungen, vol. 22.) Leipzig: Kommissionsverlag O. Harrassowitz, 1939.

Shakhovskoi, S. V. *Iz arkhiva Kniazia S. V. Shakhovskago: Materialy dlia istorii nedavniago proshlago pribaltiiskoi okrainy, 1885–1894 gg.* St. Petersburg: V. Eriks, 1909–10. 3 vols.

Shevyrev, S. P. *Istoriia russkoi slovesnosti.* Moscow: Universitetskaia Tipo-grafiia, 1846–60. 4 vols.

————. "Vzgliad russkago no sovremennoe obrazovanie Evropy," *Moskvitianin,* 1841, Part I, No. 1, pp. 219–96.

Shishkov, A. S. *Razsuzhdenie o krasnorechii Sviashchennago pisaniia, i o tom, v chem sostoit bogatsvo, obilie, krasota i sila Rossiiskago iazyka.* St. Peters-burg: Izdanie Imperatorskoi Rossiiskoi Akademii, 1811.

————. *Razsuzhdenie o starom i novom sloge Rossiiskago iazyka.* St. Peters-burg: Imperatorskaia Tipografiia, 1803.

————. *Zapiski, mneniia i perepiska Admirala A. S. Shishkova,* ed. N. Kiselev and Iu. Samarin. Berlin: B. Behr's Buchhandlung, 1870. 2 vols.

Shtrange, M. M. *Russkoe obshchestvo i frantsuzskaia revoliutsiia 1789–1794 gg.* Moscow: Akademiia Nauk, 1956.

Simmons, E. J. *Dostoevski: The Making of a Novelist.* New York: Oxford Uni-versity Press, 1940.

Smirnov, V. D. *Aksakovy, ikh zhizn' i literaturnaia deiatel'nost'.* St. Petersburg: "Obshchestvennaia Pol'za," 1895.

Solov'ev, V. S. *Sobranie sochinenii,* ed. E. L. Radlov. St. Petersburg: To-varishchestvo "Obshchestvennaia Pol'za," 1901–7. 9 vols.

Steinmann, F., and Hurwicz, E. *Konstantin Petrovitsch Pobjedonoszew der*

Staatsman der Reaktion unter Alexander III. Königsberg–Berlin: Ost-Europa Verlag, 1933.

Stephany, M. *Konversion und Rekonversion in Livland.* (*Abhandlungen der Herder-Gesellschaft und des Herder-Instituts zu Riga,* Vol. IV, No. 8.) Riga, 1931.

Strakhov, N. N. *Bednost' nashei literatury.* St. Petersburg: Tipografiia Nekliudova, 1868.

———. *Bor'ba s zapadom v nashei literature.* 2nd ed.; St. Petersburg: Tipografiia Brat. Panteleevykh, 1887–96. 3 vols.

———. *Filosofskie ocherki.* 2nd ed.; Kiev: Izdanie I. P. Matchenko, 1906.

———. *Iz istorii literaturnago nigilizma, 1861–1865 gg.* St. Petersburg: Tipografiia Brat. Panteleevykh, 1890.

———. *Kriticheskiia stat'i 1861–1894 gg.* Kiev: Izdanie I. P. Matchenko, 1902.

———. *Kriticheskiia stat'i ob I. S. Turgeneve i L. N. Tolstom, 1862–1885 gg.* St. Petersburg: Tipografiia Brat. Panteleevykh, 1885.

———. *Mir kak tseloe: Cherty iz nauki o prirode.* 2nd ed.; St. Petersburg: Tipografiia Brat. Panteleevykh, 1892.

——— (ed.). "Novyia pis'ma Apollona Grigor'eva," *Epokha* (February, 1865), pp. 152–82.

———. "Pis'ma N. N. Strakhova k N. Ia. Danilevskomu," ed. I. P. Matchenko, *Russkii Vestnik,* CCLXXI (January, 1901), 127–42, (February) 453–69, and CCLXXII (March, 1901), 125–41.

———. "Pis'ma N. N. Strakhova k M. N. Katkovu," *Russkii Vestnik,* CCLXXIII (June, 1901), 460–62.

———. "Pis'ma Tolstogo s N. N. Strakhovym," *Literaturnoe Nasledstvo,* Nos. 37–38 (1939), pp. 151–88.

——— (ed.). *Sochineniia Apollona Grigor'eva.* Vol. I. St. Petersburg: Tovarishchestvo "Obshchestvennaia Pol'za," 1876.

———. *Vospominaniia i otryvki.* St. Petersburg: Tipografiia Brat. Panteleevykh, 1892.

———. "Vospominaniia ob Apollone Aleksandroviche Grigor'eve," *Epokha* (September, 1864), pp. 1–50.

———. "Vospominaniia o Fedore Mikhailoviche Dostoevskom," *Biografiia, pis'ma i zametki iz zapisnoi knizhki F. M. Dostoevskago.* St. Petersburg: A. S. Suvorin, 1883, pp. 179–329.

———. *Zametki o Pushkine i drugikh poetakh.* St. Petersburg: Tipografiia Brat. Panteleevykh, 1888.

Strémooukhoff, D. *Vladimir Soloviev et son oeuvre messianique.* (Publications de la Faculté des Lettres de l'Université de Strasbourg, fasc. 69.) Paris: Société d'édition Les Belles Lettres, 1935.

Stupperich, R. "Motive und Massnahmen in der livländischen Bauernbewegung der Jahre 1845–47," *Kyrios,* 4ter Jahrgang, Heft 1, 1939, pp. 39–56.

Temkin, O. "German Concepts of Ontogeny and History around 1800," *Bulletin of the History of Medicine,* XXIV (1950), 227–46.

Thaden, E. C. "Natural Law and Historicism in the Social Sciences," *Social Science,* XXXII (January, 1957), 32–38.

———. "The Beginnings of Romantic Nationalism in Russia," *American Slavic and East European Review,* XIII (December, 1954), 500–21.

Tikhomirov, L. A. *Monarkhicheskaia gosudarstvennost'.* Moscow: Universitetskaia Tipografiia, 1905. 4 vols.

————. "Russkie idealy i K. N. Leont'ev," *Russkoe Obozrenie*, XXIX (October, 1894), 867–88.

Tiutcheva (Aksakova), A. F. *Pri dvore dvukh imperatorov: Vospominaniia-dnevnik*. Moscow: Izdanie M. i S. Sabashnikovykh, 1928–29. 2 vols.

Tolstovskii Muzei. Tom II: *Perepiska L. N. Tolstogo s N. N. Strakhovym, 1870–1894 gg.*, ed. B. L. Modzalevskii. St. Petersburg: Izdanie Obshchestva Tolstovskago Muzeia, 1914.

[Trubachev, S.] "R. A. Fadeev i ego sochineniia," *Russkii Vestnik*, CCXVI (September, 1891), 117–41, (October) 320–35, and CCXVII (November, 1891), 281–99.

————. "R. A. Fadeev kak voennyi deiatel' i pisatel'," *Russkii Vestnik*, CCXIX (April, 1892), 90–122, and CCXX (May, 1892), 124–65.

Trubetskoi, S. "Razocharovannyi slavianofil," *Vestnik Evropy*, CLVII (October, 1892), 772–810.

Usov, P. S. "Vospominaniia o R. A. Fadeeve," *Istoricheskii Vestnik*, XV (February, 1884), 371–79.

Ustrialov, N. V. "Politicheskaia doktrina slavianofil'stva: Ideia samoderzhaviia v slavianofil'skoi postanovke," *Izvestiia Iuridicheskogo Fakul'teta* of the Vysshaia Shkola, Harbin, Manchuria, I (1925), 47–74.

————. "Natsional'naia problema u pervykh slavianofilov," *Russkaia Mysl'* (October, 1916), Section II, pp. 1–22.

Uvarov, S. S. *Desiatiletie ministerstva narodnago prosveshcheniia, 1833–1843 gg.* St. Petersburg: Tipografiia Imperatorskoi Akademii Nauk, 1864.

Venevitinov, D. V. *Polnoe sobranie sochinenii*. Moscow–Leningrad: "Academia," 1934.

Vengerov, S. A. "Molodaia redaktsiia *Moskvitianina*," *Vestnik Evropy*, CXVII (February, 1886), 381–612.

Vsepoddanneishii otchet ober-prokurora sviateishago sinoda po vedomstvu pravoslavnago ispovedaniia. Published annually by the Sviateishii pravitel'st-vuiushchii sinod. St. Petersburg: Sinodal'naia Tipografiia, 1837–1916.

Witte, S. Iu. *Vospominaniia*. Moscow–Petrograd–Leningrad: Gosizdat, 1923–24. 3 vols.

Zaionchkovskii, P. A. *Voennye reformy 1860–1870 godov v Rossii*. Moscow: Izdatel'stvo Moskovskogo Universiteta, 1952.

Zamotin, I. I. *Romantizm dvadtsatykh godov XIX stoletiia v russkoi literature*. 2nd ed.; St. Petersburg: M. O. Wolf, 1911–13. 2 vols.

Zenkovskii, V. V. *A History of Russian Philosophy*. Translated by G. L. Kline. New York: Columbia University Press, 1953. 2 vols.

"Tserkov' i russifikatsiia buriato-mongol pri tsarizme," ed I. Shpitsberg, *Krasnyi Arkhiv*, LIII (1932), 100–26.

Znamenskii, P. *Na pamiat' o Nikolae Ivanoviche Il'minskom*. Kazan: Izdanie Bratstva Sviatitelia Guriia, 1892.

Zyzniewski, S. J. "Miliutin and the Polish Question," *Harvard Slavic Studies*, IV (1957), 237–48.

Index

Agassiz, Louis, 105
Aksakov, Constantine S.: and Stankevich circle, 29; as Slavophile, 32, 33, 130, 132, 186, 214n37
Aksakov, Ivan S.: as Slavophile, 12, 35–39, 49, 59, 94, 130, 157, 163, 165, 170, 177, 179, 180, 181, 185–86, 201, 231n1, 231n5, 233n47, 234n50, 234n55, 234n62; as journalist, 132; and problem of the western borderlands, 137, 139; as Pan-Slavist, 138–39; and anti-Semitism, 140–41; and autocracy, 141; and reactionaries, 141–42; and decline of Slavophilism, 145; and Fadeev, 149; and Pobedonostsev, 185–86
Aksakova, Anna F. See Tiutchev, Anna F.
Aksakovs, 36, 163
Alexander I (1777–1825), 10, 13, 18
Alexander II (1818–81), 11, 14, 32, 40, 44, 48, 52, 53, 76, 80, 94, 103, 131, 134, 165, 184, 187, 195, 196
Alexander III (1845–94), 37, 52, 56, 98, 162, 183, 184, 185, 189, 195, 196, 197, 203, 205
Alexander Nevskii, 16
Aleksandrov, A. A., 177
Annals of the Fatherland (Otechestvennyia Zapiski), 30
Anti-Semitism: Dostoevskii and, 85, 122, 223n63; Aksakov and, 140–41, 180; conservative nationalists and, 181; Pobedonostsev and, 199
Arakcheev, A. A., 18
Autocracy: historic origins, 8–9; popularized by Orthodox Church, 16; described by Uvarov, 20; Karamzin and, 26, 91; Slavophiles and, 33, 141, 143;

praised by Katkov, 46; Dostoevskii and, 75, 76–77; Strakhov and, 91; Danilevskii and, 109; Fadeev and, 156; Leont'ev and, 172, 173, 174; Pobedonostsev and, 184
Averkiev, D. V., 71–72, 164

Baader, Franz von, 32
Baer, K. E. von, 105
Bakhmeteva, A. N., 202
Bakunin, M. A., 29
Baltic provinces, problem of: under official nationality, 20, 21, 22, 24; Katkov's opposition to special rights for Baltic Germans, 49; Strakhov and, 97; Danilevskii and, 113; Samarin and, 131, 133–35; Leont'ev and, 169; Pobedonostsev and, 185, 195, 198–99, 232n22
Bariatinskii, Prince A. I., 147, 160, 161, 162
Barrès, Maurice, 204
Belinskii, V. G.: and Grigor'ev, 65; and Dostoevskii, 73, 74; mentioned, 29, 36, 80, 86, 164
—*Letter to Gogol*, 65; *Literary Reveries*, 65
Benckendorff, A. Kh., 11
Benda, Julien, 180, 241n72
Berdiaev, N. A., 178, 181
Bestuzhev-Riumin, K. N., 29, 230n26
Bibikov commission, 137
Birzhevskiia Vedomosti. See Stock Exchange News
Bismarck, Otto von, 182, 204
Bluntschli, J. K., 43
Bock, Woldemar von, 134, 232n19

University of St. Petersburg. *See* St. Petersburg University
Ustrialov, N., 145
Utin, B. I., 79
Uvarov, Count S. S.: and official nationality, 19–20; mentioned, 11

Valuev, P. A., 51, 56, 157
Venevitinov, D. V.: and romantic nationalism, 28–29
Vest'. See News
Vestnik Evropy. See Messenger of Europe
Vestnik Iugo-zapadnoi Rossii. See Messenger of Southwestern and Western Russia
Vladimir, Saint and Grand Prince of Kiev, 16
Voice (Golos), 169
Vorontsov-Dashkov, Count I. I., 160

Vremia. See Time

War of 1812, 11, 13
Weber, Alfred, 102
Western provinces, problem of: under official nationality, 21; Katkov and, 47, 53; Samarin and, 137; Aksakov and, 138–39
Westerners, 60, 65, 85, 164, 165
Wigand, Alfred, 104

Zaria. See Dawn
Zasulich, Vera I., 52, 188
Zederbaum, Alexander, 248n81
Zemskii sobor: Dostoevskii and, 86; Aksakov and, 142, 234n62. *See also* Council of the Land
Zemstvos, 44, 45, 53, 54, 157, 159, 194
Zenkovskii, V. V., 73
Zoe Palaeologus, 16

.